INSTANT POT COOKBOOK:

A Collection of 555 Delicious & Healthy Instant Pot Recipes

Table of Contents

DESCRIPTION 1

INTRODUCTION 2

CHAPTER 1 – BREAKFAST 3
1. Potato Egg Frittata.........................3
2. Extra Thick Almond Milk Yogurt 3
3. Blueberry Breakfast Oats 4
4. Instant Pot Banana Bread.................4
5. Egg and Broccoli Casserole 4
6. Blueberry French Toast 5
7. Bacon and Cheese Crustless Quiche 5
8. Eggs Benedict Casserole.................6
9. Instant Pot Huevos Rancheros 6
10. Mexican-Style Quiche.................7
11. Breakfast Brownie Muffins 7
12. Avocado and Bacon Muffins 8
13. Onion and Spinach Omelet with Goat Cheese ..8
14. Blackberry Cobbler 9
15. Plantain Bread.................9
16. Cottage Cheese and Pine Nut Egg Pie.............9
17. Scotch Eggs 10
18. Almond Flour Breakfast Bread.................10
19. Breakfast Plum Cake 11
20. Jalapeno Popper Keto Frittata 11
21. Breakfast Biscuit.................12
22. Burrito Casserole 12
23. Breakfast Oatmeal.................13
24. Chocolate Oatmeal.................13
25. Blueberry and Yogurt Bowl.................13
26. Breakfast Cauliflower Pudding 14
27. Scotch Eggs 14
28. Celeriac and Bacon Breakfast 14
29. Meat Quiche 15
30. Cinnamon Oatmeal 15
31. Cauliflower Congee 16
32. Breakfast Avocado Cups 16
33. Chicken Liver Spread.................16
34. Cheesy Grits 17
35. Tasty Breakfast 17
36. Mushroom Pate 17
37. Ricotta Cheese Spread 18

38. Breakfast Salad 18
39. Breakfast Potatoes 19
40. Pecan Sweet Potatoes 19
41. Barbecue Tofu.................19
42. Potatoes and Tofu Breakfast.................20
43. Pumpkin Butter 20
44. Tofu Breakfast.................21
45. Tofu Scramble 21
46. Chocolate Zucchini Muffin Bites.................21
47. Instant Pot Rice Pudding Recipe 22
48. Instant Pot Cinnamon Banana Oatmeal 23
49. Chocolate Instant Bircher Muesli.................24
50. Green Chile Breakfast Tacos 24
51. Pressure Cooker Breakfast Hash.................25
52. Instant Pot Cheesy Bacon Ranch Potatoes....25
53. Instant Pot Monkey Bread Recipe 26
54. Instant Pot French Toast Casserole.............26
55. Sauteed Caramelized Pears.................27
56. Instant Pot Apple Bread with Salted Caramel Icing.................27
57. Spice Oatmeal 28
58. Special Oatmeal 28
59. Walnut Oatmeal.................29
60. Healthy Quinoa Bowl 29
61. Delicious Quinoa.................29
62. Broccoli Egg Casserole.................30
63. Banana Oatmeal 30
64. Delicious Cornmeal Porridge.................31
65. Mushroom and Eggs Casserole.................31
66. Mix Beans Rice.................32
67. Strawberry Oatmeal.................32
68. Korean Style Steamed Eggs 32
69. Almond Quinoa 33

CHAPTER 2 – BEANS AND GRAINS 34
70. White Beans and Broccoli.................34
71. Italian Bean Stew.................34
72. Stewed Spicy Cannellini Beans.................35
73. One-Minute Quinoa and Veggies.................35
74. Mexican Quinoa with Cilantro Sauce.................35
75. Quinoa Fried Rice 36

76. INSTANT POT QUINOA PILAF 37

77. QUINOA WITH MUSHROOMS AND VEGETABLES 37

78. BASIC INSTANT POT MILLET 37

79. INSTANT POT MILLET PORRIDGE 38

80. CREAMY MILLET BREAKFAST PORRIDGE 38

81. HIBACHI FRIED RICE 38

82. INSTANT POT MEXICAN RICE 39

83. INSTANT POT CREAMY MUSHROOM WILD RICE SOUP.39

84. RICE WITH CHICKEN AND BROCCOLI 40

85. INSTANT POT MUSHROOM RISOTTO 40

86. PROOFING WHOLE WHEAT BREAD IN INSTANT POT41

87. INSTANT POT COCONUT OATMEAL 41

88. BANANA WALNUT STEEL-CUT OATS 42

89. INSTANT POT APPLE SPICE OATS 42

90. PUMPKIN SPICE OAT MEAL 42

91. PEACHES AND CREAM OATMEAL 43

92. PARSLEY PUREED NAVY BEANS 43

93. MEXICAN-STYLE BLACK BEAN AND AVOCADO
SALAD 43

94. ROSEMARY GOAT CHEESE BARLEY 44

95. AFRICAN LENTIL DIP 44

96. QUINOA PILAF WITH CHERRIES 45

97. TASTY BEAN AND BACON DIP 45

98. APRICOT AND RAISIN OATMEAL 45

99. CINNAMON BULGUR WITH PECANS 46

100. PEACH QUINOA PUDDING 46

101. MUSHROOM AND FARRO BEANS 46

102. PEAR AND ALMOND OATMEAL 47

103. POTATO RICE 47

104. DELICIOUS RICE PILAF 47

105. SIMPLE SPLIT PEA CURRY 48

106. SPECIAL CHICKPEA RICE 48

107. RED BEAN CURRY 49

108. INSTANT BACON RICE 49

109. AWESOME BEAN BARLEY STEW 50

110. GREEN MUNG BEAN RISOTTO 50

111. LENTIL CORN STEW 51

112. VEGETABLE AND CORN RICE 51

113. CHICKEN AND BROWN RICE 52

CHAPTER 3 – SIDE DISHES 53

114. CAULIFLOWER AND EGGS SALAD 53

115. ASPARAGUS AND CHEESE SIDE DISH 53

116. SPROUTS AND APPLE SIDE DISH 53

117. RADISHES AND CHIVES 54

118. HOT RADISHES WITH BACON AND CHEESE 54

119. AVOCADO SIDE SALAD 55

120. SWISS CHARD AND PINE NUTS 55

121. SPINACH AND CHARD MIX 55

122. CHERRY TOMATOES AND PARMESAN MIX 56

123. ALMOND CAULIFLOWER RICE 56

124. SAFFRON CAULIFLOWER RICE 57

125. GARLIC AND PARMESAN ASPARAGUS 57

126. POACHED FENNEL 57

127. HARVEST VEGETABLES 58

128. EGGPLANT 58

129. BEETS AND GARLIC 59

130. FAVA BEAN SAUTÉ 59

131. CALAMARI AND TOMATOES 59

132. CAULIFLOWER, BROCCOLI, AND CITRUS 60

133. ISRAELI COUSCOUS 60

134. RED CABBAGE 60

135. GREEN BEANS 61

136. SAVORY BOK CHOY 61

137. EASY-TO-MAKE EGGPLANT DELIGHT 62

138. SPICY CAULIFLOWER WITH PEAS 62

139. SPINACH WITH COTTAGE CHEESE 62

140. MUSHROOM AND ZUCCHINI PLATTER 63

141. SIMPLE CABBAGE AND PEPPER SIDE 63

142. GNOCCHI WITH BUTTERNUT SQUASH AND
TOMATOES 63

143. FRASCATI AND SAGE BROCCOLI 64

144. EASY MUSHROOM PÂTÉ 64

145. LEMONY BUCKWHEAT SALAD 65

146. RICOTTA CHEESE LASAGNA WITH MUSHROOMS ...65

147. CAJUN POTATOES WITH BRUSSEL SPROUTS 66

148. TURMERIC KALE WITH SHALLOTS 66

149. LUSCIOUS SOUR CREAM VEGGIES 66

150. RED CABBAGE WITH APPLE 67

151. INSTANT POT SPICY CREAMED CORN 67

152. INSTANT POT GOBI MASALA – CAULIFLOWER IN
INDIAN SPICES V+GF 68

153. PRESSURE COOKER GREEN BEANS WITH BACON...68

154. INSTANT POT CORN ON THE COB 69

155. INSTANT POT BROCCOLI CHICKEN MAC AND
CHEESE..69

156. INSTANT POT STEAMED ASPARAGUS 70

157. INSTANT POT SCALLOPED POTATOES 70

158. INSTANT POT RISOTTO WITH PEAS AND
ARTICHOKES 71

159. INSTANT POT BLACKK-EYED PEAS 72

160. INSTANT POT HUMMUS NO SOAK 72

161. INSTANT POT CILANTRO LIME RICE 73

162. INSTANT POT REFRIED BEANS 73

163. MUSHROOM QUINOA SALAD 74

164. SWEET HONEY CARROTS 74

165. Famous Bok Choy 75
166. Mushrooms and Butternut Squash 75
167. Veg Chickpea Salad 76
168. IP Seasoned Potatoes 76
169. Steamed Broccoli 77
170. Fresh Mushrooms 77
171. Cauliflower and Potato Mash 77
172. Healthy Chickpea Hummus 78
173. Chickpea Bowl 78
174. Awesome Asparagus Sticks.....................79
175. Cheesy Potatoes 79

CHAPTER 4 – SOUPS AND STEWS.....................80
176. Italian Sausage Stew 80
177. Enchilada Chicken Stew 80
178. Instant Pot Goulash 81
179. Instant Pot Carne Guisada 81
180. Instant Pot Turkey Chili 82
181. Classic Beef Chili 82
182. Instant Pot Chipotle Chili 83
183. Instant Pot Cowboy Chili 83
184. Curried Cauliflower Soup 84
185. Easy Everyday Chicken Soup 84
186. Creamy Chicken & Tomato Soup..............84
187. Tomato & Basil Soup 85
188. Beef & Cabbage Soup 85
189. 3 Ingredients Vegetable Beef Soup 86
190. Clam Chowder 86
191. Mushroom Soup 86
192. Seafood Soup 87
193. Cream of Broccoli & Mushroom Soup........87
194. Beef & Vegetable Soup 88
195. Fast Bean Stew 88
196. Sweet Potato Stew 88
197. Simple Turkey Stew 89
198. Mushroom and Beef Stew 89
199. Drunken Lamb Stew 90
200. German Stew 90
201. Oxtail Stew 91
202. Okra Stew 91
203. Lamb Stew 91
204. Beef and Root Vegetables Stew 92
205. Italian Sausage Stew 92
206. Beef and Barley Soup 93
207. Instant Pot Chicken Tortellini Soup 93
208. Shortcut Instant Pot Chicken Chile Verde Soup..94
209. Instant Pot Taco Soup 94

210. Instant Pot Creamy Tomato Tortellini Soup ..95
211. Chunky Potato Cheese Soup 96
212. Instant Pot Tuscan Chicken Stew 96
213. Instant Pot Pasta E Fagioli 97
214. Instant Pot Lebanese Chicken Soup...........98
215. Instant Pot Spicy White Bean and Chard Stew 98
216. Instant Pot Chicken Tortilla Soup 99
217. Bacon and Veggie Soup 100
218. Veggie Soup..100
219. Lentil Spinach Soup 101
220. Pepper Lamb Stew 101
221. Carrot Soup 102
222. Mouthwatering Green Bean Soup...........102
223. Special Turkey Soup 103
224. Instant Chicken Soup 103
225. Tomato Soup 104
226. Zuppa Toscana 104

CHAPTER 5 – BEEF, LAMB AND PORK.................106
237. 3-Ingredient Pork Chops 106
238. Shortcut Pork Posole 106
239. Moo Shu Pork 106
240. Instant Pot Asian Pork Belly 107
241. Instant Pot Pork Stroganoff....................107
242. Hungarian Pork Paprikash 108
243. Simple General Tso's Pork 108
244. Peppercorn Pork Brisket 108
245. Ginger Pork Shogayaki 109
246. Chile Pork Stew......................................109
247. Chinese BBQ Pork Char Siu 109
248. Balsamic Spiced Apple Pork 110
249. Sweet Chili Sauce Braised Pork.............110
250. Bolognese Stuffed Squash 111
251. Garlicky Cumin Slow Cooked Chili 111
252. Mexican Zucchini Boats 112
253. Peanut Butter and Lemon Pepper Beef 112
254. Smothered Beef Patties in Onion and Worcestershire 113
255. Spiced Mini Pies the Jamaican Way...........113
256. Cauliflower and Beef Goulash................114
257. Eggplant and Beef in a Tomato and Mozzarella Sauce................................114
258. Minty Lamb Chops in a Cranberry Sauce 115
259. Cheesy Pork Loin Pie 115
260. Middle Eastern Lamb Cutlets with a Tangy Salad 116
261. Pork Tostadas...116

262. Pork Carnitas...117
263. Pork with Orange and Honey 117
264. Pork with Hominy 118
265. Kalua Pork 118
266. Meatloaf 119
267. Beef Meatloaf 119
268. Sausage and Red Beans........................120
269. Meatballs and Tomato Sauce..................120
270. Pork Sausages and Mashed Potatoes 121
271. Meatball Delight 121
272. Pork Roast with Mushrooms in Beer Sauce .122
273. Lovely Rutabaga & Apple Pork Loins 122
274. Homemade Apple-flavored Pork Ribs 122
275. Tasty Pork Butt with Mushrooms and
     Celery 123
276. Easy Pork Chops with Brussel Sprouts 123
277. Braised Red Cabbage and Bacon 123
278. Quick Pineapple Pork Loin 124
279. Happy Pork Cutlets with Baby Carrots......124
280. Savory Ground Pork with Cabbage and
     Veggies 125
281. Ground Pork and Sauerkraut 125
282. Herby Pork Butt and Yams 125
283. Instant Pot BBQ Pulled Pork 126
284. Instant Pot Italian Bean & Pork Stew 126
285. Instant Pot Italian Beef 127
286. Instant Pot French Dip 128
287. Easy Low-Carb Instant Pot Meatballs.......129
288. Instant Pot HK Garlic Beef Rice Bowl Pot
     in Pot 130
289. Instant Pot Barbacoa Beef 131
290. Instant Pot Mongolian Beef 132
291. Instant Pot Pot Roast 133
292. Picante Lamb Chops.............................134
293. Greek Lamb Recipe 134
294. Famous Beef Pot Roast 135
295. Mouthwatering Pork Roast Tacos 135
296. Special Beef Carne Asada.......................136
297. Instant Pork Brisket.............................136

CHAPTER 6 – POULTRY AND CHICKEN...............137
298. Instant Pot Jamaican Jerk Chicken 137
299. Instant Pot Chicken Creole 137
300. Instant Pot Chicken Piccata 137
301. Root Beer Chicken Wings 138
302. Instant Pot Alfredo Chicken Noodles 138
303. Chicken with Mushrooms and Mustard....139
304. Quick Hoisin Chicken 139

305. Sticky Chicken and Chilies 140
306. Instant Pot Herbed Chicken......................140
307. Yakitori Chicken Wings 140
308. Balsamic Orange Chicken Drumsticks 141
309. French Style Chicken Potatoes 141
310. Garlicky Chicken Nuggets 142
311. Gingery Wings in Minty Chutney..............142
312. Chicken Liver Pate with Radishes 143
313. Crockpot Chicken and Tomato Chowder....143
314. Ranch Chicken Meatballs........................143
315. Chicken and Shrimp on a Spinach Bed 144
316. Chicken Thighs in a Balsamic Sauce 144
317. Italian Chicken Thighs 145
318. Taco Chicken 145
319. Barbecue Chicken 145
320. Pina Colada Chicken.............................146
321. Chicken Curry with Eggplant and Squash .146
322. Chicken with Duck Sauce 147
323. Chicken and Dumplings 147
324. Chicken and Chickpea Masala 148
325. Sesame Chicken 148
326. Chicken and Noodles 149
327. Chicken and Pomegranate 149
328. Chicken and Shrimp 150
329. Indian Butter Chicken 150
330. Goose with Cream 151
331. Goose with Chili Sauce 151
332. Chicken and Cabbage 151
333. Chicken and Broccoli 152
334. Chicken with Corn................................152
335. Greek-Style Chicken Legs with Herbs 153
336. Hearty and Hot Turkey Soup 153
337. Chicken and Beans Casserole with Chorizo154
338. Green BBQ Chicken Wings 154
339. Homemade Cajun Chicken Jambalaya........154
340. Tasty Turkey with Campanelle and
     Tomato Sauce 155
341. Hot and Spicy Shredded Chicken 155
342. Creamy Turkey Breasts with Mushrooms..156
343. Hot and Buttery Chicken Wings 156
344. Simple Pressure Cooked Whole Chicken 156
345. Chicken Bites Snacks with Chili Sauce 157

CHAPTER 7 – FISH AND SEAFOOD 158
346. Steamed Crab Legs................................158
347. Lobster with Wine and Tomatoes.............158
348. Instant Pot Mussels...............................158
349. Instant Pot Boiled Octopus 159

350. Instant Pot Lobster Roll 159
351. Instant Pot Easy Scallops 160
352. Instant Pot Tuna Casserole 160
353. Steamed Fish Patra Ni Maachi 160
354. Salmon on a Veggie Bed 161
355. Gruyere Lobster Keto Pasta 161
356. Sea Bass in a Tomato Feta Sauce 161
357. Stewed Scallops and Mussels 162
358. ParmesanCrusted Salmon 162
359. Fish Soup...163
360. Saucy Trout with Chives 163
361. Cheesy Tuna and Noodles 164
362. Wrapped Zesty and Herbed Fish...............164
363. Creamy Crabmeat 164
364. Shrimps with Tomatoes and Feta 165
365. Shrimp with Risotto and Herbs 165
366. Spicy Shrimp and Rice..........................166
367. Shrimp Scampi 166
368. Octopus and Potatoes 166
369. Seafood Gumbo 167
370. Stuffed Squid 167
371. Squid Masala 168
372. Octopus Stew......................................168
373. Greek Octopus 169
374. Braised Squid 169
375. Squid Roast..170
376. Superior Prawns and Fish Kabobs.............170
377. Glazed Orange Salmon 170
378. Light Clams in White Wine 171
379. Almond-Crusted Fresh Tilapia..................171
380. Mediterranean Salmon Fillet 172
381. Fancy Shrimp Scampi with Soy Sauce 172
382. Pleasing Tuna and Pea Cheesy Noodles 172
383. Alaskan Cod with Fennel, Olives and
        Potatoes 173
384. Instant Pot Shrimp and Lentil Stew..........173
385. Instant Pot Louisiana Seafood, Chicken,
        and Sausage Gumbo 174
386. Instant Pot Cioppino Seafood Stew..........175
387. Easy Coconut Red Curry Shrimp 176
388. Instant Pot Lemon Pepper Salmon 176
389. Instant Pot Salmon Tortellini Soup..........177
390. Seafood Gumbo 177
391. Shrimp Corn Chowder...........................178
392. Tomato Clam and Shrimps 178
393. Quick Seafood Platter 179
394. Salmon Teriyaki...................................179
395. Amazing Clam Chowder 180

396. Buttery Shrimp Risotto 180
397. Tasty Creamy Shrimp Grits 181
398. Yummy Alfredo Tuscan Shrimp 181

CHAPTER 8 – VEGETARIAN 183
399. Bell Pepper Gumbo 183
400. Italian Bell Pepper Platter 183
401. 2Minutes Broccoli...............................184
402. Brilliant Cheesy Broccoli.......................184
403. EasytoPrepare Broccoli........................184
404. Luscious Broccoli Casserole 185
405. BetterThanReal Mash..........................186
406. Spicy Cauliflower 186
407. Veggie Mac and Cheese 186
408. Keto Soufflé 187
409. Indian Veggie Platter 187
410. Okra Pilaf 188
411. Okra and Corn 188
412. Fennel Risotto 189
413. Kale and Bacon 189
414. Steamed Leeks....................................190
415. Crispy Potatoes 190
416. Turnips and Carrots 190
417. Spicy Turnips 191
418. Roasted Potatoes 191
419. Zucchinis and Tomatoes 191
420. Stuffed Tomatoes 192
421. Sweet Potato and Baby Carrot Medley 192
422. The Easiest Ratatouille 192
423. Tamari Tofu with Sweet Potatoes and
        Broccoli 193
424. On-the-go Tomato Zoodles 193
425. Delightful Leafy Green Risotto 194
426. Tropical Salsa Mash..............................194
427. Roasted Potatoes with Gorgonzola 194
428. White Wine Red Peppers 195
429. Leek and Swiss Chard Relish 195
430. Cheesy Acorn Squash Relish 196
431. Pickled Pepperoncini and Parmesan Dip 196
432. Instant Pot Vegan Jackfruit with Potato
        Curry..196
433. Vegan Baked Beans...............................197
434. Vegan Carrot Giger Soup.........................198
435. Vegan Black Eyed Peas Curry....................198
436. 5 Ingredient Vegan Queso 199
437. Instant Pot Vegan Refried Beans.............199
438. Instant Pot Vegetable Soup 200
439. Instant Pot Vegan Butter Chicken with

Tofu 201
440. Chickpea Potato Soup in Instant Pot 202
441. Instant Pot Vegan Curried Butternut Squash Soup 202
442. Instant Pot Mac and Cheese 203
443. Instant Pot Vegan Quinoa Burrito Bowls 204
444. Easy Ratatouille 204
445. Vegetable Teriyaki 205
446. IP Vegetable Barley 205
447. BBQ Mushroom Tacos 206
448. Delicious Potato Scallion Stew 206
449. Spaghetti Squash. 207
450. Cauliflower and Broccoli Florets 207
451. Awesome Vegetable Lasagne 208
452. Veg Bean Rice 208
453. Instant Veg Quinoa 209
454. Fruit Stew Recipe 209

CHAPTER 9 – STOCKS AND SAUCES 211
455. Elderberry Sauce.........................211
456. Fennel Sauce 211
457. Melon Sauce 211
458. Peach Sauce 212
459. Parsley Sauce 212
460. Cilantro Sauce 212
461. Peach and Whiskey Sauce 213
462. Leek Sauce 213
463. Chestnut Sauce 213
464. Quince Sauce 214
465. Corn Sauce............................214
466. Rhubarb Sauce 214
467. Instant Pot Vegetable Stock 215
468. Instant Pot Marinara Fresh Tomato Sauce .215
469. Instant Pot Lasagna......................216
470. Instant Pot Spaghetti and Meatballs 218
471. Instant Pot Meatball Pasta Dinner..........218
472. Instant Pot Spaghetti and Meat Sauce 219
473. Instant Pot Sunday Sauce 220
474. Beef Bacon Stock Recipe 221
475. Chicken with Herbs Stock Recipe...............221
476. Pork Bone Stock Recipe 222
477. Mushroom Sauce Recipe 222
478. Super Quick Garlic Sauce Recipe 223
479. Green Hot Sauce Recipe 223
480. Beef Pepper Stock Recipe 223
481. Chicken Green Beans Stock Recipe 224
482. Bolognese Eggplant Sauce Recipe 224
483. Chicken Corn Stock Recipe 225

484. Watermelon BBQ Sauce Recipe 225
485. Bolognese Lentil Sauce Recipe 226
486. Red Hot Sauce Recipe.........................226
487. Fish Anchovy Stock Recipe 227
488. Beef Vegetable Stock Recipe 227
489. Chicken Bone Broth 228
490. Leftover Turkey Stock.....................228
491. Bolognese Sauce 228
492. Spicy Beef Stock 229
493. Chicken Thyme Stock 229
494. Spicy Lamb Stock 230
495. Classic Beef Stock 230
496. Celery Lamb Stock 230
497. Butter Cheese Sauce 231
498. Cheese Onion Sauce 231
499. Enchilada Sauce 231
500. Curry Tomato Sauce 232
501. Parmesan Basil Sauce 232
502. Tomato Goat Cheese Sauce 233
503. Marinara Sauce 233
504. Onion Apple Sauce........................234
505. Pasta Sauce 234

CHAPTER 10 – DESSERTS 235
506. Maple Crème Brulee 235
507. Sweet Rice Pudding 235
508. Coconut, Cranberry, And Quinoa Crockpot Breakfast 236
509. Caramel and Pear Pudding....................236
510. Double Dark Chocolate Cake 236
511. Apple Cinnamon Cake 237
512. Fruit Salad Jam 237
513. Pumpkin Spice Chocolate Chip Cookies.......238
514. Instant Pot Sweetened Rhubarb 238
515. Vanilla Mousse Cups 238
516. Rich & Creamy Fat Bomb Ice Cream 239
517. English Toffee Treats 239
518. Fudgy Peanut Butter Squares 239
519. Lemon Squares & Coconut Cream 240
520. Rich Almond Butter Cake & Chocolate Sauce 240
521. Peanut Butter Cake Covered in Chocolate Sauce 241
522. Mint Custard 241
523. Keto Carrot Cake 242
524. Chocolate Bundt Cake 242
525. Raspberry Mug Cake.......................242
526. Melon Cream 243

527. PEACH CREAM 243
528. PEACHES AND SWEET SAUCE 244
529. CHESTNUT CREAM 244
530. CHEESECAKE 244
531. BANANA CAKE..245
532. PUMPKIN CAKE 245
533. APPLE CAKE 246
534. STICKY PUDDING 246
535. PINA COLADA PUDDING..............................247
536. QUICK FLAN..247
537. RHUBARB COMPOTE 248
538. SIMPLE CHOCOLATE CAKE 248
539. POACHED FIGS 248
540. LEMON CRÈME POTS...................................249
541. SIMPLE CARROT PUDDING...........................249
542. CORN PUDDING..250
543. EGGNOG CHEESECAKE 250
544. SUPER SWEET CARROTS 251
545. PINEAPPLE AND GINGER RISOTTO DESSERT 251
546. CHOCOLATE MOLTEN LAVA CAKE 251
547. BUTTERY BANANA BREAD 252
548. PEACHES WITH CHOCOLATE BISCUITS 252
549. APRICOTS WITH BLUEBERRY SAUCE.................252
550. HOT MILK CHOCOLATE FONDUE......................253
551. TUTTY FRUITY SAUCE...................................253
552. DELICIOUS STUFFED APPLES 253
553. COCONUT CRÈME CARAMEL 254
554. HOMEMADE EGG CUSTARD 254
555. POACHED PEARS WITH ORANGE AND CINNAMON .255

CONCLUSION...**256**

Description

Instant Pot is a modern-day panacea for all your cooking struggles. This all-in-one kitchen appliance takes care of your needs for nutrient-rich wholesome meals along with saving your precious time. With automated cooking, multiple cooking functions, and technologically-advanced features, there is nothing more one can ask from this amazing kitchen gadget. It is easy to operate, convenient to use cooking settings and effortless to clean.

The book aims at delivering a special collection of the Top 555 Instant Pot recipes to prepare in almost no time and maintain your optimum health.

This book covers the following recipes:

- Breakfast
- Beans & Grains
- Side dishes
- Soups & stews
- Beef, lamb & pork
- Chicken & poultry
- Fish & seafood
- Vegetarian
- Stocks & sauces
- Desserts

I sincerely hope that the versatile recipes covered in the book will help you make heavenly delicious breakfasts, soups, stews, desserts, and more at the comfort of your home. The recipes are easy to follow and suit both the beginners as well as expert cooks.

Instant Pot offers great flexibility, when it comes to preparing a wide variety of meals. You can also experiment with the recipes by adding your favorite ingredients and create your own customized dishes.

Thank you and have a great time enjoying the delicious recipes!

Happy Instant Pot Cooking!

Introduction

Instant Pots are quite amazing in what they can do and how they function. Gone are the days of unsafe, hard to use pressure cookers that were unreliable and didn't make food as perfectly as you may hope. Gone are the days of needing several different large appliances, each of which only cooked foods in one way. Gone are the days when a new, deluxe appliance was out of your price range or too advanced for your cooking abilities. The Instant Pot changed all of that.

Instant Pots are definitely one of the best and most useful kitchen appliances you can purchase. With their multi-functional abilities, quick cooking times and ease of use, it is a machine that you will find yourself using all the time. So, weather you are looking for a new way to make healthier foods, want to start making delicious foods faster or are just super excited for this new trendy kitchen tool, you need to get an Instant Pot as soon as possible. It is a purchase you will not regret.

Grab that Instant Pot you have been eyeing in the store and find a nice spot for it on your counter (you are going to want it out all the time!). Now, open up this cookbook and get ready to create some fantastic meals that will surprise and delight you. The hardest part about using the Instant Pot is deciding what to make first!

Chapter 1 – Breakfast

1. Potato Egg Frittata

Serves: 4
Preparation Time: 5 minutes
Cooking Time: 10 minutes

Ingredients

¼ cup milk
6 large eggs, beaten
1 teaspoon tomato paste
1 tablespoon butter, melted
Salt and pepper to taste
4 ounces French fries
¼ cup onions, diced
1 clove of garlic, minced
¾ cup cheddar cheese, grated

Directions

1. In a mixing bowl, mix together the milk, eggs, tomato paste, and butter. Season with salt and pepper to taste. Set aside.
2. Place the French fries in the bottom of the Instant Pot.
3. Add the onions and garlic.
4. Pour the milk mixture and pour in the cheddar cheese.
5. Close the lid and seal off the vent.
6. Press the Manual button and add the adjust the cooking time to 10 minutes.
7. Do natural pressure release.

Nutritional Values Per serving:

Calories: 420
Carbohydrates: 26.3g
Protein: 24.7g
Fat: 24.3g
Fiber: 0.9g

2. Extra Thick Almond Milk Yogurt

Serves: 4
Preparation Time: 10 minutes
Cooking Time: 8 hours

Ingredients

4 cups almond milk
1/3 cup raw cashews
2 tablespoons arrowroot powder
¼ cup yogurt source of live culture
1 tablespoon maple syrup

Directions

1. Place the almond milk, cashews and arrowroot powder in a blender. Pulse until smooth.
2. Transfer to a saucepan and heat over a medium flame while stirring constantly until the mixture simmers. Allow simmering for 5 minutes.
3. Remove from the heat to cool.
4. Transfer to the Instant Pot and add the yogurt with live culture.
5. Close the lid and press the Yogurt button. Adjust the cooking time to 8 hours.
6. Once the timer beeps, place the yogurt in clean mason jars and refrigerate before serving.
7. When ready to serve, drizzle with maple syrup or your favorite fruits.

Nutritional Values Per serving:

Calories: 285
Carbohydrates: 36.5g
Protein: 4.6g
Fat: 14.7g
Fiber: 1.7g

3. Blueberry Breakfast Oats

Serves: 1
Preparation Time: 3 minutes
Cooking Time: 6 minutes

Ingredients

- 1/3 cup old-fashioned oats
- 1/3 cup almond milk, unsweetened
- 1/3 cup Greek yogurt
- 1/3 cup blueberries
- 1 tablespoon chia seeds
- 2 tablespoons brown sugar
- A dash of salt
- A dash of cinnamon

Directions

1. Place all ingredients in the Instant Pot and give a good stir.
2. Close the lid and seal the vent.
3. Press the Manual button and adjust the cooking time to 6 minutes.
4. Do natural pressure release.
5. Give a good stir before serving.

Nutritional Values Per serving:

Calories:343
Carbohydrates: 66.8g
Protein: 19.3g
Fat: 6.9g
Fiber: 9.9g

4. Instant Pot Banana Bread

Serves: 4
Preparation Time: 10 minutes
Cooking Time: 50 minutes

Ingredients

- 2 eggs, beaten
- 1 stick soft butter
- ½ cup sugar
- 4 bananas, mashed
- 1 tablespoon vanilla extract
- 2 cups flour
- 1 teaspoon baking powder

Directions

1. Place a steamer rack in the Instant Pot and pour a cup of water into the pot.
2. In a mixing bowl, combine the eggs, butter, and sugar until creamy. Add the vanilla and bananas. Stir to mix well.
3. In another bowl, mix the flour and baking powder.
4. Gradually add the dry ingredients to the wet ingredients. Fold to combine everything.
5. Pour the batter into a greased baking dish that will fit inside the Instant Pot. Put foil over the top.
6. Place the baking dish on the steamer rack.
7. Close the lid and seal off the vent.
8. Press the Manual button and adjust the cooking time to 50 minutes.
9. Do quick pressure release and allow the banana bread to cool before serving.

Nutritional Values Per serving:

Calories: 554
Carbohydrates: 8g
Protein: 13.3g
Fat: 29.6g
Fiber: 6.7g

5. Egg and Broccoli Casserole

Serves: 6
Preparation Time: 5 minutes
Cooking Time: 15 minutes

Ingredients

- 3 cups cottage cheese
- 6 eggs, beaten
- 1/3 cup all-purpose flour
- ¼ cup butter, melted
- Salt and pepper to taste
- 3 cups broccoli florets
- 2 tablespoons chopped onions
- 2 cups cheddar cheese, grated

Directions

1. In a mixing bowl, mix together the cottage cheese, eggs, all-purpose flour, butter, salt, and pepper. Mix until well-combined.
2. Place the broccoli and onions in the Instant

Pot.

3. Pour over the egg mixture and sprinkle with grated cheese on top.
4. Close the lid and press the Manual button. Adjust the cooking time to 15 minutes.
5. Do natural pressure release.

Nutritional Values Per serving:

Calories:407
Carbohydrates: 15.8g
Protein: 27.8g
Fat: 25.7g
Fiber: 0.9g

6. Blueberry French Toast

Serves: 10
Preparation Time: 8 minutes
Cooking Time: 10 minutes

Ingredients

8 large eggs, lightly beaten
½ cup yogurt
1/3 cup sour cream
1 teaspoon vanilla extract
½ teaspoon ground cinnamon
1 cup milk
1-pound French bread, cubed
1 ½ cup blueberries
12 ounces cream cheese, cubed
1/3 cup maple syrup

Directions

1. In a mixing bowl, combine the eggs, yogurt, sour cream, vanilla, cinnamon, and milk until well-combined.
2. Grease the inner pot of the Instant Pot with cooking spray.
3. Arrange the French bread, blueberries, and cream cheese in the Instant Pot.
4. Pour over the egg mixture and drizzle with maple syrup.
5. Close the lid and seal off the vent.
6. Press the Manual button and adjust the cooking time to 10 minutes.

7. Do natural pressure release.

Nutritional Values Per serving:

Calories: 363
Carbohydrates: 43.1g
Protein: 15g
Fat: 19g
Fiber:1.7 g

7. Bacon and Cheese Crustless Quiche

Serves: 6
Preparation Time: 5 minutes
Cooking Time: 10 minutes

Ingredients

6 eggs, lightly beaten
1 cup milk
Salt and pepper to taste
2 cups Monterey Jack cheese, grated
1 cup bacon, cooked and crumbled

Directions

1. Spray the inner pot of the Instant Pot with cooking spray.
2. In a mixing bowl, mix together the eggs, milk, salt, and pepper until well-combined.
3. Place the bacon and cheese in the Instant Pot and pour over the egg mixture.
4. Close the lid and press the Manual button. Adjust the cooking time to 10 minutes.
5. Do natural pressure release.

Nutritional Values Per serving:

Calories: 396
Carbohydrates: 5.5g
Protein: 23.7g
Fat: 31.3g
Fiber: 0.7g

8. Eggs Benedict Casserole

Serves: 6
Preparation Time: 10 minutes
Cooking Time: 10 minutes

Ingredients

- 1 tablespoon olive oil
- 6 large eggs, beaten
- 2 ½ cups milk
- 1 ½ teaspoon dried mustard
- 1 ½ cup heavy cream
- 6 English muffins, cubed
- 1 leek, chopped
- 1 cup bacon, cooked and crumbled
- 2 tablespoons chives
- ½ teaspoon cayenne pepper
- 1 stick butter
- 8 egg yolks, at room temperature
- 1 tablespoon lemon juice
- 1 teaspoon Dijon mustard
- ½ cup heavy cream
- ½ teaspoon salt
- ¼ teaspoon black pepper

Directions

1. Grease the Instant Pot with olive oil.
2. In a mixing bowl, mix together the eggs, milk, dried mustard, and heavy cream until well-combined. Set aside.
3. Place the English muffins in the Instant Pot. Add the leeks, bacon, chives, and cayenne pepper.
4. Pour over the egg mixture.
5. Close the lid and seal off the vent. Press the Manual button and adjust the cooking time to 10 minutes.
6. Meanwhile, prepare the hollandaise sauce by combining all ingredients in a bowl. Place the bowl over a double boiler and continue whisking until the mixture is thick enough to coat the back of the spoon.
7. Once the Instant Pot is done cooking the casserole, do natural pressure release.
8. Drizzle with the hollandaise sauce before serving.

Nutritional Values Per serving:

Calories: 314
Carbohydrates: 15g
Protein: 21g
Fat: 20g

Fiber: 6.3g

9. Instant Pot Huevos Rancheros

Serves: 8
Preparation Time: 5 minutes
Cooking Time: 15 minutes

Ingredients

- 1 tablespoon butter
- 10 eggs, beaten
- 1 cup light cream
- 8 ounces Mexican blend cheese, grated
- ½ teaspoon pepper
- ¼ teaspoon chili powder
- 1 clove of garlic, crushed
- 1 can green chilies, drained
- 8 tortillas
- 1 can red enchilada sauce

Directions

1. Grease the inside of the Instant Pot with butter.
2. In a large bowl, mix together the eggs, cream, Mexican cheese, pepper, and chili powder. Stir in the garlic and chilies.
3. Pour into the Instant Pot and close the lid. Press the Manual button and adjusts the cooking time to 15 minutes.
4. Do natural pressure release.
5. Assemble the dish by spooning the egg casserole to tortillas and serving with enchilada sauce.

Nutritional Values Per serving:

Calories:182
Carbohydrates: 4g
Protein: 9g
Fat: 14g
Fiber: 2.6g

10. Mexican-Style Quiche

Serves: 8
Preparation Time: 5 minutes

Cooking Time: 25 minutes

Ingredients

Prepared pie crust
6 eggs, beaten
¼ teaspoon chili powder
Salt and pepper to taste
4 green onions, chopped
1 can cannelloni beans, drained and rinsed
2 cups cheddar cheese, grated
1 cup salsa

Directions

1. Make sure that the pie crust fits the Instant Pot.
2. Place a steamer rack in the Instant Pot and pour a cup of water.
3. In a mixing bowl, combine the eggs, chili powder, salt, and pepper.
4. Place the onion and beans in the pie crust.
5. Pour over the egg mixture and pour cheddar cheese on top. Place a foil on top.
6. Place the quiche on the steamer rack.
7. Close the lid and seal the vent.
8. Press the Steam button and adjust the cooking time to 25 minutes.
9. Do natural pressure release.
10. Serve with salsa.

Nutritional Values Per serving:

Calories: 318
Carbohydrates: 26.5g
Protein: 15.6g
Fat: 17.1g
Fiber: 3.7g

11. Breakfast Brownie Muffins

Preparation Time: 30 MIN
Serves: 6

Ingredients:

1 Egg
1 cup Flaxseed Meal
2 tbsp. Coconut Oil, melted

¼ cup Cocoa Powder, unsweetened
1 tsp Apple Cider Vinegar
1 tsp Vanilla
½ cup Pumpkin Puree
¼ cup Sugar Free Caramel Syrup
½ tsp Salt
¼ cup Slivered Almonds
1 ½ cups Water

Directions:

1. Pour the water into the Instant Pot and lower the trivet.
2. Combine the dry ingredients in one bowl, and whisk the wet ones in another.
3. Combine the two mixtures gently.
4. Divide the mixture between 6 silicone muffin cups.
5. Top with the almonds.
6. Place the muffin cups into the IP.
7. Close the lid and cook on MANUAL for 20 minutes.
8. Do a quick pressure release.
9. Let cool before serving.
10. Enjoy!

Nutritional Value

Calories 193
Fats 14g
Carbohydrates: 4.4g
Protein 7g

12. Avocado and Bacon Muffins

Preparation Time: 40 MIN
Serves: 16

Ingredients:

5 Bacon Slices, cooked and crumbled
5 Eggs, beaten
1 ½ cups Coconut Milk
2 Avocados, diced
4 ½ ounces grated Cheese
½ cup Almond Flour
2 tbsp. Butter
¼ cup Flaxseed Meal
1 ½ tbsp. Phylum Husk Powder

1 ½ tbsp. Lemon Juice
3 Spring Onions, diced
1 tsp Oregano
1 tsp minced Garlic
1 tsp Onion Powder
1 tsp Salt
Pinch of Pepper
1 tsp Baking Powder
1 ½ cups Water

Directions:

1. Pour the water into the Instant Pot and lower the trivet.
2. Whisk together the wet ingredients.
3. Gradually and gently, stir in the dry ingredients until smooth.
4. Stir in the avocado, bacon, onions, and cheese.
5. Divide the mixture into 16 small or medium muffin cups.
6. Place half of them inside your IP. Close the lid and cook on HIGH for 12 minutes.
7. Do a quick pressure release.
8. Repeat the process one more time.
9. Serve and enjoy!

Nutritional Value

Calories 144
Fats 11g
Carbohydrates: 1.7g
Protein 6.2g

13. Onion and Spinach Omelet with Goat Cheese

Preparation Time: 25 MIN
Serves: 1

Ingredients:

2 tbsp. Butter
¼ Onion, sliced
1 Spring Onion, chopped
2 cups Spinach
3 Eggs, beaten
1 ounce Goat Cheese

¼ tsp Garlic Salt
Pinch of Pepper
1 ½ cups Water

Directions:

1. Melt the butter in the Instant Pot on SAUTE.
2. Add onions and cook for 3 minutes.
3. Stir in spinach and spices and cook for 1 more minute.
4. Transfer the mixture to a greased baking dish.
5. Pour the eggs over and stir in the cheese.
6. Pour the water into the IP and lower the rack.
7. Place the baking dish inside and close the lid.
8. Cook on HIGH for 12 minutes.
9. Serve and enjoy!

Nutritional Value

Calories 321
Fats 54g
Carbohydrates: 4.8g
Protein 36g

14. Blackberry Cobbler

Preparation Time: 40 MIN
Serves: 2

Ingredients:

2 tbsp. Heavy Cream
¼ cup Coconut Flour
2 tbsp. Coconut Oil
2 tsp Lemon Juice
10 drops of Liquid Stevia
5 Egg Yolks
¼ tsp Baking Powder
¼ cup Blackberries
2 tbsp. Erythritol
½ tsp Lemon Zest
Pinch of Sea Salt
1 ½ cups Water

Directions:

1. Pour the water into the Instant Pot and lower the trivet.
2. Whisk together the yolks, coconut oil, butter, stevia, lemon juice, heavy cream, erythritol, and salt.
3. Stir in the wet ingredients, gradually, until smooth.
4. Divide the mixture between 2 greased ramekins.
5. Push the blackberries into the batter.
6. Place the ramekins inside the IP.
7. Cook on HIGH for 10 minutes.
8. Release the pressure quickly.
9. Serve and enjoy!

Nutritional Value

Calories 459
Fats 44g
Carbohydrates: 4.9g
Protein 9g

15. Plantain Bread

Preparation Time: 55 MIN
Serves: 12

Ingredients:

2 cups Almond Flour
4 Plantains, mashed
1 tsp Baking Powder
2 Eggs, beaten
1 tbsp. Vanilla
3 tbsp. Butter, melted
Sweetener, to taste
1 ½ cup Water

Directions:

1. Pour the water into the Instant Pot and lower the trivet.
2. Whisk the eggs, plantains, butter, and vanilla.
3. Stir in the dry ingredients and mix until smooth.

4. Grease a loaf pan with cooking spray and pour the mixture inside.
5. Place in the IP and close the lid.
6. Cook on MANUAL for 40 minutes.
7. Serve and enjoy!

Nutritional Value

Calories 102
Fats 3.8g
Carbohydrates: 8.4g
Protein 1.6g

16. Cottage Cheese and Pine Nut Egg Pie

Preparation Time: 40 MIN
Serves: 6

Ingredients:

6 Eggs, beaten
2 tbsp. chopped Pine Nuts
1 Tomato, diced
¼ cup Heavy Cream
2 tbsp. chopped Basil
¼ cup grated Parmesan Cheese
1 cup Cottage Cheese
Pinch of Salt
Pinch of Pepper
1 ½ cups Water

Directions:

1. Pour the water into the Instant Pot and lower the trivet.
2. Combine all of the ingredients in a large bowl.
3. Grease a baking dish and pour the mixture inside.
4. Place the dish inside the IP and close the lid.
5. Cook for 30 minutes on MANUAL.
6. Release the pressure quickly.
7. Serve and enjoy!

Nutritional Value

Calories 182
Fats 13g
Carbohydrates: 3g
Protein 13g

17. Scotch Eggs

Preparation Time: 15 MIN
Serves: 2

Ingredients:

2 Hardboiled Eggs
1 Egg, beaten
4 Bacon Slices
2 tbsp. Coconut Flour
1 tbsp. Coconut Oil
2 tbsp. grated Parmesan Cheese
½ tbsp. Olive Oil

Directions:

1. Peel your hardboiled eggs.
2. In a shallow bowl, combine the flour, and parmesan cheese.
3. Wrap the eggs in one bacon slice horizontally, and in one slice vertically.
4. Dip in the beaten egg first and then coat in flour/parmesan mixture.
5. Melt the coconut oil along with the olive oil in your IP on SAUTE.
6. Add the eggs and cook until golden and crispy.
7. Serve and enjoy!

Nutritional Value

Calories 477
Fats 42g
Carbohydrates: 2.95g
Protein 19g

18. Almond Flour Breakfast Bread

Preparation Time: 40 MIN
Serves: 15

Ingredients:

2 ½ cups Almond Flour
6 tbsp. Milk
½ tsp Baking Soda
¼ cup WheyProtein Powder
1 tsp Xanthan Gum
½ cup Oat Fiber
1 tbsp. Erythritol
6 ounces Yogurt
4 Eggs
6 tbsp. Butter, softened
2 tsp Baking Powder
Pinch of Salt
1 ½ cups Water

Directions:

1. Pour the water into the Instant Pot and lower the trivet.
2. Combine the dry ingredients in one bow, and whisk the wet ones in another.
3. Gently combine the two mixtures.
4. Grease loaf pan that can fit into the IP, with cooking spray.
5. Pour the batter into the loaf pan.
6. Place the pan inside the IP and close the lid.
7. Cook on HIGH for 30 minutes.
8. Release the pressure quickly.
9. Serve and enjoy!

Nutritional Value

Calories 180
Fats 11 g
Carbohydrates: 2.9 g
Protein 12 g

19. Breakfast Plum Cake

Preparation Time: 40 MIN
Serves: 8

Ingredients:

½ cup Butter, softened
1 ½ cups almond Flour
2 tsp Baking Powder
½ cup Coconut Flour
½ cup Granulated Sweetener

3 Eggs
1 tbsp. Vanilla
¾ cup Almond Milk
4 Plums, pitted and halved
¼ tsp Almond Extract
Pinch of Sea Salt
¼ tsp Xanthan Gum
1 ½ cups Water

Directions:

1. Pour the water into the Instant Pot and lower the rack.
2. Beat the butter and sweetener until the mixture becomes smooth.
3. Beat in the eggs, one at a time.
4. Beat in the extracts and milk.
5. Combine the dry ingredients in a bowl, and gradually beat this mixture into the wet one.
6. Grease a baking dish with cooking spray and pour the batter into it.
7. Top with the plumscut side down.
8. Place the dish inside the IP and close the lid.
9. Cook for 25 minutes on HIGH.
10. Serve and enjoy!

Nutritional Value

Calories 296
Fats 25g
Carbohydrates: 6.5g
Protein 9g

20. Jalapeno Popper Keto Frittata

Preparation Time: 40 MIN
Serves: 8

Ingredients:

Cream Cheese Mixture:

2 tbsp. chopped Jalapeno Peppers
6 ounces Cream Cheese, softened
¼ cup shredded Cheddar Cheese
2 tbsp. Salsa Verde

Egg Mixture:

6 Eggs
2 tbsp. Heavy Cream
¼ tsp Salt
1/3 cup Milk
Pinch of Pepper

Toppings:

1 tbsp. sliced Jalapeno Peppers
6 Bacon Slices, chopped and cooked
½ cup shredded Cheddar Cheese

Directions:

1. Pour some water into your Instant Pot, about 1 ½ cups, and lower the trivet.
2. Grease a baking dish with some cooking spray.
3. Whisk together the cream cheese mixture ingredients. Place in a microwave and microwave for a minute, to soften.
4. Drop spoonfuls of that mixture to the bottom of the dish.
5. Whisk the egg mixture ingredients and pour over the cream cheese.
6. Place the toppings on top.
7. Cover the baking dish with a foilthis is optional, and place in the IP.
8. Cook on HIGH for 20 minutes.
9. Do a quick pressure release and serve.

Nutritional Value

Calories 361
Fats 40g
Carbohydrates: 3g
Protein 24g

21. Breakfast Biscuit

Preparation Time: 40 MIN
Serves: 8

Ingredients:

1 cup Coconut Flour
½ cup Butter
1 tbsp. SugarFree VanillaProtein Powder

¼ tsp Xanthan Gum
2 tbsp. GlutenFree Baking Mix
1 ½ tsp Baking Powder
¾ cup Milk
3 Eggs
½ tsp Salt
1 ½ cups Water

Directions:

1. Pour the water into the Instant Pot and lower the trivet.
2. Combine the dry ingredients in a bowl.
3. Add the butter and rub the mixture with your fingers, until crumbly.
4. Stir in the wet ingredients and knead with your hand.
5. Roll out the dough and cut into 8 equal pieces.
6. Place on a greased baking tray and in the IPDo NOT overcrowd. Work in batches if needed.
7. Close the lid and cook on HIGH for 10 minutes.
8. Do a quick pressure release.
9. Serve and enjoy!

Nutritional Value

Calories 198
Fats 16g
Carbohydrates: 4g
Protein 5g

22. Burrito Casserole

Preparation Time: 10 minutes
Cooking Time: 13 minutes
Serves: 6

Ingredients:

2 pound celeriac, peeled and cubed
4 eggs
¼ cup yellow onion, chopped
1 jalapeno, chopped
6 ounces ham, chopped
A pinch of salt and black pepper

¼ teaspoon chili powder
¾ teaspoon taco seasoning
Keto salsa for serving
1 cup water+ 1 tablespoon

Directions:

1. In a bowl, mix eggs with onion, jalapeno, celeriac, ham, salt, pepper, chili powder and taco seasoning and stir.
2. Add 1 tablespoon water, stir again and pour everything into a casserole.
3. Add the water to your instant pot, add the trivet, and casserole, cover pot and cook on Manual for 13 minutes.
4. Divide between plates and serve for breakfast with some keto salsa on top. Enjoy!

Nutritional Values

Per servingcalories 213
fat 4
fiber 6
carbs 7
protein 7

23. Breakfast Oatmeal

Preparation Time: 10 minutes
Cooking Time: 10 minutes
Serves: 2

Ingredients:

¼ cup chia seeds
¼ cup coconut, unsweetened and shredded
1/3 coconut, flaked
1/3 cup almonds, flaked
½ cup coconut milk
1 teaspoon vanilla extract
1 cup water
2 tablespoons swerve

Directions:

1. In your instant pot, mix coconut with almonds, coconut milk, vanilla, water and swerve, stir, cover and cook on High for 6 minutes.

2. Add chia seeds, stir, cover the pot and leave it aside for 4 minutes more.
3. Divide into bowls and serve for breakfast. Enjoy!

Nutritional Values

Per servingcalories 173
fat 3
fiber 4
carbs 5
protein 6

24. Chocolate Oatmeal

Preparation Time: 10 minutes
Cooking Time: 10 minutes
Serves: 4

Ingredients:

1 cup coconut milk
2 and ½ tablespoon cocoa powder
4 cups water
2 cups coconut, shredded
1 teaspoon vanilla extract
1 teaspoon cinnamon powder
10 ounces cherries, pitted

Directions:

1. In your instant pot, mix coconut milk with water, cocoa powder, coconut, vanilla extract, cinnamon and cherries, stir, cover and cook on High for 10 minutes.
2. Stir your chocolate oatmeal once again, divide into bowls and serve for breakfast. Enjoy!

Nutritional Values

Per servingcalories 183
fat 4
fiber 2
carbs 5
protein 7

25. Blueberry and Yogurt Bowl

Preparation Time: 10 minutes
Cooking Time: 6 minutes
Serves: 1

Ingredients:

1/3 cup coconut milk
1/3 cup coconut, unsweetened and flaked
1/3 cup yogurt
1/3 cup blueberries
1 tablespoon chia seeds
½ teaspoon stevia
¼ teaspoon vanilla extract
A sprinkle of cinnamon powder
1 and ½ cups water

Directions:

1. In a heatproof jar, mix coconut milk with coconut, yogurt, blueberries, chia, stevia, vanilla and cinnamon, stir well and cover with tin foil.
2. Put the water in your instant pot, add the jar, cover and cook on High for 6 minutes.
3. Transfer blueberry mix to a bowl and serve. Enjoy!

Nutritional Values

Per servingcalories 152
fat 3
fiber 3
carbs 4
protein 6

26. Breakfast Cauliflower Pudding

Preparation Time: 10 minutes
Cooking Time: 10 minutes
Serves: 6

Ingredients:

2 cups coconut milk
1 and ¼ cups water
1 cup cauliflower rice
¾ cup coconut cream
2 tablespoons swerve
1 teaspoon vanilla extract

Directions:

1. In your instant pot, mix coconut milk with water, swerve and cauliflower rice, stir, cover and cook on High for 10 minutes.
2. Add cream and vanilla extract, stir, divide into bowls and serve for breakfast. Enjoy!

Nutritional Values

Per servingcalories 153
fat 3
fiber 2
carbs 6
protein 7

27. Scotch Eggs

Preparation Time: 10 minutes
Cooking Time: 12 minutes
Serves: 4

Ingredients:

1 pound sausage, ground
4 eggs
1 tablespoon olive oil
2 cups water

Directions:

1. Put 1 cup water in your instant pot, add the steamer basket, add eggs inside, cover, cook on High for 6 minutes, transfer eggs to a bowl filled with ice water, cool them down and peel.
2. Divide sausage mix into 4 pieces, place them on a cutting board and flatten them.
3. Divide eggs on sausage mix, wrap well and shape 4 balls.
4. Add the oil to your instant pot, set on sauté mode, heat it up, add scotch eggs and brown them on all sides.
5. Clean the pot, add 1 cup water, and the steamer basket, and scotch eggs inside, cover the pot and cook on High for 6

minutes.
6. Serve them for breakfast. Enjoy!

Nutritional Values

Per servingcalories 192
fat 4
fiber 2
carbs 4
protein 7

28. Celeriac and Bacon Breakfast

Preparation Time: 10 minutes
Cooking Time: 9 minutes
Serves: 6

Ingredients:

2 teaspoons parsley, dried
3 bacon strips
2 pounds celeriac, peeled and cubed
4 ounces cheddar cheese, shredded
1 teaspoon garlic powder
A pinch of salt and black pepper
2 tablespoons water

Directions:

1. Set your instant pot on sauté mode, add bacon, stir and cook for a couple of minutes.
2. Add garlic powder, salt, pepper, water and parsley and stir.
3. Add celeriac, stir, cover and cook on Manual for 7 minutes.
4. Divide between plates and serve for breakfast.

Enjoy!

Nutritional Values

Per servingcalories 164
fat 3
fiber 2
carbs 6
protein 7

29. Meat Quiche

Preparation Time: 10 minutes
Cooking Time: 30 minutes
Serves: 4

Ingredients:

½ cup coconut milk
A pinch of salt and black pepper
6 eggs, whisked
4 bacon slices, cooked and crumbled
1 cup sausage, ground and cooked
½ cup ham, chopped
2 green onions, chopped
1 cup cheddar cheese, shredded
1 cup water

Directions:

1. In a bowl, mix eggs with salt, pepper, milk, sausage, bacon, ham, green onions and cheese and stir well.
2. Pour this into a soufflé dish and spread.
3. Add the water to your instant pot, add the trivet, add soufflé dish inside, cover pot and cook on High for 30 minutes.
4. Serve hot for breakfast.
   Enjoy!

Nutritional Values

Per servingcalories 200
fat 3
fiber 3
carbs 6
protein 6

30. Cinnamon Oatmeal

Preparation Time: 10 minutes
Cooking Time: 5 minutes
Serves: 2

Ingredients:

1 and ½ cups water
½ cup coconut, unsweetened and flaked
½ teaspoon cinnamon powder
2 apples, cored, peeled and chopped
¼ teaspoon ginger powder
Stevia to the taste

Directions:

1. In your instant pot, mix water with coconut, cinnamon, apples, ginger and stevia to the taste, stir, cover and cook on High for 5 minutes.
2. Stir again, divide into bowls and serve for breakfast.
   Enjoy!

Nutritional Values

Per servingcalories 172
fat 4
fiber 2
carbs 6
protein 6

31. Cauliflower Congee

Preparation Time: 10 minutes
Cooking Time: 20 minutes
Serves: 4

Ingredients:

1 cup cauliflower rice
3 cups veggie stock
2 cups bok choy, chopped
2 tablespoons ginger, grated
2 cups shitake mushrooms, chopped
2 garlic cloves, minced
1 cup water
1 tablespoon coconut aminos

Directions:

1. In your instant pot, mix cauliflower rice with veggie stock, bok choy, mushrooms, garlic, water and aminos, stir, cover and cook on Manual for 20 minutes.
2. Divide into bowls and serve for breakfast.
   Enjoy!

Nutritional Values

Per servingcalories 183
fat 3
fiber 2
carbs 6
protein 3

32. Breakfast Avocado Cups

Preparation Time: 10 minutes
Cooking Time: 5 minutes
Serves: 4

Ingredients:

2 avocados, cut into halves and pitted
1 cup water
A drizzle of olive oil
1 tablespoon chives, chopped
A pinch of salt and black pepper
4 eggs

Directions:

1. Arrange all avocado cups on a cutting board and drizzle some olive oil over them.
2. Crack an egg into each avocado cup, season with salt and pepper and sprinkle chives all over.
3. Add the water to your instant pot, add the trivet, add avocado cups inside, cover and cook on High for 5 minutes.
4. Divide avocado cups between plates and serve for breakfast.
   Enjoy!

Nutritional Values

Per servingcalories 200
fat 3
fiber 3
carbs 7
protein 5

33. Chicken Liver Spread

Preparation Time: 5 minutes
Cooking Time: 15 minutes

Serves: 8

Ingredients:

1 teaspoon extra virgin olive oil
¾ pound chicken livers
1 yellow onion, peeled and chopped
1 bay leaf
¼ cup red wine
2 anchovies
1 tablespoons capers, drained and chopped
1 tablespoon butter
Salt and ground black pepper, to taste

Directions:

Put the olive oil into the Instant Pot, add the onion, salt, pepper, chicken livers, bay leaf and wine. Stir, cover the Instant Pot, and cook on the Manual setting for 10 minutes. Release the pressure, add the anchovies, capers, and butter. Stir, transfer to a blender and pulse several times. Add the salt and pepper, blend again, transfer to a bowl, and serve with toasted bread slices.

Nutritional Values Per serving

Calories: 150
Fat: 12
Fiber: 0
Carbs: 5
Sugar: 2
Protein: 4

34. Cheesy Grits

Preparation Time: 10 minutes
Cooking Time: 10 minutes
Serves: 4

Ingredients:

2 tablespoons coconut oil
1¾ cup half and half
1 cup stone ground grits
3 cups water
2 teaspoons salt
3 tablespoons butter
4 ounces cheddar cheese, grated
Butter, for serving

Directions:

Set the Instant Pot on Sauté mode, add the grits, stir, and toast them for 3 minutes. Add the oil, half and half, water, salt, butter, and cheese, stir, cover and cook on Manual mode for 10 minutes. Release the pressure naturally, set the cheesy grits aside for 15 minutes, transfer to bowls, add the butter on top, and serve.

Nutritional Values Per serving

Calories: 280
Fat: 13
Fiber: 1
Carbs: 26
Sugar: 2
Protein: 13.2

35. Tasty Breakfast

Preparation Time: 10 minutes
Cooking Time: 25 minutes
Serves: 4

Ingredients:

3 cups green tea
1 tablespoon ground cinnamon
1 cup red lentils, soaked for 4 hours and drained
2 apples, diced
1 teaspoon ground cloves
1 teaspoon turmeric
Maple syrup, for serving
Coconut milk, for serving

Directions:

Put lentils into the Instant Pot, add the tea and stir, cover, and cook on the Manual setting for 15 minutes. Release the pressure, uncover the Instant Pot, add the cinnamon, apples, turmeric, and cloves, stir, cover and cook on the Manual setting for 15 minutes. Release pressure, divide lentils between bowls and add some maple syrup and coconut milk.

Nutritional Values Per serving

Calories: 140

Fat: 1.2
Fiber: 8.4
Carbs: 35
Sugar: 14
Protein: 5

36. Mushroom Pate

Preparation Time: 6 minutes
Cooking Time: 18 minutes
Serves: 6

Ingredients:

1-ounce dried porcini mushrooms
1 pound button mushrooms, sliced
1 cup boiled water
1 tablespoon butter
1 tablespoon extra virgin olive oil
1 shallot, peeled and diced
¼ cup white wine
Salt and ground black pepper, to taste
1 bay leaf
1 tablespoon truffle oil
3 tablespoons Parmesan cheese, grated

Directions:

Put the porcini mushrooms in a bowl, add 1 cup boiling water over them, and set aside. Set the Instant Pot on Sauté mode, add the butter and olive oil and heat them. Add the shallots, stir and cook for 2 minutes. Add the porcini mushrooms and their liquid, button mushrooms, wine, salt, pepper, and bay leaf. Stir, cover the Instant Pot and cook on the Manual setting for 16 minutes. Release the pressure, remove the bay leaf and some of the liquid, transfer everything to a blender and pulse until smooth. Add the truffle oil and grated Parmesan cheese, blend again, transfer to a bowl, and serve.

Nutritional Values Per serving

Calories: 220
Fat: 15
Fiber: 0
Carbs: 15
Sugar: 3
Protein: 5

37. Ricotta Cheese Spread

Preparation Time: 10 minutes
Cooking Time: 5 minutes
Serves: 4

Ingredients:

10 ounces canned diced tomatoes with green chilies
1¾ cups Italian sausage, ground
4 cups processed cheese, cut into chunks
4 tablespoons water

Directions:

In the Instant Pot, mix the tomatoes and chilies with the water, ground sausage, and cheese. Stir, cover and cook on the Manual setting for 5 minutes. Release the pressure naturally for 5 minutes, uncover the Instant Pot, stir the spread, transfer to a bowl, and serve.

Nutritional Values Per serving

Calories: 294
Fat: 18
Fiber: 1
Carbs: 4
Protein: 7

38. Breakfast Salad

Preparation Time: 10 minutes
Cooking Time: 4 minutes
Serves: 4

Ingredients:

6 potatoes, peeled and cubed
4 eggs
1½ cups water
1 cup mayonnaise
¼ cup onion, peeled and diced
1 tablespoon dill pickle juice
2 tablespoons parsley, diced
1 tablespoon mustard
Salt and ground black pepper, to taste

Directions:

Put the potatoes, eggs and the water into the steamer basket of the Instant Pot, cover, and cook on Manual mode for 4 minutes. Release the pressure, transfer the eggs to a bowl filled with ice water and set aside to cool. In a bowl, mix the mayonnaise with the pickle juice, onion, parsley, and mustard, and stir well. Add the potatoes and toss to coat. Peel the eggs, chop them, add them to salad, and toss again. Add salt and pepper, stir, and serve your salad with toasted bread slices.

Nutritional Values Per serving

Calories: 150
Fat: 8
Fiber: 1.3
Carbs: 11
Protein: 3

39. Breakfast Potatoes

Preparation Time: 5 minutes
Cooking Time: 7 minutes
Serves: 2

Ingredients:

4 Yukon gold potatoes, washed
2 teaspoons Italian seasoning
1 tablespoon bacon fat
1 cup chives, chopped, for serving
Water
Salt and ground black pepper, to taste

Directions:

Put the potatoes into the Instant Pot, add enough water to cover them, cover the Instant Pot and cook on the Manual setting for 10 minutes. Release the pressure naturally, transfer potatoes to a working surface, and set aside to cool. Peel the potatoes, transfer them to a bowl, and mash them with a fork. Set the Instant Pot on Sauté mode, add the bacon fat and heat. Add the potatoes, Italian seasoning, salt and pepper, stir, cover the Instant Pot and cook on the Manual setting for 1 minute. Release the pressure, stir the potatoes again, divide them between plates, and serve with chives sprinkled on top.

Nutritional Values Per serving

Calories: 90
Fat: 3
Fiber: 1
Carbs: 11
Protein: 1

40. Pecan Sweet Potatoes

Preparation Time: 10 minutes
Cooking Time: 10 minutes
Serves: 8

Ingredients:

1 cup water
1 tablespoon lemon peel
½ cup brown sugar
¼ teaspoon salt
3 sweet potatoes, peeled and sliced
¼ cup butter
¼ cup maple syrup
1 cup pecans, chopped
1 tablespoon cornstarch
Whole pecans, for garnish

Directions:

Put the water into the Instant Pot, add the lemon peel, brown sugar, and salt and stir. Add the potatoes, cover the Instant Pot and cook on the Manual setting for 15 minutes. Release the pressure and transfer the potatoes to a serving plate. Select Sauté mode on the Instant Pot, add the butter and melt it. Add the pecans, maple syrup, and cornstarch and stir well. Pour this over the potatoes, garnish with the whole pecans, and serve.

Nutritional Values Per serving

Calories: 230
Fat: 13
Fiber: 4
Carbs: 15
Protein: 6

41. Barbecue Tofu

Preparation Time: 10 minutes
Cooking Time: 10 minutes
Serves: 6

Ingredients:

28 ounces firm tofu, cubed
12 ounces barbecue sauce
2 tablespoons extra virgin olive oil
4 garlic cloves, peeled and minced
1 yellow onion, peeled and chopped
1 celery stalk, chopped
1 red bell pepper, chopped
1 green bell pepper, chopped
Salt, to taste
Curry powder

Directions:

Set the Instant Pot on Sauté mode, add the oil and heat it up. Add the bell peppers, garlic, onion and celery, and stir. Add the salt and curry powder, stir, and cook for 2 minutes. Add the tofu, stir, and cook 4 minutes. Add the barbecue sauce, stir, cover the Instant Pot and cook on the Manual setting for 5 minutes. Release the pressure, uncover the Instant Pot, transfer to plates, and serve.

Nutritional Values Per serving

Calories: 200
Fat: 11
Fiber: 3
Carbs: 14.1
Protein: 14.4

42. Potatoes and Tofu Breakfast

Preparation Time: 10 minutes
Cooking Time: 4 minutes
Serves: 4

Ingredients:

3 purple potatoes, cubed
1 yellow onion, peeled and chopped
2 garlic cloves, peeled and minced

1 carrot, peeled and chopped
1 ginger root, peeled and grated
½ pound firm tofu, cubed
3 tablespoons water
1 tablespoon tamari
Mexican spice blend, to taste
1½ cups Brussels sprouts

Directions:

Set the Instant Pot on Sauté mode, add the onion and brown it for 1 minute. Add the potatoes, ginger, garlic, tofu, carrots, tamari, spices, Brussels sprouts, and water, cover, and cook on the Manual setting for 2 minutes. Release the pressure, uncover the Instant Pot, uncover the Instant Pot, transfer to plates, and serve.

Nutritional Values Per serving

Calories: 156
Fat: 10
Fiber: 3
Carbs: 11.4
Protein: 13

43. Pumpkin Butter

Preparation Time: 15 minutes
Cooking Time: 10 minutes
Serves: 18

Ingredients:

30 ounces pumpkin puree
3 apples, peeled, cored and chopped
1 tablespoon pumpkin pie spice
1 cup sugar
A pinch of salt
12 ounces apple cider
½ cup honey.

Directions:

In the Instant Pot, mix the pumpkin puree with the pumpkin pie spice, apple pieces, sugar, honey, cider and a pinch of salt. Stir well, cover the Instant Pot, and cook on the Manual setting for 10 minutes. Release the pressure naturally for 15 minutes, transfer the butter to small jars,

and keep it in the refrigerator until serving.

Nutritional Values Per serving

Calories: 50
Fat: 1
Fiber: 0
Carbs: 10
Sugar: 9
Protein: 1

44. Tofu Breakfast

Preparation Time: 10 minutes
Cooking Time: 7 minutes
Serves: 4

Ingredients:

1 bunch kale leaves, chopped
1 leek, cut into halves lengthwise and sliced thin
1 teaspoon paprika
1 tablespoon olive oil
½ cup water
Salt, to taste
Cayenne pepper
2 teaspoons sherry vinegar
3 ounces tofu, cubed and baked
¼ cup almonds, chopped

Directions:

Set the Instant Pot on Sauté mode, add the oil and heat it up. Add the leeks, stir and sauté them for 5 minutes. Add the paprika, stir and cook for 1 minute. Add the water, kale, salt, and cayenne, cover the Instant Pot and cook on the Manual setting for 2 minutes. Release the pressure, add the tofu and vinegar and more salt, if needed, stir, and transfer to plates. Sprinkle the almonds on top, and serve.

Nutritional Values Per serving

Calories: 170
Fat: 12
Fiber: 7
Carbs: 18
Protein: 16

45. Tofu Scramble

Preparation Time: 10 minutes
Cooking Time: 7 minutes
Serves: 4

Ingredients:

1 yellow onion, peeled and sliced thin
1 teaspoon walnut oil
3 garlic cloves, peeled and minced
¼ cup vegetable stock
1 cup carrot, peeled and chopped
1 block firm tofu, drained
12 ounces canned tomatoes, diced
1 teaspoon cumin
2 tablespoons red bell pepper, chopped
1 tablespoon Italian seasoning
1 teaspoon nutritional yeast
Salt and ground black pepper, to taste

Directions:

Set the Instant Pot on Sauté mode, add the oil and heat it up. Add the onion, carrot, and garlic, stir, and cook for 3 minutes. Crumble the tofu, add it to pot, and stir. Add the stock, bell pepper, tomatoes, cumin, Italian seasoning, salt, and pepper, stir, cover the Instant Pot and cook on the Manual setting for 4 minutes. Release the pressure, transfer to bowls, and serve with nutritional yeast on top.

Nutritional Values Per serving

Calories: 144
Fat: 5.7
Fiber: 3.1
Carbs: 11.8
Protein: 13

46. Chocolate Zucchini Muffin Bites

Preparation Time: 38 minutes

Ingredients

2 organic or pastured eggs
3/4 to 1 cup evaporated cane juice
1/2 cup coconut oil
2 teaspoons vanilla extract
1 tablespoon grass-fed butter melted
3 tablespoons cocoapowder
1 cupsprouted einkorn flour learn how to sprout your grains
1/2 teaspoon baking soda
1/4 teaspoon seasalt
3/4 teaspoon ground cinnamon
1 cups zucchini or s□uash, grated
1/3 cup chocolate chips
1 cup pure water

Directions

1. Combine eggs, sweetener, coconut oil, and vanilla extract in a medium-sized mixing bowl.
2. Stir well.
3. Next, add cocoa powder to melted butter.
4. Mix until it looks like a thick but smooth dark paste.
5. Then, add chocolate mixture to egg mixture and stir well.
6. Add flour, baking soda, seasalt, and cinnamon to the bowl.
7. Stir well.
8. Fold in grated zucchini and chocolate chips.
9. Then, add trivet and 1 cup of water to the inner pot of your Instant Pot or other pressure cooker.
10. Cover with a glass lid toprevent evaporation.
11. If using an electriccooker such as the Instant Pot, put it on sauté so it can pre-heat.
12. If using a stovetopcooker, turn on the burner to medium to begin pre-heat.
13. Using a small cookie scoop, fill silicone muffin cupsabout 2/3 full. The 6-quart Instant Pot fits 16 muffin cups at a time. This means you'll have batter left over. Either pressure cook these muffins after the first batch is done, or cook them in theoven at the same time *see oven adaptation below.
14. Then, layer muffin cups inside inner pot of pressurecooker.

15. Once bottom layer is full, cover with piece of parchment paper and piece of aluminum foil. Both should becut in a circle to thesizeof the inner pot.

16. Cover with a plateor another trivet.

17. Then put the rest of the muffin cups inside to fill up the second layer. Try to keepall the muffin cups level!

18. Again, cover with parchment paper and aluminum foil, then a plate.

19. Cover thepressurecooker, checking that the seal and other parts are in good shape.

20. If using an electriccooker, set to high for 8 minutes.

21. If using a stovetop cooker, bring to low pressure and maintain for 8 minutes.

22. When cooking time isover, if using an electric cooker, let it sit for 10 to 15 minutes while it depressurizes naturally.

23. If using a stovetop cooker, remove from heat and let it sit for 10 to 15 minutes to depressurize naturally.

24. Then, if anypressure remains, cover release valve with a towel and quick release.

25. Next check for doneness with a toothpick.

26. Finally, carefully unpack your lovely, moist chocolate-y muffins!

27. For special occasions or just for fun, topyour pressurecooker muffins with this chocolate cream cheese frosting!

Nutritional Values

Per serving Servings Per Recipe: 9
Serving Size: 1 serving
Calories 131.2
Sugars14.4 g
Protein 3.2 g

47. Instant Pot Rice Pudding Recipe

Prep+Cook Time 19 minutes
Serves:5

Ingredients

 1 c uncooked rice

 1/2 c sugar
 1 c water
 1.5 tbsp butter
 2 c milk or whole is best
 1 egg
 1/4-1/2 c evaporated milk add 1/4 c. first and at theend if you want moreadd the additional 1/4 c. until desired texture isachieved
 1/2 tsp vanilla
 1/2 tspalmond extract - optional
 pinch of nutmeg - optional
 pinch of cinnamon - optional

Directions

1. Put Instant Pot on saute and add butter until melted.

2. Add rice and stir so rice is coated.

3. Add milk, water, vanilla, cinnamon, almond extract if desired and sugar. Stir until combined.

4. Put lid on IP and close steam valve.

5. Set to manual, pressure, high, for 14 minutes if you like your rice more turgid set it for 12.

6. When done do a quick release

7. In a small bowl whisk egg and 1/4 c evaporated milk together.

8. Spoon a spoonful of rice pudding mixture intoegg mixture and stir, add another warm spoonful of rice mixture and stir.

9. Then add bowl full of egg mixture into your IP or pressure cooker and set tosaute.

10. Allow to get hot enough where it bubbles for about 30-60 seconds, stir slowly when it starts to bubble so it doesn't stick to bottom. Add more evaporated milk if desired.

11. It will begin to thicken.

12. When it has reached the perfect consistency for you pour contents into a bowl or small serving bowls immediatelyso it doesn't continue tocook and get a bit mushy.

13. Serve warm or chilled, top with cinnamon or nutmeg.

Nutritional Value

Per Serving:Calories 198
Calories from Fat 72
Total Fat 8g
Saturated Fat 4g
Cholesterol 55mg
Sodium 101mg
Potassium 179mg

48. Instant Pot Cinnamon Banana Oatmeal

Preparation Time: 25 minutes
Serves: 3 servings

Ingredients

1 cupold fashioned oatmeal
1 cup milk
1 cup water
2 bananas
2 tspcinnamon
1 Tbsp brown sugar

Directions

1. Spray the bottom of your Instant Pot lightly with non-stick cooking spray. Add in the oatmeal, milk and water.
2. Slice up 1 of the bananas and add it into thepot. Add in cinnamon and brown sugar. Stir.
3. Set the manual button to 5 minutes. Once the timer beeps let the pressure release naturally for 10 minutesand then carefully release the rest of thepressure. Be careful though since grainscan really get foamy. The best way to release extra pressure is to gently move the valve halfway between "sealing" and "venting." If any foam comesout move the valve back to venting and wait for 20 seconds and then try again.
4. Stir the oatmeal and scoop into bowls. Slice the second bananaand add fresh slices to the top of each bowl.

Nutrition Info:

Calories 278
Calories from Fat 54

Total Fat 6g
Total Carbohydrates 45g

49. Chocolate Instant Bircher Muesli

Prep+Cook Time 20 min
Serves: 2 people

Ingredients

1 1/2 Cup greek yogurt
Dollop of honeyor maple syrup
1 Teaspoon vanilla essence
1 Cup rolled oats Organic
1 Cup milk
1 Tablespoon chia seeds
Handful Toasted almonds &chopped
Fresh raspberries or your favourite fruit
1/2 Cup orange juice
1 Tablespoon heaped cocoapowder
Some dak chocolate chips / dark chopped chocolate

Directions

1. Blend chiaseedsand milk together for 2 minutes continuosly. Keep it aside.
2. Toast almonds in a pan, chop it , keep it aside
3. Take a bowl + greek yogurt + rolled oats +honey or maple syrup + vanilla essence + mix well and now add chiaseeds mixture + cocoa powder + orange juice. Mix all well and keep it in the refrigerator for 8-10 minutes toset. Serve it with raspberries , chopped toasted almonds + dark chocolate on top

Recipe Notes

You can add 1 teaspoon more cocoa if you really want more chocolaty flavour.

Nutritional Values

Per serving Calories 270.6
Total Fat 2.8 g

50. Green Chile Breakfast Tacos

Prep+Cook Time 2 hours 5 mins

Ingredients

Instant Pot Green Chile

2 to 3 lb. pork shoulder
¾ cupchicken broth
1 14 oz can roasted crushed tomatoes
2 mild hatch green chiles
2 hot hatch green chiles
1 onion, chopped
3 tbs lard or bacon fat
1 ½ tspcumin
salt and pepper to taste

Breakfast Tacos

8 oz green chile
3 eggs, scrambled
2 Siete Foods Tortillasor anyother paleo tortilla
sliced avocado, mayo, cilantro and lime wedges
for garnish

Directions

Instant Pot Green Chile

1. Season pork with salt, pepper and cumin and set aside.
2. Melt lard in Instant Pot set to SAUTE setting on HIGH
3. Once lard has melted, saute onions until browned, almost carmelized.
4. Sear pork on all sides in the instant pot to get a nice crust. Remove pork from instant pot.
5. Deglaze instant pot with chicken broth scraping upany brown bits with a wooden spoon.
6. Add green chiles, diced tomatoesand pork to the instant pot. Seal and cook on MANUAL setting on HIGH pressure for 90 minutes.
7. Release pressureand shred pork using two forks.

Breakfast Tacos

1. Heat a medium skillet over medium heat and add green chile. Reheat until pork is crispy.
2. Add scrambled eggsand green chile to tortillas, garnish with sliced avocado, mayo, cilantro and juice from a lime wedge.
3. Enjoy!

Nutrition Info:

Calories440.8
Total Fat30.8 g

51. Pressure Cooker Breakfast Hash

Preparation Time: 30 minutes, Serving: 4

Ingredients

cooking oil
6 small potatoes, peeled if desired
6 eggs
1/4 cup water
1 cup shredded American cheese
1 cupchopped breakfast ham

Directions

1. Set the pressure cooker to "saute" and add a thin layer of oil to the bottom of thepan. While the pressure cooker is heating, finely shred the potatoes in a food processor. Squeeze out anyexcess moisture then add the shredded potatoes to the hot oil. Let the potatoes brown in the hot oil without stirring.
2. Meanwhile, beat theeggsand set aside.
3. Once the potatoes have browned on the bottom, break them up with a wooden spoon. Add the water, eggs, cheese, and ham. Stir gently.
4. Lock thecover on thepressurecooker and bring to high pressure. Let cook for 1 minute then use the quick release method to release thesteam.

5. Serve the breakfast hash immediately with toast, if desired.
6. shareon facebook shareon twitter share on pinterest save toyummly

Nutritional Values

Per serving 445 calories
23 grams fat
34 gramscarbohydrates
25 grams protein per serving.

52. Instant Pot Cheesy Bacon Ranch Potatoes

Preparation Time: 22 minutes
Serves6

Ingredients

3 medium red potatoes we used Washington potatoes
3 medium baking potatoes
1 packet ranch dressing mix powdered mix, 1 oz.
3/4 c chicken broth
1/3 c bacon bits we used real bacon bits
1 c cheddar cheese grated
1/3 c parmesan cheese
3 chives diced, optional

Directions

1. Wash potatoes. Leave the skin on and dice intoapprox. into 1" pcs.
2. Put them inside your Instant Pot and sprinkle your powdered ranch dressing mix on topof them. alternatively to get them all really coated put potatoesand dry mix in a bowl and mix to coat and then add intoyour pressure cooker.
3. Sprinkle your bacon bits on topof that and pour your chicken broth over everything.
4. Close your lid and steam valve and set topressure high for 7 minutes.
5. Do a quick release.
6. Lift lid and sprinkle parmesan cheese, then grated cheese over your potatoes. Put lid back on for a few minutessocheesecan melt.
7. Lift lid, gently stir and serve!!

Nutritional Values

Per serving Calories 231
Calories from Fat 90
Total Fat 10g
Saturated Fat 6g
Cholesterol 31mg
Sodium 828mg
Potassium 544mg
Total Carbohydrates 22g

53. Instant Pot Monkey Bread Recipe

Prep+Cook Time: 30 minutes
Servings: 6 servings

Ingredients

¼ cup white sugar
¼ cup brown sugar
½ tsp vanilla
½ cup butter
2 packages of biscuit dough one butter, one regular flavor cut intosmall pieces
1 Tbsp ground cinnamon
1 Tbsp powdered sugar
1½ cups of water

Directions

1. To get started, add the 1½ cupof water to the Instant pot and add the trivet that came with your pressure cooker.
2. Add the whitesugar, cinnamon, and biscuit dough to the ziplock bag. Then shake well until everything iscoated.
3. Place a long strip of foil that is rolled into the Instant pot over the trivet with the sides coming up to the top. Place the mixture into your bundt pan, and then place the bundt pan over the foil on the trivet. We will be using the foil stripas makeshift handles when we remove the bundt pan from thepot after cooking.
4. Place the lid and turn until locked. Set the manual mode for 20 minutes and allow your bread to cook.
5. Once the time has finished, do a quick releaseand carefully remove the monkey bread from the Instant Pot. Be careful as

your bundt pan will still be hot.

6. Over medium heat melt the butter, vanilla, and brown sugar. Place the monkey bread on a plate, and then drizzle the top with the butter and brown sugar.

Nutritional Values

Per serving Calories: 244kcal
Fat: 16g
Saturated fat: 9g
Cholesterol: 40mg
Sodium: 225mg
Carbohydrates: 24g

54. Instant Pot French Toast Casserole

Preparation Time: 35 mins, **Servings:** 4

Ingredients

1/2 loaf challah bread, cubed
2 eggs
1 1/2 cups milk
1/2 cup brown sugar
1/4 teaspoon nutmeg
1 teaspoon cinnamon
1 teaspoon vanilla
2 tablespoons butter, melted
1 cup water for the bottom of Instant Pot

Directions

1. Whisk together eggs, milk, brown sugar, nutmeg, cinnamon, vanilla and melted butter.

2. Coat an oven safe 7-inch bowl or 7-inch cakepan with non stick cooking spray.

3. Add cubed bread to the bowl. Pour egg mixture over the bread and gentlypress bread down tocoat with the egg mixture.

4. Pour the cup of water in the Instant Pot. Place the trivet into the Instant Pot.

5. Place the bowl or cake pan on topof the trivet. Close the lid and lock. Set time to 25 minutes Pressure Cook setting.

6. Once donecooking, do a quick pressure release. Once the valve drops, carefully remove the lid.

7. Remove the bowl from the Instant Pot. Optional: Top with a sprinkle of powdered sugar and maplesyrup.

Notes
For easy bowl removal, take 4 long strips of foil placeon topof the trivet creating a sling. Place bowl on topof foil strips. I am able to carefully remove the bowl without the sling by tilting the Instant pot once it'sslightlycooled and using pot holders.

Nutritional Value Per Serving:

Calories: 424kcal
Carbohydrates: 59g
Protein: 12g
Fat: 15g
Saturated Fat: 7g
Cholesterol: 175mg

55. Sauteed Caramelized Pears

Preparation Time: 20 mins, **Servings:** 4 servings

Ingredients

2 large Bartlett pears a bit under-ripe, peeled and sliced
1/2 cup heavy cream preferably raw or coconut cream can be used
1/4 cup butter preferably pasture-raised, or coconut oil, ghee or lard
1/4 cup maplesyrup
1 Tablespoon vanilla extract
1/8 teaspoon sea salt

Directions

1. Melt butter in large cast iron skillet over medium-high heat. Add pearsand sea salt. Saute until pears begin to brown and soften a bit, about 8-10 minutes.

2. Reduce heat to low. Add maplesyrup, stirring to coat. Becareful; thepan'scontents will sizzle and steam a bit. Add vanilla. Add cream and de-glaze thepan, using thesteam and your spatula toscrape up any bits that are stuck to thepan. Stir in bits, and turn off heat.

3. Garnish bread pudding with pears and sauce.

56. Instant Pot Apple Bread with Salted Caramel Icing

Prep+Cook Time: 1 hour 10 minutes
Serving 10

Ingredients

3 cups apples Peeled, Cored, and cubed
1 cup sugar
2 eggs
1 tbs vanilla
1 tbs applepiespice
2 cups flour
1 stick butter
1 tbs baking powder

For the topping:

1 stick salted butter
2 cups brown sugar
1 cup heavy cream
2 cupspowdered sugar

Directions

1. In your mixer cream together eggs, butter, applepiespice, and sugar until creamy and smooth.

2. Stir in your apples. In another bowl mix flour and baking powder. Add your flour mix to your wet mix. I added half of my mix at a time.

3. The batter was thick. Pour into your 7" springform pan.

4. Place your trivet in the bottom of your Instant pot and onecupof water.

5. Place your pan on the trivet.

6. Put on manual high pressure for 70 minutes.

7. Do a ☐uick release. Remove and top with Icing.

8. Icing Instructions: Melt butter in a small saucepan add brown sugar and let come to a boil continue cooking for 3 minutesor until sugar is melted. Stir in heavy cream.

continue cooking for 2-3 minutes. until slightly thickens. Remove from heat and let completelycool. Mix in powdered sugar with a whisk until creamy with no lumps.

Nutritional ValuesPer serving

Calories: 551
Saturated Fat: 5g
Cholesterol: 65mg
Sodium: 38mg
Carbohydrates: 113g
Fiber: 1g
Sugar: 90g
Protein: 4g

57. Spice Oatmeal

Preparation Time: 18 minutes
Serves: 2

Ingredients

1 cup old-fashioned rolled oats
1/4 cup grated extra-sharp cheddar
1 scallion; chopped.
2 cups water
1/4 tsp. paprika
kosher salt and black pepper

Directions:

1. Add all the Ingredients to Instant Pot; except cheese,

2. Secure the lid of instant pot and press *Manual* function key.

3. Adjust the time to 3 minutes and cook at high pressure,

4. When it beeps; release the pressure naturally and remove the lid. Stir in shredded cheese and serve.

Nutrition Values Nutritional Values Per serving

Calories:- 210
Carbohydrate:- 27.9g
Protein:- 9g
Fat:- 7.3g
Sugar:- 0.7g

58. Special Oatmeal

Preparation Time: 11 minutes
Serves: 4

Ingredients

2 cups old-fashioned oats
2 ¼ cups water
2 ¼ cups milk
1 tbsp. dried cranberries
1 tbsp. dried cherries
1 tbsp. roasted pistachios
1/2 tsp. salt
1/4 tsp. nutmeg
1 tbsp. honey

Directions:

1. Add all the Ingredients to Instant Pot; except for cranberries, cherries and pistachios,
2. Secure the lid of instant pot and press *Manual* function key.
3. Adjust the time to 6 minutes and cook at high pressure,
4. When it beeps; release the pressure naturally and remove the lid.
5. Stir the prepared oatmeal and serve in a bowl. Garnish with cranberries, cherries and pistachios on top.

Nutrition Values Nutritional Values Per serving

Calories:- 415
Carbohydrate:- 66.8g
Protein:- 15g
Fat:- 8.9g
Sugar:- 12.9g
Sodium:- 0.36g

59. Walnut Oatmeal

Preparation Time: 11 minutes
Serves: 6

Ingredients

1/2 cup walnuts; chopped fine
2 cups steel-cut oats
4 cups water
2 cups unsweetened almond milk
4 tbsp. ground flaxseeds
4 tbsp. chia seeds
2 large ripe bananas; mashed
4 tbsp. pure maple syrup
2 tsp. ground cinnamon
2 tsp. pure vanilla extract
Pinch salt

Directions:

1. Add all the Ingredients to Instant Pot. Reserve some banana slices and walnuts for topping.
2. Secure the lid of instant pot and press *Manual* function key.
3. Adjust the time to 6 minutes and cook at high pressure,
4. When it beeps; release the pressure naturally and remove the lid.
5. Stir the prepared oatmeal and serve in a bowl. Garnish with banana slices and chopped walnuts on top.

Nutrition Values Nutritional Values Per serving

Calories:- 284
Carbohydrate:- 37.2g
Protein:- 8.2g
Fat:- 12.4g
Sugar:- 1o.6g
Sodium:- 58mg

60. Healthy Quinoa Bowl

Preparation Time: 15 minutes
Serves: 3

Ingredients

3/4 cup quinoa; soaked in water at least 1 hour
1/2 tsp. cocoa powder
2 tbsp. honey

1 8 oz. can milk
3/4 cup water
1 pinch of salt
Toppings:
Chocolate chips
Whipped cream

Directions:

1. Add all the Ingredients for quinoa to Instant Pot.
2. Secure the lid of instant pot and press *Rice* function key.
3. Adjust the time to 10 minutes and cook at low pressure,
4. When it beeps; release the pressure naturally and remove the lid.
5. Stir the prepared quinoa well and serve in a bowl. Add chocolate chips and whipped cream on top.

Nutrition Values Nutritional Values Per serving

Calories:- 373
Carbohydrate:- 41.1g
Protein:- 7.9g
Fat:- 20.5g
Sugar:- 11.2g
Sodium:- 17mg

61. Delicious Quinoa

Preparation Time: 17 minutes
Serves: 3

Ingredients

3/4 cup quinoa; soaked in water for at least 1 hour
1 8 oz. can almond milk
3/4 cup water
1/2 cup banana; peeled and sliced
2 tbsp. honey
1 pinch of salt
1 tsp. vanilla extract

Topping:

6 banana slices
Grated chocolate

Directions:

1. Add all the Ingredients for quinoa to Instant Pot.
2. Secure the lid of instant pot and press *Rice* function key.
3. Adjust the time to 12 minutes and cook at low pressure,
4. When it beeps; release the pressure naturally and remove the lid.
5. Stir the prepared quinoa well and serve in a bowl. Add banana slices and grated chocolate on top.

Nutrition Values Nutritional Values Per serving

Calories:- 371
Carbohydrate:- 41.4g
Protein:- 7.3g
Fat:- 20.4g
Sugar:- 10.3g
Sodium:- 17mg

62. Broccoli Egg Casserole

Preparation Time: 30 minutes
Serves: 3

Ingredients

1/2 lb. broccoli florets
3 eggs
1/2 small onion chopped.
1/2 cup cooked ham or bacon
1/4 cup heavy cream
1/2 cup cheddar cheese
Sea salt and pepper; to taste

Directions:

1. Add 1 cup water to Instant Pot and place the trivet inside,
2. Add all the Ingredients to a bowl except cheese and whisk well.
3. Take a heatproof container and pour the egg mixture into it.
4. Place the container over the trivet.

5. Secure the lid of instant pot and press *Manual* function key.

6. Adjust the time to 20 minutes and cook at high pressure,

7. When it beeps; release the pressure naturally and remove the lid. Drizzle shredded cheese on top and serve hot.

Nutrition Values Nutritional Values Per serving

Calories:- 203
Carbohydrate:- 11.1g
Protein:- 6.2g
Fat:- 7.6g
Sugar:- 2.3g
Sodium:- 66mg

63. Banana Oatmeal

Preparation Time: 11 minutes
Serves: 4

Ingredients

2 bananas sliced
2 cups old-fashioned oats
2 ¼ cups water
2 ¼ cups milk
1 tbsp. sugar
2 tbsp. molasses
4 tbsp. chopped toasted pecans

Directions:

1. Add oats, milk, water and sugar into Instant Pot.

2. Secure the lid of instant pot and press *Manual* function key.

3. Adjust the time to 6 minutes and cook at high pressure,

4. When it beeps; release the pressure naturally and remove the lid.

5. Stir the prepared oatmeal. Serve with banana slices and pecans on top. Then drizzle molasses on it.

Nutrition Values Nutritional Values

Per serving

Calories:- 518
Carbohydrate:- 72.9g
Protein:- 16g
Fat:- 18g
Sugar:- 17.4g
Sodium:- 75mg

64. Delicious Cornmeal Porridge

Preparation Time: 21 minutes
Serves: 6

Ingredients

1 ¼ cups yellow cornmeal; fine
6 cups water
1 ¼ cups coconut milk
2 ½ sticks cinnamon
1 ¼ tsp. vanilla extract
3/4 tsp. coconut flakes
3/4 cup sweetened condensed milk

Directions:

1. Add 5 cups of water and all the coconut milk to Instant Pot.

2. Mix the cornmeal with 1 cup of water and add the mixture to the pot.

3. Stir in vanilla extract, coconut flakes and cinnamon sticks,

4. Secure the lid of instant pot and press *Manual* function key.

5. Adjust the time to 6 minutes and cook at high pressure,

6. After it beeps; release the pressure naturally and remove the lid.

7. Stir in sweetened condensed milk. Serve and enjoy.

Nutrition Values Nutritional Values Per serving

Calories:- 253
Carbohydrate:- 46.2g
Protein:- 6.9g
Fat:- 3.1g
Sugar:- 17.2g

Sodium:- 0.17g

65. Mushroom and Eggs Casserole

Preparation Time: 15 minutes
Serves: 3

Ingredients

1/2 cup cremini mushrooms; cooked and sliced
3 eggs
1/2 small onion chopped.
1/2 cup cooked ham or bacon
1/4 cup heavy cream
1/2 cup cheddar cheese
Sea salt and pepper; to taste

Directions:

1. Add 1 cup water to Instant Pot and place the trivet inside,
2. Add all the Ingredients to a bowl except cheese and whisk well.
3. Take a heatproof container and pour the egg mixture into it.
4. Place the container over the trivet.
5. Secure the lid of instant pot and press *Manual* function key.
6. Adjust the time to 10 minutes and cook at high pressure,
7. When it beeps; release the pressure naturally and remove the lid. Drizzle the shredded cheese on top and serve hot.

Nutrition Values Nutritional Values Per serving

Calories:- 218
Carbohydrate:- 3.3g
Protein:- 14.6g
Fat:- 16.3g
Sugar:- 1.2g
Sodium:- 0.47g

66. Mix Beans Rice

Preparation Time: 27 minutes
Serves: 4

Ingredients

1 cup whole mung beans
1 cup white basmati rice
1/2 tsp. turmeric powder
1/2 tsp. sea salt
2 inches ginger; grated or chopped.
3 tsp. shredded coconut
bunch of cilantro; chopped.
6 cups water
1/2 cup cremini mushrooms; sliced

Directions:

1. Add all the Ingredients to Instant Pot.
2. Secure the lid of instant pot and press *Manual* function key.
3. Adjust the time to 15 minutes and cook at high pressure,
4. When it beeps; release the pressure naturally and remove the lid.
5. Stir the prepared mixture and serve in a bowl. Garnish with mushroom slices on top.

Nutrition Values Nutritional Values Per serving

Calories:- 202
Carbohydrate:- 41g
Protein:- 7g
Fat:- 1.3g
Sugar:- 0.4g
Sodium:- 0.25g

67. Strawberry Oatmeal

Preparation Time: 11 minutes
Serves: 4

Ingredients

2 cups old-fashioned oats
8 strawberries; chopped.
2 ¼ cups water
2 ¼ cups milk
1/2 tsp. salt
1/2 tsp. ground cinnamon
1/4 cup sugar

Directions:

1. Add all the Ingredients to Instant Pot. Save a few strawberry slices for garnishing.
2. Secure the lid of instant pot and press *Multigrain option.*
3. Adjust the time to 6 minutes and let it cook.
4. After it beeps; release the pressure naturally and remove the lid. Serve with chopped strawberries on top.

Nutrition Values Nutritional Values Per serving

Calories:- 436
Carbohydrate:- 70g
Protein:- 14.7g
Fat:- 8g
Sugar:- 22g
Sodium:- 0.36g

68. Korean Style Steamed Eggs

Preparation Time: 11 minutes
Serves: 2

Ingredients

3 large eggs
1/2 cup cold water
Pinch of sesame seeds
Pinch of garlic powder
3 tsp. chopped scallions
Salt and pepper to taste

Directions:

1. Add 1 cup water to Instant Pot and place the trivet inside,
2. Add all the Ingredients in a bowl and whisk well.
3. Take a heatproof bowl and pour the egg mixture into it.
4. Place the bowl over the trivet.
5. Secure the lid of instant pot and press *Manual* function key.
6. Adjust the time to 5 minutes and cook at high pressure,
7. When it beeps; release the pressure

naturally and remove the lid. Serve immediately with rice,

Nutrition Values Nutritional Values Per serving

Calories:- 443
Carbohydrate:- 26.5g
Protein:- 13.2g
Fat:- 14.2g
Sugar:- 3.4g
Sodium:- 0.21g

69. Almond Quinoa

Preparation Time: 15 minutes
Serves: 3

Ingredients

3/4 cup quinoa; soaked in water at least 1 hour
1 8 oz. can almond milk
3/4 cup water
1/2 tsp. crushed almonds
1 tsp. vanilla extract
2 tbsp. honey
1 pinch of salt

Topping:

1/4 cup almonds; soaked, peeled and chopped.

Directions:

1. Add all the Ingredients for quinoa, to Instant Pot.
2. Secure the lid of instant pot and press *Rice* function key.
3. Adjust the time to 10 minutes and press cook at low pressure,
4. When it beeps; release the pressure naturally and remove the lid.
5. Stir the prepared quinoa well and serve in a bowl. Add chopped almonds on top.

Nutrition Values Nutritional Values Per serving

Calories:- 376
Carbohydrate 39.7g

Protein:- 7.9g
Fat:- 21.3g
Sugar:- 10.5g
Sodium:- 17 mg

Chapter 2 – Beans and Grains

70. White Beans and Broccoli

Serves: 7
Preparation Time: 5 minutes
Cooking Time: 25 minutes

Ingredients

3 tablespoons olive oil
2 anchovy fillets, packed in oil
4 cloves of garlic, sliced
2 cans cannellini beans, rinsed
¼ cup parsley, chopped
1 cup chicken broth
Salt and pepper to taste
1 head broccoli, cut into florets
2 tablespoons parmesan cheese, grated

Directions

1. Press the Sauté button on the Instant Pot.
2. Add the oil and sauté the anchovy fillets and garlic until fragrant.
3. Add the beans and parsley. Pour in the broth. Season with salt and pepper to taste
4. Close the lid and seal off the vent.
5. Press the Manual button and adjust the cooking time to 20 minutes.
6. Do natural pressure release.
7. Once the lid is open, press the Sauté button and add the broccoli florets. Stir and allow to simmer for 5 minutes until the vegetables are done.
8. Sprinkle with parmesan cheese.

Nutritional Values Per serving:

Calories: 66
Carbohydrates: 1.6g
Protein: 1.1g
Fat: 6.4g
Fiber: 1.3g

71. Italian Bean Stew

Serves: 9
Preparation Time: 5 minutes
Cooking Time: 25 minutes

Ingredients

½ cup olive oil
4 cloves of garlic, chopped
½ teaspoon red pepper flakes
2 medium carrots, chopped
2 stalks of celery, chopped
1 leek white part, chopped
1 can tomatoes
3 cans cannellini beans, rinsed
1 bay leaf
1 sprig thyme
5 cups chicken broth
Salt and pepper to taste
1 bunch collard greens, chopped
½ cup parmesan cheese, grated

Directions

1. Press the Sauté button and pour the olive oil.
2. Sauté the garlic, red pepper flakes, carrots, celery, and leeks until fragrant.
3. Add the tomatoes and beans.
4. Stir in the bay leaf, thyme, and chicken broth.
5. Season with salt and pepper to taste.
6. Close the lid and press the Manual button. Adjust the cooking time to 25 minutes.
7. Once cooked, do quick pressure release.
8. Open the lid and press the Sauté button.
9. Stir in the collard greens and allow to simmer for 3 minutes.
10. Sprinkle with parmesan cheese on top.

Nutritional Values Per serving:

Calories: 361
Carbohydrates: 6.6g
Protein:31.2 g

Fat: 22.9g
Fiber: 1.2g

72. Stewed Spicy Cannellini Beans

Serves: 8
Preparation Time: 5 minutes
Cooking Time: 50 minutes

Ingredients

*1-pound dried cannellini beans, soaked overnight
and rinsed
1 onion, halved
1 bulb garlic, minced
1 fennel bulb, sliced
1 carrot, peeled then chopped
4 sprigs of thyme
2 dried chilies
1/3 cup olive oil
6 cups chicken broth
Salt and pepper to taste*

Directions

1. Place all ingredients in the Instant Pot.
2. Close the lid and seal off the vent.
3. Press the Bean/Chili button and adjust the cooking time to 50 minutes.
4. Do natural pressure release.

Nutritional Values Per serving:

*Calories:111
Carbohydrates: 7.1g
Protein: 1.3g
Fat: 9.2g
Fiber: 2.5g*

73. One-Minute Quinoa and Veggies

Serves: 4
Preparation Time: 2 minutes
Cooking Time: 2 minutes

Ingredients

*3 stalks of celery, chopped
1 bell pepper, chopped
1 ½ cups quinoa, rinsed
¼ teaspoon salt
4 cups spinach
1 ½ cups chicken broth
½ cup feta cheese*

Directions

1. Place all ingredients except the feta cheese in the Instant Pot.
2. Close the lid and seal off the vent.
3. Press the Manual button and adjust the cooking time to 2 minutes.
4. Do natural pressure release.
5. Once the lid is open, garnish with feta cheese on top,

Nutritional Values Per serving:

*Calories: 360
Carbohydrates: 31g
Protein: 16g
Fat: 18g
Fiber:9g*

74. Mexican Quinoa with Cilantro Sauce

Serves: 4
Preparation Time: 5 minutes
Cooking Time: 10 minutes

Ingredients

*2 tablespoons cilantro, chopped
½ clove of garlic, minced
1 tablespoon lime juice
2 tablespoons mayonnaise
1 tablespoons jalapeno, chopped
A pinch of salt
2 tablespoons olive oil
1 onion, chopped
3 cloves of garlic, minced
1 red pepper, diced
1 stalk of celery, diced
1 teaspoon cumin
1 teaspoon coriander seeds*

1 teaspoon paprika
1 teaspoon oregano
1 cup raw quinoa, rinsed
Salt and pepper to taste
½ cup corn kernels
½ cup garden peas
½ cup tomato puree
½ cup water

Directions

1. Prepare the cilantro sauce first by combining in a small bowl the first 5 ingredients. Set aside.
2. Press the Sauté button on the Instant Pot.
3. Heat the oil and sauté the onion and garlic until fragrant.
4. Add the pepper and celery. Season with cumin, coriander, paprika, and oregano.
5. Stir in the quinoa and season with salt and pepper to taste.
6. Dump the corn, peas, tomato puree, and water.
7. Close the lid and seal off the vent.
8. Press the Manual button and adjust the cooking time to 12 minutes.
9. Do natural pressure release.
10. Serve with cilantro sauce.

Nutritional Values Per serving:

Calories: 298
Carbohydrates: 40.3g
Protein: 8.7g
Fat: 12.3g
Fiber: 5.6g

75. Quinoa Fried Rice

Serves: 6
Preparation Time: 5 minutes
Cooking Time: 20 minutes

Ingredients

3 ½ cups quinoa, rinsed
3 cups water
1 tablespoon sesame oil

3 cloves of garlic, minced
1 onion, diced
1 cup frozen mixed vegetables
2 large eggs, beaten
2 tablespoons soy sauce
1 teaspoon red pepper flakes
Salt and pepper to taste

Directions

1. Place the quinoa and water in the Instant Pot.
2. Close the lid and press the Manual button. Adjust the cooking time to 12 minutes.
3. Do natural pressure release. Take the cooked quinoa out and set aside in another bowl.
4. Press the Sauté button on the pot.
5. Heat the sesame oil and sauté the garlic and onion until fragrant.
6. Add the vegetables and stir for 3 minutes. Push the vegetables to one side and add the eggs.
7. Scramble the eggs.
8. Stir in the cooked quinoa and season with soy sauce, red pepper flakes, salt, and pepper.
9. Stir to combine everything.
10. Serve warm.

Nutritional Values Per serving:

Calories: 454
Carbohydrates: 72.7g
Protein: 16.7g
Fat: 10.8g
Fiber: 9g

76. Instant Pot Quinoa Pilaf

Serves: 6
Preparation Time: 10 minutes
Cooking Time: 20 minutes

Ingredients

3 tablespoons butter
2 tablespoons onion, chopped

1 tablespoon garlic, minced
2 tablespoons chopped celery
2 cups quinoa, rinsed
2 cups chicken broth
¾ teaspoon garlic powder
¼ teaspoon paprika
Salt and pepper to taste
1 tablespoon parsley, chopped

Directions

1. Press the Sauté button on the Instant Pot.
2. Melt the butter and sauté the onion, garlic, and celery until fragrant.
3. Add the quinoa, chicken broth, garlic, powder, and paprika.
4. Season with salt and pepper to taste.
5. Close the lid and press the Manual button.
6. Adjust the cooking time to 15 minutes
7. Do natural pressure release.
8. Garnish with parsley on top

Nutritional Values Per serving:

Calories:592
Carbohydrates: 58.4g
Protein: 38.6g
Fat: 22.2g
Fiber: 6.4g

77. Quinoa with Mushrooms and Vegetables

Serves: 6
Preparation Time: 2 minutes
Cooking Time: 12 minutes

Ingredients

3 tablespoons olive oil
1 onion, diced
1 carrots, peeled and chopped
2 cups button mushrooms, sliced
Zest of ½ lemon

2 tablespoons lemon juice
1 tablespoon salt
4 cloves of garlic, minced
1 cup quinoa, rinsed
1 cup vegetable stock

Directions

1. Place all ingredients in the Instant Pot.
2. Close the lid and press the Manual button.
3. Adjust the cooking time to 12 minutes.
4. Do natural pressure release.

Nutritional Values Per serving:

Calories: 184
Carbohydrates: 22.2g
Protein: 4.5g
Fat: 8.5
Fiber: 4.3g

78. Basic Instant Pot Millet

Serves: 4
Preparation Time: 2 minutes
Cooking Time: 9 minutes

Ingredients

½ cup millet
1 cup water

Directions

1. Place all ingredients in the Instant Pot.
2. Close the lid and press the Manual button.
3. Adjust the cooking time to 9 minutes.

Nutritional Values Per serving:

Calories: 95
Carbohydrates: 18.2g
Protein: 2.8g
Fat: 1.1g
Fiber:2.1g

79. Instant Pot Millet Porridge

Serves: 3

Preparation Time: 5 minutes
Cooking Time: 10 minutes

Ingredients

3 tablespoons of prepared millet
1 ½ cups coconut milk
2 Medjool dates, chopped
1 teaspoon cinnamon powder
1 teaspoon vanilla powder
A dash of salt

Directions

1. Place all ingredients in the Instant Pot.
2. Close the lid and press the Manual button.
3. Adjust the cooking time to 10 minutes.

Nutritional Values Per serving:

Calories:374
Carbohydrates: 28.6g
Protein: 4.5g
Fat: 29.7g
Fiber: 5.1g

80. Creamy Millet Breakfast Porridge

Serves: 2
Preparation Time: 5 minutes
Cooking Time:20 minutes

Ingredients

1 cup uncooked millet
1 cup almond milk
3 cups water
2 tablespoons maple syrup
1 tablespoon vanilla extract
Chopped almonds, for garnish
Sliced strawberries, for garnish

Directions

1. Place all ingredients except for the almonds and strawberries in the Instant Pot.
2. Close the lid and press the Manual button.
3. Adjust the cooking time to 20 minutes.

Nutritional Values Per serving:

Calories:514
Carbohydrates: 98.9g
Protein: 11.9g
Fat: 6.5g
Fiber: 9.2g

81. Hibachi Fried Rice

Serves: 6
Preparation Time: 5 minutes
Cooking Time: 15 minutes

Ingredients

2 cups Jasmine rice, rinsed and drained
2 cups water
1 tablespoon butter
3 eggs, beaten
1 onion, chopped
1 cup frozen peas
1 cup corn kernels
2 tablespoons soy sauce
2 tablespoons sesame oil

Directions

1. Place the rice and water in the Instant Pot.
2. Close the lid and press the Manual button. Adjust the cooking time for 3 minutes.
3. Do natural pressure release to open the lid.
4. Fluff the rice and transfer to a serving bowl.
5. Press the Sauté button.
6. Use the same inner pot and melt the butter.
7. Scramble the eggs for a minute or two then set aside in a bowl.
8. Add the onions, peas, and corn.
9. Stir in the cooked rice and drizzle with soy sauce.
10. Add the scrambled eggs and continue stirring until the vegetables are cooked.
11. Drizzle with sesame oil last.

Nutritional Values Per serving:

Calories per serving: 298

Carbohydrates: 28.9g
Protein: 11.6g
Fat: 20.9g
Fiber: 10.1g

82. Instant Pot Mexican Rice

Serves: 12
Preparation Time: 3 minutes
Cooking Time: 8 minutes

Ingredients

2 tablespoons olive oil
¼ cup onion, chopped
4 cloves of garlic, chopped
2 cups long grain white rice, rinsed
A dash of salt
¾ cup crushed tomatoes
2 ½ cups chicken stock
½ teaspoon cumin
½ teaspoon smoked paprika
¼ cup sun-dried tomatoes

Directions

1. Press the Sauté button on the Instant Pot.
2. Pour in the oil and sauté the onion and garlic until fragrant.
3. Add the rest of the ingredients and stir to combine everything.
4. Close the lid and press the Manual button.
5. Adjust the cooking time to 8 minutes.
6. Do natural pressure release.

Nutritional Values Per serving:

Calories per serving: 158
Carbohydrates: 28.1g
Protein: 3.8g
Fat:3.5g
Fiber: 0.8g

83. Instant Pot Creamy Mushroom Wild Rice Soup

Serves: 6
Preparation Time: 5 minutes

Cooking Time: 45 minutes

Ingredients

5 carrots, chopped
5 stalks of celery, chopped
1 onion, chopped
3 cloves of garlic, minced
1 cup uncooked wild rice, rinsed
8 ounces mushrooms, diced
4 cups chicken broth
1 teaspoon salt
1 teaspoon dried thyme
6 tablespoons butter
½ cup flour
1 ½ cups milk

Directions

1. Put all ingredients in the Instant Pot except the butter, flour, and milk.
2. Close the lid and press the Manual button. Adjust the cooking time to 45 minutes.
3. Meanwhile, prepare the sauce by melting the butter in a saucepan over medium flame. Whisk in the flour and add the milk gradually. Continue stirring until the sauce thickens.
4. Once the Instant Pot timer beeps, do natural pressure release. Fluff the rice and pour the creamy sauce. Stir to combine.

Nutritional Values Per serving:

Calories per serving:670
Carbohydrates: 68.1g
Protein: 46.2g
Fat: 25.2g
Fiber:8.3g

84. Rice with Chicken and Broccoli

Serves: 6
Preparation Time: 5 minutes
Cooking Time: 15 minutes

Ingredients

2 tablespoons butter
1 ½ pounds boneless chicken breasts, sliced

2 cloves of garlic, minced
1 onion, chopped
Salt and pepper to taste
1 1/3 cups long grain rice
1 1/3 cups chicken broth
½ cup milk
1 cup broccoli florets
½ cup cheddar cheese, grated

Directions

1. Press the Sauté button on the Instant Pot.
2. Melt the butter and add the chicken pieces, garlic, and onion. Season with salt and pepper to taste.
3. Continue stirring for 5 minutes or until the chicken has slightly browned
4. Add the rice and chicken broth. Stir in the milk.
5. Stir in the broccoli florets and cheddar cheese.
6. Close the lid and seal off the vent.
7. Cook for15 minutes.
8. Do natural pressure release.

Nutritional Values Per serving:

Calories per serving: 515
Carbohydrates: 41.6g
Protein: 47.9g
Fat: 16.6g
Fiber: 2.1g

85. Instant Pot Mushroom Risotto

Serves: 6
Preparation Time: 5 minutes
Cooking Time: 10 minutes

Ingredients

3 tablespoons olive oil
4 tablespoons unsalted butter
1 onion, chopped
4 cloves of garlic, minced
3 shiitake mushrooms, sliced
1 cremini mushrooms, sliced
2 cups Arborio rice
4 ½ cups chicken stock

1 cup parmesan cheese, grated
3 tablespoons light soy sauce
¾ cup dry white wine
Salt and pepper to taste

Directions

1. Press the Sauté button on the Instant Pot.
2. Heat the oil and butter.
3. Sauté the onion and garlic until fragrant.
4. Add the mushrooms.
5. Stir in the Arborio rice and half of the chicken stock.
6. Stir until the stock has boiled.
7. Add the rest of the ingredients and give a boil.
8. Close the lid and seal off the vent.
9. Press the Manual button and adjust the cooking time to 3 minutes.
10. Do natural pressure release.
11. Once the lid is open, press the Sauté button and continue stirring until the amount of liquid has reduced and the rice has thickened.

Nutritional Values Per serving:

Calories per serving: 459
Carbohydrates: 60g
Protein: 11g
Fat:16 g
Fiber: 3g

86. Proofing Whole Wheat Bread in Instant Pot

Serves: 6
Preparation Time: 4 hours
Cooking Time: 30 minutes

Ingredients

2 ¼ cups whole wheat flour
1 cup white flour
2 tablespoons vital wheat gluten
2 tablespoons rolled oats
1 tablespoon raw millet
1 tablespoon flax seeds

1 tablespoon sunflower seeds
1 ½ teaspoon salt
1 teaspoon instant yeast
1 ½ cups water, room temperature

Directions

1. In a bowl, mix together the wheat flour, white flour, gluten, oats, millet, flax seed, sunflower seeds, salt, and yeast.
2. Add water gradually and mix until the dough becomes tacky but not too overly wet.
3. Place on top of a parchment paper and place inside the Instant Pot.
4. Close the lid without sealing the vent.
5. Press the Yogurt button. Adjust the screen until it reads 24:00. Set the pressure to low.
6. Adjust the time to 4:30 and once the timer beeps off after 4 hours, the bread should have proofed.
7. Form a ball and place back on the parchment paper.
8. Heat the oven to 450 degrees Fahrenheit.
9. Place the bread in the oven and cook for 30 minutes.

Nutritional Values Per serving:

Calories: 261
Carbohydrates: 51.9g
Protein: 9.5g
Fat: 3.1g
Fiber: 6.2g

87. Instant Pot Coconut Oatmeal

Serves: 2
Preparation Time: 2 minutes
Cooking Time: 3 minutes

Ingredients

1 cup steel-cut oats
2 cups water
1 cup coconut milk
½ cup coconut sugar
1 apple, cored and sliced

Directions

1. Place all ingredients in the Instant Pot.
2. Stir to combine.
3. Close the lid and press the Manual button.
4. Adjust the cooking time to 3 minutes.
5. Do natural pressure release.

Nutritional Values Per serving:

Calories:536
Carbohydrates: 75.3g
Protein: 11.1g
Fat: 32.1g
Fiber: 12.1g

88. Banana Walnut Steel-Cut Oats

Serves: 3
Preparation Time: 2 minutes
Cooking Time: 6 minutes

Ingredients

1 cup steel-cut oats
2 cups water
1 cup almond milk
¼ cup walnut, chopped
2 tablespoons flaxseed
2 tablespoons chia seeds
1 large banana, sliced
2 tablespoons pure maple syrup
1 teaspoon cinnamon powder
1 teaspoon pure vanilla extract
A pinch of salt

Directions

1. Place all ingredients in the Instant Pot.
2. Stir to combine.
3. Close the lid and press the Manual button.
4. Adjust the cooking time to 6 minutes.
5. Do natural pressure release.

Nutritional Values Per serving:

Calories: 295
Carbohydrates: 52.7g
Protein: 9.3g

Fat: 11.6g
Fiber:10.3 g

89. Instant Pot Apple Spice Oats

Serves: 2
Preparation Time: 2 minutes
Cooking Time: 6 minutes

Ingredients

½ cup steel cut oats
1 medium apple, peeled and chopped
1 ½ cups water
1 teaspoon ground cinnamon
¼ teaspoon allspice
1/8 teaspoon nutmeg
3 tablespoons maple syrup

Directions

1. Place all ingredients in the Instant Pot.
2. Stir to combine.
3. Close the lid and press the Manual button.
4. Adjust the cooking time to 6 minutes.
5. Do natural pressure release.

Nutritional Values Per serving:

Calories: 188
Carbohydrates: 49.5g
Protein: 4.4g
Fat: 1.9g
Fiber: 6.6g

90. Pumpkin Spice Oat Meal

Serves: 6
Preparation Time: 2 minutes
Cooking Time: 10 minutes

Ingredients

1 can pumpkin puree
1 ¼ cups steel-cut oats
3 tablespoons brown sugar
1 ½ teaspoons pumpkin pie spice
1 teaspoon ground cinnamon
¾ teaspoon salt

3 cups water
1 ½ cups milk

Directions

1. Place all ingredients in the Instant Pot.
2. Stir to combine.
3. Close the lid and press the Manual button.
4. Adjust the cooking time to 10 minutes.
5. Do natural pressure release.

Nutritional Values Per serving:

Calories:127
Carbohydrates: 26.g
Protein: 6.3g
Fat:3.7g
Fiber: 5.7g

91. Peaches and Cream Oatmeal

Serves: 8
Preparation Time: 2 minutes
Cooking Time: 10 minutes

Ingredients

4 cups old-fashioned oats
3 ½ cups water
3 ½ cups milk
1 teaspoon salt
1 teaspoon ground cinnamon
1/3 cup sugar
4 peaches

Directions

1. Place all ingredients in the Instant Pot.
2. Stir to combine.
3. Close the lid and press the Manual button.
4. Adjust the cooking time to 10 minutes.
5. Do natural pressure release.

Nutritional Values Per serving:

Calories:222
Carbohydrates: 47.1g

Protein: 11.7g
Fat: 6.8g
Fiber: 7.8g

92. Parsley Pureed Navy Beans

Preparation Time: 35 minutes
Serves: 6

Ingredients

1 ½ cups Water
1 ½ tsp Garlic powder
1 cup Red Onions, peeled and chopped
2 ¼ cups dry Pinto Beans, soaked
3 tsp Vegetable Oil
¼ tsp Black Pepper
1 tsp Chipotle powder
¼ tsp Red Pepper
½ tsp Sea Salt
½ cup fresh Cilantro, roughly chopped

Directions

1. Heat the oil on SAUTÉ at High. Cook the onions, cilantro, garlic, and chipotle powders, for about 2-3 minutes. Add in the beans and the water. Season with salt, black and red pepper.
2. Seal the lid, select BEANS/CHILI mode and cook for 25 minutes at High pressure.
3. Do a quick release. Puree the beans using a potato masher. Season with black pepper and salt.

Nutritional Values Per serving:

Calories 302
Carbs 45g
Fat 2g
Protein 18g

93. Mexican-Style Black Bean and Avocado Salad

Preparation Time: 35 minutes
Serves: 4

Ingredients

1 tsp Garlic, smashed
2 Avocados, diced
½ tsp freshly cracked Black Pepper
1 tsp Salt
2 tbsp Wine Vinegar
½ cup fresh Cilantro, chopped
1 tsp dried Dill Weed
¼ tsp hot Pepper Sauce
¼ tsp Chili powder
1 tbsp ground Cumin
½ cup Olive Oil
2 cups Black Beans, soaked overnight
1 ½ cups Water
1 Lime, juiced
1 cup Red Onions, peeled and coarsely chopped

Directions

1. Pour water and add black beans in the pressure cooker. Select BEANS/CHILI mode and cook for 25 minutes at High Pressure. Do a quick pressure release, and drain the beans.
2. Add in the remaining ingredients. Serve chilled with diced avocado.

Nutrition Value Per serving

Calories 485
Carbs 62g
Fat 29g
Protein 19g

94. Rosemary Goat Cheese Barley

Preparation Time: 30 minutes
Serves: 6

Ingredients

2 cups Barley
6 cups Stock
1 Butter Stick, melted
1 cup Spring Onions, chopped
½ cup Goat Cheese
¼ tsp Black Pepper
½ tsp Salt
2 tsp Rosemary

Directions

1. Melt butter on SAUTÉ at High. Add onions and cook until soft, for about 3 minutes. Stir in the remaining ingredients, except the cheese. Seal the lid and cook for 15 minutes on PRESSURE COOK/MANUAL at High.
2. When ready, do a quick pressure release. Stir in the goat cheese and serve.

Nutrition Value Per serving

Calories 570
Carbs 53g
Fat 31g
Protein 21g

95. African Lentil Dip

Preparation Time: 15 minutes
Serves: 12

Ingredients

2 cups dry Green Lentils, rinsed
½ tsp Dukkah
3 Garlic Cloves, minced
¼ cup Tomato Paste
2 tbsp tahini
2 tbsp Vegetable Oil
1 tsp Maple Syrup
½ tsp ground Black Pepper
1 tsp Salt
1 tsp dry Thyme, minced
¼ tsp Cardamom
4 cups Water

Directions

1. Pour 4 cups water, and add lentils to the pressure cooker. Cook on PRESSURE COOK/MANUAL for 5 minutes at High. Allow for a natural pressure release, for 10 minutes. Stir in the remaining ingredients, and serve.

Nutrition Value Per serving

Calories 185
Carbs 19g

Fat 7g
Protein 12g

96. Quinoa Pilaf with Cherries

Preparation Time: 20 minutes
Serves: 4

Ingredients

1 ½ cups Quinoa
½ cup Almonds, sliced
¼ cup Cherries, chopped
1 Celery Stalk, chopped
½ Onion, chopped
14 ounces Chicken Broth
¼ cup Water
1 tbsp Butter

Directions

1. Melt butter on SAUTÉ at High, and cook the onions for 2 minutes, until translucent. Add celery and cook for 2 more, until soft. Stir in the remaining ingredients. Seal the lid and cook for 8 minutes on RICE at High.
2. Release the pressure quickly and serve.

Nutrition Value Per serving

Calories 281
Carbs 44g
Fat 7g
Protein 11g

97. Tasty Bean and Bacon Dip

Preparation Time: 30 minutes
Serves: 12

Ingredients

20 ounces frozen Lima Beans
4 Bacon slices, cooked and crumbled
3 tsp Butter, melted
½ tsp Cayenne Pepper
Salt and Black Pepper, to taste

Water, as needed

Directions

1. Place the beans in the pressure cooker and cover with water. Seal the lid and cook on BEANS/CHILI for 25 minutes at High. Do a quick pressure release. Transfer to a food processor along with the remaining ingredients.
2. Process until smooth.

Nutrition Value Per serving

Calories 105
Carbs 12g
Fat 4g
Protein 5g

98. Apricot and Raisin Oatmeal

Preparation Time: 15 minutes
Serves: 4

Ingredients

2 ¼ cups Water
1 ½ cups Steel Cut Oats
1 ½ cups Almond Milk
A handful of Raisins
8 Apricots, chopped
1 tsp Vanilla Paste
¾ cup Brown Sugar

Directions

Combine all ingredients in your pressure cooker. Set it to RICE mode, seal the lid, and cook for 8 minutes, at High pressure. Once cooking is over, do a quick pressure release.

Nutrition Value Per serving

Calories 325
Carbs 78g
Fat 4g
Protein 8g

99. Cinnamon Bulgur with Pecans

Preparation Time: 20 minutes
Serves: 8

Ingredients

2 cups Bulgur Wheat
¼ cup Pecans, chopped
½ tsp Cloves
1 tsp Cinnamon
¼ tsp Nutmeg
½ cup Honey
6 cups Water

Directions

Place all ingredients in your pressure cooker. Stir to combine well. Seal the lid and cook on PRESSURE COOK/MANUAL mode for 15 minutes at High. When ready, do a quick pressure release.

Nutrition Value Per serving

Calories 105
Carbs 21g
Fat 2g
Protein 2g

100. Peach Quinoa Pudding

Preparation Time: 20 minutes
Serves: 4

Ingredients

2 cups Quinoa
2 Peaches, diced
2 tbsp Raisins
2 cups Milk
2 tsp Peanut Oil
½ tsp Cardamom
2 cups Water
A pinch of Nutmeg
A pinch of Ground Star Anise
2 tbsp Honey

Directions

Combine all ingredients, except peaches and honey, in the pressure cooker. Seal the lid and cook on RICE for 13 minutes, at High. Quick-release the pressure, and stir in the peaches. Drizzled with honey.

Nutrition Value Per serving

Calories 456
Carbs 76g
Fat 10g
Protein 16g

101. Mushroom and Farro Beans

Preparation Time: 25 minutes
Serves: 4

Ingredients

1 ¼ cups Navy Beans
¾ cup Farro
2 ½ cups Mushrooms, sliced
4 Green Onions, chopped
1 tsp Garlic, minced
½ Jalapeno, minced
1 cup Tomatoes, diced
3 cups ChickenBroth

Directions

Combine all ingredients in your pressure cooker. Seal the lid and cook on BEANS/CHILI mode for 25 minutes at High pressure. When ready, do a quick pressure release.

Nutrition Value Per serving

Calories 408
Carbs 75g
Fat 3g
Protein 23g

102. Pear and Almond Oatmeal

Preparation Time: 15 minutes
Serves: 4

Ingredients

½ cup Almonds, chopped

1 ½ cups Oats
½ cup Milk
2 ½ cups Water
2 Pears, sliced
1 tbsp Maple Syrup
2 tsp Butter
½ tsp Vanilla
A pinch of Sea Salt

Directions

Place all ingredients, except the pears, in the pressure cooker. Seal the lid and cook for 8 minutes on RICE mode at High. Do a quick pressure release. Top with pears, to serve.

Nutrition Value Per serving

Calories 180
Carbs 42g
Fat 5g
Protein 8g

103. Potato Rice

Preparation Time: 15 minutes
Serves: 3

Ingredients

3 medium-sized potatoes; diced
1 cup basmati rice; rinsed
1 ½ tbsp. olive oil
1/2 large onion; diced small
1 ½ tbsp. chopped cilantro stalks
1 large garlic clove; finely diced
1/2 tsp. turmeric powder
1 cup chicken stock
1 tsp. butter
Salt; to taste

Directions:

1. Add oil and all the vegetables to Instant Pot and *Sauté* for 5 minutes,

2. Stir in all the remaining Ingredients except the butter.

3. Cover and secure the lid. Turn its pressure release handle to the sealing position.

4. Cook on the *Manual* function with high

pressure for 5 minutes,

5. When it beeps; do a Natural release for 7 minutes,

6. Stir in butter and let it melt into the rice, Serve warm.

Nutrition Values Nutritional Values Per serving

Calories:- 466
Carbohydrate:- 86.1g
Protein:- 9g
Fat:- 9.2g
Sugar:- 3.9g
Sodium:- 0.33g

104. Delicious Rice Pilaf

Preparation Time: 15 minutes
Serves: 8

Ingredients

4 cups raw short-grain white rice; rinsed
5 cups chicken stock
2 rice wine
2 tbsp. vegetable oil
2 cups leftover meat; chopped
2 tbsp. soy sauce
2 tbsp. oyster sauce
4 potatoes; cubed
4 carrots; chopped.
2 lbs. white mushrooms; halved
2 lbs. green beans; chopped
4 kale greens; chopped.
Chopped green onion for garnish

Directions:

1. Add all the Ingredients to Instant Pot; except green onions and oyster sauce,

2. Cover and secure the lid. Turn its pressure release handle to the sealing position.

3. Cook on the *Bean/Chili* function for 10 minutes,

4. When it beeps; do a Natural release for 10 minutes,

5. Stir in oyster sauce and green onions, Let it sit for 5 minutes, Serve hot.

Nutrition Values Nutritional Values Per serving

Calories:- 567
Carbohydrate:- 105.9g
Protein:- 24.7g
Fat:- 5.8g
Sugar:- 6.6g
Sodium:- 0.88g

105. Simple Split Pea Curry

Preparation Time: 24 minutes
Serves: 3

Ingredients

1 cup split yellow peas; rinsed well
1/2 tbsp. olive oil
1/2 medium white onion; diced
1/2 medium carrot; diced into small cubes
1/2 celery stick; diced into cubes
3 garlic cloves; diced finely
1 bay leaf
1/2 tsp. paprika powder
3/4 tsp. cumin powder
1/4 tsp. salt
1/8 tsp. cinnamon powder
1/8 tsp. chili powder or cayenne pepper
1/4 cup chopped tinned tomatoes
2 tbsp. lemon juice
2 cups vegetable stock

Directions:

1. Add oil, onion, celery and garlic to Instant Pot and *Sauté* for 4 minutes,

2. Add all the remaining Ingredients to the cooker.

3. Cover and secure the lid. Turn its pressure release handle to the sealing position.

4. Cook on the *Manual* function with high pressure for 10 minutes,

5. When it beeps; do a Natural release and remove the lid. Stir and serve.

Nutrition Values Nutritional Values Per serving

Calories:- 206

Carbohydrate:- 33.5g
Protein:- 11g
Fat:- 3.4g
Sugar:- 3.4g
Sodium:- 0.24g

106. Special Chickpea Rice

Preparation Time: 48 minutes
Serves: 8

Ingredients

4 1/2 cups brown rice; rinsed and drained
1/2 cup chickpeas; soaked
8 bacon strips; chopped
4 tbsp. cooking oil
2 onions; minced
6 cups vegetable broth
1/2 cup chopped cilantro

Directions:

1. Add oil and onion to Instant Pot. *Sauté* for 3 minutes,

2. Stir in bacon. Sauté for 5 minutes,

3. Add all the remaining Ingredients to the cooker.

4. Cover and secure the lid. Turn its pressure release handle to the sealing position.

5. Cook on the *Manual* function with high pressure for 30 minutes,

6. When it beeps; do a Natural release and remove the lid. Stir and serve warm.

Nutrition Values Nutritional Values Per serving

Calories:- 637
Carbohydrate:- 92.6g
Protein:- 21.4g
Fat:- 19.4g
Sugar:- 3g
Sodium:- 1.02g

107. Red Bean Curry

Preparation Time: 34 minutes

Serves: 4

Ingredients

1/2 cup raw red beans
1 ½ tbsp. cooking oil
1/2 cup chopped onions
1 bay leaf
1/2 tbsp. grated garlic
1/4 tbsp. grated ginger
3/4 cup water
1 cup fresh tomato puree
1/2 green chili; finely chopped.
1/4 tsp. turmeric
1/2 tsp. coriander powder
1 tsp. chili powder
1 cup chopped baby spinach
Salt; to taste
1/2 cup fresh cilantro

Directions:

1. Add oil and onions to Instant Pot. *Sauté* for 5 minutes,

2. Stir ginger, garlic paste, green chili and bay leaf. Cook for 1 minute then add all the spices,

3. Add red beans, tomato puree and water to the pot.

4. Cover and secure the lid. Turn its pressure release handle to the sealing position.

5. Cook on the *Manual* function with high pressure for 15 minutes,

6. When it beeps; do a Natural release for 20 minutes,

7. Stir in spinach and cook for 3 minutes on the *Sauté* setting. Serve hot with boiled white rice,

Nutrition Values Nutritional Values Per serving

Calories:- 163
Carbohydrate:- 22.8g
Protein:- 7g
Fat:- 5.7g
Sugar:- 4.4g

108. Instant Bacon Rice

Preparation Time: 48 minutes
Serves: 8

Ingredients

  4 1/2 cups brown rice; rinsed and drained
  8 bacon strips; chopped
  8 dried mushrooms; soaked
  4 tbsp. cooking oil
  2 onions; minced
  6 cups vegetable broth
  1/2 cup chopped cilantro

Directions:

1. Add oil and onion to Instant Pot. *Sauté* for 3 minutes,

2. Stir in mushrooms and bacon. *Sauté* for 5 minutes,

3. Add all the remaining Ingredients to the cooker.

4. Cover and secure the lid. Turn its pressure release handle to the sealing position.

5. Cook on the *Manual* function with high pressure for 30 minutes,

6. When it beeps; do a Natural release and remove the lid. Stir and serve warm.

Nutrition Values Nutritional Values Per serving

Calories:- 594
Carbohydrate:- 85.6g
Protein:- 19.6g
Fat:- 18.6g
Sugar:- 2g
Sodium:- 1.01g

109. Awesome Bean Barley Stew

Preparation Time: 30 minutes
Serves: 4

Ingredients

  1/2 cup Cannellini beans; soaked and rinsed
  1/4 cup barley; soaked and rinsed
  1/2 cup chickpeas; soaked and rinsed
  1 garlic clove; chopped.
  1/2 tbsp. olive oil
  4 pepper kernels
  3 coriander seeds
  2 cups water
  1 clove
  Salt and pepper to taste
  Tea infuser to hold the spices

Directions:

1. Add oil, water, garlic, barley, salt, chickpeas and the tea infuser filled with all the spices to Instant Pot.

2. Set a steamer trivet above it and place the cannellini beans into it.

3. Secure the lid and select the *Manual* function with high pressure for 15 minutes,

4. When it beeps; do a Natural release and remove the lid.

5. Remove the steamer trivet and transfer the beans to the pot.

6. Remove the tea infuser. Stir well and cook for 5 minutes on the *Sauté* setting. Serve hot.

Nutrition Values Nutritional Values Per serving

Calories:- 196
Carbohydrate:- 32.1g
Protein:- 10.5g
Fat:- 3.5g
Sugar:- 3.2g
Sodium:- 0.16g

110. Green Mung Bean Risotto

Preparation Time: 50 minutes
Serves: 6

Ingredients

  1 ½ cup green mung beans
  2 tsp. ground coriander
  1 tsp. cayenne

1/2 tsp. black pepper
8 cups water
2 tsp. lemon juice
1 cup brown basmati rice
1 tsp. coconut oil
1 tsp. cumin seeds
1 red onion; chopped
2 cans crushed tomatoes
3 cloves of garlic
2-inch ginger; peeled and chopped.
2 tsp. turmeric
2 tsp. salt

Directions:

1. Add tomatoes, garlic, onions, spices and 2 tbsp. water to a food processor and blend to form a puree,

2. Pour some oil into Instant Pot and heat it on the *Sauté* setting.

3. *Sauté* the cumin seeds in the heated oil and stir in the tomato puree, Let it cook for 15 minutes,

4. Add the green mung beans and rice, Secure the lid.

5. Cook on the *Manual* function for 15 minutes at high pressure,

6. When it beeps; do a Natural release and remove the lid. Stir and serve with crackers,

Nutrition Values Nutritional Values Per serving

Calories:- 205
Carbohydrate:- 41g
Protein:- 7.2g
Fat:- 1.4g
Sugar:- 4.3g
Sodium:- 0.21g

111. Lentil Corn Stew

Preparation Time: 24 minutes
Serves: 3

Ingredients

1/2 cup fresh or frozen corn

1/3 cup dried lentils
1/2 medium onion; chopped
1 medium carrot; sliced
3 1/2 cups water
1 medium tomato
1 tbsp. tamari or soy sauce
1/2 cup cooked brown rice
Salt and pepper; to taste

Directions:

1. Add oil, onion and carrots to Instant Pot and *Sauté* for 4 minutes,

2. Add water, lentils, tomatoes and corn to the cooker.

3. Cover and secure the lid. Turn its pressure release handle to the sealing position.

4. Cook on the *Manual* function with high pressure for 10 minutes,

5. When it beeps; do a Natural release and remove the lid.

6. Stir in cooked rice, tamari sauce, salt and pepper. Serve warm.

Nutrition Values Nutritional Values Per serving

Calories:- 239
Carbohydrate:- 47.4g
Protein:- 10.1g
Fat:- 1.5g
Sugar:- 4.2g
Sodium:- 0.36g

112. Vegetable and Corn Rice

Preparation Time: 14 minutes
Serves: 3

Ingredients

1 cup basmati rice; rinsed
1 ½ tbsp. olive oil
1/2 cup frozen sweet corn kernels
1/2 large onion; diced small
Salt; to taste
1 ½ tbsp. chopped cilantro stalks
1/2 cup carrots; chopped.

1/4 cup green onions; chopped
1/4 cup bell peppers; chopped.
1/2 cup frozen garden peas
1 cup chicken stock
1 large garlic clove; finely diced
1/2 heaped tsp. turmeric powder
Dollop of butter; to finish

Directions:

1. Add oil and all the vegetables to Instant Pot and *Sauté* for 5 minutes,

2. Stir in all the remaining Ingredients except the butter.

3. Cover and secure the lid. Turn its pressure release handle to the sealing position.

4. Cook on the *Manual* function with high pressure for 4 minutes,

5. When it beeps; do a Natural release for 7 minutes,

6. Stir in butter and let it melt into the rice, Serve warm.

Nutrition Values Nutritional Values Per serving

Calories:- 423
Carbohydrate:- 66g
Protein:- 7.8g
Fat:- 14.9g
Sugar:- 5.9g
Sodium:- 0.29g

113. Chicken and Brown Rice

Preparation Time: 43 minutes
Serves: 6

Ingredients

2 lbs. chicken thigh; boneless, skinless
2 cups brown rice; raw
1 medium onion
3 garlic cloves
2 cups baby carrots
2 cups cremini mushrooms
1 tbsp. olive oil
2 ¼ cups chicken broth
1/8 tsp. salt

1/8 tsp. ground black pepper
10 oz. soup; cream of chicken, canned, condensed
2 tbsp. Worcestershire sauce
1 tbsp. fresh thyme

Directions:

1. Add oil, garlic, vegetables and onions to Instant Pot. *Sauté* for 2 minutes,

2. Add all the remaining Ingredients to the cooker. Place the chicken pieces on top.

3. Cover and secure the lid. Turn its pressure release handle to the sealing position.

4. Cook on the *Manual* function with high pressure for 31 minutes,

5. When it beeps; do a Natural release for 7 minutes,

6. Remove the chicken and shred its meat. Add the meat back to the rice, Stir and serve warm.

Nutrition Values Nutritional Values Per serving

Calories:- 606
Carbohydrate:- 58.8g
Protein:- 52.4g
Fat:- 16.6g
Sugar:- 4.7g
Sodium:- 0.89g

Chapter 3 – Side Dishes

114. Cauliflower and Eggs Salad

Preparation Time: 10 minutes
Cooking Time: 5 minutes
Serves: 10

Ingredients:

21 ounces cauliflower, florets separated
1 cup red onion, chopped
1 cup celery, chopped
½ cup water
Salt and black pepper to the taste
2 tablespoons balsamic vinegar
1 teaspoon stevia
4 eggs, hard-boiled, peeled and chopped
1 cup mayonnaise

Directions:

1. Put the water in your instant pot, add steamer basket, add cauliflower, cover pot and cook on High for 5 minutes.
2. Transfer cauliflower to a bowl, add eggs, celery and onion and toss.
3. In a separate bowl, mix mayo with salt, pepper, vinegar and stevia and whisk well.
4. Add this to your salad, toss, divide between plates and serve as a side dish.
   Enjoy!

Nutritional Values Per serving

calories 171
fat 6
fiber 2
carbs 6
protein 3

115. Asparagus and Cheese Side Dish

Preparation Time: 10 minutes
Cooking Time: 6 minutes
Serves: 4

Ingredients:

10 ounces asparagus, cut into medium pieces
Salt and black pepper to the taste
2 tablespoons parmesan, grated
1/3 cup Monterey jack cheese, shredded
2 tablespoons mustard
2 ounces cream cheese
1/3 cup coconut cream
3 tablespoons bacon, cooked and crumbled

Directions:

1. In your instant pot, mix asparagus with salt, pepper, parmesan, Monterey jack cheese, mustard, cream cheese, coconut cream and bacon, stir, cover and cook on High for 6 minutes.
2. Divide between plates and serve as a side dish.
   Enjoy!

Nutritional Values Per serving

calories 156
fat 3
fiber 2
carbs 5
protein 7

116. Sprouts and Apple Side Dish

Preparation Time: 10 minutes
Cooking Time: 7 minutes
Serves: 4

Ingredients:

1 green apple, cored and julienned
1 and ½ teaspoons olive oil
4 cups alfalfa sprouts
Salt and black pepper to the taste
¼ cup coconut milk

Directions:

1. Set your instant pot on sauté mode, add oil, heat it up, add apple and sprouts, stir, cover pot and cook on High for 5 minutes.
2. Add salt, pepper and coconut milk, stir, cover pot again and cook on High for 2 minutes more.
3. Divide between plates and serve as a side dish.
   Enjoy!

Nutritional Values Per serving

calories 120
fat 3
fiber 1
carbs 3
protein 3

117. Radishes and Chives

Preparation Time: 10 minutes
Cooking Time: 7 minutes
Serves: 2

Ingredients:

2 cups radishes, cut into quarters
½ cup chicken stock
Salt and black pepper to the taste
2 tablespoons ghee, melted
1 tablespoon chives, chopped
1 tablespoon lemon zest, grated

Directions:

1. In your instant pot, mix radishes with stock, salt, pepper and lemon zest, stir, cover pot and cook on High for 7 minutes.
2. Add melted ghee, toss a bit, divide between plates, sprinkle chives on top and serve as a side dish.
   Enjoy!

Nutritional Values Per serving

calories 102
fat 4
fiber 1

carbs 6
protein 5

118. Hot Radishes with Bacon and Cheese

Preparation Time: 10 minutes
Cooking Time: 10 minutes
Serves: 1

Ingredients:

7 ounces red radishes, halved
½ cup veggie stock
2 tablespoons coconut cream
2 bacon slices, chopped
1 tablespoon green onion, chopped
1 tablespoon cheddar cheese, grated
Hot sauce to the taste
Salt and black pepper to the taste

Directions:

1. Set your instant pot on sauté mode, add bacon, stir and cook for a couple of minutes.
2. Add radishes, salt, pepper and stock, stir, cover and cook on High for 4 minutes.
3. Add green onion, cream, cheese and hot sauce, stir, cover the pot again and cook on High for 2 minutes more.
4. Divide between plates and serve as a side dish.
   Enjoy!

Nutritional Values Per serving

calories 170
fat 16
fiber 3
carbs 6
protein 12

119. Avocado Side Salad

Preparation Time: 10 minutes
Cooking Time: 7 minutes
Serves: 4

Ingredients:

4 cups mixed lettuce leaves, torn
4 eggs
2 cups water
2 teaspoons mustard
1 avocado, pitted and sliced
¼ cup mayonnaise
2 garlic cloves, minced
1 tablespoon chives, chopped
Salt and black pepper to the taste

Directions:

1. Put the water in your instant pot, add steamer basket, add eggs inside, cover pot, cook on High for 7 minutes, cool them down, chop and transfer to a bowl.
2. Add lettuce, avocado, garlic, chives, salt and pepper and toss.
3. In a small bowl, mix mustard with mayo, salt and pepper, whisk well, add to salad, toss to coat and serve as a side salad.
   Enjoy!

Nutritional Values Per serving

calories 134
fat 7
fiber 4
carbs 7
protein 10

120. Swiss Chard and Pine Nuts

Preparation Time: 10 minutes
Cooking Time: 5 minutes
Serves: 4

Ingredients:

1 bunch Swiss chard, cut into strips
2 tablespoons olive oil
1 tablespoon balsamic vinegar
1 small yellow onion, chopped
¼ teaspoon red pepper flakes
¼ cup pine nuts, toasted
¼ cup raisins
1 tablespoon balsamic vinegar
Salt and black pepper to the taste

Directions:

1. Set your instant pot on sauté mode, add oil, heat it up, add onion and chard, stir and cook for 2 minutes.
2. Add pepper flakes, salt, pepper and vinegar, stir, cover and cook on High for 3 minutes.
3. Add raisins and pine nuts, toss, divide between plates and serve as a side dish.
   Enjoy!

Nutritional Values Per serving

calories 120
fat 2
fiber 1
carbs 2
protein 4

121. Spinach and Chard Mix

Preparation Time: 10 minutes
Cooking Time: 6 minutes
Serves: 4

Ingredients:

1 apple, cored and chopped
1 yellow onion, sliced
4 tablespoons pine nuts, toasted
3 tablespoons olive oil
¼ cup raisins
6 garlic cloves, chopped
¼ cup balsamic vinegar
2 and ½ cups baby spinach
2 and ½ cups Swiss chard, roughly torn
Salt and black pepper to the taste
A pinch of nutmeg

Directions:

1. Set your instant pot on sauté mode, add oil, heat it up, add onion and apple, stir and cook for 3 minutes.
2. Add garlic, raisins, spinach, chard and vinegar, stir, cover and cook on High for 3 minutes.
3. Add salt, pepper, nutmeg and pine nuts,

stir, divide between plates and serve as a side dish.

Enjoy!

Nutritional Values Per serving

calories 140
fat 1
fiber 2
carbs 3
protein 3

122. Cherry Tomatoes and Parmesan Mix

Preparation Time: 10 minutes
Cooking Time: 7 minutes
Serves: 8

Ingredients:

1 jalapeno pepper, chopped
4 garlic cloves, minced
Salt and black pepper to the taste
2 pounds cherry tomatoes, cut into halves
1 yellow onion, cut into wedges
¼ cup olive oil
½ teaspoon oregano, dried
1 and ½ cups chicken stock
¼ cup basil, chopped
½ cup parmesan, grated

Directions:

1. Set your instant pot on sauté mode, add oil, heat it up, add onion and garlic, stir and cook for 2-3 minutes.
2. Add jalapeno, tomatoes, oregano, salt, pepper and stock, stir, cover and cook on High for 4 minutes.
3. Add basil and parmesan, toss a bit, divide between plates and serve as a side dish. Enjoy!

Nutritional Values Per serving

calories 120
fat 2
fiber 3

carbs 5
protein 4

123. Almond Cauliflower Rice

Preparation Time: 10 minutes
Cooking Time: 7 minutes
Serves: 4

Ingredients:

½ cup yellow onion, finely chopped
1 tablespoon ghee
1 celery stalk, chopped
1 and ½ cups cauliflower rice
4 ounces chicken stock
Salt and black pepper to the taste
½ cup almonds, toasted and chopped
2 tablespoons parsley, chopped

Directions:

1. Set your instant pot on Sauté mode, add ghee, melt it, add celery and onion, stir and sauté for 3 minutes.
2. Add cauliflower, salt, pepper and stock, stir, cover and cook on High for 4 minutes.
3. Add parsley and almonds, toss, divide between plates and serve as a side dish. Enjoy!

Nutritional Values Per serving

calories 172
fat 3
fiber 5
carbs 7
protein 12

124. Saffron Cauliflower Rice

Preparation Time: 10 minutes
Cooking Time: 7 minutes
Serves: 6

Ingredients:

2 tablespoons olive oil
½ teaspoon saffron threads, crushed

½ cup onion, chopped
2 tablespoons coconut milk
1 and ½ cups cauliflower rice
2 cups veggie stock
Salt and black pepper to the taste
1 tablespoon stevia
1 cinnamon stick
1/3 cup almonds, chopped

Directions:

1. In a bowl, mix milk with saffron and stir.
2. Set your instant pot on sauté mode, add oil, heat it up, add onion, stir and cook for 2 minutes.
3. Add cauliflower rice, stock, saffron mix, stevia, almonds, salt, pepper and cinnamon, stir, cover and cook on High for 5 minutes.
4. Stir your rice one more time, discard cinnamon, divide between plates and serve as a side dish.

    Enjoy!

Nutritional Values Per serving

calories 162
fat 4
fiber 3
carbs 7
protein 4

125. Garlic and Parmesan Asparagus

Preparation Time: 5 minutes
Cooking Time: 8 minutes
Serves: 4

Ingredients:

3 garlic cloves, peeled and minced
1 bunch asparagus, trimmed
1 cup water
3 tablespoons butter
3 tablespoons Parmesan cheese, grated

Directions:

Put the water into the Instant Pot. Place the asparagus on aluminum foil, add the garlic and butter and seal the edges of the foil. Place this into the pot, cover it and cook on the Manual setting for 8 minutes. Release the pressure, arrange the asparagus on plates, sprinkle with cheese, and serve.

Nutritional Values Per serving

Calories: 70
Fat: 5.2
Fiber: 1.8
Carbs: 3.8
Protein: 4

126. Poached Fennel

Preparation Time: 5 minutes
Cooking Time: 6 minutes
Serves: 3

Ingredients:

2 big fennel bulbs, sliced
2 tablespoons butter
1 tablespoon white flour
2 cups milk
Ground nutmeg
Salt, to taste

Directions:

Set the Instant Pot on Sauté mode, add the butter, and melt it. Add the fennel slices, stir, and cook until slightly browned. Add the flour, salt, pepper, nutmeg, and milk, stir, cover, and cook on Manual for 6 minutes. Release the pressure, transfer the fennel to plates, and serve.

Nutritional Values Per serving

Calories: 140
Fat: 5
Fiber: 4.7
Carbs: 12
Protein: 4.4

127. Harvest Vegetables

Preparation Time: 10 minutes
Cooking Time: 6 minutes
Serves: 4

Ingredients:

2 yellow bell peppers, seeded and sliced thin
1 green bell pepper, seeded and sliced thin
2 red bell peppers, seeded and sliced, thin
2 tomatoes, cored and chopped
2 garlic cloves, peeled and minced
1 red onion, peeled and sliced thin
Salt and ground black pepper, to taste
1 bunch parsley, diced
Extra virgin olive oil

Directions:

Set the Instant Pot on Sauté mode, add a drizzle of oil, and heat it up. Add the onions, stir, and cook for 3 minutes. Add the red, yellow and green peppers, stir, and cook for 5 minutes. Add the tomatoes, salt and pepper, stir, cover and cook on the Manual setting for 6 minutes. Release the pressure, uncover the Instant Pot, transfer the peppers and tomatoes to a bowl, add more salt and pepper with the garlic, parsley, and a drizzle of oil. Toss to coat, and serve.

Nutritional Values Per serving

Calories: 146
Fat: 2.2
Fiber: 8.1
Carbs: 28.1
Protein: 4.5

128. Eggplant

Preparation Time: 40 minutes
Cooking Time: 13 minutes
Serves: 4

Ingredients:

2 eggplants, cubed
Salt and ground black pepper, to taste
2 tablespoons extra virgin olive oil
1 garlic clove, peeled and crushed
Red pepper flakes
1 bunch oregano, chopped
½ cup water
2 anchovies, chopped

Directions:

Sprinkle the eggplant pieces with salt, place them in a strainer, press them with a plate, set aside for 30 minutes, and then drain them. Set the Instant Pot on Sauté mode, add the oil and the garlic and heat it up. Add the anchovies, oregano, and a pinch of pepper flakes, stir and cook for 5 minutes. Discard the garlic, add the eggplant, salt and pepper, toss to coat, and cook for 5 minutes. Add the water, stir, cover the Instant Pot and cook on the Manual setting for 3 minutes. Release the pressure, transfer the eggplant mixture to plates, and serve.

Nutritional Values Per serving

Calories: 130
Fat: 5
Fiber: 10
Carbs: 12
Protein: 15

129. Beets and Garlic

Preparation Time: 10 minutes
Cooking Time: 15 minutes
Serves: 4

Ingredients:

3 beets, greens cut off and washed
Water to cover
1 tablespoon extra virgin olive oil
Salt, to taste
2 garlic cloves, peeled and minced
1 teaspoon lemon juice

Directions:

Put beets into the Instant Pot, add enough

water to cover, add salt, cover the Instant Pot, and cook on the Manual setting for 15 minutes. Release the pressure naturally for 10 minutes, strain the beets, peel them, and chop them. Heat up a pan with the oil over medium-high heat, add the beets, stir, and cook for 3 minutes. Add the garlic, lemon juice, and salt, stir, take off heat, divide among plates, and serve.

Nutritional Values Per serving

Calories: 70
Fat: 1
Fiber: 3.8
Carbs: 13
Protein: 2.2

130. Fava Bean Sauté

Preparation Time: 10 minutes
Cooking Time: 7 minutes
Serves: 4

Ingredients:

3 pounds fava beans, shelled
1 teaspoon extra virgin olive oil
Salt and ground black pepper, to taste
4 ounces bacon, chopped
½ cup white wine
3 parsley sprigs, chopped
¾ cup water

Directions:

Set the Instant Pot on Sauté mode, add the oil and heat up. Add the bacon, stir, and cook until it browns. Add the wine, stir and cook for 2 minutes. Add the water and fava beans, stir, cover, and cook on the Bean/Chili setting for 7 minutes. Release pressure, transfer the beans to plates, add the parsley, salt and pepper, stir, and serve.

Nutritional Values Per serving

Calories: 140
Fat: 3
Fiber: 1
Carbs: 23
Protein: 13

131. Calamari and Tomatoes

Preparation Time: 10 minutes
Cooking Time: 32 minutes
Serves: 4

Ingredients:

1½ pounds calamari, washed, tentacles separated, and cut into strips
Salt and ground black pepper, to taste
14 ounces canned tomatoes, chopped
1 bunch parsley, chopped
1 garlic clove, peeled and crushed
½ cup white wine
1 cup water
2 anchovies
Juice of 1 lemon
2 tablespoons extra virgin olive oil
Red pepper flakes

Directions:

Set the Instant Pot on Sauté mode, add oil, pepper flakes, garlic and anchovies, stir, and cook for 3 minutes. Add the calamari, stir, and cook for 5 minutes. Add the wine, stir, and cook 3 minutes. Add tomatoes, 1 cup water, half of the parsley, salt, and pepper. Stir, cover the Instant Pot and cook on the Manual setting for 20 minutes. Release the pressure, add the rest of the parsley, lemon juice, salt, and pepper, stir, divide among plates, and serve.

Nutritional Values Per serving

Calories: 230
Fat: 6.5
Fiber: 1.2
Carbs: 11
Protein: 24

132. Cauliflower, Broccoli, and Citrus

Preparation Time: 10 minutes
Cooking Time: 6 minutes
Serves: 4

Ingredients:

1 cauliflower, florets separated
1 pound broccoli, florets separated
1 romanesco cauliflower, florets separated
2 oranges, peeled and sliced
Zest from 1 orange
Juice from 1 orange
Red pepper flakes
4 anchovies
1 tablespoon capers, chopped
Salt and ground black pepper, to taste
4 tablespoons extra virgin olive oil
1 cup water

Directions:

In a bowl, mix the orange zest with orange juice, pepper flakes, anchovies, capers, salt, pepper, and olive oil, stir well and set the dish aside. Place the cauliflower and broccoli in the steamer basket of you Instant Pot, add 1 cup water to the Instant Pot, cover and cook on Steam mode for 6 minutes. Release the pressure, uncover the Instant Pot, transfer florets to a bowl and mix with orange slices. Add the orange vinaigrette, toss to coat, and divide among plates and serve.

Nutritional Values Per serving

Calories: 260
Fat: 2.9
Fiber: 6.5
Carbs: 33
Protein: 4.2

133. Israeli Couscous

Preparation Time: 10 minutes
Cooking Time: 5 minutes
Serves: 10

Ingredients:

16 ounces harvest grains blend
Salt and ground black pepper, to taste
2½ cups chicken stock
2 tablespoons butter
Parsley leaves, chopped, for serving

Directions:

Set the Instant Pot on Sauté mode, add the butter, and melt it. Add the grains and stock and stir. Cover the Instant Pot and cook on the Multigrain setting for 5 minutes. Release the pressure, fluff the couscous with a fork, season with salt and pepper, divide among plates, sprinkle parsley on top, and serve.

Nutritional Values Per serving

Calories: 190
Fat: 1
Fiber: 2
Carbs: 34
Protein: 6

134. Red Cabbage

Preparation Time: 10 minutes
Cooking Time: 10 minutes
Serves: 4

Ingredients:

4 garlic cloves, peeled and minced
½ cup yellow onion, peeled and chopped
1 tablespoon vegetable oil
6 cups red cabbage, chopped
1 cup water
1 tablespoon apple cider vinegar
1 cup applesauce
Salt and ground black pepper, to taste

Directions:

Set the Instant Pot on Sauté mode, add the oil and heat it up. Add the onions, stir, and cook for 4 minutes. Add the garlic, stir, and cook for 1 minute. Add the cabbage, water, applesauce, vinegar, salt, and pepper, stir, cover, and cook on the Manual setting for 10 minutes. Release the pressure, uncover the Instant Pot, stir the cabbage, add more vinegar, salt, and pepper, if needed, divide among plates, and serve.

Nutritional Values Per serving

Calories: 160
Fat: 12

Fiber: 2.2
Crabs 10.2
Protein: 5.6

135. Green Beans

Preparation Time: 10 minutes
Cooking Time: 5 minutes
Serves: 4

Ingredients:

2 cups tomatoes, cored and chopped
1 tablespoon extra virgin olive oil
1 garlic clove, peeled and crushed
1 pound green beans, trimmed
1 teaspoon extra virgin olive oil
Salt, to taste
½ cup basil leaves, chopped

Directions:

Set the Instant Pot on Sauté mode, add 1 tablespoon of oil and heat it up. Add the garlic, stir, and cook for 1 minute. Add the tomatoes, stir, and cook for 1 minute. Place the green beans in the steamer basket and place it in the Instant Pot. Add the salt, cover the Instant Pot and cook on the Manual setting for 5 minutes. Release the pressure, transfer the green beans from the basket into the Instant Pot, and toss to coat. Transfer to plates, sprinkle with the basil, and drizzle 1 teaspoon oil on them and serve.

Nutritional Values Per serving

Calories: 55
Fat: 3.2
Fiber: 2.6
Carbs: 1.6
Protein: 1.6

136. Savory Bok Choy

Preparation Time: 10 minutes
Cooking Time: 10 minutes
Serves: 4

Ingredients:

5 bok choy bunches, ends cut off
5 cups water
2 garlic cloves, peeled and minced
1 teaspoon ginger, grated
1 tablespoon coconut oil
Salt, to taste

Directions:

Put the bok choy into the Instant Pot, add the water, cover the Instant Pot and cook on the Manual setting for 7 minutes. Release the pressure, drain the bok choy, chop it, and put them in a bowl. Heat up a pan with the oil over medium heat, add the bok choy, stir, and cook for 3 minutes. Add more salt, garlic, and ginger, stir, and cook for 2 minutes. Divide among plates, and serve.

Nutritional Values Per serving

Calories: 60
Fat: 0.4
Fiber: 1.3
Carbs: 6.5
Protein: 2.4

137. Easy-to-make Eggplant Delight

Preparation Time: 40 minutes
Serves: 4

Ingredients

2 cups Eggplants, cubed
¼ cup Olive Oil
½ cup freshly Basil, chopped
2 tsp Garlic, minced
1 cup Red Onion, sliced
2 tbsp Red Wine
½ cup Water
1 tbsp Salt

Directions

1. Sprinkle the eggplants with the salt and place them in a colander for 20 minutes. Rinse and squeeze them, reserving the liquid. Heat oil on SAUTÉ mode at High.

2. Cook the eggplants, garlic, and onion for a

few minutes, until soft and lightly browned. Pour in the wine, water, and reserved liquid. Seal the lid and cook for 7 minutes on PRESSURE COOK/MANUAL at High.

3. When ready, release the pressure quickly. Serve topped with freshly chopped basil.

Nutrition Value Per serving

Calories 183
Carbs 6g
Fat 18g
Protein 1g

138. Spicy Cauliflower with Peas

Preparation Time: 25 minutes
Serves: 8

Ingredients

2 Tomatoes, diced
2 ¼ cups Green Peas
2 pounds Cauliflower, broken into florets
2 tbsp Garlic, minced
7 cups Stock
2 Yams, cubed
2 tbsp Butter
½ tsp Salt
¼ tsp Pepper
½ tsp Paprika
½ tsp Chili Powder
¼ tsp Red Pepper Flakes
¼ tsp Cayenne Pepper
½ tsp Onion Powder

Directions

Melt butter on SAUTÉ at High, and cook the garlic and spices for 1 minute. Stir in the remaining ingredients. Seal the lid and set for 10 minutes on PRESSURE COOK/MANUAL at High. Do a quick release, drain and serve

Nutrition Value Per serving

Calories 173
Carbs 24g
Fat 4g

Protein 10g

139. Spinach with Cottage Cheese

Preparation Time: 25 minutes
Serves: 4

Ingredients

18 ounces Spinach, chopped
10 ounces Cottage Cheese
1 Onion, chopped
8 Garlic Cloves, minced
1 tbsp Butter
2 tbsp Corn Flour
1 tsp Cumin
½ cup Water
½ tsp Coriander
1 tsp grated Ginger

Directions

1. Melt the butter on SAUTÉ mode at High, and cook the onions, ginger, and garlic for 2 minutes, until soft. Stir in the spices and spinach and cook for 2 minutes, until tender.

2. Pour in the water and stir in flour. Seal the lid, and cook for 3 minutes on STEAM at High. When ready, do a quick pressure release, and stir in the cottage cheese.

Nutrition Value Per serving

Calories 152
Carbs 15g
Fat 6g
Protein 13g

140. Mushroom and Zucchini Platter

Preparation Time: 25 minutes
Serves: 8

Ingredients

12 ounces Mushrooms, sliced
4 medium Zucchinis, sliced
15 ounces canned Tomatoes, undrained

1 cup chopped Onion
1 Garlic Clove, minced
1 tbsp chopped Parsley
¼ tsp Red Pepper Flakes
2 tbsp Butter

Directions

1. Melt butter on SAUTÉ mode at High. Add onion and garlic and cook for 2 minutes, until soft and crispy. Add mushrooms and cook for 5 minutes, until soft. Add zucchini and top with tomatoes. Seal the lid.

2. Cook for 2 minutes on STEAM at High. Quick release the pressure. Stir in parsley and flakes and season to taste.

Nutrition Value Per serving

Calories 44
Carbs 5g
Fat 2g
Protein 2g

141. Simple Cabbage and Pepper Side

Preparation Time: 20 minutes
Serves: 8

Ingredients

2 pounds Cabbage, shredded
1 cup Bell Peppers, diced sliced
¼ cup White Wine
½ cup Veggie Stock
1 cup Scallions, chopped
¼ cup Parsley, chopped
1 tbsp Oil
½ tsp Salt
¼ tsp Pepper

Directions

1. Heat oil on SAUTÉ mode at High. Add scallions and cook until soft, for about 3 minutes. Stir in the remaining ingredients. Seal the lid and cook for 10 minutes on STEAM mode at High.

2. Once done, release the pressure quickly. Serve topped with freshly chopped parsley.

Nutrition Value Per serving

Calories 60
Carbs 10g
Fat 2g
Protein 2g

142. Gnocchi with Butternut Squash and Tomatoes

Preparation Time: 20 minutes
Serves: 4

Ingredients

1 lb Potato Gnocchi
10 oz Butternut squash, peeled, deseeded and diced
1 cup Green Onions, white parts only
1 cup Bell Peppers, stemmed, cored, and chopped
1 ½ cups Water
1 sprig dry Rosemary, crushed
¼ tsp ground Black Pepper
¼ tsp Salt
½ tsp Garlic powder
3 tsp Olive Oil
20 ounces canned diced Tomatoes

Directions

1. Heat oil on SAUTÉ at High and add in the leeks. Cook for 3-4 minutes, stirring constantly.

2. Stir in squash and bell peppers, and continue to cook for 2 more minutes. Add in tomatoes, rosemary, water, garlic powder, salt, black pepper, and wine vinegar. Press CANCEL.

3. Throw in the gnocchi and stir with a wooden spoon until it is well coated. Seal the lid, switch the pressure release valve to close and set to PRESSURE COOK/MANUAL mode, for 8 minutes, for al dente taste.

4. Once done, do a quick pressure release. Serve topped with fresh chives and grated

parmesan.

Nutrition Value Per serving

Calories 485
Carbs 67g
Fat 12g
Protein 21g

143. Frascati and Sage Broccoli

Preparation Time: 15 minutes
Serves: 6

Ingredients

1 ½ pounds Broccoli, broken into florets
1 large Sweet Onion, sliced
1 cup Frascati, Italian White Wine
½ cup Water
2 tsp Sage
3 tsp Olive Oil
1 tsp Garlic Paste
Salt and Pepper, to taste

Directions

1. Heat the oil on SAUTÉ at High and cook the onions until soft, for about 3 minutes. Add garlic paste and cook for 1 minute until fragrant. Stir in the remaining ingredients.
2. Seal the lid and cook for 4 minutes on PRESSURE COOK/MANUAL at High pressure. Do a quick release.

Nutrition Value Per serving

Calories 73
Carbs 9g
Fat 3g
Protein 4g

144. Easy Mushroom Pâté

Preparation Time: 30 minutes
Serves: 8

Ingredients

½ cup White Wine
2 Onions, peeled and sliced
1 ½ pounds Button Mushrooms, thinly sliced
1 ½ cups boiling Water
½ tsp Salt
¼ tsp Black Pepper, freshly cracked
1 cup dried Porcini Mushrooms, washed
3 tbsps Butter

Directions

1. Combine the mushrooms and boiling water in a heatproof cup. Cover and set aside. The mushrooms will soak up the water. Melt butter on SAUTÉ at High. Add in onions and cook for 3 minutes, until soft.
2. Stir in mushrooms and sauté them until golden brown, for about 4 minutes. Pour in wine and let it fully evaporate. Stir in the soaked mushrooms and adjust the seasoning. Seal the lid.
3. Select PRESSURE COOK/MANUAL and cook for 10 minutes at High. Do a quick release. To prepare the paté, blend the ingredients with an immersion blender, for about 5 minutes. Refrigerate and serve chilled.

Nutrition Value Per serving

Calories 55
Carbs 4g
Fat 4g
Protein 1g;

145. Lemony Buckwheat Salad

Ready in: 15 minutes + chilling time
Serves: 6

Ingredients

¼ cup Extra-Virgin Olive Oil
¼ cup fresh Basil, minced
½ tsp Sea Salt
1 tsp Cayenne Pepper
5 cups Water
3 tsp Vegetable Oil
¼ cup fresh Lemon Juice
2 cups Buckwheat, rinsed and drained

½ cup Green Bell Pepper, seeded and chopped
1 cup Red Onions, minced
1 ½ cups Zucchini, diced
Sea Salt and freshly cracked Black Pepper

Directions

1. Add water, buckwheat, salt, oil, and cayenne pepper into your pressure cooker. Seal the lid, set on PRESSURE COOK/MANUAL, and cook for 8 minutes at High.
2. Once cooking is over, allow for a natural pressure release, for about 10 minutes. Carefully open the lid, and stir in the remaining ingredients. Refrigerate and serve chilled.

Nutrition Value Per serving

Calories 286
Carbs 51g
Fat 9g
Protein 12g

146. Ricotta Cheese Lasagna with Mushrooms

Preparation Time: 40 minutes
Serves: 6

Ingredients

2 Cloves Garlic, minced
2 pounds dry lasagna Noodles
2 cups Pasta Sauce
2 cups Ricotta Cheese
1 tsp Red Pepper flakes, crushed
½ tsp Sea Salt
½ tsp dried Oregano
½ tsp ground Black Pepper
2 cups Mushrooms, thinly sliced
¼ cup chopped fresh Basil, plus more for garnish
Non-stick Cooking Spray, for greasing
2 cups Water

Directions

1. Grease spring-form pan with cooking spray. Place the lasagna noodles at the bottom and spread the pasta sauce evenly on top. Then place a layer of ricotta cheese and sprinkle roughly with mushrooms.
2. Season with garlic, herbs, and spices and repeat the process until you run out of products. Cover with aluminum foil. Place the trivet at the bottom of your cooker, and pour 2 cups water.
3. Place down the spring-form pan on the trivet and seal the lid. Cook for 25 minutes on BEANS/CHILI at High pressure. Do a quick pressure release. Garnish with basil to serve.

Nutrition Value Per serving

Calories 613
Carbs 86g
Fat 11g
Protein 28g

147. Cajun Potatoes with Brussel Sprouts

Preparation Time: 20 minutes
Serves: 6

Ingredients

1 ½ pounds Potatoes, chopped
½ pound Brussel Sprouts, halved
1 tsp Cajun Seasoning
½ Onion, chopped
1 Garlic Clove, minced
1 ½ cups Chicken Stock
1 tbsp Oil

Directions

1. Heat oil on SAUTÉ at High, and cook the onions and garlic for 2 minutes, until soft and fragrant. Pour the stock and add potatoes. Seal the lid and cook for 6 minutes on PRESSURE COOK/MANUAL at High pressure.
2. When ready, release the pressure, add the Brussel sprouts, and continue cooking for 4 more minutes, lid off, on SAUTÉ at High. Drain and transfer to a plate. Season with Cajun, and serve.

Nutrition Value Per serving

Calories 131
Carbs 27g
Fat 1g
Protein 5g

148. Turmeric Kale with Shallots

Preparation Time: 20 minutes
Serves: 3

Ingredients

10 ounces Kale, chopped
5 Shallots, chopped
1 tsp Turmeric Powder
2 tsp Olive Oil
½ tsp Coriander Seeds
½ tsp Cumin
Salt and Black Pepper, to taste
1 cup Water

Directions

1. Pour 1 cup of water and place the kale in the steaming basket. Seal the lid and cook on STEAM for 3 minutes at High pressure. When ready, do a quick pressure release.
2. Transfer to a plate. Discard the water and heat the oil on SAUTÉ at High. Add the spices and shallots and cook until soft, for about 5-6 minutes. Stir in the kale, serve and enjoy!

Nutrition Value Per serving

Calories 102
Carbs 14g
Fat 4g
Protein 5g

149. Luscious Sour Cream Veggies

Preparation Time: 20 minutes
Serves: 4

Ingredients

4 Bacon slices, chopped
2 Carrots, chopped
½ Onion, chopped
1 Garlic Clove, minced
2 Potatoes, chopped
1 cup Broccoli Florets
1 cup Cauliflower Florets
1 tbsp Lemon Juice
1 tbsp Olive Oil
1 cup Sour Cream
1 ½ cups Chicken Stock
Salt and Pepper, to taste

Directions

1. Cook the bacon until crispy on SAUTÉ mode at High. Remove to a plate. Add the onion and garlic and cook for 2 minutes, until soft. Add the potatoes and carrots and cook for 2 more minutes.
2. Pour the stock and seal the lid. Cook for 5 minutes on PRESSURE COOK/MANUAL at High pressure. Do a quick release. Stir in sour cream and lemon juice. Adjust the seasoning. Serve topped with crispy bacon slices.

Nutrition Value Per serving

Calories 399
Carbs 42g
Fat 21g
Protein 12g

150. Red Cabbage with Apple

Preparation Time: 30 minutes
Serves: 4

Ingredients

1 small head Red Cabbage, shredded and stems removed
1 ½ cups Vegetable Stock
½ cup dry Red wine
1 Onion, diced
¼ tsp Allspice
½ tsp ground Black Pepper
1 tsp Salt
2 tbsp Olive Oil
2 apples, peeled, cored and diced

½ tbsp Cornstarch dissolved in 6 tsp dry Red Wine

Directions

1. Warm the oil on SAUTÉ at High. Stir in the apples, and onions and sauté until soft, for about 5 minutes.

2. Add in the remaining ingredients, except for cornstarch slurry. Select BPRESSURE COOK/MANUAL mode and cook for 15 minutes at High. Do a quick pressure release. Stir in the already prepared cornstarch slurry.

3. Boil for another 5 minutes, lid off, on SAUTÉ. It has to thicken before it is ready to be served. Serve hot.

Nutritional Values Per serving:

Calories 183
Carbs 18g
Fat 5g
Protein 5g

151. Instant Pot Spicy Creamed Corn

Preparation Time: 15 mins
Servings: 8 servings

Ingredients

32 oz. corn canned, fresh or frozen
8 oz. cream cheesecubed
1 stick butter 1/2 cup, cubed
1/2 cup milk
1/2 cup heavycream
1 tbsp. bacon grease
1-2 tsp. cayennepepper
1/2 tsp. black pepper
1 tbsp. sugar
1 tsp. salt

Directions

1. Combine all Ingredients in the Instant Pot.

2. Set topressure cook on LOW for 10 minutes.

3. Let pressure releaseand serve hot.

Nutritional Values Per serving

Serving Size 4 oz
Serves 8
Calories 376
Total Fat 29.8g
Cholesterol 77.7mg
Sodium 411.4mg
Total Carbohydrate 25.8g
Sugars 11g
Protein 6.6g

152. Instant Pot Gobi Masala – Cauliflower in Indian Spices V+GF

Preparation Time: 7 minutes
Serves: 4

Ingredients

1 Large Cauliflower - cleaned & cut into florets or you can use those readymade florets bags
2 Tbsp Olive Oil - you can use any other light oil
1 Large Onion - finely chopped - you may use white or any other kind
1 Tsp Grated Ginger - you may use 1/2 tsp ginger powder
1 Cup Water - remove 2tbsp to make dry gobhi or use whole 1 cup to make it slightly thick
4 Tbsp Chopped Cilantro - optional

Spices:

½ Tsp Turmeric Powder
1 Tsp Cumin Seeds
1 Tbsp Coriander Powder
1 Tbsp Cumin Powder
½ teaspoon Garam Masala
½ teaspoon Chili Powder
1 Tsp Salt - use as per choice

Directions

1. Turn On the Instant Pot to Saute mode.

2. Once hot indication ison, add oil, cumin seedsand sauté for 30 secs.

3. Now, add onionsand saute for a minuteor till onions are golden.

4. Add all thespicesand saute for 30 seconds.

5. Now, add the cauliflower florets and saute

everything evenly.

6. Add water and put Instant Pot lid on with pressure valve toseal.

7. Cook manually on high for 3 mins.

8. Once the timer is off, quick release the steam or pressure valve.

9. Add chopped cilantro. and mix evenly using a fork thecauliflower will be tender, so please don't put much pressureor it will mash up easily.

10. Transfer to serving dish and garnish some more with cilantroon top.

11. Serve with choice of side.

Notes

Now, in an Instant-Pot, you'd need toadd some minimum amount of water to make it steam properly, hence I'm adding a cupof water. However, once your Gobi is cooked and you open the pot, if you see extra water, you can:

Lightly Saute the gobi while the instant pot is still plugged in and in saute mode. This way, you can cook most of the water making the gobi crisp.

Nutritional Values Per serving

Calories 305
Total Fat 7g
Saturated Fat 1g
Cholesterol 2mg
Sodium 364mg
Carbohydrates 54g
Sugar 16g
Protein 19g

153. Pressure Cooker Green Beans with Bacon

Preparation Time: 25 mins
Servings: 4

Ingredients

1 cup onion diced
5 slices bacon diced
6 cups green beans cut in half
1 teaspoon salt

1 teaspoon pepper
1/4 cup water

Directions

1. You could either put all the Ingredients in thepressure cooker in the order listed, or you could follow the steps below.

2. Turn your Instant Pot or pressure cooker on Sauté, and follow thesteps in this order.

3. Cut up the bacon and put it in the hot pressurecooker.

4. Start dicing theonion and put it in as you cut it.

5. Stir the bacon and onions and start cutting up the green beans.

6. Add the beans, water, salt and pepper to the pot.

7. Cook on high pressure for 4 minutes, and releaseall pressure immediately.

8. Taste and add salt and pepper as needed beforeserving.

Nutritional Values Per serving

122kcal, Fat: 7g, Saturated fat: 2g, Cholesterol: 12mg, Sodium: 517mg, Protein: 4g

154. Instant Pot Corn on the Cob

Preparation Time: 12 mins
Serves: 1 - 10

Ingredients

1-10 ears Corn on the Cob you can cook just 1, or as many as you can fit in the pot

Directions

1. Cut the endsoff of the ears of corn you can fit more in this way. Shuck it if you want to.

2. Place the trivet in thepot, and pour in 1 1/2 cupsof water 2 cups for the 8 qt

3. Stack the ears of corn in thepot. Close the lid and set thesteam release knob to the sealing position.

4. Press the Pressure Cook/Manual button or dial, then the + or - button or dial to select 2 minutes 3 to 4 minutes for unshucked corn.

5. When the cooking cycle is finished, turn the steam release knob to the Venting position to do a Quick Release of the pressure.

6. When the pin in the lid drops down, open the lid and carefully remove thecorn. Slather with butter and sprinkle with salt, and enjoy!

Nutritional Values Per serving

Calories 96
Protein 3.4 g
Carbs 21 g

155. Instant Pot Broccoli Chicken Macand Cheese

Preparation Time: 18 minutesplus 5 minute**NPR Serving:** 6 servings

Ingredients

Between 1 and 1 1/2 lbs boneless, skinless chicken breasts depending on how much meat you like
1 Tbsp butter
3 garliccloves, minced
3/4 pound 12 oz cavatappi, cellentani or elbow macaroni noodles
3 cups water or for more flavor you can use broth
1 tsp ground mustard
1/2 tsp salt
1/2 pound 8 oz fresh broccoli florets
3/4 cup half and half, heavycream, milk or evaporated milk
1/2 pound 8 oz grated medium or sharp cheddar see note below
Cornstarch, if needed

Directions

1. Turn your Instant Pot to the saute setting. While it is heating up cut up your chicken into bite-sizepieces. When the Instant Pot displaysays HOT add in the butter. When it is melted add in thechicken and saute lightly for 1-2 minutes. Add in the garlic and saute for 30 seconds. Turn off thesaute function.

2. Add in the pasta into a flat, even layer. Pour the water over the top tocover thepastaas much aspossible. Sprinkle in the ground mustard and the salt.

3. Create a foil packet byplacing broccoli floretssee note below in the center of a pieceof foil large enough to enclose the food one and a half times. Pull over oneside, folding theedges to seal. Then fold the remaining two edges. Don't seal the packet too tightly: you want to leave some room for the steam to expand. Place the foil packet on topof the pasta.

4. Cover the Instant Pot and secure the lid. Make sure valve is set to "sealing." Set the manual/pressure cook button to 3 minutes. When the time is up let the pot sit there for an additional 5 minutes and then move the valve to "venting." Remove the lid, when you can.

5. Use hot pads to open up the foil packet. Stir the broccoli into thepot. Stir in the milk your choice and the cheese until it is melted.

6. If the mixture is too liuidy then you can prepare a cornstarch slurry by mixing 1-2 tablespoons of cornstarch with 1-2 tablespoons of cold water until smooth. Stir the mixture into thepot and turn thepot to the saute function. Stir constantly until thick. The mac and cheese will thicken up in a minute or two.

7. Salt and pepper to taste. Serve and enjoy!

Nutritional Value Per Serving:

Serving Size: 1/6 of recipe
Calories: 582
Sugar: 4 g
Sodium: 88 mg
Fat: 23 g
Carbohydrates: 48 g
Protein: 45 g

156. Instant Pot Steamed Asparagus

Preparation Time: 5 minutes
Servings: 4 Servings

Ingredients

1 pound fresh asparagus rinsed and tough ends removed
1 cup water

Directions

1. Place asparagus in a steaming rack, set inside your pressure cooker insert and add the water.
2. Twist the lid into the Locked position, turn the knob to the Sealing position.
3. Plug in the Instant Pot, press the Steam button and adjust the cooking time to 2 minutes. When the timer beeps, turn Off thepressure cooker and release thesteam.
4. Lift the steamer basket out of the Instant Pot and place asparagus in a serving bowl.
5. Season as desired and serve immediately.

Nutrition Info:

Calories: 22kcal
Carbohydrates: 4g
Protein: 2g
Sodium: 5mg
Potassium: 229mg
Fiber: 2g
Sugar: 2g

157. Instant Pot Scalloped Potatoes

Preparation Time: 40 minutes
Serves8

Ingredients

2 lbspotatoes peeled, sliced thin
1 c half and half
1/2 c chicken broth
2 tbsp flour
1 tsp garlicpowder
1 tsp salt
1/2 tsp pepper
1 c mozzarella cheese shredded
1 c cheddar cheeseshredded add another 3/4 c if you want to top it with morecheeseasseen in pic.
1/2 c parmesan cheese grated, shredded

Directions

1. In a bowl mix half and half, broth, flour and spices, mix well.
2. In another bowl mix cheeses.
3. Spray inside of springform pan, slice potatoes and place 1/3 in the bottom of thepan, there will be 3 layers total.
4. Pour half of the li□uid on thepotatoes, sprinkle with 1/2 of cheese. Layer another layer of potatoes.
5. Sprinkle with cheese, lay remaining potatoes on topand pour remaining li□uid on top.
6. Create a foil sling and put under pan.
7. Pour 2 c of water into your Instant pot and put trivet at bottom.
8. Lower pan on to trivet and close lid and steam valve.
9. Set on pressure high for 25 minutes.
10. Do a quick release.
11. Sprinkleanother 3/4 c of cheeseon very top and put under broiler for about 4 minutesor until melted and lightly browned if you want toadd even more cheese!!

Nutritional Value Per Serving:

Calories 242
Calories from Fat 117
Total Fat 13g
Total Carbohydrates 17g
Dietary Fiber 2g
Protein 12g

158. Instant Pot Risotto with Peas and Artichokes

Preparation Time: 35 minutes
Serves: 5

Ingredients

2 tablespoons extra virgin olive oil
1 small yellow onion, peeled and diced
3 cloves garlic, minced
1 1/2 cups arborio, carnaroli, or vialone rice
4 cups vegetablestock, plus more if needed
1 1/2 cups frozen peas, thawed
1 12 oz. jar artichoke hearts, drained
salt, to taste
freshly ground black pepper, to taste
1/4 cup Nutrition Infoal yeast or a pinch of trufflesalt optional
fresh Italian parsleyor basil, for garnish optional

Directions

1. Heat theoliveoil in the Instant Pot with the saute mode. Add theonion and saute until tender and golden brown, about 5 minutes. Add the garlic and saute another minute longer. Add the rice and stir to toast for about one minute. Add the vegetablestock. Place the lid on the Instant Pot and make sure the valve isset to sealing. Cook on manual for 5 minutes.

2. Quick release the pressure bycarefullyand slowly pulsing the valve to venting so that the juices don't sprayout. Remove the lid away from you. Stir the risottoand add more broth if needed to loosen it up. Stir in thepeasand artichokes. Season with salt and pepper. Lock the lid back on for a few minutes to heat up the peasand artichokes. Stir again and season to taste with salt and pepper, and Nutrition Infoal yeast, if using.

Nutritional Values Per serving

Calories: 228
Saturated Fat: 0g
Cholesterol: 0mg
Sodium: 0mg

159. Instant Pot Blackk-Eyed Peas

Preparation Time: 52 mins

Serves: 4 servings

Ingredients

1 Tbsp Olive Oil
1 small Onion, chopped
2 Celery Ribs Stalks, diced
1 Bell Pepper, red or green
2 small Bay Leaves
2 sprigs Fresh Thyme, or 1/2 tsp dried
1 Tbsp Smoked Paprika
1/2 tsp Black Pepper
1 tsp Coarse Salt, or 3/4 tsp tablesalt
4 cloves Garlic, pressed or minced
1 Jalapeño Pepper, seeded and diced small
3 1/2 cups Chicken Broth, low sodium
2 tsp Balsamic Vinegar
1-2 slices Bacon, chopped
1 small Ham Hock or meaty ham bone
1 1/4 cups Black-Eyed Peas, dry*
2 cups Collard Greens, optional chopped in 2" pieces

Directions

1. Turn the pressure cooker on to the Sauté function. When the display reads Hot, add the oil.

2. Add the onion, celery, and bell pepper, and bay leaves. Cook, stirring occasionally, until the onion starts to turn translucent.

3. Add the thyme, smoked paprika, pepper, and salt. Stir.

4. Add the garlicand jalapeño. Cook for about 30 seconds, stirring fre□uently.

5. Add the broth, balsamic vinegar, bacon, and ham hock.

6. Stir in the black-eyed peas, and collard greens, if using.

7. Place the lid on the pressure cooker, locking it in place. Set thesteam release knob to the Sealing position.

8. Cancel the Sauté function.

9. Press the Pressure Cook/Manual button or dial and use the + or - button or dial toselect 17 minutes for firmer beans choose 14 minutes.

10. When thecooking cycle has ended and thepot beeps, let it sit undisturbed for 15

minutes 15 minute Natural Release, then turn the steam release knob to the Venting position to release the remaining steam/pressure.

11. When the pin in the lid drops down, open it and give the contents a stir. Discard bay leaves and ham hock the ham hock won't be tender, it is for flavor, but if you can get some meat off of it, add it to the pot!.

12. Serve

Nutritional Values Per serving

Calories: 324 kcal

160. Instant Pot Hummus NO Soak

Preparation Time: 1 hr
Serves: 12 servings

Ingredients

BEANS:

> *1 pound dried garbanzo beans rinsed*
> *12 cups filtered water*

HUMMUS:

> *3 cupscooked garbanzo beans, still warm*
> *1/2 cup warm bean cooking liquid*
> *1/4 cup tahini*
> *2 medium cloves garlic*
> *1 large lemon juiced*
> *1 teaspoon kosher salt*
> *1/2 teaspoon ground cumin*
> *1/4 teaspoon smoked paprika*
> *1/4 cup extra virgin oliveoil highest ⬚uality*

Directions

1. beansand discard any stones. Place in Instant Pot insert along with 12 cups of filtered water.

2. Close lid, makesure vent isset to "sealed" and set Instant Pot to manual for 35 minutes.

3. Allow Instant Pot to naturally release pressure when done this can take up to 1/2 hour. If you are pressed for time, allow IP

to release pressure naturally for at least 15 minutesand then do a slow quick pressure release.

4. Carefully drain the beans, making sure to reserve the liquid!

!HUMMUS:

1. Transfer 3 cupsof warm drained, cooked garbanzo beans to the bowl of food processor fitted with the chopping blade. Add all other Ingredients EXCEPT olive oil.

2. Process until smooth and slowlyadd the olive in through the tube, 1 T at a time.

3. Hummus should be smooth, creamyand tastealmost whipped.

4. Serve topped with Za'atar, smoked paprika and a splash of olive oil and Enjoy!

Nutritional Value Per Serving:

Calories 106
Calories from Fat 63
Protein 2g

161. Instant Pot Cilantro Lime Rice

Preparation Time: 8 mins, **Servings:** 8 servings

Ingredients

> *2 cups uncooked Long Grain White Rice rinsed*
> *2 cups water*
> *Zest of one lime*
> *½ cup fresh chopped cilantro*
> *1 tspsalt*
> *2 Tbsp fresh squeezed lime juice moreor less to taste*

Directions

1. Place rice and water in Instant Pot. Place lid on pot and lock. Set vent to SEALING. Select MANUAL/PRESSURE COOK and set to 3 minutes on HIGH PRESSURE. Allow rice to NATURALLY PRESSURE RELEASE will take approx. 15-20 mins to release naturally.

2. Fluff rice with fork or the rice paddle that came with Instant Pot. Stir in lime zest,

cilantroand salt. Add lime juicestart with a small amount and adjust to meet your tastes. Serve warm.

Nutrition Info:

Calories 171
Calories from Fat 3
Total Fat 0.3g
Sugars 0.2g
Protein 3.5g

162. Instant Pot Refried Beans

Preparation Time: 1 hour 35 minutes, **Servings:** 4 -6

Ingredients

1 pound 454g pinto beans , rinsed and drained
1 323g largeonion , roughly diced
4 cloves 13.7g garlic , minced
4 cups 1L unsalted chicken stock vegan option: use vegetablestock
2 tablespoons 30ml olive oil, lard or bacon fat
½ - 1 teaspoon 1.3g - 2.7g chilli powder
1 teaspoon 2.7g ground cumin
1 teaspoon 1.1g dried oregano
Salt to taste

Garnish:

Cilantro
Jalapeno optional

Directions

1. Saute Onion, Spices, and Garlic: Heat up Instant Pot using Sauté More function. Wait until it says HOT. Add in 2 tbsp olive oil, bacon fat, or lard. Add roughly diced onion and cook until softened. Then add ½ - 1 tsp chili powder, 1 tsp ground cumin, 1 tsp dried oregano, and minced garlic to Instant Pot. Cook for another minute until fragrant.

2. Deglaze: Pour roughly ½ cup unsalted chicken stock in Instant Pot and deglaze by scrubbing all the brown bits off the bottom of the pot with a wooden spoon. Give it a ⬜uick mix.

3. Pressure Cook Beans: Add well-drained pinto beans in Instant Pot and pour in remaining 3 ½ cups unsalted chicken stock. Pressure Cook at High Pressure for 40 mins tender with a bite or 50 minssilkysmooth & tender, then 25 mins Natural Release.

4. Drain Beans Liquid: Strain the beans li⬜uid with a strainer. Place beans back in Instant Pot. Keep the beans li⬜uid in a mixing bowl.

5. Mash Beans: Create Instant Pot Refried Beans by mashing the beans with a potato masher or immersion blender until desired consistency. Tasteand season with salt FYI: we used 4 pinchesof salt. Add drained beans li⬜uid back to the mashed beans until desired consistency.

6. Garnish Refried Beans: Give it a final taste and garnish. You can spice it up with some jalapeno.

Nutritional Values Per serving

Calories: 202kcal
Carbohydrates: 27g
Protein: 10g
Fat: 6g
Saturated Fat: 1g
Sodium: 54mg

163. Mushroom Quinoa Salad

Preparation Time: 11 minute
Serves: 4

Ingredients

1/2 cup cremini mushrooms; diced
1/2 cup quinoa; rinsed
1/2 carrot; peeled and shredded
1/2 cup green onions
1 tbsp. lime juice
1 tbsp. vegetable oil
1 tbsp. freshly grated ginger
1 tbsp. sesame oil
Pinch of red pepper flakes
3/4 cup water
1/4 tsp. salt

Directions:

1. Add the quinoa, salt and water to Instant Pot.
2. Secure the lid and select the *Manual* function with high pressure for 1 minute,
3. When it beeps; do a quick release and remove the lid.
4. Meanwhile; add the remaining Ingredients to a bowl and mix well.
5. Add the cooked quinoa to the prepared mixture and mix well. Serve as a salad.

Nutrition Values Nutritional Values Per serving

Calories:- 156
Carbohydrate:- 17.6g
Protein:- 3.7g
Fat:- 8.2g
Sugar:- 1.1g
Sodium:- 0.15g

164. Sweet Honey Carrots

Preparation Time: 10 minutes
Serves: 3

Ingredients

1 lb. carrots; peeled and cut into chunks
1/2 tbsp. honey
2 tbsp. golden raisins
⅔ tsp. red pepper flakes; crushed
1/2 tbsp. unsalted butter; melted
1/2 cup water
Salt to taste

Directions:

1. Add raisins, water and carrots to Instant Pot
2. Secure the lid and select the *Manual* function for 5 minutes with low pressure,
3. When it beeps; do a quick release then remove the lid.
4. Strain the carrots and transfer them to a large bowl.

5. Put the remaining Ingredients into the bowl and mix well. Serve warm.

Nutrition Values Nutritional Values Per serving

Calories:- 109
Carbohydrate:- 22.8g
Protein:- 1.5g
Fat:- 2g
Sugar:- 13.9g
Sodium:- 0.17g

165. Famous Bok Choy

Preparation Time: 12 minutes
Serves: 2

Ingredients

1 bunch bok choy; trimmed
1 cup or more water
1 garlic clove; smashed
Salt and pepper to taste

Directions:

1. Add water, garlic and bok choy to Instant Pot.
2. Secure the lid and select the *Manual* function for 7 minutes with high pressure,
3. When it beeps; do a Quick release and remove the lid.
4. Strain the cooked bok choy and transfer it to a platter.
5. Sprinkle some salt and pepper on top. Serve.

Nutrition Values Nutritional Values Per serving

Calories:- 27
Carbohydrate:- 5g
Protein:- 3.1g
Fat:- 0.5g
Sugar:- 1g
Sodium:- 0.13g

166. Mushrooms and Butternut Squash

Preparation Time: 50 minutes
Serves: 4

Ingredients

8 oz. white mushrooms; sliced
2 cups butternut squash; peeled and diced
1 tbsp. olive oil
1/2 cup onion; chopped.
3 garlic cloves; minced
1 red bell pepper; diced
1 ½ cups Arborio rice
3 1/2 cup vegetable broth
1/2 cup dry white wine
1 tsp. salt
1 tsp. black pepper
1/4 tsp. oregano
1 ½ a tbsp. nutritional yeast

Directions:

1. Add the oil to the insert of the Instant Pot and select the *Sauté* function.
2. Put the onion, bell pepper, butternut squash and garlic to the oil and sauté for 5 minutes,
3. Now stir in rice, broth, salt, pepper, mushrooms, oregano, coriander and wine,
4. Secure the lid and select the *Bean* function with 30 minutes cooking time,
5. When it beeps; do a Natural release for 10 minutes then remove the lid.
6. Add nutritional yeast; cook for another 5 minutes on *Sauté* setting. Serve warm.

Nutrition Values Nutritional Values Per serving

Calories:- 422
Carbohydrate:- 72g
Protein:- 14.5g
Fat:- 5.5g
Sugar:- 5.5g
Sodium:- 1.29g

167. Veg Chickpea Salad

Preparation Time: 30 minutes
Serves: 4

Nutrition Values Nutritional Values Per serving

Calories:- 164
Carbohydrate:- 24.1g
Protein:- 6g
Fat:- 5.4g
Sugar:- 7.5g
Sodium:- 0.16g

Ingredients

1/2 cup chickpeas; soaked and rinsed
1/2 bunch kale; chopped.
1/2 carrot; peeled and shredded
1/2 cup cabbage; sliced
1/2 cup green onions; chopped.
1/2 cup red onions; sliced
1 cup water
1 tbsp. brown sugar
2 tablespoons; balsamic vinegar
1 tbsp. vegetable oil
1 tbsp. ginger; grated
1 tbsp. sunflower seeds
1 garlic clove; minced
Black pepper to taste
1/4 tsp. salt

Directions:

1. Add chickpeas, salt and water to Instant Pot.
2. Secure the lid and select the *Manual* function with high pressure for 20 minutes,
3. When it beeps; do a quick release and remove the lid.
4. Meanwhile; add the remaining Ingredients to a bowl and mix well.
5. Strain the cooked chickpeas and add to the prepared mixture and stir. Serve as a salad.

168. IP Seasoned Potatoes

Preparation Time: 30 minutes

Serves: 6

Ingredients

3 lbs. russet potatoes
1/2 cup avocado oil
1 tsp. onion powder
2 tsp. garlic powder
1/2 tsp. ground black pepper
2 cups chicken broth
2 tsp. sea salt
1/2 tsp. paprika

Directions:

1. Add oil to the insert of the Instant Pot and select *Sauté* function on it.
2. Add diced potatoes to the oil and sauté for 8 minutes,
3. Now stir in all the remaining ingredients,
4. Secure the lid and select the *Manual* function with 10 minutes cooking time,
5. When it beeps; do a *Quick release* and remove the lid. Sprinkle additional seasoning on top and serve.

Nutrition Values Nutritional Values Per serving

Calories:- 200
Carbohydrate:- 38.2g
Protein:- 5.9g
Fat:- 3.1g
Sugar:- 3.3g
Sodium:- 0.89g

169. Steamed Broccoli

Preparation Time: 15 minutes
Serves: 6

Ingredients

6 cups broccoli florets
2 tbsp. peanut oil
2 tbsp. Chinese rice wine
1 cup water
1/2 garlic cloves; minced
Fine Sea Salt to taste

Directions:

1. Pour a cup of water into the insert of the Instant Pot.
2. Place the steamer trivet inside,
3. Arrange the broccoli florets over the trivet.
4. Secure the lid and select the *Manual* function with low pressure for 5 minutes,
5. When it beeps; do a Natural release and remove the lid.
6. Strain the florets and return them back to the pot. Add the remaining Ingredients to the broccoli.
7. Select *Sauté* and stir-fry for 5 minutes, Garnish with lemon slices and serve.

Nutrition Values Nutritional Values Per serving

Calories:- 72
Carbohydrate:- 6.1g
Protein:- 2.6g
Fat:- 4.8g
Sugar:- 1.6g
Sodium:- 76mg

170. Fresh Mushrooms

Preparation Time: 11 minutes
Serves: 6

Ingredients

2 lbs. fresh mushrooms; sliced
2 tbsp. olive oil
⅓ cup white wine
6 garlic cloves; minced
⅓ cup balsamic vinegar
Salt to taste
Black pepper to taste

Directions:

1. Add the oil and garlic to Instant Pot and Select the *Sauté* function to cook for 1 minute,
2. Now add all the remaining Ingredients to the cooker.
3. Switch the cooker to the *Manual* function

with high pressure and 5 minutes cooking time,

4. When it is done; do a Quick release then remove the lid. Sprinkle some salt and black pepper if desired then serve.

Nutrition Values Nutritional Values Per serving

Calories:- 91
Carbohydrate:- 6.5g
Protein:- 5g
Fat:- 5.1g
Sugar:- 2.8g
Sodium:- 40mg

171. Cauliflower and Potato Mash

Preparation Time: 30 minutes
Serves: 8

Ingredients

16 oz. cauliflower florets
4 lbs. potatoes peeled
3 cups water
1 tsp. coarse rock salt
2 tbsp. full cream
additional salt and pepper to taste

Directions:

1. Add water, potatoes, cauliflower and salt to Instant Pot.

2. Secure the lid and select the *Manual* function for 25 minutes with high pressure,

3. When it beeps; do a Natural release in 10 minutes and remove the lid.

4. Drain the water from the pot and leave the potatoes and cauliflower inside,

5. Use a potato masher to mash the cauliflower and potatoes in the pot.

6. Stir in cream, pepper and additional salt. Mix well. Serve and enjoy.

Nutrition Values Nutritional Values Per serving

Calories:- 204
Carbohydrate:- 38.7g

Protein:- 6.6g
Fat:- 2.1g
Sugar:- 6.4g
Sodium:- 64mg

172. Healthy Chickpea Hummus

Preparation Time: 25 minutes
Serves: 4

Ingredients

1/2 cup dry chickpeas; soaked
1 bay leaf
1/4 tsp. powdered cumin
1/4 bunch Parsley; chopped.
1/4 tsp. paprika
2 garlic cloves
1 tbsp. tahini
1/2 lemon; juiced
1/4 tsp. sea salt
1 tbsp. olive oil

Directions:

1. Add 3 cups of water, chickpeas, bay leaf and garlic cloves to Instant Pot.

2. Secure the lid and select the *Manual* function for 18 minutes with high pressure,

3. When it beeps; do a Natural release and remove the lid.

4. Strain and rinse the cooked chickpeas, Discard the bay leaf.

5. Add oil and all the remaining Ingredients to Instant Pot and *Sauté* for 2 minutes,

6. Return the chickpeas to the pot and use an immerse blender to form a smooth puree, Stir and serve.

Nutrition Values Nutritional Values Per serving

Calories:- 149
Carbohydrate:- 17.4g
Protein:- 5.7g
Fat:- 7.1g
Sugar:- 2.9g
Sodium:- 0.12g

173. Chickpea Bowl

Preparation Time: 35 minutes
Serves: 3

Ingredients

1/2 cup dried chickpeas; rinsed, soaked and drained
1/2 tbsp. olive oil
1/2 onion; chopped
1/2 tbsp. fresh ginger; minced
1/2 tbsp. garlic; minced
1/2 tsp. ground coriander
1 medium tomato; chopped finely
1/2 tsp. curry powder
1/2 tsp. ground cumin
1/2 cup water
Pinch of salt
Freshly ground black pepper to taste
1 tbsp. fresh parsley; chopped

Directions:

1. Add oil and onion to Instant Pot and Select the *Sauté* function to cook for 3 minutes,
2. Now add the garlic, ginger and spices to cook for another 2 minutes,
3. Add water and chickpeas to the pot then secure the lid.
4. Switch the cooker to the Manual function with high pressure and 20 minutes cooking time,
5. When it is done; do a Quick release then remove the lid.
6. Sprinkle some salt and black pepper on top and garnish with parsley. Serve hot.

Nutrition Values Nutritional Values Per serving

Calories:- 211
Carbohydrate:- 26.2g
Protein:- 7.8g
Fat:- 9.4g
Sugar:- 4.8g
Sodium:- 66mg

174. Awesome Asparagus Sticks

Preparation Time: 13 minutes
Serves: 3

Ingredients

1lb. thick Asparagus sticks
1 cup water
8 oz. thinly sliced Prosciutto*
Pepper to taste
Salt to taste

Directions:

1. Wrap each prosciutto slice over the asparagus sticks,
2. Pour a cup of water into Instant Pot.
3. Arrange a steamer trivet inside,
4. Place the wrapped asparagus sticks over the trivet.
5. Secure the lid and select *Manual* with high pressure for 3 minutes,
6. When it beeps; do a natural release then remove the lid.
7. Transfer the steamed asparagus sticks to the platter. Sprinkle salt and pepper then serve.

Nutrition Values Nutritional Values Per serving

Calories:- 164
Carbohydrate:- 9.6g
Protein:- 17.6g
Fat:- 5.7g
Sugar:- 3g
Sodium:- 0.33g

175. Cheesy Potatoes

Preparation Time: 30 minutes
Serves: 5

Ingredients

5 medium potatoes
2 cups water
1/4 cup cheddar cheese; shredded
1/4 cup mozzarella cheese; shredded
1 tsp. red pepper flakes
1 ½ tbsp. butter

Salt and Pepper to taste

Directions:

1. Prick all the potatoes in the center and create a slit on top.
2. Top the potatoes with cheese, butter, salt, pepper and pepper flakes,
3. Add water to Instant Pot and place a steamer trivet inside,
4. Arrange the stuffed potatoes over the trivet with their pricked side up.
5. Secure the lid and cook on *Manual* function for 20 minutes with high pressure,
6. When the timer goes off; do a Natural release and remove the lid.
7. Transfer the potatoes to the platter and sprinkle with some salt and pepper. Serve and enjoy.

Nutrition Values Nutritional Values Per serving

Calories:- 205
Carbohydrate:- 33.8g
Protein:- 5.5g
Fat:- 5.9g
Sugar:- 2.5g
Sodium:- 85mg

Chapter 4 – Soups and stews

176. Italian Sausage Stew

Serves: 4
Preparation Time: 5 minutes
Cooking Time: 30 minutes

Ingredients

2 tablespoons butter
½ pound ground pork
½ teaspoon onion powder
½ teaspoon garlic powder
1 ½ teaspoon basil
½ teaspoon thyme
¼ teaspoon cumin
½ teaspoon marjoram
¼ teaspoon cayenne
2 carrots, diced
2 stalks of celery, chopped
½ cup wine
1 can diced tomatoes
4 cups bone broth
Salt and pepper
A handful of kale, chopped
½ cup parmesan cheese, grated

Directions

1. Press the Sauté button on the Instant Pot.
2. Melt the oil and add the ground pork. Stir in the onion powder, garlic powder, basil, thyme, cumin, marjoram, and cayenne.
3. Continue stirring the pork until lightly golden.
4. Stir in the carrots, celery, wine, tomatoes, and bone broth.
5. Season with salt and pepper.
6. Close the lid and press the Manual button.
7. Adjust the cooking time to 25 minutes.
8. Do quick pressure release.
9. Once the lid is open, press the Sauté button and stir in the kale. Simmer until wilted.
10. Sprinkle with parmesan cheese.

Nutritional Values Per serving:

Calories: 304
Carbohydrates: 8.9g
Protein:21.3g
Fat:19.4 g
Fiber: 2.7g

177. Enchilada Chicken Stew

Serves: 6
Preparation Time: 5 minutes
Cooking Time: 20 minutes

Ingredients

2 tablespoons coconut oil
1 onion, chopped
3 cloves of garlic, minced
2 pounds chicken breasts
1 green bell pepper, chopped
1 can jalapenos, chopped
1 can green chilies, chopped
1 can diced tomatoes
1 can tomato sauce
1 tablespoon cumin
1 tablespoon chili powder
2 teaspoons dried oregano
Salt and pepper to taste

Directions

1. Press the Sauté button on the Instant Pot.
2. Heat the oil and sauté the onion and garlic until fragrant.
3. Add in the chicken breasts and continue stirring until lightly brown.
4. Add the rest of the ingredients
5. Give a good stir.
6. Close the lid and press the Manual button.
7. Adjust the cooking time to 15 minutes.
8. Do natural pressure release.
9. Serve with avocado slices if desired.

Nutritional Values Per serving:

Calories: 385
Carbohydrates:17.1 g
Protein:34.2 g
Fat: 19.3g
Fiber:5.8 g

178. Instant Pot Goulash

Serves: 5
Preparation Time: 5 minutes
Cooking Time: 20 minutes

Ingredients

1 tablespoon olive oil
1 onion, chopped
3 cloves of garlic, minced
1-pound ground beef
2 carrots, chopped
3 cups beef broth
2 cans tomato sauce
2 cans diced tomatoes
1 tablespoon Worcestershire sauce
½ teaspoon dried thyme
½ teaspoon oregano
1 cup dry elbow pasta
Salt and pepper to taste

Directions

1. Press the Sauté button on the Instant Pot.
2. Heat the oil and sauté the onion and garlic until fragrant.
3. Stir in the ground beef and stir for 3 minutes.
4. Add the rest of the ingredients.
5. Close the lid and press the Manual button.
6. Adjust the cooking time to 15 minutes.
7. Do quick pressure release.

Nutritional Values Per serving:

Calories:651
Carbohydrates: 81.5g
Protein: 32.3g
Fat: 18.9g
Fiber:18.1g

179. Instant Pot Carne Guisada

Serves: 5
Preparation Time: 5 minutes
Cooking Time: 35 minutes

Ingredients

2 tablespoons olive oil
1 onion, chopped
3 cloves of garlic, minced
1-pound beef stew meat, cut into chunks
1 Serrano peppers, minced
1 bay leaf
1 teaspoon ground cumin
1 teaspoon chili powder
1 teaspoon paprika
½ teaspoon chipotle powder
½ teaspoon oregano
1 cup beef broth
½ cup tomato sauce
Salt and pepper

Directions

1. Press the Sauté button on the Instant Pot.
2. Heat the oil and sauté the onion and garlic until fragrant.
3. Stir in the beef and stir for 3 minutes.
4. Add the rest of the ingredients.
5. Close the lid and press the Manual button.
6. Adjust the cooking time to 30 minutes.
7. Do quick pressure release.

Nutritional Values Per serving:

Calories:189
Carbohydrates: 15.9g
Protein:1.9g
Fat:13.4 g
Fiber: 3.1g

180. Instant Pot Turkey Chili

Serves: 6
Preparation Time: 5 minutes
Cooking Time: 15 minutes

Ingredients

- 1 tablespoon olive oil
- 1-pound lean ground turkey
- 1 onion, chopped
- 1 tablespoon chili powder
- 2 teaspoons chipotle pepper
- 2 teaspoons ground cumin
- 1 teaspoon garlic powder
- 2 medium sweet potatoes, peeled and sliced thickly
- 1 medium red bell pepper, diced
- 1 can crushed tomatoes
- 2 cans beans, drained and rinsed
- 1 ½ cups chicken broth
- Salt and pepper to taste

Directions

1. Press the Sauté button on the Instant Pot.
2. Heat the oil and sauté the ground turkey meat.
3. Stir in the onions, chili powder, chipotle pepper, cumin, and garlic powder until fragrant.
4. Add the rest of the ingredients.
5. Scrape the bottom to remove the browning.
6. Close the lid and press the Manual button.
7. Adjust the cooking time to 10 minutes.
8. Do quick pressure release.
9. Serve with cilantro or avocado slices

Nutritional Values Per serving:

Calories: 346
Carbohydrates: 49g
Protein: 31g
Fat: 4g
Fiber: 14g

181. Classic Beef Chili

Serves: 6
Preparation Time: 5 minutes
Cooking Time: 20 minutes

Ingredients

- 1-pound ground beef
- 1 onion, diced
- 3 cloves of garlic, minced
- 1 bell pepper, diced
- 1 tablespoon chili powder
- 2/3 tablespoon cumin
- 1 teaspoon ground cumin
- ½ tablespoon brown sugar
- 1 teaspoon hot sauce
- 1/3 cup red wine
- 2 cans kidney beans, undrained
- 1 can diced tomatoes, undrained
- 1 can green chilies, drained
- ¼ cup ketchup
- Salt and pepper

Directions

1. Press the Sauté button and add in the beef, onions, and garlic.
2. Break the beef and stir for 3 minutes.
3. Add the rest of the ingredients.
4. Give a good stir.
5. Close the lid and press the Manual button.
6. Adjust the cooking time to 15 minutes.
7. Do quick pressure release.
8. Serve with cilantro or avocado slices

Nutritional Values Per serving:

Calories: 249
Carbohydrates: 22.2g
Protein:27 g
Fat: 5.5g
Fiber: 6.9g

182. Instant Pot Chipotle Chili

Serves: 6
Preparation Time: 5 minutes
Cooking Time: 60 minutes

Ingredients

- 1 tablespoon oil
- 1-pound ground beef
- 1 onion, chopped
- 6 cloves of garlic, minced

½ teaspoon chipotle chili powder
1 tablespoon red chili powder
1 teaspoon oregano
1 teaspoon cumin powder
2 cups tomatoes, chopped
1 cup dry kidney beans, soaked overnight and rinsed
2 cups chicken broth
Salt and pepper to taste

Directions

1. Press the Sauté button and heat the oil.
2. Stir in the ground beef. Break the beef and stir for 3 minutes.
3. Add the onions and garlic until fragrant.
4. Add the rest of the ingredients.
5. Give a good stir.
6. Close the lid and press the Manual button.
7. Adjust the cooking time to 60 minutes.
8. Do quick pressure release.

Nutritional Values Per serving:

Calories: 405
Carbohydrates: 13.5g
Protein: 40.2g
Fat: 20.6g
Fiber: 3.9g

183. Instant Pot Cowboy Chili

Serves: 8
Preparation Time: 5 minutes
Cooking Time: 15 minutes

Ingredients

1-pound breakfast sausage, chopped
1-pound ground beef
2 onions, diced
2 tablespoons chili powder
1 teaspoon garlic powder
1 teaspoon onion powder
½ teaspoon paprika
1 ½ cups tomatoes, chopped

1 ½ cups carrots, diced
1 cup water
Salt and pepper

Directions

1. Press the Sauté button and add the breakfast sausages, ground beef, and onions.
2. Stir for 3 minutes until the meat has rendered some of its fat.
3. Add the rest of the ingredients.
4. Give a good stir.
5. Close the lid and press the Manual button.
6. Adjust the cooking time to 15 minutes.
7. Do quick pressure release.

Nutritional Values Per serving:

Calories: 312
Carbohydrates:8.7 g
Protein: 24.7g
Fat: 19.5g
Fiber:2.6g

184. Curried Cauliflower Soup

Preparation Time: 25 minutes
Serve: 6

Ingredients:

1 tbsp olive oil
1 medium spring onion
1 cup cauliflower, steamed
1 cup beef stock
1/2 cup coconut milk
10 cashew nuts
½ tsp coriander
½ tsp turmeric
½ tsp cumin
2 tbsp fresh parsley, finely chopped
salt and pepper, to taste

Directions:

1. Place the cauliflower and onion in a large pot and add chicken stock. Stir in coriander, turmeric, cumin and a pinch of salt. Bring to a boil and let boil for 5 minutes.
2. Remove from heat. Using a hand blender, puree ingredients in the pot until smooth. Stir in the coconut milk. Serve with roasted cashew nuts and top with parsley.

Nutritional Value

Calories 258
Fats 12.6g
Carbohydrates: 10.8g
Protein 27g

185.Easy Everyday Chicken Soup

Preparation Time: 5 HR
Serve: 8

Ingredients:

3 skinned, bonein chicken breasts
6 skinned and boned chicken thighs
1 tsp salt
1/2 tsp freshly ground pepper
1/2 tsp chicken spice seasoning
34 carrots sliced
4 celery ribs, sliced
1 sweet onion, chopped
2 cans evaporated milk
2 cups chicken stock

Directions:

1. Prepare Chicken: Rub chicken pieces with salt, pepper, and chicken spice seasoning. Place breasts in a slow cooker, top with thighs.
2. Add carrots and next 3 ingredients. Whisk evaporated milk and stock until smooth. Pour soup mixture over vegetables.
3. Cover with lid and cook on high 3 and half hours.
4. Remove chicken from slow cooker and allow to cool for 10 minutes.
5. Using fork shred the chicken.

6. Stir shredded chicken into the soupandvegetable mixture.
7. Cover again with lid and cook on HIGH for 1 hour.

Nutritional Value

Calories 282
Fats 18g
Carbohydrates: 5.6g
Protein 24g

186.Creamy Chicken & Tomato Soup

Preparation Time: 9 HR 10 minutes
Serve: 8

Ingredients:

8 frozen skinless boneless chicken breast
2 tbsp Italian Seasoning
1 tbsp dried basil
2 cloves garlic, minced
1 large onion, chopped
2 can of coconut milkfull fat, shake before opening can avoid separation
2 cans diced tomatoes and juice
2 ¼ cups of chicken stock
1 small can of tomato paste
Sea salt and pepper to taste

Directions:

1. Put all the above ingredients into the slow cooker, cook for 9 hours on low.
2. After 9 hours take two forks and shred the chicken, set the slow cooker on warm till ready to serve

Nutritional Value

Calories 227
Fats 3.8g
Carbohydrates: 6.37g
Protein 30g

187.Tomato & Basil Soup

Preparation Time: 7 HR 45 minutes

Serve: 6

Ingredients:

2 cans diced tomatoes, with juice
1 cup finely diced celery
1 cup finely diced carrots
1 cup finely diced onions
1 tsp dried oregano or 1 T fresh oregano
1 tbsp dried basil or 1/4 cup fresh basil
4 cups chicken stock
½ tsp bay leaf
1 cup Parmesan cheese
½ cup butter
2 cups full cream milk
1 tsp salt
¼ tsp black pepper
¼ cup almond flour or ground chia seeds

Directions:

1. Add tomatoes, celery, carrots, chicken stock, onions, oregano, basil, and bay leaf to a large slow cooker.
2. Cover and cook on low for 57 hours, until flavors, are blended and vegetables are tender.
3. About 30 minutes before serving, Melt butter over low heat and add almond flour. Stir constantly with a whisk for 57 minutes.
4. Slowly stir in 1 cup hot soup. Add another 3 cups and stir until smooth. Add all back into the slow cooker.
5. Stir and add the Parmesan cheese, milk, salt, and pepper.
6. Cover and cook on LOW for another 30 minutes or so until ready to serve.

Nutritional Value

Calories 269
Fats 11g
Carbohydrates: 4.86g
Protein 35.71g

188.Beef & Cabbage Soup

Preparation Time: 8 HR 15 minutes
Serve: 8

Ingredients:

2 tbsp olive or coconut oil
lbs ground beef mince
1/2 large onion, chopped
5 cups chopped cabbage
cups water
tins tomato puree
beef stock cubes
1 1/2 tsp ground cumin
1 tsp salt
1 tsp pepper

Directions:

1. Heat oil in a large pot.
2. Add ground beef and onion, and cook until beef brown and crumbled.
3. Transfer mince with fat to a slow cooker. Add cabbage, water, tomato sauce, bouillon, cumin, salt, and pepper. Stir to dissolve stock cubes and cover.
4. Cook on high setting for 4 hours, or on low setting for 6 to 8 hours. Stir occasionally.

Nutritional Value

Calories 165
Fats 8g
Carbohydrates: 13.7g
Protein 11.54g

189.3 Ingredients Vegetable Beef Soup

Preparation Time: 8 HR 45 minutes
Serve: 4

Ingredients:

lbs ground beef mince
cups tomatovegetable juice cocktail
packages frozen mixed vegetables

Directions:

1. Place ground beef mince in a slow cooker. Cook over mediumhigh heat until evenly brown and crumble.
2. Add juice cocktail and mixed vegetables.

3. In a slow cooker oven, simmer for 30 minutes.
4. In a slow cooker, cook 1 hour on High.
5. Then reduce heat to Low and simmer 6 to 8 hours.

Nutritional Value

Calories 251
Fats 12g
Carbohydrates: 13.5g
Protein 21.3g

190.Clam Chowder

Preparation Time: 11 HR 15 MIN
Serve: 8

Ingredients:

2 can minced clams in brine
4 slices bacon, cut into small pieces
3 sweet potatoes, peeled and cubed
1 cup chopped onion
1 carrot, grated
1 punnet mushrooms fried in butter and blended finely with a hand blender
1/4 tsp ground black pepper
2 cans evaporated milk

Directions:

1. In a small bowl, drain the clams and reserve the juice.
2. Add water to the juice as needed to total 1 3/4 cups liquid. Cover the clams and put in refrigerator for later.
3. In a slow cooker combine the bacon, sweet potatoes, onion, carrot, mushrooms, ground black pepper, evaporated milk and reserved clam juice with water.
4. Cover and cook on low setting for 9 to 11 hours or on high setting for 4 to 5 hours. Add the clams and cook on high setting for another hour.

Nutritional Value

Calories 206

Fats 9.56g
Carbohydrates: 21.42g
Protein 9.24g

191.Mushroom Soup

Preparation Time: 6 HR 55 minutes
Serve: 8

Ingredients:

2 punnets white button mushrooms, cleaned, trimmed, and quartered
1 medium onion, roughly chopped
4 cloves garlic, sliced
7 sprigs thyme, divided
2 small lemons, halved
2 tbsp olive oil
1 1/2 tbsp red wine vinegar
Salt and freshly ground black pepper
1/2 cup dry sherry
2 cups milk
1 cup heavy cream
1/2 cup sour cream
3 cups chicken stock or vegetable stock

Directions:

1. Preheat oven to 375 F.
2. Place mushrooms, onions, garlic, and 5 thyme sprigs in a large bowl. Squeeze lemons into the bowl and add the squeezed lemon halves. Add vinegar and olive oil.
3. Season with salt and pepper and toss to coat.
4. Transfer to a foillined rimmed baking sheet and spread into an even layer.
5. Roast in preheated oven until mushrooms release liquid, about 15 minutes.
6. Carefully drain liquid into a separate container and reserve.
7. Return mushrooms to oven and continue roasting until browned about 30 minutes.
8. Discard lemons and thyme sprigs.
9. Transfer mushroom mixture along with drained liquid to the slow cooker.
10. Add milk, heavy cream, sour cream, sherry, and stock, along with remaining

thyme sprigs. Stir well.

11. Cook on low for 6 hours.
12. Discard thyme sprigs.
13. Transfer soup to a blender and blend until you get desired consistency.

Nutritional Value

Calories 198
Fats 13.2g
Carbohydrates: 15.8g
Protein 5g

192.Seafood Soup

Preparation Time: 4 HR 15 minutes
Serve: 8

Ingredients:

12 slices bacon, chopped
2 cloves garlic, minced
6 cups chicken stock
3 stalks celery, diced
2 large carrots, diced
Ground black pepper to taste
1/2 tsp red pepper flakes, or to taste
2 cups onions
2 cup uncooked prawns, peeled and deveined
lbs white fish fillets like Hake or Kingklip, cut into bitesize pieces
1 can evaporate milk

Directions:

1. Fry bacon in coconut oil or olive oil, add onion and garlic. Transfer mixture to a slow cooker.
2. Pour chicken stock into slow cooker. Add celery, and carrots into the stock. Season with black pepper and red pepper flakes.
3. Set the cooker to high, cover, and cook for 3 hours.
4. Stir prawns and fish into the soup and cook 1 more hour. Stir evaporated milk into chowder, heat thoroughly, and serve.

Nutritional Value

Calories 281
Fats 9.5g
Carbohydrates: 7.8g
Protein 39g

193.Cream of Broccoli & Mushroom Soup

Preparation Time: 4 HR 15 minutes
Serve: 6

Ingredients:

1 tbsp oil
1 onion, chopped
2 packets frozen chopped broccoli, thawed
2 cans cream of celery soup
2 punnets of mushrooms fried in butter and blitzed smooth with a hand blender
1 cup shredded cheddar cheese
2 cans evaporated milk

Directions:

1. Fry the onion in coconut oil and transfer to the slow cooker.
2. Transfer the drained onion to a slow cooker.
3. Place the broccoli, cream of celery soup, mushrooms, cheddar cheese, and milk into the slow cooker.
4. Cook on low for 34 hours or until the broccoli is tender.

Nutritional Value

Calories 212
Fats 4.7g
Carbohydrates: 36.6g
Protein 10g

194.Beef & Vegetable Soup

Preparation Time: 8 HR 15 minutes
Serve: 8

Ingredients:

lbs beef chuck or neck

1 can diced tomatoes, undrained
2 medium sweet potatoes, peeled and cubed
2 medium onions, diced
3 celery ribs, sliced
2 carrots, sliced
2 cups pumpkin
3 beef stock cubes
1/2 tsp salt
1/2 tsp dried basil
1/2 tsp dried oregano
1/4 tsp pepper
3 cups water

Directions:

In a slow cooker, combine all the ingredients. Cover and cook on high for 68 hours

Nutritional Value

Calories 253
Fats 14.5g
Carbohydrates: 10g
Protein 23g

195. Fast Bean Stew

Preparation Time: 10 minutes
Cooking Time: 25 minutes
Serves: 4

Ingredients:

1 yellow onion, peeled and chopped
2 carrots, peeled and chopped
1 garlic head, halved
1 pound chickpeas, drained
22 ounces canned diced tomatoes
22 ounces water
1 teaspoon dried oregano
3 bay leaves
2 tablespoons olive oil
Salt and ground black pepper, to taste
½ teaspoon red pepper flakes
Olive oil, for serving
2 tablespoons Parmesan cheese, grated

Directions:

Put the onion, carrots, garlic, chickpeas,

tomatoes, water, oregano, bay leaves, 2 tablespoons olive oil, salt, and pepper into the Instant Pot. Cover, cook on the Meat/Stew setting for 25 minutes, and release pressure. Ladle into bowls, add the cheese, pepper flakes and a drizzle of oil on top, and serve.

Nutritional Values Per serving

Calories: 164
Fat: 2
Fiber: 9
Carbs: 28
Protein: 8.2

196. Sweet Potato Stew

Preparation Time: 10 minutes
Cooking Time: 20 minutes
Serves: 4

Ingredients:

1 onion, peeled and chopped
1 sweet potato, cubed
3 garlic cloves, peeled and chopped
1 celery stalk, chopped
2 carrots, peeled and chopped
1 cup green lentils
½ cup red lentils
2 cups vegetable stock
¼ cup raisins
14 ounces canned diced tomatoes
Salt and ground black pepper, to taste

For the spice blend:

1 teaspoon cumin
1 teaspoon turmeric
½ teaspoon ground cinnamon
1 teaspoon paprika
2 teaspoons coriander
¼ teaspoon ginger, grated
Cloves
Red chili flakes

Directions:

Set the Instant Pot on Sauté mode, add the onions and brown them for 2 minutes, adding some of the stock from time to time. Add the garlic, stir, and cook for 1 minute. Add the carrots, raisins, celery, and sweet potatoes, stir, and cook for 1 minute. Add the lentils, stock, tomatoes, salt, pepper, turmeric, cinnamon, paprika, cumin, coriander, ginger, cloves, and chili flakes, stir, cover, and cook on the Meat/Stew setting for 15 minutes. Release the pressure, uncover the Instant Pot, stir the stew, add more salt and pepper, if needed, ladle into bowls, and serve.

Nutritional Values Per serving

Calories: 150
Fat: 9
Fiber: 3
Protein: 4
Carbs: 25

197. Simple Turkey Stew

Preparation Time: 10 minutes
Cooking Time: 35 minutes
Serves: 4

Ingredients:

1 tablespoon avocado oil
1 yellow onion, peeled and chopped
3 celery stalks, chopped
2 carrots, peeled and chopped
Salt and ground black pepper, to taste
2 cups potatoes, chopped
3 cups turkey meat, already cooked and shredded
15 ounces canned tomatoes, chopped
5 cups turkey stock
1 tablespoon cranberry sauce
1 teaspoon garlic, minced

Directions:

Set the Instant Pot on Sauté mode, add the oil and heat it up. Add the carrots, celery, and onions, stir and cook for 3 minutes. Add the potatoes, tomatoes, stock, garlic, meat, and cranberry sauce, stir, cover, and cook on Meat/Stew for 30 minutes. Release the pressure, uncover the Instant Pot, add salt and pepper, stir, divide into bowls, and serve.

Nutritional Values Per serving

Calories: 210
Fat: 4
Fiber: 0
Carbs: 15
Protein: 28

198. Mushroom and Beef Stew

Preparation Time: 10 minutes
Cooking Time: 25 minutes
Serves: 6

Ingredients:

1 tablespoon olive oil
1 red onion, peeled and chopped
2 pounds beef chuck, cubed
1 teaspoon fresh rosemary, chopped
1 celery stalk, chopped
½ cup red wine
1 cup beef stock
Salt and ground black pepper, to taste
1 ounce dried porcini mushrooms, chopped
2 carrots, peeled and chopped
2 tablespoons flour
2 tablespoons butter

Directions:

Set the Instant Pot on Sauté mode, add the oil and beef, stir, and brown for 5 minutes. Add the onion, celery, rosemary, salt, pepper, wine, and stock and stir. Add the carrots and mushrooms, cover the Instant Pot and cook on the Meat/Stew setting for 15 minutes. Release the pressure, uncover the Instant Pot and set it on Manual mode. Meanwhile, heat up a pan over medium-high heat, add the butter, and melt it. Add the flour and 6 tablespoons of cooking liquid from the stew and stir well. Pour this over the stew, stir, cook for 5 minutes, divide into bowls, and serve.

Nutritional Values Per serving

Calories: 322
Fat: 18
Fiber: 3

Carbs: 12
Protein: 24

199. Drunken Lamb Stew

Preparation Time: 10 minutes
Cooking Time: 15 minutes
Serves: 6

Ingredients:

2 onions, peeled and chopped
3 pounds lamb shoulder, cut into medium chunks
2 potatoes, roughly chopped
Salt and ground black pepper, to taste
2 thyme sprigs, chopped
6 ounces dark beer
2 cups water
2 carrots, seeded and chopped
¼ cup fresh parsley, minced

Directions:

Put the onions and lamb into the Instant Pot. Add the salt, pepper, potatoes, thyme, water, beer, and carrots, stir, cover and cook on the Meat/Stew setting for 15 minutes. Release the pressure, uncover the Instant Pot, add the parsley, more salt and pepper, if needed, stir, divide into bowls, and serve.

Nutritional Values Per serving

Calories: 236
Fat: 8
Fiber: 2.5
Carbs: 22
Protein: 19

200. German Stew

Preparation Time: 10 minutes
Cooking Time: 10 minutes
Serves: 4

Ingredients:

1 pound kielbasa, cut into medium pieces
14 ounces canned diced tomatoes
2 potatoes, cut into quarters
1 small jar sauerkraut
1 onion, peeled and cut into medium chunks

Directions:

In the Instant Pot, add the kielbasa, tomatoes, potatoes, sauerkraut, and onion, stir, cover, and cook on the Manual setting for 10 minutes. Release the pressure, uncover the Instant Pot, divide stew into bowls, and serve.

Nutritional Values Per serving

Calories: 140
Fat: 4
Fiber: 2
Carbs: 11
Protein: 12

201. Oxtail Stew

Preparation Time: 10 minutes
Cooking Time: 40 minutes
Serves: 4

Ingredients:

5 pounds oxtails
1 yellow onion, peeled and chopped
Salt and ground black pepper, to taste
3 carrots, peeled and chopped
3 celery stalks, chopped
1 garlic clove, peeled and chopped
1 bunch parsley, chopped
2 cups red wine, chopped
1 cup tomatoes, cored and chopped
1 cup water
Sugar: to the taste

Directions:

In the Instant Pot, mix the oxtails with salt, pepper, onion, carrots, celery, garlic, tomatoes, red wine, parsley, water and sugar, stir, cover, and cook on Meat/Stew for 40 minutes. Release the pressure, uncover the Instant Pot, divide the oxtail stew into bowls, and serve.

Nutritional Values Per serving

Calories: 312
Fat: 12
Fiber: 14
Carbs: 15
Protein: 14
Sugar: 1

202. Okra Stew

Preparation Time: 10 minutes
Cooking Time: 20 minutes
Serves: 4

Ingredients:

1 yellow onion, peeled and chopped
1 garlic clove, peeled and minced
1 pound beef chuck, cubed
1 cardamom pod
2 cups chicken stock
14 ounces frozen okra, sliced
12 ounces tomato sauce
Salt and ground black pepper, to taste
½ cup parsley, chopped
Olive oil
Juice of ½ lemon
For the marinade:
½ teaspoon onion powder
½ teaspoon garlic powder
Salt
1 tablespoon 7-spice mix

Directions:

In a bowl, mix the meat with 7-spice mix, a pinch of salt, onion garlic, and garlic powder, toss to coat and set the dish aside. Set the Instant Pot on Sauté mode, add some olive oil, and heat it up. Add the onion, stir, and cook 2 minutes. Add the garlic and cardamom, stir, and cook for 1 minute. Add the meat, stir, and brown meat for 2 minutes. Add the stock, tomato sauce, okra, salt, and pepper, stir, cover, and cook on Meat/Stew for 20 minutes. Release the pressure, uncover the Instant Pot, add more salt and pepper, if needed, lemon juice, and

parsley, stir, divide into bowls, and serve.

Nutritional Values Per serving

Calories: 230
Fat: 10
Fiber: 8
Carbs: 15
Protein: 20

203. Lamb Stew

Preparation Time: 10 minutes
Cooking Time: 30 minutes
Serves: 4

Ingredients:

2 pounds lamb shoulder, cubed
¼ cup red wine vinegar
1 tablespoon garlic, peeled and minced
14 ounces canned diced tomatoes
2 yellow onions, peeled and chopped
1 tablespoon olive oil
2 tablespoons tomato paste
1 teaspoon dried oregano
1 teaspoon dried basil
Salt and ground black pepper, to taste
2 bay leaves
1 red bell pepper, seeded and chopped
1 green bell pepper, seeded and chopped
⅓ cup fresh parsley, chopped

Directions:

Set the Instant Pot on Sauté mode, add the oil and heat it up. Add the onions and garlic, stir, and cook for 2 minutes. Add the vinegar, stir, and cook for 2 minutes. Add the lamb, tomatoes, tomato paste, oregano, basil, salt, pepper, and bay leaves, stir, cover the Instant Pot and cook on the Meat/Stew setting for 12 minutes. Release the pressure for 10 minutes, uncover the Instant Pot, discard the bay leaves, add the bell peppers, more salt and pepper, if needed, stir, cover, and cook on Manual for 8 more minutes. Release the pressure again, uncover, add the parsley, stir and divide into bowls.

Nutritional Values Per serving

Calories: 700
Fat: 52
Fiber: 4.4
Carbs: 17
Protein: 40

204. Beef and Root Vegetables Stew

Preparation Time: 10 minutes
Cooking Time: 32 minutes
Serves: 4

Ingredients:

1 pound beef chuck, cubed
2 tablespoons olive oil
2 bacon slices, cooked and crumbled
½ cup white flour
Salt and ground black pepper, to taste
1 rutabaga, diced
1 cup cipollini onions, peeled
4 carrots, peeled and chopped
4 garlic cloves, peeled and minced
2 cups beef stock
1 tablespoon tomato paste
½ cup bourbon
A bunch of thyme, chopped
A bunch of rosemary, chopped
1 cup peas
2 bay leaves

Directions:

Mix the flour with salt and pepper and place on a plate. Dredge the meat in flour mix and set aside. Set the Instant Pot on Sauté mode, add the oil and heat up. Add the meat, brown on all sides, and transfer to a bowl. Add the garlic, bourbon, stock, thyme, rutabaga, carrots, tomato paste, rosemary, and onions, stir, and cook for 2 minutes. Return the beef to the Instant Pot, cover, and cook on the Manual setting for 10 minutes. Release the pressure, uncover the Instant Pot, add the bay leaves, bacon, peas, more salt and pepper, stir, and cook on Meat/Stew for 12 minutes. Release the pressure again, uncover the Instant Pot, stir, discard the bay leaves, divide into bowls, and serve.

Nutritional Values Per serving

Calories: 302
Fat: 9
Fiber: 6
Carbs: 33
Protein: 18

205. Italian Sausage Stew

Preparation Time: 10 minutes
Cooking Time: 20 minutes
Serves: 6

Ingredients:

1 pound Italian sausage, crumbled
½ pound cherry tomatoes, cut into halves
1 sweet onion, peeled and chopped
1½ pounds Yukon gold potatoes, cubed
¾ pound collard greens, sliced thin
1 cup chicken stock
Salt and ground black pepper, to taste
Juice of ½ lemon

Directions:

Set the Instant Pot on Sauté mode, add the sausage, stir, and cook for 8 minutes. Add the onions and tomatoes, stir, and cook 4 minutes. Add the potatoes, stock, salt, pepper, and collard greens, stir, cover the Instant Pot and cook on the Meat/Stew setting for 10 minutes. Release the pressure, uncover the Instant Pot, add more salt and pepper and lemon juice, stir, divide into bowls, and serve.

Nutritional Values Per serving

Calories: 230
Fat: 10
Fiber: 1
Carbs: 24
Protein: 28

206. Beefand Barley Soup

Preparation Time: 1 hour

Serves: 8

Ingredients

2 pounds beef chuck cut into 1/2 inch cubes
4 teaspoons oliveoil divided
1 sweet onion diced
1 stalk celery diced
2 cloves garlic minced
2 cups carrots diced
15 ounce diced tomatoes
3 red potatoes cubed
2/3 cup pearl barley
6 cups beef broth or water and bouillon
1 teaspoon salt
1/8 teaspoon black pepper
2 sprigs fresh thyme
1 bayleaf
1 cup frozen green beans
Fresh parsley for garnish

Directions

1. Season beef with salt &pepper. Place 2 teaspoons oil in the bottom of Instant Pot and set to "Saute". Once hot, work in batches to brown the beef. Placeon a plate once browned.

2. Add remaining 2 teaspoonsoil to the Instant Pot and saute theonionsand celery until softened. Add the garlic and cook 30 more seconds. Add the beef back in along with thecarrots, tomatoes, potatoes, barley, broth, salt, pepper, thyme, and bay leaf. Stir together, place lid on and set valve to "seal". Cook on HIGH PRESSURE for 15 minutes with a 15 minutes natural release followed by a ⬜uick release. Remove lid when safe.

3. Stir in the frozen green beansand place the lid back on for 5 minutes no need to mess with thesetting. Remove bay leaf and thymesprigs. Serve garnished with parsley and a side of hearty bread.

Nutritional Values Per serving

Calories 390
Calories from Fat 135
Total Fat 15g

Saturated Fat 6g
Cholesterol 78mg
Protein 28g

207. Instant Pot Chicken Tortellini Soup

Preparation Time: 18 minutes
Serves4 servings

Ingredients

4 cups low sodium chicken broth
3 large carrots peeled and sliced
2 ribs celery sliced
1 teaspoon dried parsley
1 teaspoon salt
1/2 teaspoon dried thyme
1/4 teaspoon garlic powder
1/8 teaspoon black pepper
2 cupscooked chicken chopped
2 cupscheese tortellini 1 250g package

Directions

1. Add carrots, celery, broth, parsley, salt, thyme, garlicpowder, and pepper to the Instant Pot I use a 6 ⬜uart.

2. Set to high pressure, Manual mode, for 3 minutes. It will takeabout 10 minutes to come topressureand start counting down.

3. When cook time is over, release pressure gradually use a towel to keep the steam off your hands, but keepyour hand on the valve to slowly release the pressure. Becareful becausesoup can sputter.

4. Turn the Instant Pot tosaute and add thechicken and tortellini. Cook for 5 minutesor until tortellini reaches desired tenderness.

Nutrition Info:

Calories 381
Calories from Fat 135
Total Fat 15g
Saturated Fat 4g
Cholesterol 73mg
Sugars 4g
Protein 30g

208. Shortcut Instant Pot Chicken Chile Verde Soup

Preparation Time: 45 mins

Ingredients

3 chicken breasts roughly 1.5 lbs
1 can of black beans 540mL/ 19 oz cannellini drained and rinsed
1 can green chiles 127 mL/ 4.3 oz
1 can of corn kernels 340mL/ 11.5 oz , drained
1 onion diced
3 cloves garlic minced
2 cup salsa verde *
2 teaspoons ground cumin
1 teaspoon ground coriander
1 teaspoon salt
4 cups chicken stock

After cooking

3 tablespoons cornmeal
juiceof 1 lime

To serve

yogurt
cilantro
tortillachips
shredded cheese

Directions

1. In the base of a 6 ⬜uart Instant Pot, combine all ingredients.
2. Cook on high pressure for 10 minutes. Release pressure immediately 10 minutes natural pressure release is fine, too.
3. Remove thechicken breasts and shred with two forks.
4. Stir in the cornmeal and lime juice.
5. Serve with yogurt, cilantro, tortilla chipsand/or shredded cheese.
6. Toprepare freezer packs:
7. Combine all Ingredientsexcept for thestock, cornmeal and lime juice in a large gallon-sized freezer-bag.
8. Removeas much air as possible and freeze for up to 3 months.

9. Thaw completely beforecooking using the Directions above.

Nutrition Info:

Serving: 1/8 of batch
Calories: 249kcal
Carbohydrates: 30g
Protein: 28g

209. Instant Pot Taco Soup

Preparation Time: 50 minutes
Serves: 6

Ingredients:

2 Tablespoons oliveoil
2 pounds ground beef
1 medium onion, chopped
1 15.25 oz. can corn
1 16 oz. can pinto beans, drained and rinsed
1 10 oz. can Rotel diced tomatoesand green chilies
214.5 oz. cans diced tomatoes
1 packet dry ranch seasoning mix
2 packets tacoseasoning
2 1/2 cups beef broth

Directions:

1. Set the instant pot to "Saute" and add olive oil.
2. Once hot, add the ground beef and onions, cook until meat is browed.
3. Turn off instant pot and drain meat.
4. Put the meat back into the instant pot.
5. Add corn, beans, rotel, diced tomatoes, ranch seasoning and tacoseasoning.
6. Add beef broth and stir.
7. Place the lid on and set the valve to "Sealed".
8. Press the "Soup" button and set timer for 20 minutes.
9. Once the soup is done, turn valve to "Quick Release".
10. Servesoup with shredded cheese, avocado, sour cream and Fritos.

Nutritional Value Per Serving:

Calories: 348
Calories
Total Fat: 10.6g
Cholesterol: 90.4mg
Sodium: 349.1mg
Carbohydrates: 24.9g
Fiber: 4.5g
Sugar: 4.9g
Protein: 38.2g

210. Instant Pot Creamy Tomato Tortellini Soup

Prep+Cook Time: 35 minutes
Serves: 4

Ingredients

1 tablespoon olive oil
1 pound turkeysausage, removed from casing
*optional
1 medium yellow onion, chopped
3 cloves garlic, minced
1 tablespoon tomato paste
1/2 teaspoon red pepper flakes
1/2 teaspoon dried basil
salt and pepper to taste
28 ouncescrushed tomatoes
4 cups chicken or vegetable broth
4 ounces Cabot cream cheese, room temperature
4 cups fresh cheese tortellini **use gluten-free if necessary
1/2 cup light cream
4 ounces baby greens spinach, kale, chard, etc.
4 ounces Cabot Farmhouse Reserve Cheddar, grated
Freshly chopped basil for garnish

Directions

1. Turn the Instant Pot on to sauté mode. Once hot, add the oliveoil and turkeysausage if using breaking the sausage into small pieces as it cooks with a wooden spoon or spatula.
2. Once sausage is mostly browned, add onions or start with this step if not using sausage to thepot and continue cooking another 2-3 minutes until softened.
3. Add garlic, cook an additional 30 seconds – 1 minute until fragrant then add tomatopaste, red pepper flakes, dried basil, salt and pepper. Stir to combine and cook for 20-30 seconds.
4. Add thecrushed tomatoes and broth to thepot and give everything a few stirs until well combined.
5. Place the lid of the Instant Pot on and set valve tosealing position. Press manual pressure cook button and set to 15 minutes.
6. When Instant Pot signals the end of the cooking time by beeping, release pressure manually by carefully turning the valve to venting position.
7. Oncepressure is fully released, slowly remove lid and turn the Instant Pot back on to sauté mode.
8. Add the cream cheese to the pot and stir for a few minutes until dissolved in the soup.
9. Add the tortellini to the pot and cook according topackage Instructions for al dente, usually about 7 minutes for fresh tortellini.
10. Add the cream and baby greens, stir until incorporated and greens begin to wilt.
11. Turn the Instant Pot off and add the grated cheddar right before serving.
12. Garnish each bowl with freshlychopped basil.

Nutritional Value Per Serving:

Calories383.7
Total Fat7.8 g
Saturated Fat4.9 g
Protein15.3 g

211. Chunky Potato Cheese Soup

Preparation Time: 30 minutes, 6-8 servings

Ingredients

2 tablespoons butter

1/2 cup chopped onion
6 cups peeled and cubed potatoes
2 14 oz. cans chicken broth
1 teaspoon salt
1/2 teaspoon black pepper
1/8 tsp red pepper flakes
2 tablespoons dried parsley
2 tablespoons cornstarch
2 tablespoons water
3 oz. cream cheese, cut into cubes
1 cup shredded cheddar cheese
2 cups half and half can use fat free but soup will be thinner
1 cup frozen corn
6 slicescrisp-cooked bacon, crumbled

Directions

1. Select Sauteand add butter to the pressurecooker pot. When butter is melted, add theonion and cook, stirring occasionally until the onion is tender, about 5 minutes. Add 1 can chicken broth, salt, pepper, red pepper flakes, and parsley to theonions.

2. Put thesteamer basket in the pressure cooker pot. Add the diced potatoes. Lock lid in place, select High Pressure and 4 minutes cook time and start. When timer beeps, turn off pressure cooker, wait 5 minutes, then do a quick pressure release. Carefully removepotatoesand steamer basket from the pressure cooking pot.

3. In a small bowl, dissolve cornstarch in 2 tablespoons water. Select Simmer and add cornstarch mixture to thepot stirring constantly. Add cubed cream cheese and shredded cheese. Stir until cheese is melted. Add remaining can of chicken broth, half and half, corn, crumbled bacon, and cooked potatoes, and heat through but do not bring to a boil.

Nutritional Values Per serving

Calories 220
Calories from Fat 99
Total Fat 11g
Saturated fat 4g

Cholesterol 20mg
Sodium 1020mg

212. Instant Pot Tuscan Chicken Stew

Preparation Time: 55 mins
Serves: 6

Ingredients

6-8 boneless skinless chicken thighs
2 carrots sliced
2 celery ribs sliced
1 onion diced
2 tomatoes diced
2 cloves garlic minced
12 babypotatoes halved or left whole
1 3/4 cupchicken stock
2 tablespoons white wineoptional
1 teaspoon fennel seeds crushed with the side of a knife
1/2 teaspoon salt
1 sprig rosemary

After cooking

2 tablespoons balsamic vinegar
1 tablespoon cornstarch
1/4 cup water

Directions

1. Add all ingredients not labelled 'after cooking' to the base of a 6 ☐uart Instant Pot.

2. Set the valve to 'sealing', then cook on high pressure for 10 minutes.

3. When the Instant Pot beeps, allow it to sit for 10 minutes natural pressure release. After 10 minutes, release the remaining pressure in thepot.

4. Stir together the water and cornstarch, then add to the pot with the balsamic vinegar.

5. If stew doesn't thicken, set on 'sautee' for 5 or so minutes.

6. Serve with crusty bread.

7. Toprep ahead and freeze

8. Add all ingredients not labelled 'after cooking' to a gallon sized freezer bag.

9. Removeas much air aspossible, and freeze flat for up to 3 months.
10. To cook, thaw completely before cooking as directed above.

Nutritional Values Per serving

Serving: 1/6 of batch
Calories: 316kcal
Carbohydrates: 37g
Protein: 27g

213. Instant Pot Pasta E Fagioli

Preparation Time: 15 mins
Serves: 4

Ingredients

2 Tablespoonsolive oil avocado or grapeseed oil work as well
1 largeonion chopped
3/4 pound extra-lean ground turkey
2 garliccloves minced
1/2 teaspoon dried red pepper chili flakesoptional
1 rib celery chopped
1 large carrot chopped
3 cups tomato sauce canned or homemade
28 oz canned diced tomatoes, undrained preferably fire roasted or Italian style
1/2 cup homemade beef stock or good quality no-salt beef broth
1 Tablespoon dried Italian seasoning
1 bay leaf
1/4 teaspoon fennel seeds
1/2 cupcanned kidney beans drained and rinsed, or cooked from scratch
1/2 cupcanned Great Northern beans drained and rinsed, or cooked from scratch
2 medium zucchini chopped
1/4 cup uncooked Ditalini pastaor other small pasta, use gluten-free or other small pasta use gluten-freepasta if necessary or leaveout entirely seasalt and freshly cracked black pepper to taste
2 teaspoons balsamic vinegar to taste
water as needed to thin out soup to desired consistency
2 Tablespoons fresh parsleychopped

Directions

1. Press the SAUTE button on the Instant Pot. Allow topreheat or until it beeps. Add oil to the inner pot and saute the onions for 1-2 minutes until fragrant. Add the ground turkey, garlic and red pepper flakes. Cook and crumble until meat is brown and no longer pink. Drain any fat and return thepot back to the Instant Pot.
2. Add thecelery, carrots, diced tomatoes, tomato sauce, beef broth, Italian seasoning, bay leaf, fennel seeds, kidney beans, and zucchini.
3. Press Cancel then close the lid. Press the MANUAL older models or PRESSURE COOK newer models button and set for 4 minutes. Turn the valve to SEALING.
4. After the soupcooks for 3 minutesand the instant pot beeps, allow the pressure to release naturally for 2 minutes. Then turn the valve to VENT to release thepressure.
5. Once thepressure is released, open the lid stir in the uncooked pasta. Press the SAUTE button cook for another 5-6 minutes, or until the pasta is tender and cooked.
6. If soup is too thick for your liking, add more water as needed. Season with salt and black pepper to taste and discard bay leaf. Stir in balsamic vinegar if desired.
7. Serve warm with bread, sprinkled Parmesan cheese and garnish with parsley if desired.
8. Recipe Notes : about pasta – If you plan to freeze thisor serve the next day, leaveout the pasta and cook on the side and then combine when you are ready toenjoy. This helps the pasta not get soggy.

Nutrition Info:

Calories 185
Calories from Fat 45
Total Fat 5g
Cholesterol 23mg
Sodium 721mg
Protein 15g

214. Instant Pot Lebanese Chicken Soup

Prep+CookTime:: 40 minutes, **Servings:** 4

Ingredients

2 largecarrotsdiced
1 mediumoniondiced
3 stalksscelerydiced
15 ouncescookedchickpeasdrainedandrinsed
2 six-ounce chicken breasts boneless, skinless
1 teaspoon cinnamon
1 teaspoon garlic powder
1 teaspoon salt
1/2 teaspoon pepper
1/4 cup lemon juice
8 cupschicken broth low sodium
8 cups babyspinach

Directions

1. Place thecarrots, onions, celery and chick peas in the bottom of the liner pot. Top with chicken breasts then add cinnamon, garlicpowder, salt, pepper, lemon juiceand chicken broth.

2. Close the lid, makesure the vent is closed then press "SOUP".Once the timer goes off, release the pressure naturally using NPR. This may take up to 30 minutes.

3. Remove the lid then carefully shred the chicken breasts using two forks. Stir in the spinach beforeserving, stirring it for 1-2 minutes or until it's wilted. Check for seasoning and add moresalt, pepper or lemon juice to taste.

Notes : To reduce the total sodium, use dried chick peas, homemade or salt-free chicken broth and organicchicken. ,

Nutritional Values Per serving

Calories 236
Calories from Fat 33
Total Fat 3.7g
Saturated Fat 0.3g
Total Carbohydrates 28g
Dietary Fiber 8.6g
Sugars 7.1g

Protein 27.7g

215. Instant Pot Spicy White Bean and Chard Stew

Preparation Time: 45 minutes, Serving: 8-10 servings

Ingredients:

1 lb. dried Great Northern beans
1 tablespoon extra virgin olive oil
1 yellow onion, chopped
2 medium carrots, chopped
4 cloves garlic, chopped
1/4 teaspoon red pepper flakes add up to 1/2 teaspoon more to make spicier
28 ouncecan fire roasted diced tomatoes
4 cups vegetable stock or water
1 teaspoon dried rosemary
1 teaspoon dried oregano
1 bay leaf
1 teaspoon kosher salt
1 bunch swiss chard I used rainbow chard, tough stems discarded and chopped into ribbons
salt and freshly ground black pepper, to taste
freshly grated parmesan, for garnish optional

Instructions:

Prep the beans:

1. Rinseand sort the dried beans, discarding any beans that are discolored or cracked.Place in a largesouppot and fill with water until covered by 1-2 inches.Soak the beans using theovernight or quick soak methods described below.Do not add salt.

2. Overnight soak:Cover and place in the refrigerator overnight.

3. Quick soak:Cover and bring to a boil over high heat.Once boiling, remove from heat and let stand covered for 1 hour.

4. Once soaked, drain the beans in a colander and rinse with cold water.

Prepare thestew:

1. Press the Saute button on the Instant Pot and select 6 minutes, then add

theoliveoil.When the oil is hot, add the onion and carrot and saute for 5 minutes till softened.Add the garlic and saute for 30 seconds.

2. Stir in the red pepper flakes, diced tomatoes, stock or water, rosemary, oregano, bay leaf and salt.Add the beansand stir to combine.

3. Lock the lid in placeand select the Beans/Chili button or Pressure mode for 20 minutes.When the stew has finished cooking, release the pressure slowly or □uick release.If the beans need more time, select the Saute button and cook with the lid off for another 5 minutesor so.

4. Remove the lid and press the Saute button.Season with additional kosher salt and pepper to taste, and add theswisschard cooking just until wilted, about 3 minutes.

5. Serve with grated parmesan cheese if desired and enjoy!

Nutritional Value Per Serving:

Amount Per Serving:
Calories: 179
Total Fat: 2g
Sodium: 222mg
Carbohydrates: 39g
Fiber: 12g, Sugar: 3g
Protein: 15g

216. Instant Pot Chicken Tortilla Soup

Preparation Time: 45 mins
Serves: 4

Ingredients

2 teaspoons olive oil
1 cup chopped onion
4 cloves garlic minced
4 ouncecan mild fire roasted diced green chiles
14.5 ounce can fire roasted diced tomatoes
15 ounces red enchilada sauce
1-2 teaspoons chili powder
1 teaspoon cumin
15 ounce can black beans rinsed and drained
4 cups low sodium chicken broth

1 pound bonelessskinless chicken breast
15 ounce can corn drained or 1 cup frozen corn, optional
salt and pepper to taste

For serving: lime wedges, crumbled tortilla chips, sour cream or plain Greek yogurt, shredded cheese, and/or avocado

Directions

1. Add olive oil to Instant Pot insert and turn on saute function. Add the onion and cook, stirring, until softened. Turn off Instant Pot. Stir in the minced garlic.

2. Add the diced green chiles, fire roasted diced tomatoes, enchilada sauce, chili powder, cumin, black beans and chicken broth. Stir well. Nestle thechicken into the mixture.

3. Place the lid on and set it to theclosed position. Turn thesteam valve to thesealing position.

4. Set the Instant Pot to manual/pressurecook, high pressure, for 9 minutes. When thecook time is done, allow the pressure to release naturally for 10 minutes this means just leave the Instant Pot alone for 10 minutes. Then, carefully turn the steam valve to the venting position to release the remaining pressure. I usually do this with the handle of a long spoon.

5. When the float valve drops down, thepressure has been released and it issafe toopen your instant pot. Carefully remove the lid. Remove the chicken and shred. This can be done in a bowl with two forks or even in your stand mixer – see my how to shred chicken tips.

6. Return the shredded chicken back to the pot and stir in thecorn. Season to taste with salt and pepper and serve with toppingsas desired.

Nutrition Info:

Serving: 1.5cups
Calories: 247kcal
Carbohydrates: 25g
Protein: 25g

217. Bacon and Veggie Soup

Preparation Time: 35 minutes
Serves: 3

Ingredients

   3 cooked turkey bacon slices; chopped.
   1/2 tbsp. olive oil
   1/2 small yellow onion; chopped.
   1 garlic clove; minced
   1/2 head cauliflower; chopped roughly
   1/2 green bell pepper; seeded and chopped.
   Freshly ground black pepper to taste
   2 cups homemade chicken broth
   1 cup Cheddar cheese; shredded
   1/2 cup half-and-half cream
   2 dashes hot pepper sauce

Directions:

1. Add the oil with onion and garlic in the instant pot and *Sauté* for 3 minutes

2. Stir in the broth, salt, black pepper, cauliflower and bell pepper then secure the lid.

3. Select the *soup* function and cook for 15 minutes,

4. When it beeps; *Quick Release* the steam then remove the lid.

5. Stir in the remaining Ingredients and cook on the *Sauté* function for 5 minutes, Serve hot.

218. Veggie Soup

Preparation Time: 33 minutes
Serves: 3

Nutrition Values Nutritional Values Per serving

Calories:- 455
Carbohydrate:13.9g
Protein:- 44.3g
Fat:- 27.2g
Sugar:- 4.2g
Sodium:- 1.89g

Ingredients

   3 cups homemade vegetable broth
   1 tsp. olive oil
   1/2 small yellow onion; chopped.
   1/4 cup Parmesan cheese; grated
   1/2 tbsp. garlic; minced
   1/2 tsp. dried thyme; crushed
   1/2 pound fresh Baby Bella mushrooms; chopped.
   2 cups cauliflower; chopped

Directions:

1. Put the oil, garlic and onion in the instant pot and select the *Sauté* function. Cook for 3 minutes,

2. Add the mushrooms and sauté for 5 minutes,

3. Pour in the broth and add the cauliflower to the mixture, Secure the lid.

4. Press the *Manual* key and adjust settings to high pressure, Cook for 5 minutes,

5. When done, use *Natural Release* to vent the steam.

6. Remove the lid and blend the soup with an immerse blender.

7. Add Parmesan cheese and cook for 5 minutes on the *Sauté* function. Serve hot.

Nutrition Values Nutritional Values Per serving

Calories:- 293
Carbohydrate:18.1g
Protein:- 18.1g
Fat:- 21g
Sugar:- 3.3g
Sodium:- 0.89g

219. Lentil Spinach Soup

Preparation Time: 25 minutes
Serves: 2

Ingredients

   1/2 cup dry brown lentils; rinsed well in cold water
   1 tsp. olive oil
   1/2 small yellow onion; diced
   1 medium carrot; peeled and diced

1/2 medium stalk celery; diced
2 medium garlic cloves; minced
1 tsp. ground cumin
1/2 tsp. ground turmeric
1/2 tsp. dried thyme
Kosher salt to taste
2 cups low-sodium vegetable broth
4 oz. about 6 cups baby spinach
Freshly ground black pepper to taste

Directions:

1. Select the *Sauté* function on the instant pot. Pour in the oil and add the onions, celery and carrots, Cook for 5 minutes,

2. Add the thyme, cumin, garlic, pepper and salt and sauté for 1 minute,

3. Stir in the broth, along with lentils then secure the lid.

4. Press the *Manual* key and set 12 minutes cooking time on medium pressure,

5. When it beeps; *Quick Release* the steam then remove the lid. Add the spinach, salt and pepper to taste then serve.

Nutrition Values Nutritional Values Per serving

Calories:- 190
Carbohydrate:- 30.5g
Protein:- 10.8g
Fat:- 3.5g
Sugar:- 4.2g
Sodium:- 0.46g

220. Pepper Lamb Stew

Preparation Time: 45 minutes
Serves: 3

Ingredients

1 pound grass-fed lamb shoulder; trimmed and cubed into 2-inch size
1/2 tbsp. olive oil
1/2 small yellow onion; chopped.
1/2 celery stalk; chopped
1/2 tbsp. garlic; minced
1 cup fresh tomatoes; chopped finely
1 tbsp. sugar-free tomato paste

1 ½ tbsp. fresh lemon juice
1/2 tsp. dried oregano; crushed
1/2 tsp. dried basil; crushed
1/4 cup homemade chicken broth
1/2 large green bell pepper; seeded and cut into 8 slices
1/2 large red bell pepper; seeded and cut into 8 slices
1/4 cup fresh parsley; minced
Salt and freshly ground black pepper to taste

Directions:

1. Add the oil, onion and garlic to the instant pot and select *Sauté*. Cook for 2 minutes,

2. Now add all the remaining Ingredients and secure the lid.

3. Select the *Manual* function and cook for 15 minutes on high pressure,

4. When it beeps; use *Natural Release* for 10 minutes then vent any remaining steam by using *Quick Release*.

5. Remove the lid and switch the cooker back to the *Sauté* mode,

6. Add the bell peppers and cook for 8 minutes stirring constantly. Garnish with minced parsley and serve.

Nutrition Values Nutritional Values Per serving

Calories:- 252
Carbohydrate:5.3g
Protein:- 33.1g
Fat:- 10.4g
Sugar:- 3g
Sodium:- 0.14g

221. Carrot Soup

Preparation Time: 27 minutes
Serves: 2

Ingredients

1/2 pound carrots; peeled and chopped
1 tbsp. olive oil
1/2 small yellow onion; chopped.
1/2 garlic clove; minced

1/8 tsp. dried parsley; crushed
1/8 tsp. dried basil; crushed
1 7-oz can unsweetened coconut milk
1 ½ cups homemade chicken broth
1/2 tbsp. Sriracha
1 tbsp. fresh cilantro; chopped.
Salt and freshly ground black pepper to taste

Directions:

1. Select the *Sauté* function on your instant pot then add the oil, garlic and onion and cook for 3 minutes,

2. Add the salt, carrots and black pepper and cook for another 2 minutes,

3. Pour in the broth, Sriracha sauce and coconut milk then secure the lid.

4. Set the cooker to *Manual* function at high pressure for 6 minutes,

5. Use *Natural Release* for 10 minutes then carefully remove the lid.

6. Use an immerse blender to blend the soup into a smooth puree, Serve with fresh cilantro on top.

Nutrition Values Nutritional Values Per serving

Calories:- 376
Carbohydrate:- 20g
Protein:- 7.1g
Fat:- 31.7g
Sugar:- 10.2g
Sodium:- 0.69g

222. Mouthwatering Green Bean Soup

Preparation Time: 40 minutes
Serves: 3

Ingredients

1/2 lb. fresh green beans; trimmed and cut into 1-inch pieces
1/2 lb. lean ground beef
1/2 tbsp. garlic; minced
1/2 tbsp. olive oil
1/2 medium onion; chopped.
1 tsp. dried thyme; crushed

1/2 tsp. ground cumin
1 ½ cups fresh tomatoes; chopped finely
2 cups low-sodium beef broth
Freshly ground black pepper; to taste
1/8 cup Parmesan cheese; freshly grated

Directions:

1. Select the *Sauté* function on your instant pot. Pour in the oil, add the beef and cook for 5 minutes,

2. Add the thyme, cumin and garlic then cook for 3 minutes,

3. Now stir in the beans, tomatoes and broth and secure the lid.

4. Set the *Manual* function to low pressure and cook for 20 minutes,

5. *Quick Release* the steam and remove the lid.

6. Drizzle some black pepper and Parmesan cheese on top. Serve hot.

Nutrition Values Nutritional Values Per serving

Calories:- 226
Carbohydrate:- 11.5g
Protein:- 27.9g
Fat:- 7.7g
Sugar:- 4.2g
Sodium:- 0.37g

223. Special Turkey Soup

Preparation Time: 45 minute
Serves: 3

Ingredients

1/2-pound lean ground turkey
1/2 tbsp. olive oil
1/2 small yellow onion; chopped.
1 cup carrots; peeled and shredded
1/4 head cabbage; chopped.
2 cups homemade chicken broth
2 tsp. low-sodium soy sauce
1/2 tsp. ground ginger
Freshly ground black pepper to taste

Directions:

1. Place the oil and turkey in the instant pot and select the *Sauté* function to cook for 5 minutes,
2. Select *Cancel* then add the remaining ingredients, Cover and lock the lid.
3. Set the cooker to *Manual* and select high pressure for 25 minutes,
4. After it beeps sound; *Quick Release* the steam and then remove the lid. Serve hot.

Nutrition Values Nutritional Values Per serving

Calories:- 190
Carbohydrate:- 9.2g
Protein:- 19.5g
Fat:- 8.7g
Sugar:- 4.9g
Sodium:- 0.79g

224. Instant Chicken Soup

Preparation Time: 27 minutes
Serves: 3

Ingredients

1 pound chicken breasts
1/2 onion; diced
1/2 tbsp. olive oil
2 ½ garlic cloves; minced
1/4 cup organic chicken broth
1/2 tsp. dried parsley
1/8 tsp. black pepper
1/8 cup white wine
1/2 large lemon; juiced
2 tsp. arrowroot flour
1/2 tsp. sea salt

Directions:

1. Put the oil and onion in the instant pot and cook on the *Sauté* function until the onion turns golden brown.
2. Stir in all the remaining Ingredients then switch the cooker to the *poultry* function on its default settings,
3. When done; *Quick Release* the steam and remove the lid.

4. Check if the consistency is thick enough. If not, add dissolved arrowroot flour to the soup. Serve hot in a bowl.

Nutrition Values Nutritional Values Per serving

Calories:- 333
Carbohydrate:- 3.3g
Protein:- 44.7g
Fat:- 13.7g
Sugar:- 1.1g
Sodium:- 0.50g

225. Tomato Soup

Preparation Time: 19 minutes
Serves: 4

Ingredients

1 tbsp. tomato sauce
1/2 garlic clove; minced
1 tsp. dried basil; crushed
1 ¼ cups vegetable broth
1 small onion; chopped
1 ½ lbs. fresh tomatoes; chopped.
1 tsp. dried parsley; crushed
1 tbsp. sugar
1/2 tbsp. balsamic vinegar
Freshly ground black pepper; to taste
Cilantro and fresh cream Garnish

Directions:

1. Pour some oil into the inner pan of the instant pot and select the *Sauté* function.
2. Add the garlic and onions to the oil and cook for 3 minutes,
3. Hit *Cancel* then add the tomato sauce broth, herbs, tomatoes and black pepper.
4. Secure the lid and select the *Soup* function on your instant pot. Set the timer to cook for 10 minutes,
5. When you hear the beep; *Quick Release* the steam and remove the lid.

6. Stir in the vinegar and sugar. Garnish with fresh cream and cilantro then serve hot.

Nutrition Values Nutritional Values Per serving

Calories:- 56
Carbohydrate:- 12g
Protein:- 2.4g
Fat:- 0.4g
Sugar:- 8.4g
Sodium:- 55mg

226. Zuppa Toscana

Preparation Time: 20 minutes
Serves: 2

Ingredients

1 ½ large russet potatoes; unpeeled and sliced into ¼-inch slices,
3 cups 1 ½ quarts chicken broth
1 tbsp. olive oil
1/2 medium onion; diced
1/2-pound ground; mild Italian sausage
2 cloves garlic; minced
2 tbsp. water
1 cup fresh kale; chiffonade
1/2 cup heavy cream

Directions:

1. Add the oil and onion to the instant pot and cook on the *Sauté* function for 3 minutes,
2. Add the Italian sausage and cook until it turns brown.
3. Stir in the garlic and cook for 1 minute,
4. Add the water, broth and potato slices and seal the lid.
5. Cook on *Manual* setting for 5 minutes at high pressure,
6. After 10 minutes; use *Natural Release* and then *Quick Release* to vent all the steam. Remove the lid and stir in the kale and cream. Serve hot

Nutrition Values Nutritional Values Per serving

Calories:- 784
Carbohydrate:54.8g
Protein:- 34g
Fat:- 46.5g
Sugar:- 7.5g
Sodium:- 2.14g

Chapter 5 – Beef, lamb and pork

237. 3-Ingredient Pork Chops

Serves: 2
Preparation Time: 5 minutes
Cooking Time: 25 minutes

Ingredients

2 tablespoons lemon pepper
2 pork chops, bone in
¼ cup apple juice

Directions

1. Place all ingredients in the Instant Pot.
2. Close the lid and press the Meat/Stew button.
3. Adjust the cooking time to 25 minutes.
4. Do natural pressure release.

Nutritional Values Per serving:

Calories: 342
Carbohydrates:3.5 g
Protein: 40.3g
Fat: 17.4g
Fiber: 0.1g

238. Shortcut Pork Posole

Serves: 4
Preparation Time: 5 minutes
Cooking Time: 30 minutes

Ingredients

1-pound pork shoulder, cut into chunks
1 onion, chopped
4 cloves of garlic, minced
25 ounces posole
1 can chipotle chilies
1 teaspoon dried oregano
2 teaspoon ground cumin
¾ cup water
¼ cup cilantro, chopped

Directions

1. Place all ingredients in the Instant Pot.
2. Close the lid and press the Meat/Stew button.
3. Adjust the cooking time to 30 minutes.
4. Do natural pressure release.

Nutritional Values Per serving:

Calories:391
Carbohydrates: 8.3g
Protein: 72g
Fat: 3g
Fiber: 3.4g

239. Moo Shu Pork

Serves: 4
Preparation Time: 5 minutes
Cooking Time: 30 minutes

Ingredients

2 teaspoon sesame oil
1 onion, chopped
1 tablespoon minced garlic
1-pound pork chops, cut into strips
¼ cup beef broth
3 tablespoon soy sauce
1/3 cup hoisin sauce
1 bag of shredded cabbages
2 tablespoon cornstarch + 2 tablespoons water

Directions

1. Press the Sauté button on the Instant Pot.
2. Heat the oil and sauté the onion and garlic until fragrant.
3. Add in the pork strips and sauté for 5 minutes.
4. Pour in the broth, soy sauce, and hoisin sauce.

5. Close the lid and press the Meat/Stew button.

6. Adjust the cooking time to 25 minutes.

7. Do natural pressure release.

8. Once the lid is open, stir in the shredded cabbages and cornstarch slurry.

9. Allow simmering until the sauce thickens.

Nutritional Values Per serving:

Calories: 363
Carbohydrates:18.2 g
Protein: 31.5g
Fat: 17.6g
Fiber: 1.7g

240. Instant Pot Asian Pork Belly

Serves: 9
Preparation Time: 5 minutes
Cooking Time: 45 minutes

Ingredients

3 pounds pork belly
1 thumb-size ginger, sliced thinly
3 stalks of green onions, chopped
4 cloves of garlic, minced
4 star anise
4 cloves
½ cup brown sugar
½ cup soy sauce
½ cup soy paste
½ cup Shaoxing wine

Directions

1. Place all ingredients in the Instant Pot.

2. Close the lid and press the Meat/Stew button.

3. Adjust the cooking time to 45 minutes.

4. Do natural pressure release.

Nutritional Values Per serving:

Calories: 882
Carbohydrates: 16.9g
Protein: 16.5g
Fat: 82.7g

Fiber: 0.4g

241. Instant Pot Pork Stroganoff

Serves: 4
Preparation Time: 5 minutes
Cooking Time: 40 minutes

Ingredients

1-pound pork loin, cut into strips
3 carrots, chopped
2 stalks of celery, chopped
1 onion, chopped
1 tablespoon Dijon mustard
½ cup sour cream
2 cups chicken broth
1 package egg noodles, cooked

Directions

1. Place all ingredients except for the cooked egg noodles in the Instant Pot.

2. Close the lid and press the Meat/Stew button.

3. Adjust the cooking time to 40 minutes.

4. Do natural pressure release.

5. Serve on top of cooked egg noodles

Nutritional Values Per serving:

Calories:602
Carbohydrates: 16g
Protein: 85g
Fat: 19g
Fiber: 1g

242. Hungarian Pork Paprikash

Serves: 6
Preparation Time: 4 minutes
Cooking Time: 40 minutes

Ingredients

4 pounds pork loin
1 onion, chopped

1 cup mushrooms, sliced
¼ cup chicken stock
¼ cup red wine vinegar
6 ounces tomato paste
3 cloves of garlic, minced
5 tablespoons Hungarian sweet paprika, sliced
¼ cup basil leaves
¾ cup sour cream

Directions

1. Place all ingredients in the Instant Pot.
2. Close the lid and press the Meat/Stew button.
3. Adjust the cooking time to 40 minutes.
4. Do natural pressure release.

Nutritional Values Per serving:

Calories: 726
Carbohydrates: 13.1g
Protein: 81.6g
Fat: 37.5g
Fiber: 3.5g

243. Simple General Tso's Pork

Serves: 5
Preparation Time: 5 minutes
Cooking Time: 40 minutes

Ingredients

1 ½ tablespoons rice vinegar
2 tablespoons rice wine
3 tablespoons sugar
3 tablespoons soy sauce
1-pound pork tenderloin
1 cup chicken broth
1 dried chili pods, chopped
1 onion, chopped
1 tablespoon cornstarch + 2 tablespoons water

Directions

1. Place all ingredients in the Instant Pot.
2. Close the lid and press the Meat/Stew button.
3. Adjust the cooking time to 40 minutes.
4. Do natural pressure release.

Nutritional Values Per serving:

Calories: 271
Carbohydrates: 11.1g
Protein: 35.4g
Fat: 9.9g
Fiber: 1.2g

244. Peppercorn Pork Brisket

Serves: 12
Preparation Time: 5 minutes
Cooking Time: 40 minutes

Ingredients

4 pounds pork brisket
3 tablespoons peppercorn
3 cloves of garlic, minced
2 cups red wine
2 cups chicken broth
1 tablespoon butter
1 cup mushrooms, sliced
Salt and pepper

Directions

1. Place all ingredients in the Instant Pot.
2. Close the lid and press the Meat/Stew button.
3. Adjust the cooking time to 40 minutes.
4. Do natural pressure release.

Nutritional Values Per serving:

Calories: 505
Carbohydrates: 1.1g
Protein: 46.7g
Fat: 32.5g
Fiber:0.1g

245. Ginger Pork Shogayaki

Serves: 4
Preparation Time: 5 minutes
Cooking Time: 40 minutes

Ingredients

1 tablespoon peanut oil

1-pound pork shoulder
1 onion, chopped
1 clove of garlic, minced
Salt and pepper
1 thumb-size gingers, sliced
1 tablespoon soy sauce
½ teaspoon white miso paste
2 tablespoons cooking sake
2 tablespoons mirin
¼ cup water

Directions

1. Press the Sauté button on the Instant Pot.
2. Heat the oil and sear the pork shoulder on all sides.
3. Stir in the onion and garlic. Season with salt and pepper.
4. Add the rest of the ingredients.
5. Close the lid and press the Meat/Stew button.
6. Adjust the cooking time to 40 minutes.
7. Do natural pressure release.

Nutritional Values Per serving:

Calories: 373
Carbohydrates: 5.5g
Protein: 29.6g
Fat: 24.7g
Fiber: 0.8g

246. Chile Pork Stew

Serves: 16
Preparation Time: 5 minutes
Cooking Time: 40 minutes

Ingredients

4 pounds pork loin roast, cut into 6 pieces
3 cans diced green chilies
3 poblano peppers, chopped
1 onion, diced
2 tablespoons chili powder
1 tablespoon paprika
¾ cup water
Salt and pepper
Cilantro, chopped

Directions

1. Place all ingredients except for the cilantro in the Instant Pot.
2. Close the lid and press the Meat/Stew button.
3. Adjust the cooking time to 40 minutes.
4. Do natural pressure release.

Nutritional Values Per serving:

Calories: 229
Carbohydrates: 2.4g
Protein: 30.4g
Fat: 10.3g
Fiber: 0.8g

247. Chinese BBQ Pork Char Siu

Serves: 4
Preparation Time: 5 minutes
Cooking Time: 45 minutes

Ingredients

1-pound pork butt meat,
3 tablespoons honey
2 tablespoons soy sauce
1 cup water
1 tablespoon miso paste
3 tablespoons char siu sauce
½ teaspoon sesame oil
2 tablespoons Shaoxing wine
Salt and pepper

Directions

1. Place all ingredients except for the cilantro in the Instant Pot.
2. Close the lid and press the Meat/Stew button.
3. Adjust the cooking time to 45 minutes.
4. Do natural pressure release.

Nutritional Values Per serving:

Calories: 396
Carbohydrates: 18.9g
Protein: 29.4g
Fat: 22.6g

Fiber: 0.9g

248. Balsamic Spiced Apple Pork

Serves: 8
Preparation Time: 5 minutes
Cooking Time: 45 minutes

Ingredients

3 pounds pork tenderloins
3 granny smith apples, sliced
½ cup apple cider vinegar
1 tablespoon grapeseed oil
1 cinnamon stick
2 tablespoons butter
1 cup balsamic vinegar
2 tablespoon brown sugar
1 tablespoon orange zest
Salt and pepper

Directions

1. Place all ingredients except for the cilantro in the Instant Pot.
2. Close the lid and press the Meat/Stew button.
3. Adjust the cooking time to 45 minutes.
4. Do natural pressure release.

Nutritional Values Per serving:

Calories: 359
Carbohydrates: 16.4g
Protein: 45.9g
Fat: 10.7g
Fiber: 1.9g

249. Sweet Chili Sauce Braised Pork

Serves: 4
Preparation Time: 5 minutes
Cooking Time: 45 minutes

Ingredients

1 tablespoon vegetable oil
1 onion, chopped
1-pound pork shoulder, cut into large chunks
½ cup white sugar

½ cup water
3 tablespoons sweet chili sauce
3 cloves of garlic, minced
1 tablespoon sesame oil
1 tablespoon fish sauce
1 tablespoon hoisin sauce
1 teaspoon ground ginger

Directions

1. Press the Sauté button on the Instant Pot.
2. Stir in the vegetable oil and sauté the onion.
3. Add in the pork shoulder. Stir for 3 minutes until the pork has turned golden.
4. Pour in the rest of the ingredients.
5. Close the lid and press the Meat/Stew button.
6. Adjust the cooking time to 45 minutes.
7. Do natural pressure release.

Nutritional Values Per serving:

Calories:457
Carbohydrates: 11.4g
Protein: 30.7g
Fat: 31.8g
Fiber:2.1g

250. Bolognese Stuffed Squash

Preparation Time: 70minutes
Serve: 4

Ingredients:

1 pound Ground Beef
2 pounds Spaghetti Squash, pricked with a fork
1 Green Bell Pepper, chopped
1 Portobello Mushroom, sliced
3 Garlic Cloves, minced
1 Onion, chopped
28 ounces chopped canned Tomatoes
1 tsp dried Oregano
½ tsp dried Thyme
¼ tsp Cayenne Pepper
Salt and Pepper, to taste

Directions:

1. Preheat your oven to 400 degrees F.
2. Line a baking sheet with parchment paper and arrange the squash on it.
3. Place in the oven and bake for 40 minutes.
4. Scoop out the seeds from the squash and cut in half. Set aside to cool.
5. Meanwhile, coat a pan with cooking oil, and heat it over medium heat.
6. Add mushroom and onion and cook for 5 minutes.
7. Add garlic and cook for about 30 seconds, or until fragrant.
8. Add the beef and cook for a couple of minutes more, until browned.
9. Add the bell pepper, tomatoes, and all of the herbs and spices.
10. Let the mixture cook for 10 minutes.
11. Divide the mixture between the squash halves.
12. Place them back onto the lined sheet and return to the oven.
13. Cook for 10 minutes.
14. Divide between 4 plates.
15. Serve and enjoy!

Nutritional Value

Calories 260
Fats 7 g
Carbohydrates: 4 g
Protein 10 g

251.Garlicky Cumin Slow Cooked Chili

Preparation Time: 8 hours and 15 minutes
Serve: 4

Ingredients:

1 Red Onion, chopped
6 ounces Tomato Sauce
4 tbsp Chili Powder
3 Celery Ribs, chopped
1 Bay Leaf
2 ½ pounds ground Beef
2 tbsp Cumin

1 tsp Onion Powder
1 tsp dried Oregano
1 tsp Garlic Powder
15 ounces canned Tomatoes and Green Chillies, chopped
½ cup chopped pickled Jalapenos
2 tbsp Coconut Aminos
A pinch of Cayenne Pepper
4 tbsp minced Garlic
Salt and Pepper, to taste

Directions:

1. Coat a pan with some cooking spray.
2. Add half of the onions and cook for 3 minutes.
3. Add half of the garlic and cook for one more minute.
4. Stir in the beef, and cook until browned, about 56 minutes.
5. Season with some salt and pepper.
6. Transfer the mixture to your slow cooker.
7. Add the remaining ingredients.
8. Stir to combine well.
9. Close and cook on Low for 8 hours.
10. Serve and enjoy!

Nutritional Value

Calories 274
Fats 12 g
Carbohydrates: 5 g
Protein 34 g

252.Mexican Zucchini Boats

Preparation Time: 115 MIN
Serve: 4

Ingredients:

½ cup Ghee, melted
1 ounce Salt Pork
2 cups Chicken Stock
1 tsp Red Pepper Flakes
4 ounces cooked and chopped Ham
1 Yellow Onion, chopped
¼ cup Apple Cider Vinegar
2 pounds Collard Greens, cut into strips

4 ounces dry White Wine
1 tbsp Olive Oil
Salt and Pepper, to taste

Directions:

1. Heat the olive oil in a pan over medium heat.
2. Add the onions an cook for 4 minutes.
3. Add the salt pork and collard greens.
4. Pour the wine, stock, and vinegar over. Stir to combine.
5. Bring the mixture to a boil.
6. Reduce the heat.
7. Cook covered for about 1 hour and a half.
8. Stir in ghee and discard the salt pork.
9. Cook for 10 more minutes.
10. Serve and enjoy!

Nutritional Value

Calories 150
Fats 12 g
Carbohydrates: 4 g
Protein 8 g

253. Peanut Butter and Lemon Pepper Beef

Preparation Time: 20 MIN
Serve: 6

Ingredients:

1 cup Beef Stock
3 Green Onions, chopped
1 tbsp Coconut Aminos
4 tbsp Peanut Butter
1 Green Bell Pepper, chopped
1 ½ tsp Lemon Pepper
¼ tsp Garlic Powder
¼ tsp Onion Powder
1 pound Beef Steak, cut into strips
Salt and Pepper, to taste

Directions:

1. Whisk together the stock, peanut butter,

lemon pepper, and coconut aminos, in a bowl.
2. Coat a pan with cooking spray over medium heat.
3. Season the beef with salt, pepper, garlic powder, and onions powder.
4. Add to the pan and cook until browned, about 7 minutes in total.
5. Stir in bell pepper and cook for 3 more minutes.
6. Pour the peanut butter sauce over.
7. Cook for one minute before serving.
8. Top with green onions.
Enjoy!

Nutritional Value

Calories 224
Fats 15 g
Carbohydrates: 3 g
Protein 19 g

254. Smothered Beef Patties in Onion and Worcestershire

Preparation Time: 45 MIN
Serve: 6

Ingredients:

1 Egg
10 ounces canned Onion Soup
½ cup Breadcrumbs
3 tsp Worcestershire
¼ cup Water
1 tbsp Coconut flour
¼ cup Ketchup
½ tsp Mustard Powder
1 ½ pounds ground Beef
Salt and Pepper, to taste

Directions:

1. Place the beef, egg, breadcrumbs, 1/3 of the onion soup, and some salt and pepper, in a large bowl.
2. Mix to combine well.
3. Make 6 patties out of the mixture.

4. Coat a pan with cooking spray and heat it over medium heat.

5. Add the patties and cook until they are browned on all sides.

6. Whisk together the remaining ingredients, in a bowl.

7. Pour this mixture over the patties.

8. Cover the pan, lower the heat, and let them cook for 20 minutes or so.

9. Serve and enjoy!

Nutritional Value

Calories 332
Fats 18 g
Carbohydrates: 7 g
Protein 25 g

255. Spiced Mini Pies the Jamaican Way

Preparation Time: 45 MIN
Serve: 12

Ingredients:

1 tsp Jamaican Curry Powder
½ tsp Turmeric
1 tsp Garlic Powder
1 Onion, chopped
½ pound ground Pork
½ pound ground Beef
2 Habanero Peppers, chopped
3 Garlic Cloves, minced
¼ tsp Stevia
2 tbsp Ghee
½ cup Water
1 tsp dried Thyme
2 tsp ground Coriander
½ tsp Allspice
A pinch of Clove
2 tsp Cumin

Crust:

½ tsp Baking Powder
2 tbsp Water
4 tbsp Ghee, meted
½ cup Coconut Flour

1 ½ cups Flax Meal
6 ounces Cream Cheese
1 tsp Turmeric
A pinch of Salt
¼ tsp Stevia

Directions:

1. Place the habaneros, onions, water, and garlic, in your blender. Blend until smooth.

2. Coat a pan with cooking spray and cook the pork and beef until browned.

3. Stir in the blended mixture and cook for 2 minutes.

4. Stir in the remaining filling ingredients, and cook for additional 3 minutes.

5. Combine the cream cheese, ghee, and water, in one bowl.

6. Combine the dry crust ingredients in another bowl.

7. Gently combine these two mixtures. A ball of dough should be formed.

8. Divide this dough in 12. Make balls and roll them into circles.

9. Preheat your oven to 350 degrees F and line a baking sheet with parchment paper.

10. Arrange the circles on the sheet.

11. Place the filling on one half of the circle.

12. Fold the circles making a halfmoon shape, and seal with a fork.

13. Bake the mini pies for 25 minutes.

14. Serve and enjoy!

Nutritional Value

Calories 267
Fats 23 g
Carbohydrates: 3 g
Protein 12 g

256. Cauliflower and Beef Goulash

Preparation Time: 25 MIN
Serve: 5

Ingredients:

1 tbsp Tomato Paste
2 ounces chopped Bell Pepper
1 ½ pounds ground Beef
2 cups Cauliflower Florets
¼ tsp Garlic Powder
14 ounces Water
14 ounces canned Tomatoes, undrained
¼ cup chopped Onion
Salt and Pepper, to taste

Directions:

1. Coat a pan with cooking spray and cook the beef over medium heat, until browned.
2. Stir in bell pepper and onion, and cook for 4 more minutes.
3. Stir in tomatoes and cauliflower, and simmer for 5 minutes with the pan covered.
4. Stir in the remaining ingredients and season to taste.
5. Serve and enjoy!

Nutritional Value

Calories 275
Fats 7 g
Carbohydrates: 4 g
Protein 15 g

257.Eggplant and Beef in a Tomato and Mozzarella Sauce

Preparation Time: 4 hours and 30 minutes
Serve: 12

Ingredients:

1 tbsp Olive Oil
28 ounces canned and chopped Tomatoes
16 ounces Tomato Sauce
2 cups shredded Mozzarella Cheese
2 tsp Mustard
2 pounds ground Beef
2 cups cubed Eggplant
2 tbsp chopped Parsley
1 tsp dried Oregano
2 tsp Worcestershire Sauce
Salt and Pepper, to taste

Directions:

1. Place the eggplant cubes in a bowl and season with salt and pepper.
2. Let sit for about 30 minutes.
3. Squeeze out the excess liquid, and drizzle the olive oil over them. Transfer to your crock pot.
4. Place the beef, mustard, oregano, Worcestershire, tomatoes, and tomato sauce, in the crock pot.
5. Stir to combine well.
6. Sprinkle with parsley and top with mozzarella cheese.
7. Cover, and cook on Low for 4 hours.
8. Serve and enjoy!

Nutritional Value

Calories 200
Fats 12 g
Carbohydrates: 6 g
Protein 15 g

258.Minty Lamb Chops in a Cranberry Sauce

Preparation Time: 150 MIN
Serve: 4

Ingredients:

1 tsp Garlic Powder
2 cups Beef Stock
1 Shallot, chopped
1 cup Dry White Wine
1 Bay Leaf
8 Lamb Chops
Juice of ½ Lemon
2 tbsp chopped Mint
1 tbsp Olive Oil
Salt and Pepper, to taste

Sauce:

Juice of ½ Lemon
½ cup Swerve
2 cups Cranberries
1 tsp dried Mint
1 tsp grated Ginger

½ tsp chopped Rosemary
1 tsp Harissa Paste
1 cup Water

Directions:

1. Season the lamb chops with some salt and pepper, mint, and garlic powder.
2. Heat the olive oil in a pan over medium heat, add the chops and cook until browned on all sides. Transfer to a plate.
3. Spray some cooking spray into the same pan, and cook the shallots for 3 minutes.
4. Pour the wine over, stir in the bay leaf, and cook for 4 minutes.
5. Stir in the remaining ingredients and cook for 5 minutes.
6. Return the lamb to the pan and cook for 10 minutes.
7. Meanwhile, preheat the oven to 350 degrees F.
8. Cover the pan and place it in the oven.
9. Cook for 2 hours.
10. Meanwhile, Whisk together all of the sauce ingredients in a saucepan.
11. Cook for 15 minutes.
12. Serve the sauce over the lamb chops. Enjoy!

Nutritional Value

Calories 450
Fats 34 g
Carbohydrates: 6 g
Protein 26 g

259.Cheesy Pork Loin Pie

Preparation Time: 60 MIN
Serve: 6

Ingredients:

Crust:

1 cup Almond Flour
2 cups Cracklings
2 Eggs

¼ cup Flax Meal
A pinch of Salt

Filling:

4 Eggs
12 ounces chopped Pork Loin
1 cup grated Cheddar Cheese
6 Bacon Slices
1 Red Onion, chopped
2 Garlic Cloves, minced
¼ cup chopped Chives
½ cup Cream Cheese
2 tbsp Ghee
Salt and Pepper, to taste

Directions:

1. Preheat your oven to 350 degrees F. Grease a pie pan with cooking spray.
2. Place all of the crust ingredients in a food processor and process until smooth.
3. Press this mixture into the bottom of the prepared pie pan.
4. Bake for 15 minutes.
5. Meanwhile, melt the ghee in a pan over medium heat.
6. Add onion and cook for 4 minutes.
7. Stir in garlic and cook for one more minute.
8. Add bacon slices and cook until crispy, about 6 minutes. Transfer to a plate and drain on some paper towels.
9. Add the pork and cook until browned.
10. In a bowl, combine all of the remaining ingredients.
11. Stir the pork mixture into the cream cheese mixture.
12. Crumble the bacon inside. Stir to combine.
13. Spoon the filling onto the crust and spread out evenly.
14. Return to oven and bake for 25 minutes.
15. Serve and enjoy!

Nutritional Value

Calories 455
Fats 34 g
Carbohydrates: 3 g

Protein 33 g

260.Middle Eastern Lamb Cutlets with a Tangy Salad

Preparation Time: 25 MIN
Serve: 4

Ingredients:

1 tbsp Red Wine Vinegar
2 Garlic Cloves, minced
¼ cup Olive Oil
2 tsp Paprika
8 Lamb Cutlets
¼ cup chopped Parsley
1 tsp dried Oregano
2 tbsp Sumac
2 tsp Cumin
A bunch of Radishes, sliced thinly
2 cups Lettuce Salad, chopped
½ cup Black Olives, sliced
2 tbsp Water
Salt and Pepper, to taste

Directions:

1. In a small bowl, mix paprika, sumac, oregano, garlic, water, half of the oil, and some salt, and pepper.
2. Rub this mixture into the cutlets.
3. Preheat your grill to medium.
4. Grill the lamb cutlets for about 34 minutes per side.
5. In another bowl, combine the remaining oil with the harissa, cumin, vinegar, and parsley.
6. Place the lettuce, radishes, and olives, in a bowl.
7. Pour the dressing over.
8. Divide between 4 plates.
9. Divide the cutlets between the plates. Enjoy!

Nutritional Value

Calories 330
Fats 31 g
Carbohydrates: 4 g

Protein 37 g

261. Pork Tostadas

Preparation Time: 10 minutes
Cooking Time: 30 minutes
Serves: 4

Ingredients:

4 pounds pork shoulder, boneless and cubed
Salt and ground black pepper, to taste
2 cups cola
⅓ cup brown sugar
½ cup picante sauce
2 teaspoons chili powder
2 tablespoons tomato paste
¼ teaspoon cumin
1 cup enchilada sauce
Corn tortillas, for serving
Mexican cheese, shredded for serving
Shredded lettuce, for serving
Salsa, for serving
Guacamole, for serving

Directions:

In the Instant Pot, mix 1 cup of the cola with picante sauce, salsa, sugar, tomato paste, chili powder, and cumin and stir. Add the pork, stir, cover, and cook on Meat/Stew mode for 25 minutes. Release the pressure for 15 minutes, uncover the Instant Pot, drain juice from the Instant Pot, transfer the meat to a cutting board and shred it. Return the meat to Instant Pot, add the rest of the cola and enchilada sauce, stir, set the Instant Pot on Sauté mode and heat thoroughly. Brown tortillas in the oven at 350°F for 5 minutes and place them on a working surface. Add the lettuce leaves, cheese and guacamole, fold, and serve.

Nutritional Values Per serving

Calories: 160
Fat: 3
Fiber: 3
Carbs: 13
Protein: 9

262. Pork Carnitas

Preparation Time: 10 minutes
Cooking Time: 1 hour and 10 minutes
Serves: 8

Ingredients:

- 2 tablespoons extra virgin olive oil
- 3 pounds pork shoulder, chopped
- Salt and ground black pepper, to taste
- 1 jalapeño pepper, chopped
- 1 poblano pepper, seeded and chopped
- 1 green bell pepper, seeded and chopped
- 3 garlic cloves, peeled and minced
- 1 yellow onion, peeled and chopped
- 1 pound tomatillos, cut into quarters
- 1 teaspoon dried oregano
- 1 teaspoon cumin
- 2 cups chicken stock
- 2 bay leaves
- Flour tortillas, for serving
- 1 red onion, chopped, for serving
- Shredded cheddar cheese, for serving

Directions:

Set the Instant Pot on Sauté mode, add the oil and heat it up. Add the pork, salt, and pepper and brown them for 3 minutes. Add the bell pepper, jalapeño pepper, poblano pepper, tomatillos, onion, garlic, oregano, cumin, bay leaves, and stock. Stir, cover, and cook on the Meat/Stew setting for 55 minutes. Release the pressure naturally for 10 minutes, uncover and transfer meat to a cutting board. Puree the mix from the Instant Pot using an immersion blender. Shred the meat with a fork and mix with the puree. Divide the pork mixture onto flour tortillas, add the onion and cheese, and serve.

Nutritional Values Per serving

Calories: 355
Fat: 23
Fiber: 1
Carbs: 10
Protein: 23

263. Pork with Orange and Honey

Preparation Time: 10 minutes
Cooking Time: 1 hour
Serves: 4

Ingredients:

- 1½ pounds pork shoulder, chopped
- 3 garlic cloves, peeled and minced
- 1 cinnamon stick
- Juice from 1 orange
- Salt and ground black pepper, to taste
- 1 yellow onion, peeled and sliced
- 1 tablespoon ginger, sliced
- 2 cloves
- ½ cup water
- 1 teaspoon dried rosemary
- 1 tablespoon maple syrup
- 2 tablespoons soy sauce
- 1 tablespoon vegetable oil
- 1 tablespoon honey
- 1 tablespoon water
- 1½ tablespoons cornstarch

Directions:

Set the Instant Pot on Sauté mode, add the oil, and heat it up. Add the pork, salt and pepper, stir, brown for 5 minutes on each side, and transfer to a plate. Add the onions, ginger, salt, and pepper to the Instant Pot, stir, and cook for 1 minute. Add the garlic and cook for 30 seconds. Add the orange juice, water, soy sauce, honey, maple syrup, cinnamon, cloves, rosemary, and pork pieces. Cover the Instant Pot, cook on the Meat/Stew setting for 50 minutes and release the pressure naturally. Uncover the Instant Pot, discard the cinnamon and cloves, add the cornstarch mixed with water, stir, set the Instant Pot on Sauté mode, and cook until the sauce thickens. Divide the pork and sauce among plates, and serve.

Nutritional Values Per serving

Calories: 300
Fat: 7.4
Fiber: 1
Carbs: 33
Protein: 20

264. Pork with Hominy

Preparation Time: 10 minutes
Cooking Time: 30 minutes
Serves: 6

Ingredients:

1¼ pounds pork shoulder, boneless and cut into medium pieces
2 tablespoons vegetable oil
Salt and ground black pepper, to taste
2 tablespoons chili powder
1 white onion, peeled and chopped
4 garlic cloves, peeled and minced
30 ounces canned hominy, drained
4 cups chicken stock
Avocado slices, for serving
Lime wedges, for serving
¼ cup water
2 tablespoons cornstarch

Directions:

Set the Instant Pot on Sauté mode, add 1 tablespoon oil and heat it up. Add the pork, salt, and pepper, brown on all sides, and transfer to a bowl. Add the rest of the oil to the Instant Pot and heat it up. Add the garlic, onion, and chili powder, stir, and sauté for 4 minutes. Add half of the stock, stir, and cook for 1 minute. Add the rest of the stock and return pork to pot, stir, cover, and cook on the Manual setting for 30 minutes. Release the pressure naturally for 10 minutes, transfer the pork to a cutting board, and shred with 2 forks. Add the cornstarch mixed with water to the Instant Pot and set on Sauté mode. Add the hominy, more salt and pepper, and shredded pork, stir, and cook for 2 minutes. Divide among bowls, and serve with avocado slices on top and lime wedges on the side.

Nutritional Values Per serving

Calories: 250
Fat: 8.7
Fiber: 7.7
Carbs: 29
Protein: 12

265. Kalua Pork

Preparation Time: 10 minutes
Cooking Time: 90 minutes
Serves: 5

Ingredients:

4 pounds pork shoulder, cut into half
½ cup water
2 tablespoons vegetable oil
Salt and ground black pepper, to taste
1 tablespoon liquid smoke
Steamed green beans, for serving

Directions:

Set the Instant Pot on Sauté mode, add the oil, and heat it up. Add the pork, salt, and pepper, brown for 3 minutes on each side, and transfer to a plate. Add the water and liquid smoke to the Instant Pot and stir. Return the meat, stir, cover the Instant Pot and cook on the Meat/Stew setting for 90 minutes. Release the pressure for 15 minutes, transfer the meat to a cutting board and shred it with 2 forks. Divide the pork on plates, add some of the sauce on top, and serve with steamed green beans on the side.

Nutritional Values Per serving

Calories: 243
Fat: 15
Fiber: 1
Carbs: 1
Protein: 26

266. Meatloaf

Preparation Time: 10 minutes
Cooking Time: 40 minutes
Serves: 6

Ingredients:

⅓ cup milk
½ cup panko breadcrumbs
1 yellow onion, peeled and grated
Salt and ground black pepper, to taste
2 eggs, whisked

2 pounds ground meat beef, pork, veal
2 cups water
¼ cup ketchup

Directions:

In a bowl, mix the breadcrumbs with the milk, stir and set aside for 5 minutes. Add the onion, salt, pepper, and eggs and stir. Add the ground meat and stir well. Place this on a greased aluminum foil and shape a loaf. Add the ketchup on top. Put the water into the Instant Pot, arrange meatloaf in the steamer basket of the Instant Pot, cover, and cook on the Meat/Stew setting for 35 minutes. Release the pressure for 10 minutes, uncover, take the meatloaf out, let it cool briefly for 5 minutes, slices, and serve it.

Nutritional Values Per serving

Calories: 300
Fat: 18
Fiber: 1
Carbs: 10
Protein: 24

267. Beef Meatloaf

Preparation Time: 10 minutes
Cooking Time: 25 minutes
Serves: 8

Ingredients:

2 pounds ground beef
3 bread slices
½ cup milk
¾ cup Parmesan cheese, grated
Salt and ground black pepper, to taste
2 tablespoons dried parsley
2 cups water
8 bacon slices
3 eggs, whisked
½ cup barbecue sauce

Directions:

In a bowl, mix the bread slices with milk and set aside for 5 minutes. Add the meat, cheese, salt, pepper, eggs, and parsley and stir well.

Shape into a loaf, place on aluminum foil, arrange bacon slices on top, tuck them underneath, and spread half of the barbecue sauce all over. Put the water in the Instant Pot, place the meatloaf in the steamer basket of the Instant Pot, cover and cook on Meat/Stew mode for 20 minutes. Release the pressure, uncover the Instant Pot, transfer meatloaf to a pan and spread the rest of the sauce over it. Introduce under a preheated broiler for 5 minutes, transfer to a platter, and slice.

Nutritional Values Per serving

Calories: 227
Fat: 14.5
Fiber: 1
Carbs: 8.8
Protein: 15

268. Sausage and Red Beans

Preparation Time: 15 minutes
Cooking Time: 30 minutes
Serves: 8

Ingredients:

1 pound smoked sausage, sliced
1 pound red beans, dried, soaked overnight and drained
1 bay leaf
2 tablespoons Cajun seasoning
1 celery stalk, chopped
Salt and ground black pepper, to taste
½ green bell pepper, seeded and chopped
1 teaspoon dried parsley
5 cups water
¼ teaspoon cumin
1 garlic clove, peeled and chopped
1 small yellow onion, peeled and chopped

Directions:

In the Instant Pot, mix the beans with the sausage, bay leaf, Cajun seasoning, celery, salt, pepper, bell pepper, parsley, cumin, garlic, onion, and water, stir, cover, and cook on the Bean/Chili setting for 30 minutes. Release the pressure, uncover the Instant Pot, divide mix into bowls, and serve.

Nutritional Values Per serving

Calories: 248
Fat: 5
Fiber: 12.3
Carbs: 40
Protein: 15.4

269. Meatballs and Tomato Sauce

Preparation Time: 10 minutes
Cooking Time: 10 minutes
Serves: 6

Ingredients:

1 onion, peeled and chopped
⅓ cup Parmesan cheese, grated
½ cup bread crumbs
½ teaspoon dried oregano
Salt and ground black pepper, to taste
½ cup milk
1 pound ground meat
1 tablespoon extra virgin olive oil
1 egg, whisked
1 carrot, peeled and chopped
½ celery stalk, chopped
2¾ cups tomato puree
2 cups water

Directions:

In a bowl, mix the bread crumbs with cheese, half of the onion, oregano, salt, and pepper, and stir. Add the milk and meat and stir well. Add the egg and stir again. Set the Instant Pot on Sauté mode, add the oil, and heat it up. Add the onion, stir, and cook for 3 minutes. Add the celery and carrot, tomato puree, water, and salt and stir again. Shape the meatballs and add them to the Instant Pot, toss them to coat, cover, and cook on the Meat/Stew setting for 5 minutes. Release the pressure naturally for 10 minutes, and serve with your favorite spaghetti.

Nutritional Values Per serving

Calories: 150

Fat: 3
Fiber: 1
Carbs: 4
Protein: 8

270. Pork Sausages and Mashed Potatoes

Preparation Time: 15 minutes
Cooking Time: 15 minutes
Serves: 6

Ingredients:

For the potatoes:

4 potatoes, peeled and cut into cubes
Salt and ground black pepper, to taste
1 teaspoon dry mustard
1 tablespoon butter
4 ounces milk, warmed
6 ounces water
1 tablespoon cheddar cheese, grated

For the sausages:

6 pork sausages
2 tablespoons extra virgin olive oil
½ cup onion jam
3 ounces red wine
3 ounces water
Salt and ground black pepper, to taste
1 tablespoon cornstarch mixed with 1 tablespoon water

Directions:

Put potatoes into the Instant Pot, add 6 ounces water, salt and pepper, stir, cover, and cook on Steam mode for 5 minutes. Release the pressure, drain the potatoes and put them in a bowl. Add the milk, butter, mustard, and more salt and pepper, and mash well. Add the cheese, stir again and set the dish aside. Set the Instant Pot on Sauté mode, add the oil and heat it up. Add the sausages and brown them on all sides. Add the onion jam, wine, 3 ounces water, and salt and pepper. Cover the Instant Pot and cook on the Meat/Stew mode setting for 8 minutes. Release the pressure quickly and divide sausages among plates. Add the cornstarch mixture to the Instant Pot and stir well. Drizzle the sauce over sausages, and serve them with mashed potatoes.

Nutritional Values Per serving

Calories: 435
Fat: 23
Fiber: 5
Carbs: 44.2
Protein: 15

271. Meatball Delight

Preparation Time: 10 minutes
Cooking Time: 10 minutes
Serves: 8

Ingredients:

1½ pounds ground pork
2 tablespoons fresh parsley, chopped
1 egg
2 bread slices, soaked in water
2 garlic cloves, peeled and minced
Salt and ground black pepper, to taste
¾ cup beef stock
½ teaspoon ground nutmeg
¼ cup flour
1 teaspoon Worcestershire sauce
½ teaspoon paprika
2 tablespoons extra virgin olive oil
2 carrots, peeled and chopped
¾ cup fresh peas
2 potatoes, cubed
1 bay leaf
¼ cup white wine

Directions:

In a bowl, mix the ground meat with the bread, egg, salt, pepper, parsley, paprika, garlic, and nutmeg, and stir well. Add 1 tablespoon of stock and Worcestershire sauce and stir again. Shape meatballs and dust them with flour. Set the Instant Pot on Sauté mode, add the oil and heat it up. Add the meatballs and brown them on all sides. Add the carrots, peas, potatoes, bay leaf, stock and wine, cover the Instant Pot and

cook on the Meat/Stew setting for 6 minutes. Release the pressure, uncover the Instant Pot, discard the bay leaf, divide the meatballs into bowls, and serve.

Nutritional Values Per serving

Calories: 400
Fat: 13
Fiber: 7
Carbs: 24
Protein: 17

272. Pork Roast with Mushrooms in Beer Sauce

Preparation Time: 50 minutes
Serves: 8

Ingredients

3 pounds Pork Roast
8 ounces Mushrooms, sliced
12 ounces Root Beer
10 ounces Cream of Mushroom Soup
1 package Dry Onion Soup

Directions

In the pressure cooker, whisk together soup, dry onion soup mix, and root beer. Add the mushrooms and pork. Seal the lid, and set to MEAT/STEW for 40 minutes at High. Let sit for 5 minutes before doing a quick release.

Nutritional Values Per serving:

Calories 379
Carbs 10g
Fat 16g
Protein 47g

273. Lovely Rutabaga & Apple Pork Loins

Preparation Time: 40 minutes
Serves: 4

Ingredients

1 tbsp Olive Oil
1 pound Pork Loin, cut into cubes
2 Apples, peeled and chopped
2 Rutabaga, peeled and chopped
1 Onion, diced
1 Celery Stalk, diced
1 tbsp Parsley, chopped
½ cup Leeks, sliced
1 ½ cups Beef Broth
½ tsp Cumin
½ tsp Thyme

Directions

1. Heat half of the olive oil on SAUTÉ at High. Add the beef and cook until it browned on all sides. Remove to a plate. Add leeks, onions, celery, and drizzle with the remaining oil.

2. Stir to combine and cook for 3 minutes. Add the beef back to the cooker, pour the broth over, and stir in all of the herbs and spices. Seal the lid, and cook on PRESSURE COOK/MANUAL at High pressure for 10 minutes.

3. After the beep, do a quick pressure release. Stir in the rutabaga and apples. Seal the lid again and cook for 5 minutes on PRESSURE COOK/MANUAL at High. Do a quick pressure release, and serve right away.

Nutritional Values Per serving:

Calories 421
Carbs 2g
Fat 23g
Protein 44g

274. Homemade Apple-flavored Pork Ribs

Preparation Time: 40 minutes
Serves: 4

Ingredients

½ cup Apple Cider Vinegar
2 pounds Pork Ribs

3 ½ cups Apple Juice

Directions

1. Pour apple juice and apple cider vinegar into the pressure cooker and lower the trivet. Place the pork ribs on top of the trivet and seal the lid. Cook on BEANS/CHILI at High pressure for 30 minutes.

2. Once it goes off, let the valve drop on its own for a natural release, for about 10 minutes.

Nutritional Values Per serving:

Calories 432
Carbs 28g
Fat 3g
Protein 47g

275. Tasty Pork Butt with Mushrooms and Celery

Preparation Time: 354 minutes
Serves: 8

Ingredients

1 pound Pork Butt, sliced
2 cups Mushrooms, sliced
1 ½ cups Celery Stalk, chopped
½ cup White Wine
1 tsp Garlic, minced
½ cup Chicken Broth
½ tsp Salt
¼ tsp Black Pepper
Cooking spray, to grease

Directions

1. Grease with cooking spray and heat on SAUTÉ mode at High. Brown the pork slices and for a few minutes.

2. Stir in the remaining ingredients. Season with salt and pepper. Seal the lid and cook for 25 minutes on MEAT/STEW at High. When done, do a quick release.

Nutritional Values Per serving:

Calories 318
Carbs 2g
Fat 20g
Protein 29g

276. Easy Pork Chops with Brussel Sprouts

Preparation Time: 35 minutes
Serves: 4

Ingredients

4 Pork Chops
½ pound Brussel Sprouts
¼ cup Sparkling Wine
1 ½ cups Beef Stock
2 Shallots, chopped
1 tbsp Olive Oil
1 cup Celery Stalk, chopped
1 tbsp Coriander
¼ tsp Salt
¼ tsp Black Pepper

Directions

Heat olive oil on SAUTÉ. Add the pork chops and cook until browned on all sides. Stir in the remaining ingredients. Seal the lid and cook for 25 minutes on MEAT/STEW at High. Release the pressure quickly.

Nutritional Values Per serving:

Calories 406
Carbs 7g
Fat 22g
Protein 44g

277. Braised Red Cabbage and Bacon

Preparation Time: 20 minutes
Serves: 8

Ingredients

1 pound Red Cabbage, chopped
8 Bacon Slices, chopped
1 ½ cups Beef Broth
2 tbsp Butter

1 tsp Salt
½ tsp Black Pepper

Directions

Add bacon slices in your pressure cooker, and cook for 5 minutes, until crispy, on SAUTÉ. Stir in cabbage, salt, pepper, and butter. Seal the lid, hit STEAM for 10 minutes at High. Release the pressure naturally, for 10 minutes.

Nutritional Values Per serving:

Calories 149
Carbs 5g
Fat 12g
Protein 5g

278. Quick Pineapple Pork Loin

Preparation Time: 35 minutes
Serves: 6

Ingredients

2 pounds Pork Loin, cut into 6 equal pieces
16 ounces canned Pineapple
1 cup Vegetable Broth
1 tbsp Brown Sugar
3 tbsp Olive Oil
½ cup Tomato Paste
1 cup sliced Onions
½ tsp Ginger, grated
½ tsp Garlic Salt
½ tsp Pepper
¼ cup Tamari
¼ cup Rice Wine Vinegar
½ tbsp. Cornstarch
1 tbsp. Water

Directions

1. Heat the 2 tbsp oil on SAUTÉ at High. Cook the onions a few minutes, until translucent. Add the pork and stir in the rest of the ingredients, except for water and cornstarch.

2. Seal the lid and cook for 20 minutes on SOUP/BROTH mode at High. Release the pressure quickly.

3. In a bowl, mix cornstarch and water, with a

fork, until slurry. Stir in the cornstarch slurry in the pressure cooker, and cook for 2 more minutes, or until thickened, on SAUTÉ at High. Serve hot to enjoy!

Nutritional Values Per serving:

Calories 546
Carbs 42g
Fat 21g
Protein 41g

279. Happy Pork Cutlets with Baby Carrots

Preparation Time: 35 minutes
Serves: 4

Nutritional Values Per serving:

Calories 213
Carbs 13g
Fat 9g
Protein 22g

Ingredients

1 pound Pork Cutlets
1 pound Baby Carrots
1 Onion, sliced
1 tbsp Butter
1 cup Vegetable Broth
1 tsp Garlic Powder
Salt and Black Pepper, to taste

Directions

1. Season the pork with salt and pepper. Melt butter on SAUTÉ at High, and brown the pork on all sides. Stir in carrots and onions and cook for 2 more minutes, until soft. Pour in the broth, and add garlic powder.

2. Season to taste. Seal the lid and cook for 25 minutes on MEAT/STEW at High. Release the pressure quickly.

Nutritional Values Per serving:

Calories 546
Carbs 42g
Fat 21g

Protein 41g

280. Savory Ground Pork with Cabbage and Veggies

Preparation Time: 25 minutes
Serves: 6

Ingredients

1 ¼ pounds Ground Pork
1 cup Cabbage, shredded
½ cup chopped Celery
2 Red Onions, chopped
2 large Tomatoes, chopped
1 Carrot, shredded
2 cups Water
1 Red Bell Pepper, chopped
1 Green Bell Pepper, chopped
1 Yellow Bell Pepper, chopped
¼ tsp Cumin
1 tsp Red Pepper Flakes
Salt and Black Pepper, to taste
Cooking spray, to grease
Freshly chopped Coriander leaves, for garnish

Directions

Coat with cooking spray. Add the pork and cook them until browned on SAUTÉ at High. Stir in the remaining ingredients, and pour the water. Seal the lid and set to PRESSURE COOK/MANUAL for 15 minutes at High. Do a quick pressure release. Sprinkle with freshly chopped coriander, to serve.

Nutritional Values Per serving:

Calories 352
Carbs 13g
Fat 21g
Protein 27g

281. Ground Pork and Sauerkraut

Preparation Time: 35 minutes
Serves: 4

Ingredients

1 pound Ground Pork

4 cups Sauerkraut, shredded
1 cup Tomato Puree
1 cup Chicken Stock
1 Red Onion, chopped
2 Garlic Cloves, minced
2 Bay Leaves
Salt and Pepper, to taste

Directions

Add onions, garlic, and cook until soft and fragrant, on SAUTÉ at High. Add the pork and cook it until lightly browned. Stir in the remaining ingredients, and season with salt, and black pepper.
Seal the lid and cook for 25 minutes on MEAT/STEW mode at High. When done, press CANCEL and release the pressure quickly. Discard the bay leaves, serve and enjoy.

Nutritional Values Per serving:

Calories 415
Carbs 16g
Fat 9g
Protein 33g

282. Herby Pork Butt and Yams

Preparation Time: 20 minutes
Serves: 4

Ingredients

1 pound Pork Butt, cut into 4 equal pieces
1 pound Yams, diced
2 tsp Butter
¼ tsp Thyme
¼ tsp Oregano
1 ½ tsp Sage
1 ½ cups Beef Broth
Salt and Black Pepper, to taste

Directions

1. Season the pork with thyme, sage, oregano, salt, and pepper. Melt butter on SAUTÉ mode at High.
2. Add pork and cook until brown, for a few minutes. Add the yams and pour the broth.

Seal the lid and cook for 20 minutes on PRESSURE COOK/MANUAL at High. Do a quick release and serve hot.

Nutritional Values Per serving:

Calories 488
Carbs 41g
Fat 22g
Protein 31g

283. Instant Pot BBQ Pulled Pork

Preparation Time: 1 hour 45 mins,
Serving: 3

Ingredients:

2 tablespoons smoked paprika
1 tablespoon packed light brown sugar
2 teaspoons garlic powder
1 teaspoon freshly-ground black pepper
1 teaspoon ground mustard
1 teaspoon Kosher salt
3-4 pound bonelesspork roast*, cut into 2-inch cubes
1 tablespoon olive oil
2 cups of your favorite BBQ sauce homemade or store-bought, divided
1 cup chicken stock or water

Directions:

1. Whisk together thesmoked paprika, brown sugar, garlic powder, black pepper, mustard and salt in a large bowl until evenly combined.Add the pork, then gently toss with the spice blend until it is evenly coated.Cover and refrigerate for at least 30 minutes, or overnight.

2. When you're ready to cook the pork, press "Sauté" on the Instant Pot.Add the oil.Then once it is hot it will beshimmering, add a single layer of the pork pieces.Brown the pork on all sides, then transfer thepork to a clean plateand set aside.Repeat with the remaining pieces of pork.This may take you 2 or 3 batches.

3. Once all of the pork has been browned, turn the Instant Pot off.Then add the

browned pork, chicken stock, and 1 cupof the BBQ sauce to the Instant Pot, and give the mixture a quick toss tocombineeverything.Twist on the lid, turn the vent to "Sealing", then set thepressurecooker to "Manual" for 60 minutes.Once the time is up, let the vent naturally release.Don't do the quick release option.

4. Carefully open the lid.Transfer the pork to a separate clean plate with a slotted spoon, leaving the juices behind.Press the "Sauté" button once more, and let thesaucesimmer for 10 minutesor until it has thickened and reduced by more than half.Meanwhile, shred the pork with two forks.**

5. Once thesauce has reduced a bit, skim some of the fat off of the top with a spoon or use a fat separator toseparateand discard it.Then add theshredded pork back into thesauce, and give everything a good toss so that it can soak up those tasty juices.

6. Serve immediately, topped with an extraspoonful or two of the remaining BBQ sauce.

Nutritional Value Per Serving:

Calories 258 , Calories from Fat 54 , Total Fat 6g , Saturated Fat 1g , Cholesterol 90mg , Total Carbohydrates 13g

284. Instant Pot Italian Bean & Pork Stew

Preparation Time: 45 mins Serving: 4

Ingredients

2 tablespoons of olive oil
1 medium brown onion, finely diced
2 celerysticks, diced
1 large carrot, peeled and diced intocubes
2 teaspoonssalt
0.5 lb ground pork meat 250-280 g
3.5 oz / 100 g diced smoked bacon i.e. lardons or speck
3-4 fresh thymesprigsor about 1 teaspoon of dried thyme

1/2 red chili, diced or ½ teaspoon dried chili flakes
3 large cloves of garlic, diced
1 lb / 450-500g whitepotatoes, peeled and diced
3 medium potatoes
2 cupscooked mixed beans of choice cannellini, navy beansor borlotti beans etc, canned are fine
500 g / 2 +1/2 cups tinned chopped tomatoes or tinned cherry tomatoes tomatopassata/puree can also be used, we love Mutti brand of canned tomatoes
1 cup water
2 bay leaves optional
1/4 cupchopped fresh parsley
Juice of 1/2 lemon
*To **Serve**: grated Parmesan cheeseor other cheese of choice*

Directions

1. Prepare all the Ingredientsand turn on the Instant Pot. Press the Sauté function keyand let thepot to heat upslightly. Add the olive oil, onion, celeryand carrot with 1 teaspoon of salt and cook for 5 minutes, stirring a few times.

2. Add thepork and diced bacon and cook together with the vegetables for about for 2-3 minutes, stirring through and breaking the meat apart with a spatula. Then, add the rest of the ingredients, except for fresh parsley and lemon juice, and stir through. Press Cancel/Keep Warm to stop the Sauté function.

3. Placeand lock the lid, making sure the steam valve isset to Sealing. Press Manual function, HIGH pressureand adjust the time to 6 minutes. After 3 beeps, the Instant Pot will start to build up the pressure, which will take about 5-7 minutes, and the cooking will begin. Once the timer goes off, allow 10 minutes for natural pressure release; then, use a □uick pressure release method by carefully moving the valve to Venting.

4. To finish thestew, stir in the lemon juice and parsley and serve with grated cheeseon the side if you wish.

Nutrition Info:

Total Fat 12g
Saturated Fat 4.3g
Cholesterol 49mg
Sodium 462mg
Potassium 494mg
Total Carbohydrates 12g
Dietary Fiber 3.4g.

285. Instant Pot Italian Beef

Prep+Cook Time: 1 hour 50 minutes
Servings: 6

Ingredients

1 - 3 pounds 1176g USDA choice grade chuck roast/Canada AAA grade blade roast , 2 inches 5cm thick
1 cup 250ml unsalted chicken stock or high quality unsalted beef stock
1 190g onion , sliced
1 tablespoon 15ml regular soy sauce
1 tablespoon 15ml fish sauce
1 tablespoon 15ml Worcestershire sauce
1 tablespoon 15ml olive oil
1 teaspoon 3.5g onion powder
2 teaspoons 9g garlic powder
1 teaspoon 1g dried oregano
1 teaspoon 1.2g dried basil
1 teaspoon red pepper flakes Optional

For Garnish

120 grams giardiniera

Directions

1. Brown Chuck Roast Steak: Heat up Instant Pot using Sauté More function. Wait until it says HOT ~8 mins -you really want the Instant Pot to beas hot as it can be for the maillard reaction.

2. Pat dry the chuck roast steak and lightly season one side with salt + black pepper. Drizzle the inner pot with 1 tbspolive oil. Then, place the seasoned side of the chuck roast steak in Instant Pot. Lightly season theother side with moresalt + black pepper.

3. Pro Tip: brown each side for 10 minutes to develop some awesome deep flavors.

4. Note: If you prefer a "Dump-it-all-in"

Recipe, you can skip the browning and saute steps.

5. Saute Onion and Herbs: Set browned chuck roast steak aside. If you want to serve the Italian Beef Sandwich with sauteed green bell pepper, saute then set them aside.

6. Add in sliced onions, saute until softened ~3 - 4 mins. Add in 1 tsp 1g dried oregano, 1 tsp 1.2g dried basil. If you prefer slightlyspicy Italian Beef, add 1 tsp red pepper flakes. Saute for another minute.

7. Deglaze Instant Pot: Pour 1 cup unsalted stock in Instant Pot, then deglaze by scrubbing all the flavorful brown bits off the bottom of the pot with a wooden spoon.

8. Pressure Cook Chuck Roast: Add in 1 tsp 3.5g onion powder, 2 tsp 9g garlicpowder, 1 tbsp 15ml soysauce, 1 tbsp 15ml fish sauce, and 1 tbsp 15ml Worcestershire sauce. Give it a □uick mix.

9. Place browned chuck roast steak back in Instant Pot and partially submerge it into the li□uid as best as you can. Pressure Cook at High Pressure for 45 minutes + 25 minutes Natural Release.

10. Simmer Gravy& Shred Beef: Set asidechuck roast steak in a mixing bowl, then shred the meat with 2 forks. While you areshredding the meat, bring gravy back to a boil with the "Saute" function.

11. Pro Tip: Reducing the gravy will naturally thicken it. If you find the gravy to be toooily, you can use a Fat Separator to filter out the fat.

12. Adjust Seasoning & Serve Instant Pot Italian Beef: Place the beef back in theyummy beefy gravy. Taste and adjust seasoning accordingly. Serve Italian Beef on Italian rolls.

13. Optional: Garnish with giardiniera and sauteed green bell pepper.

Nutrition Info :

Calories197.0
Total Fat5.9 g
Saturated Fat1.9 g

Cholesterol87.1 mg
Protein32.4 g

286. Instant Pot French Dip

Preparation Time: 1 hour 50 minutes
Serves: 6

Ingredients

2 - 3 pounds 965g USDA choice gradechuck roast/Canada AAA grade blade roast , 2 - 2.5 inches thick
6 18g cloves garlic , minced
3 673g onions , sliced
1 cup 250ml unsalted chicken stock or high quality beef stock
1 tablespoon 15ml regular soy sauce
1 tablespoon 15ml fish sauce
1 tablespoon 15ml Worcestershiresauce
1 tablespoon 15ml olive oil
1 pinch dried rosemary
1 pinch thyme
2 bay leaves

To Serve

1 loaf french bread
2 - 3 slices Swiss cheese

Directions

1. Brown Chuck Roast Steak: Heat up Instant Pot using Sauté More function. Wait until it says HOT ~8 mins. Pat dry thechuck roast steak and lightlyseason oneside with salt + black pepper. Drizzle the inner pot with 1 tbsp olive oil. Then, place the seasoned side of chuck roast in Instant Pot. Lightly season theother side with more salt + black pepper.

2. *Pro Tip: Brown each side for 10 minutes to developsomeawesome deep flavors.

3. *Note: If you prefer a "Dump-it-all-in" Recipe, you can skip the browning and saute steps.

4. Saute Onion & Garlic: Set browned chuck roast aside. Add in sliced onions, then saute until softened ~3 - 4 mins. Set aside roughly ? of thesoftened onions for later.

Add in minced garlic, a pinch of dried rosemary, a pinch of thyme, and 2 bay leaves. Saute for another minute.

5. *Pro Tip: Your Instant Pot will stop sauteeing after 30 minutes, turn it back on by pressing "Saute" button. ??

6. Deglaze Instant Pot: Pour 1 cup unsalted stock in Instant Pot, then deglaze byscrubbing all the flavorful brown bits off the bottom of thepot with a wooden spoon.

7. Pressure Cook Chuck Roast: Add in 1 tbsp 15ml soy sauce, 1 tbsp 15ml fish sauce, and 1 tbsp 15ml Worcestershiresauce. Give it a ⬜uick mix. Place browned chuck roast back in Instant Pot and partiallysubmerge it into the li⬜uid as best asyou can. Pressure Cook at High Pressure for 45 minutes + 25 minutes Natural Release.

8. Simmer Au Jus Sauce& Shred Beef: Set aside chuck roast in a mixing bowl, and shred the beef with 2 forks. Whileyou areshredding the beef, bring Au Jussauce back to a boil with the "Saute" function. Add in reserved onions, then let the Au Jussauce reduce for 5 - 10 minutes. Taste&adjust seasoning accordingly.

9. *Pro Tip: Reducing the Au Jus sauce will naturally thicken it. If you find the Au Jus sauce to be toooily, you can use a Fat Separator to filter out the fat.

10. Assemble & Serve Instant Pot French Dip: Optional Step - While the Au Jussauce is reducing, preheat oven to 350°F. Layer 1 loaf of french bread with slices of Swiss cheeseon top. Place it in the oven until thecheese begins to melt.

11. Layer shredded beef and onions on topof thesandwich. Serve Instant Pot French Dip with savory umami Au Jussauceon theside. Enjoy~

Nutritional Values Per serving

Calories: 369kcal
Carbohydrates: 12g
Protein: 33g
Fat: 21g
Saturated Fat: 8g

287. Easy Low-Carb Instant Pot Meatballs

An easy low-carb Instant Pot meatball and tomato sauce recipe. An easy meal for busy night with no searing re□uired.

Prep+Cook Time 23 minutes
Servings: 4

Ingredients

Tomato Sauce

- 800 g tinned/canned chopped tomatopuree
- 1 tsp onion powder
- 1 tsp garlic salt
- 1/2 tbsp Italian Seasoning
- 1/2 tsp red pepper flakes optional
- 1/2 tsp black pepper
- 2 bay leaves

Meatballs

- 700 g lean ground/mince beef
- 6 slices bacon
- 1 egg
- 1/2 onion small
- 2 tsp minced garlic
- 1/2 tsp salt
- 1/2 tsp pepper
- 1/2 tbsp parsley
- 1 tsp coconut aminos

Toasted Garlic Ricotta Topping

- 100 g ricottacheese
- 25 g mozzarellacheese
- 4 tsp minced garlic
- 2 tbsp oliveoil

Directions

Tomato Sauce

1. Beforestarting, oil the whole inside of the Instant Pot liner with oliveoil. This will prevent thesauce and meatballs from sticking.
2. Add all theIngredients for thesauce into the Instant Pot. Stir the sauce so that theseasonings are mixed into thesauce.
3. Turn the Instant Pot to sauté. While the sauce is heating upyou will want to make the meatballs.

Meatballs

1. Combine all theIngredients for the meatballs in a food processor. The food processor will finely chop the bacon and onions and help the meatballs hold their shape.
2. Next, roll the meatballs. You will want to roll a palm-sized amount of meat in your hands to form the meatballs. You want your meatballs to be about the size of a golf ball.
3. Once the meatballs are formed, arrange them in the tomato sauce in the Instant Pot. It is ok if the meatballs touch. Since the sauce is hot the meatballs won't stick together when cooked.
4. Pour 120ml1/2 cup water over thesauce, do NOT stir the water into the sauce. This will help the Instant Pot come to pressure.
5. Close the lid and turn. Turn thepressure release valve to "sealing".
6. Cook the meatballsand sauce on high pressure using the "manual" or "pressurecook" button for 8 minutes. Let the pressure release naturally.

Toasted Garlic Ricotta Topping

1. While thepressure is releasing you will want to heat your ricotta topping. Mix all the topping ingredients together in an oven safe dish.
2. Bake the topping at 400 degrees F/200 degrees C for 10-15 minutes. Remove from the oven.
3. When thepressure valve dropson the Instant Pot lid remove the lid. Give the meatballs a good stir.
4. Serve the meatballs immediately with a big dollopof ricotta topping. The meatballs are

also great served with zucchini noodles!

Nutritional Values Per serving

Calories 699
Calories from Fat 468
Total Fat 52g
Total Carbohydrates 12g
Dietary Fiber 2g
Sugars 5g
Protein 44g

288. Instant Pot HK Garlic Beef Rice Bowl Pot in Pot

Prep+Cook Time: 1 hr 20 mins
Serving: 2 - 4

Ingredients

1¼ pound 567g chuck roast steak, 1.5 inch in thickness
1 whole garlic, about 12 cloves 30g, minced
1 150g small onion, diced
1 tablespoon 15ml peanut oil
2 tablespoons 28g unsalted butter
200 grams frozen mixed vegetables
Kosher salt and ground black pepper to taste

Chicken Stock Mixture

¾ cup 188ml unsalted chicken stock
1 teaspoon 5ml Worcestershiresauce
1 tablespoon 15ml light soysauce not low sodium soysauce

Thickener

2 tablespoons 18g cornstarch
2 tablespoons 30ml cold water

Pot in Pot Rice

230 grams ~1 cup Jasmine rice
250 ml 1 cupcold running tap water

Directions

1. Prepare Pressure Cooker: Heat up your pressurecooker over medium high heat Instant Pot: press Sauté button and click the adjust button to go to Sauté More function. Make sure your pot is as hot as it can be Instant Pot: wait until the indicator says HOT.

2. Prep Ingredients: While thepressurecooker is heating up, you can prepare the ingredients. You should have about 24 mins including the time to brown thechuck steak.

3. Brown Chuck Steak: Season one side of the chuck steak generously with kosher salt and freshly ground black pepper. Add 1 tbsp 15ml peanut oil in pressurecooker. Ensure to coat the oil over whole bottom of the pot. Carefullyplace the seasoned side of chuck steak in pressurecooker. Generouslyseason the other side with kosher salt and freshly ground black pepper. Brown for 6 minson each side without flipping. Remove and set aside in a large mixing bowl.

4. Make Chicken Stock Mixture: While the chuck steak is browning in pressurecooker, mix 1 tsp 5ml Worcestershire sauceand 1 tbsp 15ml light soysauce with ¾ cup 188ml unsalted chicken stock.

5. Sauté Onion & Garlic: Change heat to medium. Instant Pot: press Cancel button, then Sauté button, and click the Adjust button until it reaches Saute Normal Setting Add diced onion 150g to the pressure cooker. Sauté for 1 minute. Add in 2 tbsp 28g unsalted butter and let the butter melt. Add minced garlic cloves and stir for roughly 90 seconds until fragrant. Do not let the garlic burn. Season with kosher salt and freshly ground black pepper if desired.

6. Deglaze: Pour in ½ cup 125ml chicken stock mixture and completely deglaze the bottom of the pot by scrubbing the flavorful brown bits with wooden spoon. Pour in the remaining ¼ cup 63ml chicken stock mixture.

7. Cut Chuck Steak: After deglazing, cut thechuck steak into 1.5 – 2 inches stew cubes. Place all chuck stew meat and the flavorful meat juice into thepressure cooker.

8. Pressure Cook Beef & Rice: Layer a

stainless steel bowl filled with 1 cup 230g of Jasmine riceon topof a steamer rack. Add 1 cup 250ml cold water in the rice bowl. Make sure all the rice iscovered with water. Close lid and pressurecook at High Pressure for 32 minutes + 10 minutes Natural Release. Turn off the heat. Release the remaining pressure. Open the lid carefully. Fluff & set asidecooked rice.

9. Thicken Sauceand Add Mixed Vegetables: Add frozen mixed vegetables in the Instant Pot. They will warm up in 30 seconds. Presscancel and sauté button to heat up the sauce. In a small mixing bowl, mix cornstarch with water and mix it into the HK Garlic Sauce one third at a time until desired thickness. Tasteand adjust theseasoning with kosher salt if necessary.

10. Serve: Place the beef & mixed vegetables over Jasmine rice and drizzle the HK Garlic Sauce. Serve immediately

Nutritional Values Per serving

Serving: 2 - 4

289. Instant Pot Barbacoa Beef

Preparation Time: 1 hour 45 mins, 8-10 servings

Ingredients:

2/3 cup beer or water
4 cloves garlic
2 chipotles in adobo sauceor more, to taste
1 small white onion, peeled and roughly chopped
1 4-ounce can chopped green chiles
1/4 cup fresh lime juice
2 tablespoonsapple cider vinegar
1 tablespoon ground cumin
1 tablespoon dried Mexican oreganoor regular oregano
2 teaspoonssalt
1 teaspoon black pepper
1/4 tsp ground cloves
1 tablespoon olive oil
3 pounds beef chuck roast* fat trimmed, cut into 2-inch chunks
3 bay leaves

Instructions:

1. Combine beer, garlic, chipotles, onion, green chiles, lime juice, vinegar, cumin, oregano, salt, pepper and cloves in a blender or food processor.Purée for 30 seconds, or until completely smooth.Set aside.

2. Press the "Sauté" setting on the Instant Pot.Add oil.Then once it is heated and shimmering, add the roast and sear — turning every 45-60 seconds or so — until the roast is browned on all sides.Press "Cancel" to turn off the heat.

3. Add the bay leavesand pureed sauce, and briefly tosseverything until the roast is evenly coated in the sauce.Close lid securely and set vent to "Sealing".

4. Press "Manual", then press "Pressure" until the light on "High Pressure" lights up, then adjust the +/- buttons until time reads 60 minutes.Cook.Then very carefully, turn the vent to "Venting" for quick release, and wait until all of the steam has released and the valve has dropped.

5. Remove the lid, and discard the bay leaves.

6. Using two forks, shred the beef into bite-sized pieces.Give the beef one more good toss in all of those juices so that it can soak them up.

7. Serve warm, or refrigerate in a sealed container for up to 3 days, or freeze for up to 3 months.

Nutrition Info:

Calories: 153 calories
Total Fat: 4.5g
Saturated Fat: g
Cholesterol: 44mg
Carbohydrates: 2g
Protein: 24g

290. Instant Pot Mongolian Beef

Prep+CookTime:30 mins, 5 servings

Ingredients

1-1.5 poundsflanksteak , slicedacrossthegrain
1 tablespooncornstarch
1 tablespoonsextravirginoliveoil
1/2 cupbrownsugaror 2/3
cupsIprefertheversionwithmoresugar
10 clovesgarlic , minced
1 tablespoonfreshginger , minced
1/2 cuplitesoysauce
1 cupwater
1 tablespoonricewine
1 teaspoonredpepperflakes
Cornstarch Slurry:
2 tablespoons cornstarch
1/2 cup water

Garnish:

1/4 cup green onions , chopped
1 teaspoon sesame seeds

Directions

1. Heat up your pressure cooker: press Sauté -> click on the Adjust button ->select More to get the Sauté More function, which means that the food will besautéed over medium-high heat. Wait for the Instant Pot indicator to read HOT.

2. Add sliced beef to a large ziplock bag, add 1 tablespoon cornstarch and shake well tocoat the beef evenly.

3. Add theoil to the hot Instant Pot, once the oil is hot, add the beef and sauté for 2-3 minutes, stirring a few times. If needed brown the beef in batches, you don't want to add to much as it will start releasing juiceand it won't brown well.

4. Note: You can also skip browning the beef and just add it to thepot!

5. If bits of beef stuck to the pot, add 1/2 cup water and deglaze thepot. Using a wooden spoon scrape the bottom of thepot. You can discard that li□uid if wanted.

6. Add the rest of theIngredients to thepot: minced garlic, minced ginger, lite soy sauce, brown sugar, water, rice wineand red pepper flakes. You can add lesssugar, based on your tasteand preference.

7. Stir well until all theIngredientsarecombined and coated in

sauce.

8. Close lid and pressurecook at High Pressure for 8 minutes + 10 minutesNatural Release. Turn off the heat. Release the remaining pressure after the 10 mins NPR. Open the lid.

9. Make the cornstarch slurry, in a small bowl mix cornstarch with water until fully combined. With the Instant Pot on the Sauté function, add the slurry to thepot, stir to combine and cook for 2-3 minutes on Sauté, stirring occasionally, until the sauce thickens. Turn off the Instant Pot and let the Mongolian Beef sit for 8-10 minutes beforeserving, in this time thesauce will settle and thicken more.

10. Serveover rice and garnish with fresh chopped green onions and sesame seeds.

Nutritional Values Per serving

Calories: 292
Fat: 9g
Saturated Fat: 2g
Cholesterol: 54mg
Sodium: 1362mg
Potassium: 409mg
Carbohydrates: 28g
Sugar: 21g
Protein: 22g

291. Instant Pot Pot Roast

Prep+Cook Time: 1 hour 30 minutes
Serves10

Ingredients

1/2 tablespoon oil
1 3 lb chuck roast
1 teaspoon kosher salt
1 teaspoon black pepper
1 teaspoon onion powder
1 tablespoon minced garlic
1/4 cup prepared horseradish
4 cups beef stock
3 pounds potatoes □uartered
1 pound carrots peeled and cut into 2 inch

chunks

Directions

1. Cooking a Fresh Pot Roast Thawed
2. Season roast with salt and pepper liberally.
3. Turn thepressurecooker to saute. Once hot, ad in theoil. Sear meat on all sides, 3-4 minutesper side. Remove meat from inner pot.
4. Pour in beef broth and scrape upany browned bits on bottom of instant pot.
5. Add roast back intopressurecooker, along with the onion powder, garlicand horseradish.
6. Cook on high pressure for 20 minutesper pound.
7. When the cook time has elapsed, allow for pressure to release for 10-20 minutes.
8. For Frozen Pot Roast
9. Place roast, beef broth, salt, pepper, onion powder, garlic and horseradish in inner pot of pressure cooker.
10. Cook on high pressure for 30 minutes per pound.
11. When cook time has elapsed, allow for pressure to release for 10-20 minutes.
12. Pot Roast with Carrots and Potatoes
13. Sear the meat as directed if using a fresh roast.
14. Add remaining ingredients into pressure cooker and cook for 20 minutes LESS than Directions state Cook for 40 minuteson high pressure for FRESH 3 pound Pot Roast or 70 minutes on high pressure for FROZEN 3 pound roast
15. Allow pressure to release naturally for 10 minutes.
16. Open instant pot and add in carrotsand potatoes, seal pressure cooker and cook on high pressure for 20 minutes.
17. Allow pressurecooker to naturally release pressure for 10-20 minutes before releasing any remaining pressure. Serve the pot roast.

Nutrition Info:

Calories 366
Calories from Fat 144
Total Fat 16g
Potassium 1351mg
Total Carbohydrates 23g
Dietary Fiber 4g

292. Picante Lamb Chops

Preparation Time: 60 minutes
Serves: 6

Ingredients

6 lamb chops; bone-in
1 ¼ apples; peeled and pieced
3 tbsp. all-purpose flour
3 tbsp. brown sugar; packed
1 ¼ cup Picante sauce
3 tbsp. olive oil

Directions:

1. Dredge the mutton chops through a bowl of flour.
2. Mix the apple slices, picante sauce and brown sugar in a bowl.
3. Pour the oil into the instant pot and select *Sauté*.
4. Add the flour covered chops to the oil and sear for 5 minutes,
5. Secure the lid and select the *meat stew* function. Cook for 35 minutes at high pressure,
6. Natural release the steam for 10 minutes then remove the lid. Serve warm.

Nutrition Values Nutritional Values Per serving

Calories:- 449
Carbohydrate:- 16.3g
Protein:- 20.1g
Fat:- 33.3g
Sugar:- 10.7g
Sodium:- 0.31g

293. Greek Lamb Recipe

Preparation Time: 70 minutes
Serves: 2

Ingredients

1 pound lamb meat; ground
4 garlic cloves
1 tsp. rosemary
1/2 small onion; chopped.
1 tsp. dried oregano
1 tsp. ground marjoram
3/4 cup water
3/4 tsp. salt
1/4 tsp. black pepper

Directions:

1. Chop the garlic, onions, rosemary and marjoram in a food processor.
2. Add the ground beef and the salt and pepper to the mixture and combine well.
3. Compress the beef mixture to make a compact loaf.
4. Cover it tightly with tin foil and make some holes in it.
5. Pour water into the instant pot and place the trivet inside,
6. Place the loaf pan over the trivet and secure the lid.
7. Cook on *Manual* at high pressure for 15 minutes,
8. *Quick Release* the steam then remove the lid. Serve warm.

Nutrition Values Nutritional Values Per serving

Calories:- 664
Carbohydrate:- 4.8g
Protein:- 56.9g
Fat:- 44.8g
Sugar:- 0.8g
Sodium:- 1.06g

294. Famous Beef Pot Roast

Preparation Time: 2 hours 25 minutes
Serves: 6

Ingredients

2 ½ lbs. beef roast
1 tbsp. avocado oil
1 tsp. garlic powder
1/2 tsp. black pepper
1 tsp. salt

Directions:

1. Select the *Sauté* function on the instant pot.
2. Combine the salt, pepper and garlic powder and stir to form an even mix. Now coat the beef roast evenly with the mix.
3. Place the beef in the pot, add the oil and cover with the lid.
4. Cook for 10 minutes then flip the roast on to the other side,
5. Cover with the lid again and cook for a further 10 minutes,
6. Lock the lid and select the *meat stew* option. Set to cook for 85 minutes,
7. Natural release the steam for 30 minutes then remove the lid. Serve warm.

Nutrition Values Nutritional Values Per serving

Calories:- 356
Carbohydrate:- 0.6g
Protein:- 57.5g
Fat:- 12.1g
Sugar:- 0.1g
Sodium:- 0.51g

295. Mouthwatering Pork Roast Tacos

Preparation Time: 1 hour 15 minutes
Serves: 6

Ingredients

2 lbs. pork sirloin tip roast
8 low-carb whole wheat tortillas
1 cup Greek salsa

2 tbsp. Greek seasoning
1 tsp. Greek oregano
6 tbsp. olive oil
4 tbsp. lemon juice
1 cup chicken stock

Directions:

1. Pour the oil into the instant pot and select the *Sauté* function.

2. Add the pork roast to the heated oil and cook until it turns brown on both sides,

3. Add all the remaining ingredients; except the tortillas and secure the lid.

4. Cook for 50 minutes at high pressure on the *Manual* setting.

5. Natural release the steam for 15 minutes then remove the lid. Stuff the tortillas with cooked pork and serve.

Nutrition Values Nutritional Values Per serving

Calories:- 432
Carbohydrate:- 22g
Protein:- 37.9g
Fat:- 21g
Sugar:- 3g
Sodium:- 1.09g

296. Special Beef Carne Asada

Preparation Time: 2 hours 25 minutes
Serves: 6

Ingredients

2 lbs. beef stew meat
3/4 tbsp. chili powder
3/4 tbsp. cumin
1 tbsp. lemon juice
1 ½ oz. tomato paste
1 ½ tbsp. olive oil
1/2 cup beef bone broth
1/2 large onion; sliced
2 tbsp. salt

Directions:

1. Season the stew meat with salt, cumin and chili powder.

2. Select the *Sauté* function on your instant pot to heat the oil.

3. Place the beef in the pot and secure the lid.

4. Cook on *Manual* function for 35 minutes at high pressure,

5. Natural release the steam and remove the lid.

6. Add the remaining Ingredients and let it sit for 5 minutes, Serve warm.

Nutrition Values Nutritional Values Per serving

Calories:- 408
Carbohydrate:- 13.4g
Protein:- 58.6g
Fat:- 15.3g
Sugar:- 3.5g
Sodium:- 2.55g

297. Instant Pork Brisket

Preparation Time: 1 hour 10 minutes
Serves: 2

Ingredients

4 lbs. pork brisket; flat cut
2 tbsp. Worcestershire sauce
2 cups barbecue sauce
4 tbsp. liquid smoke
1/2 tsp. celery salt
1/2 tsp. garlic salt
1/2 tsp. Lowry's seasoned salt
1 cup water

Directions:

1. Season the pork brisket with salt, garlic salt, celery salt, liquid smoker and Worcestershire sauce,

2. Marinate the seasoned pork overnight.

3. Put the barbecue sauce, water and marinated pork into the instant pot.

4. Select *Manual* and cook for 60 minutes at high pressure,

5. When it beeps; *Natural Release* the steam

for 15 minutes, Remove the lid and serve hot.

Nutrition Values Nutritional Values Per serving

Calories:- 321
Carbohydrate:- 27.6g

Protein:- 48.6g
Fat:- 3.2g
Sugar:- 19.1g
Sodium:- 1.61g

Chapter 6 – Poultry and chicken

298. Instant Pot Jamaican Jerk Chicken

Serves: 6
Preparation Time: 5 minutes
Cooking Time: 15 minutes

Ingredients

6 chicken drumsticks
½ cup ketchup
¼ cup dark brown sugar
¼ cup red wine vinegar
3 tablespoons soy sauce
2 tablespoons Jamaican jerk seasoning
Salt and pepper to taste

Directions

1. Place all ingredients in the Instant Pot.
2. Give a good stir to coat the chicken.
3. Close the lid and press the Poultry button.
4. Adjust the cooking time to 15 minutes.
5. Do quick pressure release.

Nutritional Values Per serving:

Calories: 209
Carbohydrates: 9g
Protein: 11g
Fat: 3g
Fiber: 7g

299. Instant Pot Chicken Creole

Serves: 6
Preparation Time: 5 minutes
Cooking Time: 15 minutes

Ingredients

½ cup butter
4 chicken breasts, boneless
1 cup chopped onion
½ cup chopped celery

½ cup green bell pepper, chopped
1 teaspoon coconut sugar
¼ teaspoon ground cloves
1 teaspoon garlic powder
½ teaspoon white pepper
½ teaspoon black pepper
½ teaspoon cayenne pepper
½ teaspoon dried basil
1 cup chopped tomatoes
1 cup tomato sauce
1 cup chicken broth
Salt to taste

Directions

1. Press the Sauté button on the Instant Pot.
2. Heat the butter and stir in the chicken breasts, onion, and celery. Stir until fragrant and the chicken lightly brown.
3. Add the rest of the ingredients.
4. Scrape the bottom of the pot to remove the browning.
5. Close the lid and press the Poultry button.
6. Adjust the cooking time to 15 minutes.
7. Do quick pressure release.

Nutritional Values Per serving:

Calories:599
Carbohydrates: 13.9g
Protein: 50.8g
Fat: 36.3g
Fiber: 3.7g

300. Instant Pot Chicken Piccata

Serves: 6
Preparation Time: 5 minutes
Cooking Time: 15 minutes

Ingredients

1 ½ pounds chicken breasts, bones, and skin removed

2 teaspoons salt
½ cup all-purpose flour
2 tablespoons olive oil
3 cloves of garlic, minced
¾ cup chicken broth
1/3 cup lemon juice, freshly squeezed
1 sprig of basil, chopped
3 ounces capers, drained
¼ cup sour cream

Directions

1. Season the chicken breasts with 1 teaspoon of salt.
2. Place in a Ziploc bag and pour in flour. Dredge the chicken pieces in the flour. Set aside.
3. Press the Sauté button on the Instant Pot.
4. Add the olive oil and place the dredged chicken pieces inside. Sear on both sides until lightly brown.
5. Add the garlic and allow to sauté for 30 seconds.
6. Stir in the chicken broth, lemon juice, basil, and capers.
7. Season with the remaining salt.
8. Close the lid and press the Poultry button.
9. Adjust the cooking time to 10 minutes.
10. Do quick pressure release.
11. Serve with sour cream.

Nutritional Values Per serving:

Calories:342
Carbohydrates: 10.2g
Protein: 32.1g
Fat: 18.4g
Fiber: 0.8g

301. Root Beer Chicken Wings

Serves: 8
Preparation Time: 5 minutes
Cooking Time: 15 minutes

Ingredients

2 pounds chicken wings
2 cans of root beer
¼ cup sugar
¼ cup soy sauce

Directions

1. Place all ingredients in the Instant Pot.
2. Give a good stir.
3. Close the lid and press the Poultry button.
4. Adjust the cooking time to 10 minutes.
5. Do quick pressure release.

Nutritional Values Per serving:

Calories: 229
Carbohydrates: 18.2g
Protein:25.5 g
Fat: 5.5g
Fiber: 0.2g

302. Instant Pot Alfredo Chicken Noodles

Serves: 4
Preparation Time: 5 minutes
Cooking Time: 15 minutes

Ingredients

1 tablespoon olive oil
2 chicken breasts, bones, and skin removed
Salt and pepper
5 cloves of garlic, minced
2 tablespoons butter
2 cups heavy cream
2 cups chicken broth
A pinch of ground nutmeg
1 package dry fettuccini noodles
½ cup parmesan cheese, grated
Fresh basil leaves for garnish

Directions

1. Press the Sauté button on the Instant Pot.
2. Pour the oil and sauté the chicken breasts. Season with salt and pepper. Cook until lightly brown.

3. Stir in the garlic until fragrant.
4. Add the butter, heavy cream, broth, nutmeg, and noodles.
5. Close the lid and press the Poultry button.
6. Adjust the cooking time to 10 minutes.
7. Do quick pressure release.
8. Do natural pressure release.
9. Open the lid and garnish with parmesan cheese and basil.

Nutritional Values Per serving:

Calories: 571
Carbohydrates: 10.5g
Protein: 38.6g
Fat: 50.3g
Fiber: 0.9g

303. Chicken with Mushrooms and Mustard

Serves: 4
Preparation Time: 5 minutes
Cooking Time: 15 minutes

Ingredients

4 chicken breasts, halved
2 tablespoons flour
2 tablespoon vegetable oil
1 tablespoon butter
1 onion, chopped
1 cup mushrooms, sliced
½ cup light cream
1 tablespoon fresh parsley, chopped
1 tablespoon Dijon mustard
1 tablespoon lemon juice, freshly squeezed
Salt and pepper

Directions

1. Pound the chicken breasts and dredge in the flour. Set aside.
2. Press the Sauté button on the Instant Pot.
3. Heat the oil and butter and add the dredged chicken pieces. Cook on all sides for 3 minutes each.
4. Add the rest of the ingredients.

5. Close the lid and press the Poultry button.
6. Adjust the cooking time to 10 minutes.
7. Do quick pressure release.

Nutritional Values Per serving:

Calories: 675
Carbohydrates: 8.4g
Protein: 62.4g
Fat: 42.6g
Fiber:1 g

304. Quick Hoisin Chicken

Serves: 6
Preparation Time: 5 minutes
Cooking Time: 15 minutes

Ingredients

6 ounces snow peas
1 can water chestnuts, cut into quarters
1-pound chicken breasts, cut into bite-sized pieces
Salt and pepper to taste
4 tablespoons hoisin sauce
2 teaspoons sugar
¼ cup soy sauce
1 tablespoon cornstarch + 2 tablespoons water

Directions

1. Place all ingredients in the Instant Pot except for the cornstarch slurry.
2. Close the lid and press the Poultry button.
3. Adjust the cooking time to 15 minutes.
4. Do quick pressure release.
5. Once the lid is open, press the Sauté button and stir in the cornstarch slurry.
6. Simmer until the sauce thickens.

Nutritional Values Per serving:

Calories: 240
Carbohydrates:19.2 g
Protein: 18.5g
Fat:9.5g
Fiber:1.4g

305. Sticky Chicken and Chilies

Serves: 8
Preparation Time: 5 minutes
Cooking Time: 15 minutes

Ingredients

8 chicken thighs
¼ cup honey
1 ½ tablespoons chili paste
½ cup chicken broth
2 cloves of garlic, minced
2 tablespoons currants
2 tablespoon olive oil
2 tablespoons balsamic vinegar
Rind from 1 small lemon

Directions

1. Place all ingredients in the Instant Pot except for the cornstarch slurry.
2. Close the lid and press the Poultry button.
3. Adjust the cooking time to 15 minutes.
4. Do quick pressure release.

Nutritional Values Per serving:

Calories:522
Carbohydrates: 11.5g
Protein: 35.5g
Fat: 36.9g
Fiber: 0.6g

306. Instant Pot Herbed Chicken

Serves: 4
Preparation Time: 5 minutes
Cooking Time: 15 minutes

Ingredients

4 chicken breasts, halved
1 package herb sprinkle of your choice
1 ½ cups long-grain rice
3 cups chicken broth
2 tablespoons oregano leaves
Salt and pepper

Directions

1. Season the chicken breasts with the herbs of your choice. Set aside.
2. Pour the rice, chicken broth, and oregano in the Instant Pot.
3. Season with salt and pepper.
4. Place the chicken meat on top.
5. Close the lid and press the Poultry button.
6. Adjust the cooking time to 15 minutes.
7. Do quick pressure release.

Nutritional Values Per serving:

Calories: 774
Carbohydrates: 55.7g
Protein: 69.3g
Fat: 28.9g
Fiber:2.9g

307. Yakitori Chicken Wings

Serves: 12
Preparation Time: 5 minutes
Cooking Time: 15 minutes

Ingredients

½ cup yakitori sauce
2 cloves of garlic, minced
1 thumb-size ginger, grated
12 chicken wings
½ cup water
1 green onion, chopped
½ teaspoon sesame seeds, toasted

Directions

1. Place the yakitori sauce, garlic, ginger, and chicken wings in the Instant Pot.
2. Pour in water and give a good stir.
3. Close the lid and press the Poultry button.
4. Adjust the cooking time to 15 minutes.
5. Do quick pressure release.
6. Once the lid is open, garnish with green

onions and sesame seeds.

Nutritional Values Per serving:

Calories: 266
Carbohydrates: 2.9g
Protein: 15.7g
Fat: 5.9g
Fiber:0.2g

308. Balsamic Orange Chicken Drumsticks

Serves: 8
Preparation Time: 5 minutes
Cooking Time: 20 minutes

Ingredients

1 tablespoon olive oil
8 chicken drumsticks
2 tablespoons balsamic vinegar
1/3 cup orange marmalade
1/3 cup orange juice, freshly squeezed
2 tablespoons honey

Directions

1. Press the Sauté button on the Instant Pot.
2. Heat the oil and place the chicken drumsticks. Stir to brown all edges.
3. Pour in the rest of the ingredients.
4. Close the lid and press the Poultry button.
5. Adjust the cooking time to 15 minutes.
6. Do quick pressure release.

Nutritional Values Per serving:

Calories: 281
Carbohydrates: 15.1g
Protein: 26.3g
Fat: 13.7g
Fiber: 0.1g

309. French Style Chicken Potatoes

Serves: 8
Preparation Time: 5 minutes

Cooking Time: 20 minutes

Ingredients

1 tablespoon unsalted butter
4 chicken thighs
2 cloves of garlic, minced
1 onion, chopped
1 teaspoon onion powder
1 teaspoon garlic powder
2 teaspoons white sugar
¼ cup Dijon mustard
1 teaspoon rosemary
1 teaspoon thyme
½ pound baby potatoes, scrubbed and halved
Salt and pepper
1 cup dry white wine
½ cup chicken stock
2 tablespoons flour + 2 tablespoons milk

Directions

1. Press the Sauté button on the Instant Pot.
2. Melt the butter and add the chicken thighs, garlic, and onion. Stir to brown the chicken meat and until fragrant.
3. Add the onion powder, garlic powder, sugar, mustard, rosemary, thyme, and baby potatoes. Season with salt and pepper to taste. Continue stirring for 2 minutes.
4. Pour into the dry white wine and chicken stock.
5. Close the lid and press the Poultry button.
6. Adjust the cooking time to 15 minutes.
7. Do quick pressure release.
8. Once the lid is open, press the Sauté button.
9. Stir in the flour mixture and allow to simmer until the sauce thickens.

Nutritional Values Per serving:

Calories: 308
Carbohydrates:9.4g
Protein: 20.8g
Fat: 20.7g
Fiber: 1.4g

310. Garlicky Chicken Nuggets

Preparation Time: 25 MIN
Serve: 2

Ingredients:

1 Egg, beaten
½ cup Ghee
2 Chicken Breasts, cut into cubes
2 tbsp Garlic Powder
½ cup Coconut Flour
Salt and Pepper, to taste

Directions:

1. Place the coconut flour, garlic powder, and some salt and pepper in a bowl. Stir to combine.
2. Dip the chicken pieces in egg first, and then coat with the coconut/garlic mixture.
3. Melt the ghee in a pan over medium heat.
4. Cook the chicken nuggets for about 5 minutes on each side.
5. Drain on paper towels before serving. Enjoy!

Nutritional Value

Calories 60
Fats 3 g
Carbohydrates: 3 g
Protein 4 g

311.Gingery Wings in Minty Chutney

Preparation Time: 45 MIN
Serve: 6

Ingredients:

1 tbsp Turmeric
1 tbsp grated Ginger
1 tbsp Paprika
1 tbsp Cumin
1 tbsp ground Coriander
2 tbsp Olive Oil
18 Chicken Wings, halved
A pinch of Cayenne Pepper
Salt and Pepper, to taste

Chutney:

1 tbsp Olive Oil
1 small piece of Ginger, chopped
1 cup Mint Leaves
1 tbsp Water
Juice of ½ Lime
1 Serrano Pepper
Salt and Pepper, to taste

Directions:

1. Place the oil and all of the spices together in a bowl.
2. Add the chicken wings and coat well.
3. Cover the bowl and place in refrigerate for 20 minutes.
4. Meanwhile, preheat your grill to medium.
5. Place all of the chutney ingredients in a blender. Blend until the mixture becomes smooth. Set aside.
6. Grill the wings for about 25 minutes in total, turning them over from time to time.
7. Serve the wings with the chutney and enjoy.

Nutritional Value

Calories 200
Fats 6 g
Carbohydrates: 6 g
Protein 14 g

312.Chicken Liver Pate with Radishes

Preparation Time: 10 MIN
Serve: 1

Ingredients:

1 tsp Thyme
3 Radishes, sliced thinly
3 tbsp Butter
Crusted Keto Bread
4 ounces Chicken Liver, sautéed
Salt and Pepper, to taste

Directions:

1. Place the liver, butter and thyme, in your food processor.

2. Mix until the mixture becomes smooth.
3. Season with salt and pepper, to taste.
4. Spread the pate over a crusted bread.
5. Top with radishes.
6. Serve and enjoy!

Nutritional Value

Calories 380
Fats 40 g
Carbohydrates: 1 g
Protein 17 g

313.Crockpot Chicken and Tomato Chowder

Preparation Time: 4 hours
Serve: 4

Ingredients:

1 cup Chicken Stock
1 Garlic Clove, minced
1 pound boneless and skinless Chicken Thighs, chopped
8 ounces Cream Cheese
1 Yellow Onion, chopped
10 ounces chopped canned Tomatoes
1 Jalapeno Pepper, chopped
Salt and Pepper, to taste
Juice from 1 Lime
2 tbsp Cilantro
Cheddar Cheese, for serving

Directions:

1. Place all of the ingredients in your crockpot.
2. Season with some salt and pepper.
3. Mix to combine well.
4. Cover the crockpot and cook on High for 4 hours.
5. Serve sprinkled with some cheddar cheese. Enjoy!

Nutritional Value

Calories 300
Fats 5 g

Carbohydrates: 3 g
Protein 26 g

314.Ranch Chicken Meatballs

Preparation Time: 25minutes
Serve: 3

Ingredients:

1 Egg
½ cup Almond Flour
1 pound Ground Chicken
2 tbsp Ranch Dressing
1 tbsp Ranch Seasoning
¼ cup grated Cheddar Cheese
¼ cup Hot Sauce
Salt and Pepper, to taste

Directions:

1. Preheat your oven to 500 degrees F.
2. Place all of the ingredients in a large bowl.
3. Season with some salt and paper.
4. Line a baking dish with a piece of parchment paper.
5. Shape the meat mixture into 9 meatballs, and arrange them on the lined dish.
6. Place in the oven and bake for about 15 minutes.
7. Serve and enjoy!

Nutritional Value

Calories 156
Fats 11 g
Carbohydrates: 2 g
Protein 26 g

315.Chicken and Shrimp on a Spinach Bed

Preparation Time: 30minutes
Serve: 4

Ingredients:

½ pound Mushrooms, chopped
¼ cup Mayonnaise

½ tsp Paprika
20 Shrimp, peeled and deveined
2 boneless and skinless Chicken Breasts
1 tsp Garlic Powder
¼ tsp Xanthan Gum
2 tsp Lime Juice
2 Handfuls of Spinach
1 Green Onion, chopped
1 tbsp Coconut Oil
½ tsp Red Pepper Flakes
Salt and Pepper, to taste

Directions:

1. Place the coconut oil in a pan and melt it over medium heat.

2. Add chicken, season with garlic powder and some salt and pepper, and cook for about 67 minutes per side. Transfer to a pate.

3. Add the mushrooms to the panspray some cooking spray in it, if needed, and cook for a couple of minutes. Season with salt and pepper.

4. In another pan, Stir in shrimp, red pepper flakes, xanthan gum, sriracha, paprika, and mayonnaise.

5. Place over medium heat and cook until the shrimp turn pink. Remove from heat.

6. Divide the spinach between two plates.

7. Top with chicken, mushrooms, and shrimp.

8. Sprinkle the green onion on top.
   Enjoy!

Nutritional Value

Calories 500
Fats 34 g
Carbohydrates: 3 g
Protein 40 g

316.Chicken Thighs in a Balsamic Sauce

Preparation Time: 30 MIN
Serves: 4

Ingredients:

1 pound Chicken Thighs
2 tbsp. Olive Oil
½ cup Balsamic Vinegar
1/3 cup Sherrysubstitute with Chicken Stock for fewerCarbohydrates
2 tbsp. chopped Cilantro
1 tsp Worcestershire Sauce
2 tbsp. minced Onion
1 tsp Garlic Powder
¼ tsp Pepper
½ tsp Salt

Directions:

1. Place everything, except the chicken, in your Instant Pot.

2. Stir to combine well.

3. Add the chicken and close the lid.

4. Cook on POULTRY for 15 minutes.

5. Release the pressure quickly.

6. Serve drizzled with the sauce.
   Enjoy!

Nutritional Value

Calories 210
Fats 12g
Carbohydrates 9g
Protein 14g

317.Italian Chicken Thighs

Preparation Time: 25 MIN
Serves: 6

Ingredients:

6 Chicken Thighs
2 cups Cherry Tomatoes
½ cup Basil
3 Garlic Cloves, minced
1 Onion, chopped
½ pound Cremini Mushrooms, sliced
½ cup Olives
1 tbsp. Tomato Paste
1 tbsp. Olive Oil
¼ cup Parsley
1 cup Chicken Broth

Directions:

1. Heat the olive oil in your IP on SAUTE.
2. Sear the chicken until golden. Set aside.
3. Add mushrooms and onions and cook for a few minutes.
4. Add garlic and cook for 30 seconds.
5. Stir in the remaining ingredients including the chicken, and close the lid.
6. Cook on HIGH for 10 minutes.
7. Do a quick pressure release.
8. Serve and enjoy!

Nutritional Value

Calories 245
Fats 25g
Carbohydrates 7g
Protein 35g

318. Taco Chicken

Preparation Time: 35 MIN
Serves: 16

Ingredients:

1 ounce Taco Seasoning
1 ½ pounds Chicken Breasts
½ cup Red Salsa
½ cup mild Salsa Verde

Directions:

1. Combine all of the ingredients in your Instant Pot.
2. Close the lid and cook on HIGH for 25 minutes.
3. Do a quick pressure release.
4. Grab two forks and shred the chicken inside the pot.
5. Stir to coat well.
6. Serve and enjoy!

Nutritional Value

Calories 240
Fats 9g
Carbohydrates 5g

Protein 33g

319. Barbecue Chicken

Preparation Time: 30 MIN
Serves: 6

Ingredients:

6 Chicken Thighs
½ cup LowCarb Barbecue Sauce
1 tsp minced Garlic
1 Onion, chopped
1 tbsp. Olive Oil
1 ½ tbsp. Arrowroot
½ cup plus 2 tbsp. Water
Salt and Pepper, to taste

Directions:

1. Set your IP to SAUTE.
2. Heat the oil in it and sauté the onions for a few minutes.
3. Add garlic and cook for another minute.
4. Stir in the barbecue sauce and ½ cup of water.
5. Place the thighs upside down.
6. Cover and cook on HIGH for 10 minutes.
7. Release the pressure quickly.
8. Transfer the chicken to a plate.
9. Set your IP to SAUTE and bring to a boil.
10. Whisk the remaining water and arrowroot and stir the mixture into the sauce.
11. Cook until thickened.
12. Add the chicken and cook for another minute.
13. Serve and enjoy!

Nutritional Value

Calories 449
Fats 12g
Carbohydrates 7g
Protein 27g

320. Pina Colada Chicken

Preparation Time: 35 MIN
Serves: 4

Ingredients:

1 cup Pineapple Chunks
2 pounds Chicken, cubed
2 tbsp. Coconut Aminos
½ cup chopped Green Onion
½ cup Coconut Cream
Pinch of Cinnamon
Pinch of Sea Salt

Directions:

1. Place everything, except the green onions, in your Instant Pot.
2. Lock the lid and set the POULTRY cooking mode.
3. Cook for 15 minutes.
4. Release the pressure quickly.
5. Serve garnished with green onions. Enjoy!

Nutritional Value

Calories 530
Fats 24g
Carbohydrates 7g
Protein 60g

321. Chicken Curry with Eggplant and Squash

Preparation Time: 10 minutes
Cooking Time: 25 minutes
Serves: 4

Ingredients:

3 garlic cloves, peeled and crushed
2 tablespoons vegetable oil
3 arbol chilies, cut into halves
1-inch piece ginger, peeled and sliced
2 tablespoons green curry paste
⅛ teaspoon cumin
¼ teaspoon coriander

14 ounces canned coconut milk
6 cups butternut squash, peeled and cubed
8 chicken pieces
1 eggplant, peeled and cubed
Salt and ground black pepper, to taste
1 tablespoon fish sauce
4 cups spinach, chopped
½ cup fresh cilantro, chopped
½ cup fresh basil, chopped
Cooked barley for serving
Lime wedges, for serving

Directions:

Set the Instant Pot on Sauté mode, add the oil, and heat it up. Add the garlic, ginger, chilies, cumin, and coriander, stir, and cook for 1 minute. Add the curry paste, stir, and cook 3 minutes. Add the coconut milk, stir, and simmer for 1 minute. Add the chicken, squash, eggplant, salt, and pepper, stir, cover and cook on the Poultry setting for 20 minutes. Release the pressure, uncover the Instant Pot, add spinach, fish sauce, more salt and pepper, basil, and cilantro, stir and divide among plates. Serve with cooked barley on the side and lime wedges.

Nutritional Values Per serving

Calories: 160
Fat: 8.2
Fiber: 4.1
Carbs: 13.2
Protein: 6

322. Chicken with Duck Sauce

Preparation Time: 10 minutes
Cooking Time: 20 minutes
Serves: 4

Ingredients:

1 chicken, cut into medium-sized pieces
Salt and ground black pepper, to taste
1 tablespoon extra virgin olive oil
½ teaspoon paprika
¼ cup white wine
½ teaspoon dried marjoram
¼ cup chicken stock

For the duck sauce:
2 tablespoons white vinegar
¼ cup apricot preserves
1½ teaspoon ginger root, grated
2 tablespoons honey

Directions:

Set the Instant Pot on Sauté mode, add the oil, and heat it up. Add the chicken pieces, brown them on all sides, and transfer to a bowl. Season them with salt, pepper, marjoram, and paprika and toss to coat. Drain the fat from pot, add the stock and wine, stir, and simmer for 2 minutes. Return the chicken, cover the Instant Pot and cook on the Poultry setting for 9 minutes. Release the pressure, transfer the chicken to serving dishes and set the dish aside. Add the apricot preserves to the Instant Pot, ginger, vinegar, and honey, set on the Sauté mode, stir, and simmer sauce for 10 minutes. Drizzle over chicken, and serve.

Nutritional Values Per serving

Calories: 170
Fat: 4
Fiber: 3
Carbs: 9
Protein: 23

323. Chicken and Dumplings

Preparation Time: 10 minutes
Cooking Time: 20 minutes
Serves: 6

Ingredients:

2 pounds chicken breasts, skinless and bone-in
4 carrots, peeled and chopped
1 yellow onion, peeled and chopped
3 celery stalks, chopped
¾ cup chicken stock
Salt and ground black pepper, to taste
½ teaspoon thyme, dried
2 eggs
⅔ cup milk
1 tablespoon baking powder
2 cups flour

1 tablespoon chives

Directions:

In the Instant Pot, add the chicken, onion, carrots, celery, stock, thyme, salt, and pepper, stir, cover, and cook on poultry mode for 15 minutes. Release the pressure, transfer chicken to a bowl and keep warm for now. In a bowl, mix the eggs with salt, milk and baking powder and stir. Add the flour gradually and stir very well. Set the Instant Pot to Sauté mode and bring the liquid to a boil. Shape dumplings from the egg mixture, drop them into stock, cover the Instant Pot and cook on the Manual setting for 7 minutes. Shred the chicken and add to the Instant Pot after you've released the pressure, stir, divide everything among plates, and serve with chives sprinkled on top.

Nutritional Values Per serving

Calories: 380
Fat: 4.2
Fiber: 2.9
Carbs: 40
Protein: 43

324. Chicken and Chickpea Masala

Preparation Time: 10 minutes
Cooking Time: 25 minutes
Serves: 4

Ingredients:

1 yellow onion, peeled and diced
2 tablespoons butter
4 garlic cloves, peeled and minced
1 tablespoon ginger, grated
1½ teaspoon paprika
1 tablespoon cumin
1½ teaspoons coriander
1 teaspoon turmeric
Salt and ground black pepper, to taste
Cayenne pepper
15 ounces canned crushed tomatoes
¼ cup lemon juice
1 pound spinach, chopped
3 pounds chicken drumsticks and thighs

½ cup fresh cilantro, chopped
½ cup chicken stock
15 ounces canned chickpeas, drained
½ cup heavy cream

Directions:

Set the Instant Pot on Sauté mode, add the butter and melt it. Add the ginger, onion, and garlic, stir and cook for 5 minutes. Add the paprika, cumin, coriander, cayenne, turmeric, salt, and pepper, stir and cook for 30 seconds. Add the tomatoes and spinach, stir and cook for 2 minutes. Add half of the cilantro, chicken pieces, and stock, stir, cover the Instant Pot and cook on the Poultry setting for 15 minutes. Release the pressure, uncover the Instant Pot, add the heavy cream, chickpeas, lemon juice, more salt, and pepper, stir, set the Instant Pot on Sauté mode again and simmer for 3 minutes. Sprinkle the rest of the cilantro on top, stir, divide among plates, and serve.

Nutritional Values Per serving

Calories: 270
Fat: 8
Fiber: 7.6
Carbs: 30
Protein: 31

325.Sesame Chicken

Preparation Time: 10 minutes
Cooking Time: 8 minutes
Serves: 4

Ingredients:

2 pounds chicken breasts, skinless, boneless, and chopped
½ cup yellow onion, peeled and chopped
Salt and ground black pepper, to taste
1 tablespoon vegetable oil
2 garlic cloves, peeled and minced
½ cup soy sauce
¼ cup ketchup
2 teaspoons sesame oil
½ cup honey
2 tablespoons cornstarch

¼ teaspoon red pepper flakes
3 tablespoons water
2 green onions, chopped
1 tablespoons sesame seeds, toasted

Directions:

Set the Instant Pot on the Sauté mode, add the oil, and heat it up. Add the garlic, onion, chicken, salt and pepper, stir, and cook for 3 minutes. Add the pepper flakes, soy sauce, and ketchup, stir, cover and cook on the Manual setting for 3 minutes. Release pressure, uncover the Instant Pot, add the sesame oil and honey and stir. In a bowl, mix the cornstarch with the water and stir well. Add this to the Instant Pot with the green onions and sesame seeds, stir well, divide among plates, and serve.

Nutritional Values Per serving

Calories: 170
Fat: 3.5
Fiber: 2.9
Carbs: 16
Protein: 7

326. Chicken and Noodles

Preparation Time: 10 minutes
Cooking Time: 20 minutes
Serves: 6

Ingredients:

8 chicken thighs, skinless and boneless
3 carrots, chopped
2 garlic cloves, minced
1 yellow onion, chopped
3 celery stalks, chopped
6 cups chicken stock
1 bay leaf
2 sage leaves, chopped
1 rosemary sprig
5 thyme sprigs
Salt and ground black pepper, to taste
1 teaspoon chicken seasoning
1 pound egg noodles
2 tablespoons cornstarch
3 tablespoons water

1 cup peas, frozen
Juice of 1 lemon
¼ cup parsley, chopped

Directions:

Set the Instant Pot on Sauté mode, add onion, garlic, and celery, stir and brown for 4 minutes. Add carrot, chicken, stock, bay leaf, thyme, rosemary, sage, chicken seasoning, salt and pepper, stir, cover the Instant Pot and cook on Low for 10 minutes. Release the pressure naturally, uncover the Instant Pot, add egg noodles, cornstarch mixed with water, peas, lemon juice, parsley and more salt and pepper if needed. Discard herbs, stir everything, divide among plates, and serve.

Nutritional Values Per serving

Calories: 560
Fat: 11.2
Fiber: 5.2
Carbs: 77
Protein: 39

327. Chicken and Pomegranate

Preparation Time: 10 minutes
Cooking Time: 15 minutes
Serves: 6

Ingredients:

10 chicken pieces
2 cups walnuts
Salt and ground black pepper, to taste
3 tablespoons extra virgin olive oil
1 yellow onion, peeled and chopped
¼ teaspoon cardamom
½ teaspoon ground cinnamon
½ cup pomegranate juice
½ cup molasses
¾ cup water
2 tablespoons sugar
Juice of ½ lemon
Pomegranate seeds for serving

Directions:

Heat up a pan over medium-high heat, add the

walnuts, stir, and toast for 5 minutes. Transfer them to a food processor, blend well, transfer to a bowl and set aside. Set the Instant Pot on Sauté mode, add the 2 tablespoons oil and heat it up. Add the chicken pieces, salt and pepper, brown them on all sides, and transfer them to a plate. Add the rest of the oil to the Instant Pot, add onion, stir, and cook for 3 minutes. Add the cardamom and cinnamon, stir, and cook for 1 minute. Add the walnuts, pomegranate juice, molasses, lemon juice, chicken and sugar, stir, cover and cook on the Poultry setting for 7 minutes. Release the pressure, uncover the Instant Pot, add more salt and pepper, stir, divide among plates, and serve with the sauce from the Instant Pot and with pomegranate seeds on top.

Nutritional Values Per serving

Calories: 200
Fat: 1
Fiber: 4
Carbs: 27
Protein: 17

328. Chicken and Shrimp

Preparation Time: 10 minutes
Cooking Time: 15 minutes
Serves: 4

Ingredients:

8 ounces shrimp, peeled and deveined
8 ounces sausages, sliced
8 ounces chicken breasts, skinless, boneless, and chopped
2 tablespoons extra virgin olive oil
1 teaspoon Creole seasoning
2 teaspoons dried thyme
Cayenne pepper
2 teaspoons Worcestershire sauce
Tabasco sauce
3 garlic cloves, peeled and minced
1 yellow onion, peeled and chopped
1 green bell pepper, seeded and chopped
3 celery stalks, chopped

1 cup white rice
1 cup chicken stock
2 cups canned diced tomatoes
3 tablespoons fresh parsley, chopped

Directions:

In a bowl, mix the Creole seasoning with thyme and cayenne and stir. Set the Instant Pot on Sauté mode, add the oil and heat it up. Add the chicken and brown for a few minutes. Add the sausage slices, stir, and cook for 3 minutes. Add the shrimp and half of the seasoning mix, stir, and cook for 2 minutes. Transfer everything to a bowl and set the dish aside. Add the garlic, onions, celery, and bell peppers to the Instant Pot. Add the rest of the seasoning mix, stir, and cook for 10 minutes. Add the rice, stock, tomatoes, Tabasco sauce, and Worcestershire sauce, stir, cover, and cook on Rice mode for 8 minutes. Release the pressure, return the chicken, sausage and shrimp, stir, cover, and leave Instant Pot aside for 5 minutes. Divide everything among plates, and serve.

Nutritional Values Per serving

Calories: 269
Fat: 5.9
Fiber: 2.4
Carbs: 23.5
Protein: 28.4

329. Indian Butter Chicken

Preparation Time: 10 minutes
Cooking Time: 15 minutes
Serves: 6

Ingredients:

10 chicken thighs, skinless and boneless
2 jalapeño peppers, chopped
28 ounces canned diced tomatoes
2 teaspoons cumin
2 tablespoons ginger, chopped
½ cup butter
Salt and ground black pepper, to taste
¾ cup heavy cream
2 teaspoons garam masala

¾ cup Greek yogurt
2 teaspoons cumin seeds, toasted and ground
2 tablespoons cornstarch
2 tablespoons water
¼ cup fresh cilantro, chopped

Directions:

In a food processor, mix the tomatoes with ginger and jalapeños and blend well. Set the Instant Pot on Sauté mode, add the butter and melt it. Add the chicken, stir, and brown for 3 minutes on each side. Transfer the chicken pieces to a bowl and set aside. Add the paprika and cumin to the Instant Pot, stir, and cook for 10 seconds. Add the tomato mix, salt, pepper, yogurt, heavy cream, and chicken pieces, stir, cover, and cook on the Manual setting for 5 minutes. Release the pressure naturally for 15 minutes, uncover the Instant Pot, add cornstarch mixed with the water, garam masala, and cumin seeds and stir well. Add the cilantro, stir, divide among plates, and serve with naan bread.

Nutritional Values Per serving

Calories: 380
Fat: 29
Fiber: 2
Carbs: 8
Sugar: 2
Protein: 24

330. Goose with Cream

Preparation Time: 10 minutes
Cooking Time: 1 hour
Serves: 5

Ingredients:

1 goose breast, fat trimmed off and cut into pieces
1 goose leg, skinless
1 goose thigh, skinless
Salt and ground black pepper, to taste
3½ cups water
2 teaspoons garlic, minced
1 yellow onion, peeled and chopped

12 ounces canned cream of mushroom soup

Directions:

Put the goose meat into the Instant Pot. Add the onion, salt, pepper, water, and garlic, stir, cover and cook on Poultry mode for 1 hour. Release the pressure, uncover the Instant Pot, add the soup, set the Instant Pot on Manual mode and cook everything for 5 minutes. Divide into bowls, and serve with toasted bread.

Nutritional Values Per serving

Calories: 345
Fat: 7.8
Fiber: 1Carbs: 1
Protein: 28.4

331. Goose with Chili Sauce

Preparation Time: 10 minutes
Cooking Time: 15 minutes
Serves: 4

Ingredients:

1 goose breast half, skinless, boneless, and cut into thin slices
¼ cup extra virgin olive oil
1 sweet onion, peeled and chopped
2 teaspoons garlic, chopped
Salt and ground black pepper, to taste
¼ cup chili sauce

Directions:

Set the Instant Pot on Sauté mode, add the oil and heat it up. Add the onion and garlic, stir, and cook for 2 minutes. Add the goose breast slices, salt and pepper, stir and cook for 2 minutes on each side. Add the chili sauce, stir, cover and cook on the Manual setting for 5 minutes. Release pressure, divide among plates, and serve.

Nutritional Values Per serving

Calories: 190
Fat: 8
Fiber: 1
Carbs: 1

Protein: 29

332. Chicken and Cabbage

Preparation Time: 10 minutes
Cooking Time: 30 minutes
Serves: 3

Ingredients:

1½ pounds chicken thighs, boneless
1 green cabbage, roughly chopped
1 tablespoon vegetable oil
Salt and ground black pepper, to taste
2 chili peppers, chopped
1 yellow onion, peeled and chopped
4 garlic cloves, peeled and chopped
3 tablespoons curry
Cayenne pepper
½ cup white wine
10 ounces coconut milk
1 tablespoon fish sauce

Directions:

Set the Instant Pot on Sauté mode, add the oil, and heat it up. Add the chicken, season with salt and pepper, stir, brown for a few minutes, and transfer to a bowl. Add the garlic, chili peppers and onions to the Instant Pot, stir, and cook for 4 minutes. Add the curry, stir, and cook for 2 minutes. Add the wine, cabbage, coconut milk, cayenne, fish sauce, chicken pieces, salt and pepper, stir, cover and cook on the Poultry setting for 20 minutes. Release the pressure naturally, uncover the Instant Pot, stir your mix, divide it among plates, and serve.

Nutritional Values Per serving

Calories: 260
Fat: 5.5
Fiber: 4.9
Carbs: 15.2
Protein: 30.2

333. Chicken and Broccoli

Preparation Time: 10 minutes
Cooking Time: 15 minutes

Serves: 6

Ingredients:

2 chicken breasts, skinless and boneless
1 tablespoon butter
1 tablespoon extra virgin olive oil
½ cup yellow onion, chopped
14 ounces canned chicken stock
Salt and ground black pepper, to taste
Red pepper flakes
1 tablespoon dried parsley
2 tablespoons water
2 tablespoons cornstarch
3 cups broccoli, steamed and chopped
1 cup cheddar cheese, shredded
4 ounces cream cheese, cubed

Directions:

Set the Instant Pot on Sauté mode, add butter and oil and heat up. Add chicken breasts, salt and pepper, brown on all sides and transfer to a bowl. Add onion to the Instant Pot, stir and cook for 5 minutes. Add more salt, pepper, stock, parsley, pepper flakes and return chicken breasts as well. Stir, cover the Instant Pot and cook on the Manual setting for 5 minutes. Release the pressure, transfer chicken to a cutting board, chop it and return to pot. Add cornstarch mixed with the water, shredded cheese and cream cheese and stir until all cheese dissolves. Add broccoli, stir, set the Instant Pot on Manual mode and cook for 5 minutes. Divide among plates, and serve.

Nutritional Values Per serving

Calories: 280
Fat: 13
Fiber: 4
Carbs: 23
Protein: 30

334. Chicken with Corn

Preparation Time: 10 minutes
Cooking Time: 25 minutes
Serves: 4

Ingredients:

8 chicken drumsticks
Salt and ground black pepper, to taste
1 teaspoon extra virgin olive oil
½ teaspoon garlic powder
3 scallions, chopped
½ yellow onion, peeled and chopped
1 tomato, cored and chopped
¼ cup fresh cilantro, chopped
1 garlic clove, peeled and minced
2 cups water
8 ounces tomato sauce
1 tablespoon chicken bouillon
2 corn on the cob, husked and cut into halves
½ teaspoon cumin

Directions:

Set the Instant Pot on Sauté mode, add the oil, and heat up. Add the onions, tomato, scallions, and garlic, stir, and cook for 3 minutes. Add the cilantro, stir, and cook for 1 minute. Add the tomato sauce, water, bouillon, cumin, garlic powder, chicken, salt, and pepper and top with the corn. Cover the Instant Pot and cook on the Poultry setting for 20 minutes. Release the pressure, uncover the Instant Pot, add more salt and pepper, if needed, divide chicken, and corn among plates, and serve.

Nutritional Values Per serving

Calories: 320
Fat: 10
Fiber: 3
Carbs: 18
Protein: 42

335. Greek-Style Chicken Legs with Herbs

Preparation Time: 35 minutes
Serves: 4

Ingredients

4 Chicken Legs, skinless
1 cup Onions, thinly sliced
2 ripe Tomatoes, chopped
1 tsp Garlic, minced
2 tbsp corn Flour

1 ½ cups Chicken broth
3 tsp Olive Oil
1 tsp ground Cumin
2 tsp dried Rosemary
Salt and ground Black Pepper
½ cup Feta Cheese, cubes for garnish
10 Black Olives for garnish

Directions

1. Season the chicken with salt, black pepper, rosemary, and cumin. Heat oil on SAUTÉ mode at High. Brown the chicken legs, for 3 minutes per side. Stir in the onions and cook for another 4 minutes.

2. Add the garlic and cook for another minute. In a measuring cup, stir the cornflour into the stock to make a slurry. When mixed, add the stock to the chicken. Add the tomatoes and give it a good stir.

3. Seal the lid and switch the pressure release valve to close. Hit POULTRY and set to 20 minutes at High. Once it goes off, release the pressure quickly. Serve with a side of feta cheese and black olives.

Nutritional Values Per serving:

Calories 317
Carbs 15g
Fat 16g
Protein 28g

336. Hearty and Hot Turkey Soup

Preparation Time: 40 minutes
Serves: 6

Ingredients

1 ½ pounds Turkey thighs, boneless, skinless and diced
1 cup Carrots, trimmed and diced
2 8 oz cans White Beans
2 Tomatoes, chopped
1 potato, chopped
1 cup Green Onions, chopped
2 Cloves Garlic, minced
6 cups Vegetable Stock
¼ tsp ground Black Pepper

¼ tsp Salt
½ tsp Cayenne Pepper
½ cup Celery head, peeled and chopped

Directions

1. Place all ingredients, except the beans, into the pressure cooker, and select SOUP/BROTH mode. Seal the lid and cook for 20 minutes at High Pressure. Release the pressure quickly.

2. Remove the lid and stir in the beans. Cover the cooker and let it stand for 10 minutes before serving.

Nutritional Values Per serving:

Calories 398
Carbs 40g
Fat 11g
Protein 51g

337. Chicken and Beans Casserole with Chorizo

Preparation Time: 35 minutes
Serves: 5

Ingredients

1 tsp Garlic, minced
1 cup Onions, chopped
1 pound Chorizo Sausage, cut into pieces
4 Chicken Thighs, boneless, skinless
3 tbsp Olive Oil
2 cups Chicken Stock
11 ounces Asparagus, quartered
1 tsp Paprika
½ tsp ground Black Pepper
1 tsp Salt
2 Jalapeno Peppers, stemmed, cored, and chopped
26 oz canned whole Tomatoes, roughly chopped
1 ½ cups Kidney Beans

Directions

1. On SAUTÉ, heat the oil and brown the sausage, for about 5 minutes per side. Transfer to a large bowl. In the same oil,

add the thighs and brown them for 5 minutes. Remove to the same bowl as the sausage.

2. In the cooker, stir in onions and peppers. Cook for 3 minutes. Add in garlic and cook for 1 minute. Stir in the tomatoes, beans, stock, asparagus, paprika, salt, and black pepper.

3. Return the reserved sausage and thighs to the cooker. Stir well. Seal the lid and cook for 10 minutes on PRESSURE COOK/MANUAL mode at High Pressure. When ready, do a quick release and serve hot.

Nutritional Values Per serving:

Calories 587
Carbs 52g
Fat 29g
Protein 29g

338. Green BBQ Chicken Wings

Preparation Time: 20 minutes
Serves: 4

Ingredients

2 pounds Chicken Wings
5 tbsp Butter
1 cup Barbeque Sauce
5 Green Onions, minced

Directions

Add the butter, ¾ parts of the sauce and chicken in the pressure cooker. Select POULTRY, seal the lid and cook for 15 minutes at High. Do a quick release. Garnish wings with onions and top with the remaining sauce.

Nutritional Values Per serving:

Calories 311
Carbs 1g
Fat 10g
Protein 51g

339. Homemade Cajun Chicken Jambalaya

Preparation Time: 30 minutes
Serves: 6

Ingredients

1 ½ pounds, Chicken Breast, skinless
3 cups Chicken Stock
1 tbsp Garlic, minced
1 tsp Cajun Seasoning
1 Celery stalk, diced
1 ½ cups chopped Leeks, white part
1 ½ cups dry White Rice
2 tbsp Tomato Paste

Directions

1. Select SAUTÉ at High and brown the chicken for 5 minutes. Add the garlic and celery, and fry for 2 minutes until fragrant. Deglaze with broth. Add the remaining ingredients to the cooker. Seal the lid.

2. Select POULTRY, and cook for 15 minutes at High. Do a quick pressure release and serve

Nutritional Values Per serving:

Calories 299
Carbs 31g
Fat 8g
Protein 41g

340. Tasty Turkey with Campanelle and Tomato Sauce

Preparation Time: 20 minutes
Serves: 4

Ingredients

3 cups Tomato Sauce
½ tsp Salt
½ tbsp Marjoram
1 tsp dried Thyme
½ tbsp fresh Basil, chopped
¼ tsp ground Black Pepper, or more to taste
1 ½ pounds Turkey Breasts, chopped

1 tsp Garlic, minced
1 ½ cup spring Onions, chopped
1 package dry Campanelle Pasta
2 tbsp Olive Oil
½ cup Grana Padano cheese, grated

Directions

Select SAUTÉ at High and heat the oil in the cooker. Place the turkey, spring onions and garlic. Cook until cooked, about 6-7 minutes. Add the remaining ingredients, except the cheese.
Seal the lid and press the PRESSURE COOK/MANUAL button. Cook for 5 minutes at High Pressure. Once cooking has completed, quick release the pressure. To serve, top with freshly grated Grana Padano cheese.

Nutritional Values Per serving:

Calories 588
Carbs 71g
Fat 11g
Protein 60g

341. Hot and Spicy Shredded Chicken

Preparation Time: 1 hour
Serves: 4

Ingredients

1 ½ pounds boneless and skinless Chicken Breasts
2 cups diced Tomatoes
½ tsp Oregano
2 Green Chilies, seeded and chopped
½ tsp Paprika
2 tbsp Coconut Sugar
½ cup Salsa
1 tsp Cumin
2 tbsp Olive Oil

Directions

1. In a small mixing dish, combine the oil with all spices. Rub the chicken breast with the spicy marinade. Lay the meat into your pressure cooker. Add the tomatoes. Seal the lid, and cook for 20 minutes on POULTRY at High.

2. Once ready, do a quick pressure release. Remove chicken to a cutting board; shred it. Return the shredded chicken to the cooker. Set to SAUTÉ at High, and let simmer for about 15 minutes.

Nutritional Values Per serving:

Calories 307
Carbs 12g
Fat 10g
Protein 38g

342. Creamy Turkey Breasts with Mushrooms

Preparation Time: 35 minutes
Serves: 4

Ingredients

20 ounces Turkey Breasts, boneless and skinless
6 ounces White Button Mushrooms, sliced
3 tbsp Shallots, chopped
½ tsp dried Thyme
¼ cup dry White Wine
⅔ cup Chicken Stock
1 Garlic Clove, minced
2 tbsp Olive Oil
3 tbsp Heavy Cream
1 ½ tbsp Cornstarch
Salt and Pepper, to taste

Directions

1. Warm half of the olive oil on SAUTÉ mode at High. Meanwhile, tie turkey breast with a kitchen string horizontally, leaving approximately 2 inches apart. Season the meat with salt and pepper.

2. Add the turkey to the pressure cooker and cook for about 3 minutes on each side. Transfer to a plate. Heat the remaining oil and cook shallots, thyme, garlic, and mushrooms until soft.

3. Add white wine and scrape up the brown bits from the bottom. When the alcohol evaporates, return the turkey to the pressure cooker. Seal the lid, and cook on MEAT/STEW for 25 minutes at High.

4. Meanwhile, combine heavy cream and cornstarch in a small bowl. Do a quick pressure release. Open the lid and stir in the mixture. Bring the sauce to a boil, then turn the cooker off. Slice the turkey in half and serve topped with the creamy mushroom sauce.

Nutritional Values Per serving:

Calories 192
Carbs 5g
Fat 12g
Protein 15g

343. Hot and Buttery Chicken Wings

Preparation Time: 20 minutes
Serves: 16

Ingredients

16 Chicken Wings
1 cup Hot Sauce
1 cup Water
2 tbsp Butter

Directions

Add in all ingredients, and seal the lid. Cook on PRESSURE COOK/MANUAL for 15 minutes at High. When ready, press CANCEL and release the pressure naturally, for 10 minutes.

Nutritional Values Per serving:

Calories 50
Carbs 1g
Fat 2g
Protein 7g

344. Simple Pressure Cooked Whole Chicken

Preparation Time: 40 minutes
Serves: 4

Ingredients

1 2-pound Whole Chicken

2 tbsp Olive Oil
1 ½ cups Water
Salt and Pepper, to taste

Directions

1. Season chicken all over with salt and pepper. Heat the oil on SAUTÉ at High, and cook the chicken until browned on all sides. Set aside and wipe clean the cooker. Insert a rack in your pressure cooker and pour the water in.
2. Lower the chicken onto the rack. Seal the lid. Choose POULTRY setting and adjust the time to 25 minutes at High pressure. Once the cooking is over, do a quick pressure release, by turning the valve to "open" position.

Nutritional Values Per serving:

Calories 376
Carbs 0g
Fat 30g
Protein 25g

345. Chicken Bites Snacks with Chili Sauce

Preparation Time: 25 minutes
Serves: 6

Ingredients

1 ½ pounds Chicken, cut up, with bones
¼ cup Tomato Sauce
Kosher Salt and Black Pepper to taste
2 tsp dry Basil
¼ cup raw Honey
1 ½ cups Water

For Chili Sauce:

2 spicy Chili Peppers, halved
½ cup loosely packed Parsley, finely chopped
1 tsp Sugar
1 clove Garlic, chopped
2 tbsp Lime juice
¼ cup Olive Oil

Directions

1. Put a steamer basket in the cooker's pot and pour the water in. Place the meat in the basket, and press PRESSURE COOK/MANUAL button. Seal the lid and cook for 20 minutes at High Pressure.

2. Meanwhile, prepare the sauce by mixing all the sauce ingredients in a food processor. Blend until the pepper is chopped and all the ingredients are mixed well. Release the pressure quickly. To serve, place the meat in serving bowl and top with the sauce.

Nutritional Values Per serving:

Calories 405
Carbs 18g
Fat 19g
Protein 31g

Chapter 7 – Fish and seafood

346. Steamed Crab Legs

Serves: 4
Preparation Time:
Cooking Time:

Ingredients

2 pounds frozen crab legs
4 tablespoons butter
1 tablespoon lemon juice, freshly squeezed

Directions

1. Place a trivet or a steamer basket in the Instant Pot. Pour a cup of water.
2. Arrange the crab legs on it.
3. Close the lid and press the Steam button.
4. Adjust the cooking time to 4 minutes.
5. Do quick pressure release.
6. Once the lid is open, check if the crab legs are bright pink.
7. Serve crab legs with butter and a drizzle of lemon juice.

Nutritional Values Per serving:

Calories:291
Carbohydrates: 0.3g
Protein: 41g
Fat: 12.3g
Fiber: 0g

347. Lobster with Wine and Tomatoes

Serves: 4
Preparation Time: 5 minutes
Cooking Time: 10 minutes

Ingredients

4 tablespoons olive oil
2 onions, diced
2 cloves of garlic, minced
1 carrot, chopped
2 lobsters, shelled
½ cup cognac
1-pound ripe tomatoes
2 tablespoon tomato paste
1/3 clam juice
1 tablespoon tarragon

Directions

1. Press the Sauté button on the Instant Pot.
2. Heat the oil and sauté the onions and garlic until fragrant.
3. Add the rest of the ingredients.
4. Stir to combine.
5. Close the lid and press the Manual button.
6. Adjust the cooking time to 10 minutes.
7. Do quick pressure release.

Nutritional Values Per serving:

Calories: 300
Carbohydrates: 13.2g
Protein: 14.9g
Fat: 14.5g
Fiber: 3.1g

348. Instant Pot Mussels

Serves: 6
Preparation Time: 3 minutes
Cooking Time: 6 minutes

Ingredients

1 cup white wine
3 Roma tomatoes, chopped
2 cloves of garlic, minced
1 bay leaf
2 pounds mussels, scrubbed
½ cup fresh parsley, chopped
Salt and pepper

Directions

1. Place all ingredients in the Instant Pot.
2. Close the lid and press the Manual button.
3. Adjust the cooking time to 6 minutes.
4. Do natural pressure release.

Nutritional Values Per serving:

Calories:155
Carbohydrates: 10.5g
Protein: 19.5g
Fat: 3.7g
Fiber: 1.1g

349. Instant Pot Boiled Octopus

Serves: 8
Preparation Time: 3 minutes
Cooking Time: 15 minutes

Ingredients

2 ½ pounds whole octopus, sliced and cleaned
Salt and pepper to taste
3 tablespoons lemon juice, freshly squeezed
1 cup water

Directions

1. Place all ingredients in the Instant Pot.
2. Close the lid and press the Manual button.
3. Adjust the cooking time to 15 minutes.
4. Do quick pressure release.

Nutritional Values Per serving:

Calories:90
Carbohydrates: 7.7g
Protein:4.6 g
Fat: 6.1g
Fiber: 0.1g

350. Instant Pot Lobster Roll

Serves: 6
Preparation Time: 5 minutes
Cooking Time: 6 minutes

Ingredients

1 ½ cups chicken broth
1 teaspoon old bay seasoning
2 pounds lobster tails, raw and in the shell
1 lemon, halved
3 scallions, chopped
½ cup mayonnaise
4 tablespoons unsalted butter
¼ teaspoon celery salt

Directions

1. Pour the broth into the Instant Pot and sprinkle with old bay seasoning.
2. Place a steamer on top and lay each lobster tail shell side down.
3. Squeeze the first half of the lemon over the lobsters.
4. Close the lid and press the Manual button.
5. Adjust the cooking time to 6 minutes.
6. While cooking, prepare the sauce by combining the rest of the ingredients in a bowl.
7. Once the timer beeps off, do quick pressure release.
8. Brush the mayo dip on the exposed meat of the lobster tails.

Nutritional Values Per serving:

Calories:392
Carbohydrates: 2.7g
Protein: 47.5g
Fat: 20.2g
Fiber: 0.6g

351.Instant Pot Easy Scallops

Serves: 3
Preparation Time: 5 minutes
Cooking Time: 6 minutes

Ingredients

1 tablespoon oil
1-pound sea scallops, shells removed

½ cup coconut aminos

3 tablespoons maple syrup

½ teaspoon garlic powder

½ teaspoon ground ginger

½ teaspoon salt

Directions

1. Place a trivet or a steamer basket in the Instant Pot. Pour a cup of water.
2. In a baking dish that will fit the Instant Pot, pour all the ingredients.
3. Place the baking dish on top of the steamer.
4. Close the lid and press the Steam button.
5. Adjust the cooking time to 6 minutes.
6. Do quick pressure release.

Nutritional Values Per serving:

Calories: 270

Carbohydrates: 2.1g

Protein: 25g

Fat:16g

Fiber: 0g

352. Instant Pot Tuna Casserole

Serves: 4

Preparation Time: 3 minutes

Cooking Time: 15 minutes

Ingredients

2 carrots, peeled and chopped

¼ cup diced onions

1 cup frozen peas

¾ cup milk

2 cans tuna, drained

1 can cream of celery soup

2 tablespoons butter

½ cup water

2 eggs beaten

Salt and pepper

Directions

1. Place all ingredients in the Instant Pot.
2. Stir to combine.
3. Close the lid and press the Manual button.

4. Adjust the cooking time to 15 minutes.
5. Do quick pressure release.

Nutritional Values Per serving:

Calories:305

Carbohydrates: 15.3g

Protein: 24.5g

Fat: 16.5g

Fiber: 2.8g

353. Steamed Fish Patra Ni Maachi

Serves: 4

Preparation Time: 3 minutes

Cooking Time: 10 minutes

Ingredients

1-pound tilapia fillets

½ cup green commercial chutney

Directions

1. Place a trivet or a steamer basket in the Instant Pot. Pour a cup of water.
2. Cut a large parchment paper and place the fish in the middle.
3. Pour over the green chutney.
4. Fold and secure the parchment paper.
5. Place on top of the steamer basket.
6. Close the lid and press the Manual button.
7. Adjust the cooking time to 10 minutes.
8. Do natural pressure release.

Nutritional Values Per serving:

Calories: 134

Carbohydrates: 11g

Protein: 22g

Fat: 3g

Fiber: 0g

354. Salmon on a Veggie Bed

Preparation Time: 30 MIN

Serves: 4

Ingredients:

4 Salmon Fillets
3 tsp Olive Oil
½ Lemon, sliced
1 Bell Pepper, julienned
1 Zucchini, julienned
1 Carrot, julienned
1 Tarragon Sprig
A handful of parsley
A handful of Basil
1 cup of Water

Directions:

1. Pour the water into the Instant Pot and place the herbs inside.
2. Arrange the veggies on the rack.
3. Top with the salmon filletsskin side down.
4. Drizzle with oil and top with lemon sliced.
5. Close the lid and cook on HIGH for 5 minutes.
6. Do a quick pressure release.
7. Serve and enjoy!

Nutritional Value

Calories 308
Fats 13g
Carbohydrates 4.3g
Protein 40.6g

355.Gruyere Lobster Keto Pasta

Preparation Time: 25 MIN
Serves: 4

Ingredients:

1 cup Half and Half
¾ cup shredded Gruyere Cheese
3 Lobster Tails
1 tbsp. Worcestershire Sauce
1 tbsp. Arrowroot
1 tbsp. chopped Tarragon
½ cup White Wine
2 cups Water
4 cups Zoodles

Directions:

1. Place the lobster in the Instant Pot.
2. Pour the water over and close the lid.
3. Cook on HIGH for 5 minutes.
4. Let cool slightly. Spoon out the meat from the tails and place in a bowl.
5. Whisk together the half and half, Worcestershire, wine, and arrowroot in the Instant Pot.
6. Cook on SAUTE for 2 minutes.
7. Stir in zoodles, lobster, and cheese.
8. Cook for 3 minutes.
9. Serve and enjoy!

Nutritional Value

Calories 280
Fats 7g
Carbohydrates 3g
Protein 17g

356.Sea Bass in a Tomato Feta Sauce

Preparation Time: 30 MIN
Serves: 4

Ingredients:

4 Sea Bass Fillets
1 cup canned diced Tomatoes
1/2 cup crumbled Feta Cheese
1 tsp chopped Parsley
1 tsp chopped Basil
1 tsp minced Garlic
1 tbsp. Olive Oil
¼ tsp salt
¼ tsp Pepper
1 ½ cups Water

Directions:

1. Season the sea bass with salt and pepper.
2. Pour the water into the Instant Pot and place the sea bass on the rack.
3. Close the lid and cook on HIGH for 5 minutes.
4. Transfer to a plate and discard the water.
5. Heat the oil in the IP on SAUTE.
6. Add garlic and cook for 1 minute.

7. Add tomatoes and cook for 1 more minute.
8. Stir in basil and parsley.
9. Add the sea bass and top with feta.
10. Cook for 1 minute.
11. Serve and enjoy!

Nutritional Value

Calories 275
Fats 8g
Carbohydrates 2g
Protein 40g

357. Stewed Scallops and Mussels

Preparation Time: 20 MIN
Serves: 4

Ingredients:

1 tbsp. Coconut Oil
1 Onion, diced
2 cups ground Cauliflower
2 cups Mussels
1 cup Scallops
2 Bell Peppers, diced
2 cups Fish Stock
A pinch of Saffron

Directions:

1. Melt the coconut oil in the Instant Pot on SAUTE.
2. Add peppers and onions and cook for 3 minutes.
3. Add scallops and saffron. Cook for 2 minutes.
4. Add the remaining ingredients and stir to combine.
5. Cook on HIGH for 6 minutes.
6. Release the pressure naturally.
7. Serve and enjoy!

Nutritional Value

Calories 195
Fats 4.5g
Carbohydrates 7.6g

Protein 20g
Fiber: 3.7g

358. ParmesanCrusted Salmon

Preparation Time: 15 MIN
Serves: 2

Ingredients:

2 Salmon Fillets
1 tbsp. Olive Oil
1 tbsp. Mayonnaise
½ cup grated Parmesan Cheese
¼ tsp Garlic Powder
½ tsp Paprika
Salt and Pepper, to taste
1 ½ tbsp. Butter
1 ½ cups Water

Directions:

1. Pour the water into the Instant Pot.
2. Season the salmon with salt and pepper and place on the steaming rack.
3. Close the lid and cook on HIGH for 4 minutes.
4. Do a quick pressure release.
5. Discard the water.
6. Combine the olive oil and mayonnaise and brush over the salmon.
7. Combine the parmesan, paprika, and garlic powder.
8. Coat the salmon with the mixture well.
9. Melt the butter in the IP on SAUTE.
10. Add salmon and cook until golden on all sides.
11. Serve and enjoy!

Nutritional Value

Calories 400
Fats 38g
Carbohydrates 0.9
Protein 33g

359. Fish Soup

Preparation Time: 30 MIN
Serves: 4

Ingredients:

1 pound skinless and boneless Halibut, chopped
1 tbsp. Coconut Oil
2 cups Chicken Stock
1 cup Water
1 Onion, chopped
1 Carrot, sliced
2 Celery Stalks, chopped
2 tbsp. minced Ginger
Salt and Pepper, to taste

Directions:

1. Melt the coconut oil in the Instant Pot on SAUTE.
2. Add onion and cook for 4 minutes.
3. Stir in the stock, ginger, carrot, celery, and water.
4. Cook on HIGH for 5 minutes.
5. Add halibut and cook for 4 more minutes.
6. Do a natural pressure release.
7. Serve and enjoy!

Nutritional Value

Calories 170
Fats 6g
Carbohydrates 4g
Protein 12g

360.Saucy Trout with Chives

Preparation Time: 15 MIN
Serves: 4

Ingredients:

4 Trout Fillets
2 tsp Lemon Juice
1 tsp Lemon Zest
6 tbsp. Butter
3 tbsp. chopped Chives
2 tbsp. Olive Oil
1 ½ cups Water

Directions:

1. Pour the water into your Instant Pot.
2. Place the trout inside the steamer basket.
3. Lower it in the IP.
4. Close the lid and cook on HIGH for 3 minutes.
5. Transfer to a plate and discard the water.
6. Mel the butter in the IP on SAUTE.
7. Meanwhile, chop the trout.
8. Add the trout in the pot along with the other ingredients.
9. Cook for 2 minutes.
10. Serve and enjoy!

Nutritional Value

Calories 320
Fats 6g
Carbohydrates 3g
Protein 18g

361.Cheesy Tuna and Noodles

Preparation Time: 10 MIN
Serves: 4

Ingredients:

½ cup shredded Cheddar Cheese
2 Tuna cans, drained
1 cup Water
½ cup Heavy Cream
4 Zucchini Noodles
4 tbsp. Cheddar Cheese

Directions:

1. Pour the water into your Instant Pot.
2. Place the zoodles, heavy cream, tuna, and cheddar, in a baking dish.
3. Stir to combine.
4. Place the dish inside the IP.
5. Close the lid and cook on HIGH for 3 minutes.
6. Divide between 4 bowls.
7. Top with parmesan cheese.

8. Serve and enjoy!

Nutritional Value

Calories 210
Fats 9.3g
Carbohydrates 2g
Protein 15g
Fiber: 0g

362. Wrapped Zesty and Herbed Fish

Preparation Time: 15 MIN
Serves: 1

Ingredients:

1 4ounce Fish Fillet
1 Rosemary Sprig
1 Thyme Sprig
1 tbsp. chopped Basil
2 tsp Lime Zest
1 tbsp. Lime Juice
1 tbsp. Olive Oil
1 tsp Dijon Mustard
¼ tsp Garlic Powder
Pinch of Salt
Pinch of Pepper
1 ½ cups Water

Directions:

1. Pour the water into your Instant Pot.
2. Season the fish with salt and paper.
3. Place on a piece of parchment paper and sprinkle with zest.
4. Whisk together the oil, juice, and mustard, and brush over.
5. Top with the herbs.
6. Wrap the fish with the parchment paper.
7. Then, wrap the wrapped fish in aluminum foil.
8. Place the fish packet inside the basket.
9. Close the lid and cook for 5 minutes on HIGH.
10. Do a quick pressure release.
11. Serve and enjoy!

Nutritional Value

Calories 250
Fats 10g
Carbohydrates 1g
Protein 30g

363. Creamy Crabmeat

Preparation Time: 12 MIN
Serves: 4

Ingredients:

½ cup Heavy Cream
¼ cup Chicken Broth
1/2 Red Onion, chopped
¼ cup Butter
½ Celery Stalk, chopped
1 pound Lump Crabmeat

Directions:

1. Melt the butter in your Instant Pot on SAUTE.
2. Add onion and celery and cook for 4 minutes.
3. Add crabmeat and broth.
4. Stir to combine and close the lid.
5. Cook on HIGH for 3 minutes.
6. Do a quick pressure release.
7. Stir in the cream.
8. Serve and enjoy!

Nutritional Value

Calories 400
Fats 10g
Carbohydrates 6g
Protein 40g

364. Shrimps with Tomatoes and Feta

Preparation Time: 5 MIN
Serves: 6

Ingredients:

2 tbsp. Butter
1 tbsp. Garlicminced
½ tsp Paprika Flakes
1½ cups Oniondiced
14 oz. Crushed Tomatoescanned
1 tsp Oregano
1 tsp Salt
1 lbs. Frozen Shelled Shrimp
1 cup Feta Cheesecrumbled
½ cup Black Olivespitted and cut into 1inch slices
¼ cup Parsleychopped

Directions:

1. Set the Instant Pot to "Sauté" and add to it butter. When butter has melted add garlic and paprika flakes. Stir well.

2. Add the onions, tomatoes, oregano and salt, and cook for 2 minutes.

3. Add the shrimps and stir to combine.

4. Place and lock the lid and manually set the **Preparation Time:** to 1 minute at low pressure.

5. When done quick release the pressure.

6. Divide to plates and garnish with feta, olives and parsley.

7. Serve with riced cauliflower.

Nutritional Value

Calories: 211
Fats: 11g
Carbohydrates: 5g
Proteins: 19g

365. Shrimp with Risotto and Herbs

Preparation Time: 10 minutes
Cooking Time: 20 minutes
Serves: 4

Ingredients:

4 tablespoons butter
2 garlic cloves, peeled and minced
1 yellow onion, peeled and chopped
1½ cups Arborio rice
2 tablespoons dry white wine
4½ cups chicken stock

Salt and ground black pepper, to taste
1 pound shrimp, peeled and deveined
¾ cup Parmesan cheese, grated
⅛ cup fresh tarragon, chopped
⅛ cup fresh parsley, chopped

Directions:

Set the Instant Pot on Sauté mode, add 2 tablespoons butter, and melt. Add the garlic and onion, stir, and cook for 4 minutes. Add the rice, stir, and cook for 1 minute. Add the wine, stir, and cook 30 seconds. Add 3 cups stock, salt, and pepper, stir, cover and cook on the Rice setting for 9 minutes. Release the pressure, uncover the Instant Pot, add the shrimp, the rest of the stock, set the Instant Pot on Sauté mode, and cook for 5 minutes, stirring occasionally. Add the cheese, the rest of the butter, tarragon, and parsley, stir, divide among plates, and serve.

Nutritional Values Per serving

Calories: 400
Fat: 8
Fiber: 4
Carbs: 15
Protein: 29

366. Spicy Shrimp and Rice

Preparation Time: 20 minutes
Cooking Time: 10 minutes
Serves: 4

Ingredients:

18 ounces shrimp, peeled and deveined
Salt, to taste
½ tablespoon mustard seeds
¼ cup vegetable oil
2 teaspoons dry mustard
1 teaspoon turmeric
2 green chilies, cut into halves lengthwise
2 onions, diced
4 ounces curd, beaten
1-inch piece of ginger, peeled and chopped
Rice, already cooked, for serving

Directions:

Put the mustard seeds in a bowl, add enough water to cover, set aside for 10 minutes, drain and grind very well. Put the shrimp in a bowl, add oil, dry mustard, turmeric, mustard paste, salt, onions, chilies, curd, and ginger, toss to coat and set aside for 10 minutes. Transfer everything to the Instant Pot, cover and cook on Steam mode for 10 minutes. Release the pressure, divide among plates, and serve with boiled rice.

Nutritional Values Per serving

Calories: 200
Fat: 2
Fiber: 1
Carbs: 7
Protein: 11

367. Shrimp Scampi

Preparation Time: 10 minutes
Cooking Time: 4 minutes
Serves: 4

Ingredients:

1 pound shrimp, cooked, peeled and deveined
2 tablespoons extra virgin olive oil
1 garlic clove, peeled and minced
10 ounces canned diced tomatoes
⅓ cup tomato paste
¼ teaspoon dried oregano
1 tablespoon fresh parsley, diced
⅓ cup water
1 cup Parmesan cheese, grated
Spaghetti noodles, already cooked, for serving

Directions:

Set the Instant Pot on Sauté mode, add the oil and heat up. Add the garlic, stir, and cook for 2 minutes. Add the shrimp, tomato paste, tomatoes, water, oregano and parsley, stir, cover, and cook on the Manual setting for 3 minutes. Release pressure, divide among plates, add spaghetti noodles, sprinkle with cheese, and serve.

Nutritional Values Per serving

Calories: 288
Fat: 20
Fiber: 0
Carbs: 0.01
Protein: 23

368. Octopus and Potatoes

Preparation Time: 10 minutes
Cooking Time: 35 minutes
Serves: 6

Ingredients:

2 pounds octopus, cleaned, head removed, emptied, tentacles separated
2 pounds potatoes
Water
3 garlic cloves, peeled and crushed
½ teaspoon peppercorns
1 bay leaf
2 tablespoons parsley, diced
5 tablespoons vinegar
Salt and ground black pepper, to taste
2 tablespoons extra virgin olive oil

Directions:

Put potatoes into the Instant Pot, add water to cover them, salt and pepper, cover the Instant Pot and cook on the Manual setting for 15 minutes. Release the pressure, transfer potatoes to a bowl, peeled and chopped. Put octopus into the Instant Pot, add more water, bay leaf, 1 garlic clove, peppercorns and more salt. Stir, cover and cook on the Manual setting for 20 minutes. Release the pressure, drain octopus, chop it and add to potatoes. In a bowl, mix olive oil with vinegar, 2 garlic cloves, salt and pepper and stir very well. Add this to octopus salad, also add parsley, toss to coat, and serve.

Nutritional Values Per serving

Calories: 300
Fat: 12
Fiber: 2
Carbs: 14
Protein: 20

369. Seafood Gumbo

Preparation Time: 10 minutes
Cooking Time: 25 minutes
Serves: 10

Ingredients:

¾ cup vegetable oil
1¼ cups flour
1 cup white onions, chopped
½ cup celery, chopped
1 cup green bell pepper, chopped
4 garlic cloves, chopped
2 tablespoons peanut oil
6 plum tomatoes, cored and chopped
Cayenne pepper
3 bay leaves
½ teaspoon onion powder
½ teaspoon garlic powder
1 teaspoon dried thyme
1 teaspoon celery seeds
1 teaspoon sweet paprika
1 pound smoked sausage, sliced
2 quarts chicken stock
24 shrimp, peeled and deveined
24 crawfish tails
24 oysters
½ pound crab meat
Salt and ground black pepper, to taste
Rice, already cooked, for serving

Directions:

Heat up a pan with the vegetable oil over medium heat, add the flour and stir for 3-4 minutes. Set the Instant Pot on Sauté mode, add the peanut oil and heat it up. Add the celery, peppers, onions and garlic, stir, and cook for 10 minutes. Add the sausage, tomatoes, stock, bay leaves, cayenne, onion powder, and garlic powder, thyme, paprika, and celery seeds, stir, and cook for 3 minutes. Add the flour mixture and stir until combined. Add the shrimp, crawfish, crab, oysters, salt and pepper, stir, cover, and cook on the Meat/Stew setting for 15 minutes. Release the pressure, uncover, divide the gumbo among bowls with rice, and serve.

Nutritional Values Per serving

Calories: 800
Fat: 58
Fiber: 3
Carbs: 35
Protein: 36

370. Stuffed Squid

Preparation Time: 10 minutes
Cooking Time: 20 minutes
Serves: 4

Ingredients:

4 squid
1 cup sticky rice
14 ounces vegetable stock
2 tablespoons sake
4 tablespoons soy sauce
1 tablespoon mirin
2 tablespoons sugar

Directions:

Chop the tentacles from 1 squid and mix with the rice. Fill each squid with rice and seal ends with toothpicks. Place squid into the Instant Pot, add the stock, soy sauce, sake, sugar, and mirin. Cover and cook on the Steam setting for 15 minutes. Release the pressure, uncover the Instant Pot, divide stuffed squid among plates, and serve.

Nutritional Values Per serving

Calories: 148
Fat: 2.4
Fiber: 1.1
Carbs: 7
Protein: 11

371. Squid Masala

Preparation Time: 10 minutes
Cooking Time: 15 minutes
Serves: 4

Ingredients:

17 ounces squid, cleaned and cut

1½ tablespoons chili powder
Salt and ground black pepper, to taste
¼ teaspoon turmeric
2 cups water
5 pieces coconut
4 garlic cloves, peeled and minced
½ teaspoons cumin seeds
3 tablespoons extra virgin olive oil
¼ teaspoon mustard seeds
1-inch ginger piece, peeled and chopped

Directions:

Put the squid into the Instant Pot. Add the chili powder, turmeric, salt, pepper, and water, stir, cover, and cook on Manual for 15 minutes. In a blender, mix the coconut with the ginger, garlic, and cumin seeds and blend well. Heat up a pan with oil over medium high heat, add the mustard seeds and toast for 2-3 minutes. Release the pressure from the Instant Pot and transfer the squid and water to the pan. Stir and mix with the coconut blend. Cook until everything thickens, divide among plates, and serve.

Nutritional Values Per serving

Calories: 255
Fat: 0
Fiber: 1
Carbs: 7
Protein: 9

372. Octopus Stew

Preparation Time: 1 day
Cooking Time: 8 minutes
Serves: 4

Ingredients:

1 octopus, cleaned, head removed, emptied, tentacles separated
1 cup red wine
1 cup white wine
1 cup water
½ cup vegetable oil
½ cup extra virgin olive oil
2 tablespoons hot sauce

1 tablespoon paprika
1 tablespoon tomato paste
Salt and ground black pepper, to taste
½ bunch fresh parsley, chopped
2 garlic cloves, peeled and minced
1 yellow onion, peeled and chopped
4 potatoes, cut into quarters.

Directions:

Put the octopus in a bowl and add the white wine, red wine, water, vegetable oil, hot sauce, paprika, tomato paste, salt, pepper, and parsley. Toss to coat, cover, and keep in refrigerated for 1 day. Set the Instant Pot on Sauté mode, add the olive oil and heat it up. Add the onions and potatoes, stir and cook for 3 minutes. Add the garlic, octopus, and marinade, stir, cover, and cook on the Meat/Stew setting for 8 minutes. Release the pressure, uncover the Instant Pot, divide stew among bowls, and serve.

Nutritional Values Per serving

Calories: 210
Fat: 9
Fiber: 0
Carbs: 4
Protein: 32

373. Greek Octopus

Preparation Time: 10 minutes
Cooking Time: 16 minutes
Serves: 6

Ingredients:

1 octopus, cleaned, head removed, emptied, tentacles separated
2 rosemary sprigs
2 teaspoons dried oregano
½ yellow onion, peeled and roughly chopped
4 thyme sprigs
½ lemon
1 teaspoon black peppercorns
3 tablespoons extra virgin olive oil
For the marinade:
¼ cup extra virgin olive oil

Juice of ½ lemon
4 garlic cloves, peeled and minced
2 thyme sprigs
1 rosemary sprig
Salt and ground black pepper, to taste

Directions:

Put the octopus into the Instant Pot. Add the oregano, 2 rosemary sprigs, 4 thyme sprigs, onion, lemon, 3 tablespoons olive oil, peppercorns and salt. Stir, cover, and cook on Manual mode for 10 minutes. Release the pressure, uncover the Instant Pot, transfer octopus on a cutting board, cut tentacles and place them in a bowl. Add ¼ cup olive oil, lemon juice, garlic, 1 rosemary sprig, 2 thyme sprigs, salt and pepper, toss to coat and set aside for 1 hour. Heat up your grill on medium heat, add the octopus, grill for 3 minutes on each side, and divide among plates. Drizzle the marinade over octopus, and serve.

Nutritional Values Per serving

Calories: 161
Fat: 1
Fiber: 0
Carbs: 1
Protein: 9

374. Braised Squid

Preparation Time: 10 minutes
Cooking Time: 20 minutes
Serves: 4

Ingredients:

1 pound squid, cleaned and cut
1 pound fresh peas
½ pounds canned crushed tomatoes
1 yellow onion, peeled and chopped
White wine
Olive oil
Salt and ground black pepper, to taste

Directions:

Set the Instant Pot on Sauté mode, add some oil and heat it up. Add the onion, stir, and cook for

3 minutes. Add the squid, stir, and cook for 3 more minutes. Add the wine, tomatoes and peas, stir, cover, and cook for 20 minutes. Release the pressure, uncover the Instant Pot, add salt and pepper, stir, divide among plates, and serve.

Nutritional Values Per serving

Calories: 145
Fat: 1
Fiber: 0
Carbs: 7
Protein: 12

375. Squid Roast

Preparation Time: 10 minutes
Cooking Time: 25 minutes
Serves: 4

Ingredients:

1 pound squid, cleaned and cut into small pieces
10 garlic cloves, peeled and minced
2-inch ginger piece, peeled and grated
2 green chilies, chopped
2 yellow onions, peeled and chopped
1 bay leaf
½ tablespoon lemon juice
¼ cup coconut, sliced
1 tablespoon coriander
¾ tablespoon chili powder
1 teaspoon garam masala
Salt and ground black pepper, to taste
Turmeric
1 teaspoon mustard seeds
¾ cup water
3 tablespoons vegetable oil

Directions:

Set the Instant Pot on Sauté mode, add the oil and heat it up. Add the mustard seeds and fry for 1 minute. Add the coconut and cook 2 minutes. Add the ginger, onions, garlic, and chilies, stir, and cook 30 seconds. Add the salt, pepper, bay leaf, coriander, chili powder, garam masala, turmeric, water, lemon juice, and squid. Stir, cover and cook on Steam mode for 25 minutes. Release pressure, uncover, divide among plates, and serve.

Nutritional Values Per serving

Calories: 209
Fat: 10
Fiber: 0.5
Carbs: 9.3
Protein: 20

376. Superior Prawns and Fish Kabobs

Preparation Time: 15 minutes
Serves: 4

Ingredients

1 lb Tuna Fillets, cubed
1 lb King Prawns, peeled and deveined
1 tbsp Salt
½ Onion, diced
1 Red Bell Pepper, diced1 tsp lemon zest
1 packet dry Ranch dressing mix
1 cup Water

Directions

1. In a large bowl, and mix the fish and shrimp. Sprinkle with some salt. Toss to spread the salt over the ingredients and leave aside for 5 minutes for decent flavoring.
2. Use wooden skewers to prick the fish and the shrimp by separating with bell pepper and slices of onion. Take the steel pot of your pressure cooker to mix water with the dressing.
3. Wait for the dressing mix to dissolve. Then, insert the trivet in the same pot. Lay the sewers over the pot crosswise. Seal the lid, set on STEAM for about 4 minutes at High.
4. When ready, do a quick release. Remove the lid so the skewers can rest and cool down.

Nutritional Values Per serving:

Calories 369

Carbs 22g
Fat 15g
Protein 40g

377. Glazed Orange Salmon

Preparation Time: 25 minutes
Serves: 4

Ingredients

4 Salmon Filets
2 tsp Orange Zest
3 tbsp Orange Juice
1 tbsp Olive Oil
1 tsp Ginger, minced
1 cup White Wine
Salt and Pepper, to taste

Directions

Whisk in everything, except the salmon, in the pressure cooker. Then, add salmon and seal the lid. Cook on STEAM and cook for 7 minutes at High pressure. When ready, release the pressure quickly.

Nutritional Values Per serving:

Calories 449
Carbs 4g
Fat 17g
Protein 65g

378. Light Clams in White Wine

Preparation Time: 17 minutes
Serves: 4

Ingredients

¼ cup White Wine
2 cups Veggie Broth
¼ cup Basil, chopped
¼ cup Olive Oil
2 ½ pounds Clams
2 tbsp Lemon Juice
2 Garlic Cloves, minced

Directions

1. Heat the olive oil, add garlic and cook for one minute, until fragrant, on SAUTÉ mode at High. Pour wine, broth, and add basil, lemon juice. Bring the mixture to a boil and let cook for one minute.

2. Add your steaming basket, and place the clams inside. Seal the lid, and set to STEAM mode and adjust the time to 6 minutes at High. Wait 5 minutes before releasing the pressure quickly.

3. Remove the clams to a bowl, discard any that did not open. Drizzle with the cooking juices to serve.

Nutritional Values Per serving:

Calories 224
Carbs 6g
Fat 14g
Protein 16g

379. Almond-Crusted Fresh Tilapia

Preparation Time: 10 minutes
Serves: 4

Ingredients

4 Tilapia Fillets
⅔ cup sliced Almonds
1 cup Water
2 tbsp Dijon Mustard
1 tsp Olive Oil
¼ tsp Black Pepper

Directions

1. Pour water into inner pot of pressure cooker and place a trivet in water. Mix olive oil, pepper, and mustard in a small bowl. Brush the fish fillets with the mustard mixture on all sides.

2. Coat the fish in almonds slices. Arrange the fish fillets on top of the trivet. Seal the lid, select STEAM and adjust the time to 10 minutes at High. When done, do a quick pressure release.

Nutritional Values Per serving:

Calories 327
Carbs 4g
Fat 15g
Protein 46g

380. Mediterranean Salmon Fillet

Preparation Time: 15 minutes
Serves: 4

Ingredients

4 Salmon Fillets
2 tbsp Olive Oil
1 Rosemary Sprig
1 cup Cherry Tomatoes
15 ounces Asparagus
1 cup Water

Directions

1. Pour in water and insert the rack. Place the salmon on top, sprinkle with rosemary, and arrange the asparagus on top. Seal the lid and cook on STEAM mode for 3 minutes at High.

2. Do a quick release, add cherry tomatoes, and cook for 2 minutes, on SAUTÉ. Drizzled with oil, to serve.

Nutritional Values Per serving:

Calories 431 Carbs 6g
Fat 31g
Protein 42g

381. Fancy Shrimp Scampi with Soy Sauce

Preparation Time: 45 minutes
Serves: 4

Ingredients

2 tbsp Butter
1 tbsp Parmesan Cheese, grated
2 Shallots, chopped
¼ cup White Wine

1 tsp Garlic, minced
2 tbsp Lemon Juice
1 pound Shrimp, peeled and deveined
For the dip Sauce:
2 tbsp Soy Sauce
1 tbsp chopped chives
½ tbsp Olive Oil

Directions

1. Melt butter on SAUTÉ at High, and cook the shallots until soft. Add garlic and cook for 1 more minute. Stir in wine and cook for another minute. Add the remaining ingredients and stir to combine.

2. Seal the lid and cook for 2 minutes on STEAM, at High pressure. When ready, release the pressure quickly. Serve on a platter with dipping sauce on the side.

Nutritional Values Per serving:

Calories 183
Carbs 4g
Fat 8g
Protein 24g

382. Pleasing Tuna and Pea Cheesy Noodles

Preparation Time: 17 minutes
Serves: 4

Ingredients

1 can Tuna, drained
3 cups Water
4 ounces Cheddar Cheese, grated
16 ounces Egg Noodles
¼ cup Breadcrumbs
1 cup Frozen Peas
28 ounces canned Mushroom Soup

Directions

1. Place the water and noodles in your pressure cooker. Stir in soup, tuna, and frozen peas.

2. Seal the lid, and cook for 5 minutes on STEAM at High pressure. When ready, do

a quick pressure release. Stir in the cheese. Transfer to a baking dish; sprinkle with breadcrumbs on top.

3. Insert a baking dish in your cooker, seal the lid, and cook 3 minutes on STEAM mode at High.

Nutritional Values Per serving:

Calories 430
Carbs 42g
Fat 22g
Protein 18g

383. Alaskan Cod with Fennel, Olives and Potatoes

Preparation Time: 40 minutes
Serves: 2 servings

Ingredients

2 tablespoons olive oil
½ medium onion, halved
1 head garlic, halved
1½ cups chicken stock
¼ cupolive brine
¼ cup canned tomato purée
Salt and pepper, to taste
½ cup green olives, pitted and crushed
1 head fennel, ⬜uartered
1 medium russet potato, cut into 6 pieces
One 12-ounce Alaskan cod fillet, cut into 3-inch blocks
¼ bunch basil, leaves torn
1 lemon, sliced, for garnish

Directions

1. Heat the Instant Pot to the Sauté function. Once it is hot, add the olive oil and place the onion and garlic halvescut-sides down in the pot. Sauté them toward the middle of the pot toac⬜uire more caramelization. Once theyarecaramelized, flip them over and add thechicken stock, olive brineand tomato purée, then turn the Sauté function off. Season the broth with salt and pepper accordingly.

2. Add theolives, fennel and potatoes to the broth. Affix the lid and cook on the Pressure Cook function with low pressure for 10 minutes. Make sure the steam release valve is closed. Once the timer goes off, release thesteam from the steam release valve.

3. Remove the lid, then remove all the vegetables carefully with a slotted spoon and reserve for plating. Leave the broth in thepot. It's OK if there are still someolivepieces left in the broth. Season thecod with salt and pepper, and place thepieces into the broth. Seal the lid and cook on the Pressure Cook function with low pressure for 4 minutes. If you have very thin pieces of fish, cook for 3 minutes. Makesure the steam release valve isclosed. Once it is finished, release thesteam with the valve, remove the lid and carefully remove the fish with a slotted spoon. Add the torn basil to broth. Fill a bowl with the fish and vegetables, and spoon the broth over the top. Serve with a sliceof lemon.

Nutrition Info:

515 cal

384. Instant Pot Shrimp and Lentil Stew

Prep+Cook Time: 22 minutes
Serves: 6 Servings

Ingredients

1 tablespoon Olive Oil
3 cloves Garlic, minced
1 Onion, chopped small
1 Red Bell Pepper, chopped
1 tablespoon Thyme
2 teaspoons Oregano
2 teaspoons Old Bay Seasoning
1/2 teaspoon Cayenne
1 cup Lentils
1 lb Shrimp, deveined and peeled
3 cups Chicken Broth or vegetable
1 15 oz can Diced Tomatoes, drain slightly

1/2 cup Tomato Sauce
2 tablespoons Worcestershire Sauce
1 cup Frozen Riced Broccoli

Directions

1. Set your Instant Pot to the "saute" setting and add the Olive Oil, Garlic, Onion, and Bell Pepper and saute for 5 minutes, or until Ingredientsaresoftened. Add the Thyme, Oregano, Old Bay, and Cayenne and toss to mix. Continue tosaute for an additional 1 minute.

2. Place the Lentils, Shrimp, Chicken Broth, Diced Tomatoes, Tomato Sauce, Worcestershire Sauce and Riced Broccoli into the Instant Pot. Using the "manual" setting set the temperature to "high" and cook for 12 minutes. Release the steam and season with Salt and Pepper.

*Notes:*Don't add the salt and pepper to thestew until AFTER it's done with cooking because the lentils will fall apart otherwise.

Nutritional Values Per serving

Serving Size: Serves 6
Calories: 198
Sugar: 5 g
Sodium: 573 mg
Fat: 3 g

385. Instant Pot Louisiana Seafood, Chicken, and Sausage Gumbo

Preparation Time: 1 hour, Servings 6

Ingredients

White Rice

1 1/2 cups water
1 cup long grain enriched white rice

Gumbo

2 6 oz skinless chicken breasts
1 pound raw shrimp
1 chicken andouille sausage link sliced into pieces
1 cup green peppers chopped
1 cup celery chopped

1 cupyellow onion chopped
1-2 cups frozen okrachopped
1 tbsp minced garlic I used jarred
1-2 tbsp Better Than Bouillon Chicken Base 2
tablespoons will have it on thesaltier side
1 14.5 oz can reduced-sodium chicken broth
2 tsp oliveoil
4 tbsp butter
1 cup water
4 tbspall-purpose flour
1/2 cup diced tomatoesoptional

Seasonings

1 bay leaf
1 tsp ground basil
1 tsp cayenne pepper
1 tsp oregano
1 tbsp Creole Seasoning I used Tony Chachere
1/2 tsp thyme
1 tbsp worcestershire sauce
salt and pepper to taste

Directions

White Rice

1. Add 1 1/2 cups of water and the rice to the Instant Pot. Close and seal thepot. Cook on Manual High-Pressure Cooking for 12 minutes

2. When complete, allow thesteam to release naturally for 10 minutes instead of quick release.

Gumbo

1. Turn the Instant Pot on the Saute function. Add 1 tbspof theolive oil to the pot. Then add thechicken sausage. Cook for 2-3 minutes.

2. Remove the chicken sausage from the pot. Add the butter and remaining tbsp of olive oil to the pot. While it melts add the flour in 3 phases. Add the first phase and whisk. Add the second phase, and so on.

3. Continue to whisk until the roux turns peanut butter brown. It should turn brown within a few minutes of whisking. Press Keep Warm/Cancel on the Instant Pot so the roux does not burn.

4. Add the green peppers, celery, and onions. Stir and cook for 2-3 minutes until the veggie are soft.

5. Add all of theseasonings, garlic, and worcestershire sauce to thepot.

6. Next add thechicken broth, diced tomatoes, okra, and Better Than Bouillon. Stir. Add the water.

7. Place thechicken breasts in the pot and return the chicken sausage to the pot.

8. Close thepot and seal. Cook on Manual High-Pressure Cooking for 15 minutes. When complete, allow thesteam to release naturally for 10 minutes instead of quick release.

9. Remove the chicken from the pot and shred.

10. Place the Instant Pot on the Saute function. Add the raw shrimpand shredded chicken to thepot.

11. Cook for a few minutes until the shrimp turns bright pink.

12. Serve the gumbo alongside the cooked white rice.

Nutritional Values Per serving

Calories 390 kcal

386. Instant Pot Cioppino Seafood Stew

Preparation Time: 30 mins, **Servings:** 4

Ingredients

For the Stew Base

1/4 cup vegetable oil
14.5 ounces canned fire-roasted tomatoes
1 cup diced onion
1 cup chopped carrots or 1 cup chopped bell pepper
1 cup water
1 cup white wineor broth
2 bay leaves
1 tablespoon tomatopaste
2 tablespoons minced garlic

2 teaspoons fennel seeds toasted and ground
1 teaspoon dried oregano
2 teaspoonssalt
1 teaspoon red pepper flakes

For Finishing

4 cups mixed seafood such as fish chunks,
shrimp, bayscallops, musselsand calamari rings
1-2 tablespoons fresh lemon juice

For serving

toasted, crusty bread

Directions

1. For thestew base: Place oil, tomato, onions, carrots or bell pepper, water, wine, bay leaves, tomatopaste, garlic, oregano, ground fennel seeds, salt and pepper into the inner liner of the Instant pot. Stir well.

2. Set Instant Pot at High pressure for 15 minutes. When cook time iscomplete, let pot sit undisturbed for 10 minutes, and then releaseany remaining pressure. You can complete these stepsand put thesoupaway in the refrigerator, to finish later. This really helps the flavors in thesoup develop, but if you're ready to eat, it's not necessary.

3. Turn the pot to sauté and add fish, mussels, bayscallops, and calamari rings to thepot. Once the pot boils, add in theshrimpand cook until all theseafood is cooked through. Add lemon juice right beforeserving.

4. Serve with crusty bread to mop up all the delicious, savory broth you've just created.

Nutrition Info :

241kcal
Fat: 10g
Saturated fat: 7g
Carbohydrates: 10g
Fiber: 2g
Sugar: 4g
Protein: 18g

387. Easy Coconut Red Curry Shrimp

Prep+Cook Time: 30 minutes, Servings 6

Ingredients

For the Marinade:

1/4 cup coconut milk canned
1 tspcumin
1 tsp paprika
2 tspcurryspice
3 tbsp fresh lime juice
1/2 tspseasalt
1 tsp freshly grated ginger
1 clove garlic minced
2 lbs large shrimp peeled and deveined

For the Sauce:

2 tbsp coconut oil or olive oil
1 small white onion diced
2 tsp freshly grated ginger
2 cloves garlic minced
1 28 oz can of diced tomatoes
3 tbsp red Thai curry paste
1 14 oz coconut milk
1 tsp sea salt
1/3 cup freshly chopped cilantro for garnish optional

Directions

1. Begin my making your marinade. Placecoconut milk, spices, lime juice, seasalt, ginger, and garlic in a large bowl. Whisk together, then add shrimp. Toss to coat and let sit while you prepare the sauce.

2. Select the saute function on your Instant Pot. Once hot, add oil to coat the bottom of thepan. Now add onion, ginger, and garlic. Let saute for a few minutes, then select cancel. Now add tomatoes, currypaste, coconut milk, and salt. Place lid on the IP and secure. Make sure the valve is sealed. Select the manual function, and cook on high pressure for 7 minutes.

3. Once sauce is complete, use a quick releaseon your IP. Remove the lid once all thesteam has been released, and select

cancel. Now select, saute function and add in shrimp plus juices from the marinade.

4. Simmer until theshrimp iscooked through and no longer pink, about 2-5 minutes. Serve with optional cilantro, salt to taste, and over riceor cauliflower rice.

Nutritional Values Per serving

Servings Per Recipe: 4
Serving Size: 1 serving
Calories239.6
Total Fat10.7 g
Saturated Fat6.7 g

388. Instant Pot Lemon Pepper Salmon

Preparation Time: 15 minutes
Serves3 -4

Ingredients

¾ cup water
A few sprigsof parsley dill, tarragon, basil or a combo
1 pound salmon filet skin on
3 teaspoons ghee or other healthy fat divided
¼ teaspoon salt or to taste
½ teaspoon pepper or to taste
1/2 lemon thinly sliced
1 zucchini julienned
1 red bell pepper julienned
1 carrot julienned

Directions

1. Put water and herbs in the Instant Pot and then put in the steamer rack making sure the handles are extended up.
2. Placesalmon, skin down on rack.
3. Drizzle salmon with ghee/fat, season with salt and pepper, and cover with lemon slices.
4. Close the Instant Pot and make sure vent is turned to "Sealing". Plug it in, press "Steam" and press the + or – buttons to set it to 3 minutes.
5. While salmon cooks, julienneyour veggies.

6. When the Instant Pot beeps that it's done, quick release the pressure, being careful tostayout of the wayof the steam that will shoot up. Press the "Warm/Cancel" button. Remove lid, and using hot pads, carefully remove rack with salmon and set on a plate.
7. Remove herbs and discard. Add veggies and put the lid back on. Press "Sauté" and let the veggiescook for just 1 or 2 minutes.
8. Serve veggies with salmon and add remaining teaspoon of fat to the pot and pour a little of the sauce over them if desired.

Nutrition Info:

Calories 296kcal
Fat 15g
Saturated fat 4g
Cholesterol 95mg
Sodium 284mg
Potassium 1084mg
Carbohydrates 8g
Fiber 2g

389. Instant Pot Salmon Tortellini Soup

Preparation Time: 20 minutes Serving: serves 4

Ingredients

2/3 cup diced onion
2 cloves garlic, minced
1-2 strips bacon, diced
12-16 ounces frozen bonelesssalmon
1 10 oz package frozen mixed vegetables
10 ounces frozen tortellini
1 ▢uart chicken or vegetable broth
1 tsppaprika
1 tsp Old Bayseasoning optional
2-3 handfuls fresh baby spinach

Directions

1. Set theInstant Pot to sauteand add chopped bacon, onions and garlic to thepot. Saute for 3 minutes, stirring constantly.

2. Switch Instant Pot off. Add frozen salmon cut into 3-4 pieces if not already portioned, frozen vegetables, frozen tortellini, broth and seasonings to the pot and stir.

3. Cover and use the manual or pressurecook button toset timer for 6 minutes.

4. Use□uick release once finished, flake salmon into chunks with a fork and stir in fresh baby spinach.

Notes

You can usesalmon with the skin on, just pull the pieces of salmon out after cooking, remove theskin, flake into chunks and return to the pot.

Nutrition Info:

Total Fat 4.9g
Saturated Fat 2g
Cholesterol 27mg
Sodium 1540mg
Potassium 407mg
Total Carbohydrates 33g
Dietary Fiber 3.4g.

390. Seafood Gumbo

Preparation Time: 32 minutes
Serves: 4

Ingredients

1/2 lb. large shrimp; peeled and deveined
1/2 lb. scallops
1/2 lb. crabmeat
1 red bell pepper; seeded and chopped.
4 tbsp. olive oil; divided
1/2 onion; chopped.
1 ½ celery stalks; chopped.
2 garlic cloves; minced
1 smoked sausage; chopped
1 tbsp. dried thyme; crushed
3 1/2 cups low-sodium chicken broth; divided
¼ cup all-purpose flour
Freshly ground black pepper; to taste

Directions:

1. Select the *Sauté* function on your Instant Pot then add the oil, onion, celery, bell pepper, garlic and cook for 5 minutes,

2. Hit *Cancel* then stir in 3 cups chicken broth, black pepper, sausage and thyme,

3. Secure the cooker lid then select the *Manual* function with medium pressure for 10 minutes,

4. When it beeps; do a Quick release then remove the lid.

5. Meanwhile; add the oil to a skillet and set it on a medium-low heat. Add flour to the oil then cook for 5 minutes while stirring constantly.

6. Turn off the heat then stir in remaining chicken broth to the flour. Mix well to avoid lumps,

7. Now add this flour mixture and seafood to Instant Pot and secure the lid.

8. Cook on the *Manual* function at medium pressure for 2 minutes,

9. When it beeps; do a Quick release then remove the lid. Serve immediately.

Nutrition Values Nutritional Values Per serving

Calories:- 429
Carbohydrate:25.4g
Protein:- 35g
Fat:- 20.3g
Sugar:- 5.8g
Sodium: - 0.96mg

391. Shrimp Corn Chowder

Preparation Time: 22 minutes
Serves: 8

Ingredients

16 oz. cremini mushrooms cut in half
2 lbs. Shrimp
4 tbsp. melted butter
2 cups onions; chopped.
6 cloves fresh garlic minced
3 cups corn kernels
4 cups carrots chopped

4 cups string beans cut in half
2 lbs. potatoes peeled and cubed
4 cups chicken broth
1/2 cup dry sherry wine
2 fresh lemons
1/4 tsp. white pepper
1/4 tsp. crushed red pepper flakes
1 cup heavy whipped cream
1/2 tsp. ground black pepper
3 tsp. sea salt

Directions:

1. Put the butter, onions and garlic to the insert of the Instant Pot and *Sauté* for 3 minutes,

2. Add all the ingredients, except shrimp and cream, to the pot and secure the lid.

3. Select the *Manual* function with high pressure and 7 minutes cooking time,

4. When it beeps; do a Natural release and remove the lid.

5. Stir in shrimp to the vegetable sauce, Cook on the *Sauté* function for 3 minutes,

6. Then add whipped cream into the cooking sauce, Serve hot in a bowl.

Nutrition Values Nutritional Values Per serving

Calories:- 449
Carbohydrate:52.5g
Protein:- 36.4g
Fat:- 10.1g
Sugar:- 10g
Sodium:- 1.47g

392. Tomato Clam and Shrimps

Preparation Time: 20 minutes
Serves: 2

Ingredients

4 cups Tomato Clam Cocktail
1 cup shrimp; deveined
1 chopped onion
2 tbsp. butter
1/2 cup grated Parmesan
1/2 tsp. ground black pepper

1 tsp. dried oregano
1 tbsp. smoked paprika
1 ½ cup Arborio rice
1/2 tsp. salt

Directions:

1. Select the *Sauté* function on your Instant pot then add oil to its insert.

2. Add the onions to the heated oil, cook for 3 minutes then add all the seasoning.

3. Cook for another 2 minutes then add rice to the pot.

4. Pour in Tomato Clam Cocktail to the rice then cover the lid.

5. Secure the cooker lid and set it on the *Manual* settings at high pressure for 10 minutes,

6. When it beeps; do a Quick release then remove the lid.

7. Stir in shrimp to the rice soup. Cover the lid and let it stay for 5 minutes, Drizzled grated parmesan on top then serve.

Nutrition Values Nutritional Values Per serving

Calories:490
Carbohydrate:60.4g
Protein:- 15.2g
Fat:- 20.8g
Sugar:- 22.4g
Sodium:- 1.96g

393. Quick Seafood Platter

Preparation Time: 45 minutes
Serves: 4

Ingredients

1/2 lb. shell on shrimp; deveined
1/2 lb. mussels; fresh or frozen
1/2 lb. medium sized red potatoes; halved
1 cup seafood stock
1 ½ tbsp. Cajun's shrimp boil
1/2 lb. clams; fresh frozen
1 lemon; quartered
1/2 lb. smoked Kielbasa; cut into 2-inch pieces

1 tbsp. chopped parsley
Cilantro and lemon wedges Garnish

Directions:

1. Add the seafood stock, boiling spice and potatoes to Instant Pot.
2. Cover the lid and let it *Slow Cook* for 30 minutes till the potatoes get tender.
3. Remove the lid and add clams, shrimp, mussels, Kielbasa and lemon to the pot.
4. Cook for 10 minutes if you are using frozen seafood, else cook for only 5 minutes,
5. Garnish with cilantro and lemon wedges on top. Serve,

Nutrition Values Nutritional Values Per serving

Calories:432
Carbohydrate:30.7g
Protein:- 41.8g
Fat:- 15.9g
Sugar:- 3.9g
Sodium:- 1.85g

394. Salmon Teriyaki

Preparation Time: 18 minutes
Serves: 4

Ingredients

4 8 oz. thick salmon fillets,
1 cup soy sauce
1/2 cup water
1/2 cup mirin
2 tbsp. sesame oil
4 tsp. sesame seeds
4 tbsp. brown sugar
1 tbsp. corn starch
4 green onions; minced
2 cloves garlic; minced
2 tbsp. freshly grated ginger

Directions:

1. Put the soy sauce, sesame oil, sesame seeds, mirin, ginger, water, garlic, green onions and brown sugar to a small bowl. Mix

them well.
2. In a shallow dish place the salmon fillets and pour half of the prepared mixture over the fillets, Let it marinate for 30 minutes in a refrigerator.
3. Pour 1 cup of water into the insert of your Instant pot and place trivet inside it.
4. Arrange the marinated salmon fillets over the trivet and secure the lid.
5. Select the *Manual* settings with high pressure and 8 minutes cooking time,
6. Meanwhile; take a skillet and add the remaining marinade mixture in it.
7. Let it cook for 2 minutes then add corn starch mixed with water. Stir well and cook for 1 minute,
8. Check the pressure cooker; do a Quick release if it is done,
9. Transfer the fillets to a serving platter and pour the sesame mixture over it. Garnish with chopped green chilies then serve hot.

Nutrition Values Nutritional Values Per serving

Calories:- 491
Carbohydrate:33.7g
Protein:- 46.2g
Fat:- 20.5g
Sugar:- 18.3g
Sodium:- 3.95g

395. Amazing Clam Chowder

Preparation Time: 12 minutes
Serves: 2

Ingredients

2 pieces of bacon; chopped
1 8 oz. can tomatoes; smashed
1 medium potatoes; peeled and diced
1/2 onion; chopped
1/2 clove minced garlic
1/4 cup green pepper; chopped
1 tbsp. flour
1/4 cup chopped celery
1 tsp. nutmeg

1 ½ tbsp. parsley
1 ½ cups clam juice
1 bay leaf
1/2 cup minced clam

Directions:

1. Add the bacon to Instant Pot and cook on the *Sauté* settings until it gets crispy.
2. Now add onion, green pepper and garlic to the pot. Cook for 3 minutes,
3. Add clam juice, tomatoes, potatoes, celery, parsley, bay leaf, salt, pepper and nutmeg in the pot and stir well.
4. Secure the lid and select the *Manual* function for 5 minutes with high pressure,
5. When it beeps; do a Quick release then remove the lid.
6. Remove the bay leaves from the mixture and add clams into it. Let it stay for 5 minutes and then serve hot.

Nutrition Values Nutritional Values Per serving

Calories:- 381
Carbohydrate:54.7g
Protein:- 22.1g
Fat:- 9.2g
Sugar:- 12.2g
Sodium:- 1.68g

396. Buttery Shrimp Risotto

Preparation Time: 15 minutes
Serves: 3

Ingredients

1/2 lb. frozen raw shrimp
1/2 cup jasmine rice
1/2 cup water
1 tbsp. melted butter
1/2 tbsp. lemon juice
1/4 cup frozen vegetables
1/4 cup shredded Parmesan cheese
Salt; to taste
Pepper; to taste

Directions:

1. Add butter, salt, pepper, lemon juice, water and rice to the insert of the Instant Pot.
2. Place frozen vegetables and frozen shrimp in the pot. Secure the cooker lid.
3. Only use frozen shrimp and vegetables to match the cooking time for rice,
4. Now select the *Manual* function for 5 minutes at high pressure,
5. When it beeps; do a Quick release then remove the lid. Stir in Parmesan cheese then serve.

Nutrition Values Nutritional Values Per serving

Calories:- 240
Carbohydrate:26.8g
Protein:- 19g
Fat:- 5.7g
Sugar:- 0.5g
Sodium:- 0.22g

397. Tasty Creamy Shrimp Grits

Preparation Time: 20 minutes
Serves: 8

Ingredients

24 oz. tail-on Shrimp
1 tbsp. oil
2 cups Quick Grits
12 oz. parmesan shredded cheese
4 cups water
1 stick butter
2 cups heavy cream
2 tbsp. Old Bay seasoning
Pinch of ground black pepper

Directions:

1. Add a tbsp. of oil to Instant Pot. Select *Sauté* function for cooking.
2. Add the shrimp to the oil and drizzle old bay seasoning over it.
3. Cook the shrimp for 3-4 minutes while stirring then set them aside,

4. Now add water, cream and quick grits to the pot. Select the *Manual* function for 3 minutes at high pressure,

5. When it beeps; do a Quick release then remove the lid.

6. Add the shredded cheese and butter to the grits then stir well.

7. Take a serving bowl; first pour in the creamy grits mixture then top it with shrimp. Sprinkle black pepper on top then serve hot.

Nutrition Values Nutritional Values Per serving

Calories:- 637
Carbohydrate:34.6g
Protein:- 39.2g
Fat:- 37.8g
Sugar:- 0g
Sodium:- 1.50g

398. Yummy Alfredo Tuscan Shrimp

Preparation Time: 20 minutes
Serves: 4

Ingredients

1 lbs. of shrimp
1 ½ tsp. Tuscan seasoning
1 jar of alfredo sauce
1 box of penne pasta
1 ½ cups of fresh spinach
1 cup of sun-dried tomatoes
3 cups water

Directions:

1. Add water and pasta to a pot over a medium heat, boil until it cooks completely. Then strain the pasta and keep it aside,

2. Select the *Sauté* function on the Instant Pot and add tomatoes, shrimp, Tuscan seasoning and alfredo sauce into it.

3. Stir and cook until shrimp turn pink in color.

4. Now add spinach leaves to the pot and cook for 5 minutes,

5. Add pasta to the pot and stir well. Serve hot.

Nutrition Values Nutritional Values Per serving

Calories:- 593
Carbohydrate:75.9g
Protein:- 42.8g
Fat:- 11.7g
Sugar:- 7.1g
Sodium:- 1.13g

Chapter 8 – Vegetarian

399. Bell Pepper Gumbo

Preparation Time: 20 minutes
Serves: 3

Ingredients:

*tbsp. olive oil
4 minced garlic cloves
½ tsp cumin seeds
1 seeded and cut into long strips green bell pepper
1 seeded and cut into long strips red bell pepper
1 seeded and cut into long strips yellow bell pepper
1 seeded and cut into long strips bell pepper
½ tsp red chili powder
¼ tsp ground turmeric
Salt and freshly ground black pepper, to taste
¼ cup water
½ tbsp. fresh lemon juice*

Directions:

1. Place the oil in the Instant Pot and select "Sauté". Then add the garlic and cumin and cook for about 1 minute.
2. Select the "Cancel" and stir in remaining ingredients except for lemon juice.
3. Secure the lid and place the pressure valve to "Seal" position.
4. Select "Manual" and cook under "High Pressure" for about 2 minutes.
5. Select the "Cancel" and carefully do a "Quick" release.
6. Remove the lid and select "Sauté".
7. Stir in lemon juice and cook for about 12 minutes.
8. Select the "Cancel" and serve.

Nutritional Value

*Calories 101
Total Fat 5.3g
Carbohydrates 4.6g*

Protein 2g

400. Italian Bell Pepper Platter

Preparation Time: 20 minutes
Serves: 5

Ingredients:

*tbsp. olive oil
1 cut into thin strips yellow onion
5 seeded and cut into long strips green bell peppers
very finely chopped medium ripe tomatoes
chopped garlic cloves
2 tbsp. fresh parsley
Salt and freshly ground black pepper, to taste*

Directions:

1. Place the oil in the Instant Pot and select "Sauté". Then add the onion and cook for about 34 minutes.
2. Add the bell peppers and garlic clove and cook for about 5 minutes.
3. Select the "Cancel" and stir in remaining ingredients.
4. Secure the lid and place the pressure valve to "Seal" position.
5. Select "Manual" and cook under "High Pressure" for about 56 minutes.
6. Select the "Cancel" and carefully do a "Quick" release.
7. Remove the lid and serve.

Nutritional Value

*Calories 82
Total Fat 3.2g
Carbohydrates 2.7g
Protein 12.4g*

401.2Minutes Broccoli

Preparation Time: 12 minutes
Serves: 4

Ingredients:

4 cups broccoli florets
Salt and freshly ground black pepper, to taste

Directions:

1. In the bottom of Instant Pot, arrange a steamer basket and pour 1 cup of water.
2. Place the broccoli into the steamer basket.
3. Secure the lid and place the pressure valve to "Seal" position.
4. Select "Manual" and cook under "High Pressure" for about 2 minutes.
5. Select the "Cancel" and carefully do a "Natural" release.
6. Remove the lid and transfer the broccoli to serving plates.
7. Sprinkle with salt and black pepper and serve.

Nutritional Value

Calories 31
Total Fat 0.3g
Carbohydrates 1.52g
Protein 2.6g

402. Brilliant Cheesy Broccoli

Preparation Time: 25 minutes
Serves: 2

Ingredients:

For Broccoli:

2 cups broccoli florets
1 tbsp. olive oil
2 tsp garlic powder
½ tbsp. smoked paprika
Salt and freshly ground black pepper, to taste

For Cheese Sauce:

3 tbsp. butter
2 tbs. almond flour
½ cups unsweetened almond milk

1 cup shredded cheddar cheese
1 tsp garlic powder
Salt, to taste

Directions:

1. For broccoli: in a bowl, add all ingredients and toss to coat well.
2. In the bottom of Instant Pot, arrange a steamer basket and pour 1 cup of water.
3. Place the broccoli into the steamer basket.
4. Secure the lid and place the pressure valve to "Seal" position.
5. Select "Manual" and cook under "Low Pressure" for about 10 minutes.
6. Select the "Cancel" and carefully do a "Natural" release.
7. Meanwhile, for cheese sauce: in a medium pan, melt butter over mediumhigh heat.
8. Add flour, beating continuously.
9. Slowly, add almond milk, beating continuously.
10. Cook for about 23 minutes or until thickened, stirring continuously.
11. Add cheese, garlic powder and salt and stir until smooth.
12. Remove the lid of Instant Pot and transfer broccoli ono serving plates.
13. To wit cheese sauce and serve.

Nutritional Value

Calories 536
Total Fat 47.9g
Carbohydrates 5g
Protein 19.3g

403. EasytoPrepare Broccoli

Preparation Time: 15 minutes
Serves: 4

Ingredients:

4 cups broccoli florets
6 minced garlic cloves
1 tbsp. butter

1 tbsp. fresh lime juice
Salt, to taste

Directions:

1. In the bottom of Instant Pot, arrange a steamer basket and pour 1 cup of water.
2. Place the broccoli into the steamer basket.
3. Secure the lid and place the pressure valve to "Seal" position.
4. Select "Manual" and cook under "Low Pressure" for about 10 minutes.
5. Select the "Cancel" and carefully do a "Natural" release.
6. Remove the lid and transfer the broccoli to a plate.
7. Remove water from the pot and with paper towels, pat dry.
8. Place the butter in the Instant Pot and select "Sauté". Then add the garlic and cook for about 30 seconds.
9. Add the broccoli and lime juice and cook for about 30 seconds.
10. Stir in salt and cook for about 1 minute.
11. Select the "Cancel" and serve.

Nutritional Value

Calories 64
Total Fat 3.2g
Carbohydrates 1.9g
Protein 2.9g

404. Luscious Broccoli Casserole

Preparation Time: 1 HOUR 4 minutes
Serves: 6

Ingredients:

2 tbsp. butter
1 chopped small yellow onion
4 minced garlic cloves
1 cup chopped broccoli florets
4 organic eggs
¼ cup unsweetened coconut milk
Salt, to taste
1 tsp freshly grated lemon zest

1 tbsp. chopped fresh Italian parsley
1 tsp chopped fresh thyme
1½ cups shredded cheddar cheese

Directions:

1. Grease 1½ quart casserole dish that will fit in an Instant Pot. Keep aside.
2. Place the butter in the Instant Pot and select "Sauté". Then add the onion and garlic, and cook for about 7 minutes.
3. Add the broccoli and cook for about 4 minutes.
4. Select the "Cancel" and transfer the broccoli mixture to a large bowl.
5. In a large bowl, add remaining ingredients except for cheese and beat until well combined.
6. Add broccoli mixture and cheese and stir to combine.
7. Place the mixture into prepared casserole dish evenly.
8. With the glass lid, cover the casserole dish.
9. In the bottom of Instant Pot, arrange a steamer trivet and pour 1 cup of water.
10. Place the casserole dish on top of the trivet.
11. Secure the lid and place the pressure valve to "Seal" position.
12. Select "Manual" and cook under "High Pressure" for about 23 minutes.
13. Select the "Cancel" and carefully do a "Natural" release.
14. Remove the lid and serve warm.

Nutritional Value

Calories 226
Total Fat 18.6g
Carbohydrates 0.68g
Protein 11.7g

405. BetterThanReal Mash

Preparation Time: 18 minutes
Serves: 8

Ingredients:

½ cup homemade chicken broth
1 chopped head cauliflower
2 tbsp. plain Greek yogurt
Salt and ground black pepper, to taste
2 tsp melted butter
2 tbsp. chopped chives

Directions:

1. In the bottom of Instant Pot, arrange a steamer basket and pour broth.
2. Place the cauliflower into the steamer basket.
3. Secure the lid and place the pressure valve to "Seal" position.
4. Select "Manual" and cook under "High Pressure" for about 3 minutes.
5. Select the "Cancel" and carefully do a "Quick" release.
6. Remove the lid and transfer the cauliflower into a food processor.
7. Add yogurt, salt and black pepper and pulse until smooth.
8. Transfer the mashed cauliflower to a serving bowl.
9. Drizzle with melted ghee and serve with the garnishing of chives.

Nutritional Value

Calories 40
Total Fat 1.2g
Carbohydrates 0.75g
Protein 2.7g

406. Spicy Cauliflower

Preparation Time: 22 minutes
Serves: 4

Ingredients:

2 roughly chopped tomatoes
½ chopped small onion
1 green chile
1 tsp olive oil
1 tsp ground cumin
½ tsp ground turmeric
½ tsp paprika
Salt and freshly ground black pepper, to taste

1 cut into small florets large head cauliflower
½ cup water
1 tbsp. chopped fresh cilantro

Directions:

1. In a food processor, add tomato, onion and green chile and pulse until smooth.
2. Place the oil in the Instant Pot and select "Sauté". Then add the pureed onion mixture and cook for about 23 minutes.
3. Add spices and cook for about 1 minute.
4. Select the "Cancel" and stir in cauliflower and water.
5. Secure the lid and place the pressure valve to "Seal" position.
6. Select "Manual" and cook under "Low Pressure" for about 23 minutes.
7. Select the "Cancel" and carefully do a Quick release.
8. Remove the lid and serve.

Nutritional Value

Calories 74
Total Fat 1.7
Carbohydrates 3.37g
Protein 4.5g

407. Veggie Mac and Cheese

Preparation Time: 23 minutes
Serves: 4

Ingredients:

2 cups grated into rice consistency cauliflower
½ cup shredded sharp cheddar cheese
½ cup halfandhalf
2 tbsp. cream cheese
Salt and freshly ground black pepper, to taste

Directions:

1. In a heatproof bowl that will fit in an Instant Pot, add all ingredients and stir to combine.
2. With a piece of foil, cover the bowl.
3. In the bottom of Instant Pot, arrange a

steamer trivet and pour 1½ cups of water.

4. Place the casserole dish on top of the trivet.
5. Secure the lid and place the pressure valve to "Seal" position.
6. Select "Manual" and cook under "Low Pressure" for about 5 minutes.
7. Meanwhile, preheat the oven to broiler.
8. Select the "Cancel" and carefully do a "Natural" release for about 10 minutes and then do a "Quick" release.
9. Remove the lid transfer the bowl to a counter.
10. Remove the foil and broil for about 23 minutes.
11. Remove from oven and serve hot.

Nutritional Value

Calories 126
Total Fat 10g
Carbohydrates 1.07g
Protein 5.8g

408.Keto Soufflé

Preparation Time: 27 minutes
Serves: 6

Ingredients:

2 eggs
2ounce softened cream cheese
1 cup sharp cheddar cheese
½ cup Asiago cheese
½ cup plain yogurt
2 tbsp. heavy cream
1 chopped head cauliflower
¼ cup minced fresh chives
2 tbsp. softened butter

Directions:

1. Grease 1¼ quart casserole dish that will fit in an Instant Pot. Keep aside.
2. In a food processor, add eggs, cream cheese, cheddar cheese, Asiago cheese, yogurt and heavy cream and pulse until smooth and frothy.

3. Add cauliflower and pulse until chunky.
4. Gently, fold in chives and butter.
5. Transfer the mixture to prepared casserole dish.
6. In the bottom of Instant Pot, arrange a steamer trivet and pour 1 cup of water.
7. Place the casserole dish on top of the trivet.
8. Secure the lid and place the pressure valve to "Seal" position.
9. Select "Manual" and cook under "High Pressure" for about 12 minutes.
10. Select the "Cancel" and carefully do a "Natural" release for about 10 minutes and then do a "Quick" release.
11. Remove the lid and serve.

Nutritional Value

Calories 234
Total Fat 17.5g
Carbohydrates 1.48g
Protein 11.7g

409.Indian Veggie Platter

Preparation Time: 22 minutes
Serves: 6

Ingredients:

4 dried red chilies
2 tbsp. shredded coconut
1 tsp coriander seeds
1 tsp cumin seeds
½ tsp mustard seeds
¼ tsp fenugreek seeds
½ tsp paprika
2 roughly chopped tomatoes
½ roughly chopped small yellow onion
5 chopped garlic cloves
Salt, to taste
2 tbsp. butter
3 cups cauliflower
3 cups green beans
1 cup seeded and chopped bell pepper
2 cups water

Directions:

1. Heat a nonstick frying pan over medium heat and sauté red chilies, coconut and spices for about 12 minutes.
2. Remove from heat and keep aside to cool slightly.
3. In a spice grinder, add coconut mixture and grind into a coarse powder.
4. In a blender, add spice mixture, tomato, onion, garlic and salt and pulse until smooth.
5. Place the butter in the Instant Pot and select "Sauté". Then add the pureed tomato mixture and cook for about 45 minutes.
6. Select the "Cancel" and stir in veggies and water.
7. Secure the lid and place the pressure valve to "Seal" position.
8. Select "Manual" and cook under "Low Pressure" for about 1415 minutes.
9. Select the "Cancel" and carefully do a Natural release.
10. Remove the lid and serve.

Nutritional Value

Calories 93
Total Fat 4.9g
Carbohydrates 1.95g
Protein 3.1g

410. Okra Pilaf

Preparation Time: 10 minutes
Cooking Time: 25 minutes
Serves: 4

Ingredients:

2 cups okra, sliced
4 bacon slices, chopped
2 teaspoons paprika
1 cup brown rice
1 cup tomatoes, cored and chopped
2¼ cups water
Salt and ground black pepper, to taste

Directions:

Set the Instant Pot on Sauté mode, add the bacon, and brown it for 2 minutes. Add the okra, stir, and cook for 5 minutes. Add the paprika and rice, stir, and cook for 2 minutes. Add the salt, pepper, water, and tomatoes, stir, cover, and cook for 16 minutes. Release the pressure, uncover the Instant Pot, divide pilaf among plates, and serve.

Nutritional Values Per serving

Calories: 300
Fat: 11
Fiber: 4.2
Carbs: 41
Protein: 7.8

411. Okra and Corn

Preparation Time: 10 minutes
Cooking Time: 17 minutes
Serves: 6

Ingredients:

1 pound okra, trimmed
6 scallions, chopped
3 green bell peppers, seeded and chopped
Salt and ground black pepper, to taste
2 tablespoons vegetable oil
1 teaspoon sugar
28 ounces canned diced tomatoes
1 cup corn kernels

Directions:

Set the Instant Pot on Sauté mode, add the oil, and heat it up. Add the scallions and bell peppers, stir, and cook for 5 minutes. Add the okra, salt, pepper, sugar, and tomatoes, stir, cover, and cook on the Manual setting for 10 minutes. Release the pressure fast, uncover, add the corn, cover the Instant Pot again and cook on the Manual setting for 2 minutes. Release the pressure, transfer the okra mixture on plates, and serve.

Nutritional Values Per serving

Calories: 140
Fat: 5
Fiber: 6

Carbs: 22
Protein: 4
Sugar: 9

412. Fennel Risotto

Preparation Time: 10 minutes
Cooking Time: 10 minutes
Serves: 2

Ingredients:

1½ cups Arborio rice
1 yellow onion, peeled and chopped
3 cups chicken stock
1 fennel bulb, trimmed and chopped
2 tablespoons butter
1 tablespoon extra virgin olive oil
¼ cup white wine
Salt and ground black pepper, to taste
½ teaspoon thyme, dried
3 tablespoons tomato paste
⅓ cup Parmesan cheese, grated

Directions:

Set the Instant Pot on Sauté mode, add the butter and melt it. Add the fennel and onion, stir, sauté for 4 minutes, and transfer to a bowl. Add the oil to the Instant Pot and heat it up. Add the rice, stir, and cook for 3 minutes. Add the tomato paste, stock, fennel, onions, wine, salt, pepper, and thyme, stir, cover, and cook on the Manual setting for 8 minutes. Release the pressure, uncover, add cheese, stir, divide among plates, and serve.

Nutritional Values Per serving

Calories: 200
Fat: 10
Fiber: 2
Carbs: 20
Protein: 12

413. Kale and Bacon

Preparation Time: 10 minutes

Cooking Time: 10 minute
Serves: 4

Ingredients:

6 bacon slices, chopped
1 tablespoon vegetable oil
1 onion, peeled and sliced thin
6 garlic cloves, peeled and chopped
1½ cups chicken stock
1 tablespoon brown sugar
2 tablespoons apple cider vinegar
10 ounces kale leaves, chopped
1 teaspoon red chili peppers
1 teaspoon liquid smoke
Salt and ground black pepper, to taste

Directions:

Set the Instant Pot on Sauté mode, add the oil, and heat it up. Add the bacon, stir, and cook for 1-2 minutes. Add the onion, stir, and cook for 3 minutes. Add the garlic, stir, and cook for 1 minute. Add the vinegar, stock, sugar, liquid smoke, red chilies, salt, pepper, kale, stir, cover, and cook on the Manual setting for 5 minutes. Release the pressure fast, uncover, divide among plates, and serve.

Nutritional Values Per serving

Calories: 140
Fat: 7
Fiber: 1
Carbs: 7
Protein: 2

414. Steamed Leeks

Preparation Time: 10 minutes
Cooking Time: 10 minutes
Serves: 4

Ingredients:

4 leeks, washed, roots and ends cut off
Salt and ground black pepper, to taste
⅓ cup water
1 tablespoon butter

Directions:

Put the leeks into the Instant Pot, add the water, butter, salt, and pepper, stir, cover, and cook on the Steam setting for 5 minutes. Release the pressure, uncover the Instant Pot, set it on Sauté mode, and cook the leeks for 5 minutes. Divide among plates, and serve.

Nutritional Values Per serving

Calories: 70
Fat: 4
Fiber: 1.4
Carbs: 10
Protein: 1.2

415. Crispy Potatoes

Preparation Time: 10 minutes
Cooking Time: 7 minutes
Serves: 4

Ingredients:

½ cup water
1 pound Yukon gold potatoes, cubed
Salt and ground black pepper, to taste
2 tablespoons butter
Juice of ½ lemon
¼ cup parsley leaves, chopped

Directions:

Put the water into the Instant Pot, add the potatoes in the steamer basket, cover, and cook on the Steam setting for 5 minutes. Release the pressure naturally, uncover the Instant Pot, and set it on Sauté mode. Add the butter, lemon juice, parsley, salt, and pepper, stir, and cook for 2 minutes. Transfer to plates, and serve.

Nutritional Values Per serving

Calories: 132
Fat: 1
Fiber: 0
Carbs: 23
Protein: 3

416. Turnips and Carrots

Preparation Time: 5 minutes
Cooking Time: 9 minutes
Serves: 4

Ingredients:

2 turnips, peeled and sliced
3 carrots, peeled and sliced
1 small onion, peeled and chopped
1 teaspoon cumin
1 tablespoon extra virgin olive oil
1 cup water
Salt and ground black pepper, to taste
1 teaspoon lemon juice

Directions:

Set the Instant Pot on Sauté mode, add the oil, and heat it up. Add the onion, stir, and sauté for 2 minutes. Add the turnips, carrots, cumin, and lemon juice, stir, and cook for 1 minute. Add the salt, pepper, and water, stir, cover, and cook on the Steam setting for 6 minutes. Release the pressure, uncover the Instant Pot, divide the turnips and carrots among plates, and serve.

Nutritional Values Per serving

Calories: 70
Fat: 0
Fiber: 1
Carbs: 0.4
Protein: 2

417. Spicy Turnips

Preparation Time: 10 minutes
Cooking Time: 22 minutes
Serves: 4

Ingredients:

20 ounces turnips, peeled and chopped
1 teaspoon garlic, peeled and minced
1 teaspoon ginger, grated
2 yellow onions, peeled and chopped
2 tomatoes, cored and chopped
1 teaspoon sugar
1 teaspoon cumin

1 teaspoon coriander
2 green chilies, chopped
½ teaspoon turmeric
1 cup water
2 tablespoons butter
Salt, to taste
½ cup fresh cilantro, chopped

Directions:

Set the Instant Pot on Sauté mode, add the butter, and melt it. Add the green chilies, garlic, and ginger, stir, and cook for 1 minute. Add the onions, stir, and cook 3 minutes. Add the salt, tomatoes, turmeric, cumin, and coriander, stir, and cook 3 minutes. Add the turnips and water, stir, cover, and cook on Steam mode for 15 minutes. Release the pressure, uncover the Instant Pot, add the sugar, and coriander, stir, divide among plates, and serve.

Nutritional Values Per serving

Calories: 80
Fat: 2.4
Fiber: 4
Carbs: 12
Protein: 3

418. Roasted Potatoes

Preparation Time: 10 minutes
Cooking Time: 17 minutes
Serves: 4

Ingredients:

2 pounds baby potatoes
5 tablespoons vegetable oil
Salt and ground black pepper, to taste
1 rosemary sprig
5 garlic cloves
½ cup stock

Directions:

Set the Instant Pot on Sauté mode, add the oil, and heat it up. Add the potatoes, rosemary, and garlic, stir, and brown them for 10 minutes. Prick each potato with a fork, add the stock, salt, and pepper, to the Instant Pot, cover, and

cook on the Manual setting for 7 minutes. Release the pressure, uncover the Instant Pot, divide the potatoes among plates, and serve.

Nutritional Values Per serving

Calories: 50
Fat: 1.4
Fiber: 1
Carbs: 7.4
Protein: 1

419. Zucchinis and Tomatoes

Preparation Time: 10 minutes
Cooking Time: 12 minutes
Serves: 4

Ingredients:

6 zucchini, roughly chopped
2 yellow onions, chopped
1 tablespoon vegetable oil
1 cup tomato puree
1 pound cherry tomatoes, cut into halves
A drizzle of olive oil
Salt and ground black pepper, to taste
2 garlic cloves, minced
1 bunch basil, chopped

Directions:

Set the Instant Pot on Sauté mode, add the vegetable oil, and heat it up. Add the onion, stir, and cook for 5 minutes. Add the tomatoes, tomato puree, zucchini, salt, and pepper, stir, cover, and cook on the Steam setting for 5 minutes. Release the pressure, uncover the Instant Pot, add the garlic and basil, stir, and divide among plates. Drizzle some olive oil at the end, and serve.

Nutritional Values Per serving

Calories: 155
Fat: 2
Fiber: 4
Carbs: 12
Protein: 22

420. Stuffed Tomatoes

Preparation Time: 10 minutes
Cooking Time: 10 minutes
Serves: 4

Ingredients:

4 tomatoes, tops cut off and flesh removed
Salt and ground black pepper, to taste
1 yellow onion, peeled and chopped
1 tablespoon butter
2 tablespoons celery, chopped
½ cup mushrooms, chopped
1 slice of bread, crumbled
1 cup cottage cheese
¼ teaspoon caraway seeds
1 tablespoon fresh parsley, chopped
½ cup water

Directions:

Chop the tomato flesh and put it in a bowl. Heat up a pan with the butter over medium-high heat, add the onion and celery, stir, and cook for 3 minutes. Add the tomato flesh, and mushrooms, stir, and cook for 1 minute. Add the salt, pepper, bread, cheese, caraway seeds, and parsley, stir, and cook for 4 minutes. Fill each tomato shell with this mix and arrange them in the steamer basket of the Instant Pot. Add the water to the Instant Pot, cover, and cook on the Manual setting for 2 minutes. Release the pressure fast, uncover the Instant Pot, transfer stuffed tomatoes to plates, and serve.

Nutritional Values Per serving

Calories: 140
Fat: 3
Fiber: 1.4
Carbs: 10
Protein: 4

421. Sweet Potato and Baby Carrot Medley

Preparation Time: 30 minutes
Serves: 4

Ingredients

1 tsp dried Oregano
2 tbsp Olive Oil
½ cup Veggie Broth
1 Onion, finely chopped
2 pounds Sweet Potatoes, cubed
2 pounds Baby Carrots, halved

Directions

Heat olive oil and cook onions for 3 minutes, on SAUTÉ mode at High. Stir in the carrots and cook for 3 more minutes. Add potatoes, carrots, broth, and oregano. Seal the lid, set on PRESSURE COOK/MANUAL for 15 minutes at High. Once the cooking is over, do a quick pressure release.

Nutritional Values Per serving:

Calories 415
Carbs 78g
Fat 8g
Protein 7g

422. The Easiest Ratatouille

Preparation Time: 20 minutes
Serves: 4

Ingredients

1 Zucchini, sliced
2 Tomatoes, sliced
1 tbsp Balsamic Vinegar
1 Eggplant, sliced
1 Onion, sliced
1 tbsp dried Thyme
2 tbsp Olive Oil
2 Garlic Cloves, minced
1 cup Water

Directions

1. Add the garlic to a springform pan. Arrange the veggies in a circle. Sprinkle them with thyme and drizzle with olive oil. Pour water in your pressure cooker. Place the pan inside on a trivet. Seal the lid.
2. Cook for 6 minutes on PRESSURE

COOK/MANUAL at High. Release the pressure naturally, for 10 minutes.

Nutritional Values Per serving:

Calories 104
Carbs 11g
Fat 7
Protein 2g

423. Tamari Tofu with Sweet Potatoes and Broccoli

Preparation Time: 10 minutes
Serves: 4

Ingredients

1 pound Tofu, cubed
3 Garlic Cloves, minced
2 tbsp Tamari
2 tbsp Sesame Seeds
2 tsp Sesame Oil
2 tbsp Tahini
1 tbsp Rice Vinegar
1 cup Vegetable Stock
2 cups Onion slices
2 cups Broccoli Florets
1 cup diced Sweet Potato
2 tbsp Sriracha

Directions

Heat oil and cook onion and sweet potatoes for 2 minutes, on SAUTÉ mode at High. Add garlic and half of the sesame seeds, and cook for a minute. Stir in tamari, broth, tofu, and vinegar. Seal the lid, select PRESSURE COOK/MANUAL for 8 minutes at High pressure. Do a quick pressure release. Open the lid and add in broccoli, and cook for 2 minutes, lid off. Stir in sriracha and tahini before serving.

Nutritional Values Per serving:

Calories 250
Carbs 22g
Fat 12g
Protein 17g

424. On-the-go Tomato Zoodles

Preparation Time: 20 minutes
Serves: 4

Ingredients

4 cups Zoodles
2 Garlic Cloves, minced
8 cups Boiling Water
1 tbsp Olive Oil
½ cup Tomato Paste
2 cups canned Tomatoes, diced
2 tbsp chopped Basil

Directions

1. Place the zoodles in a bowl filled with boiling water. After one minute, drain them and set aside. Heat oil and cook garlic for about a minute, until fragrant, on SAUTÉ mode at High.
2. Add tomato paste, and 1 cup water and basil. Stir in the zoodles, coating them well with the sauce. Seal the lid, cook for 8 minutes on PRESSURE COOK/MANUAL at High. Do a quick pressure release.

Nutritional Values Per serving:

Calories 102
Carbs 10g
Fat 4g
Protein 2g

425. Delightful Leafy Green Risotto

Preparation Time: 20 minutes
Serves: 6

Ingredients

3 ½ cups Veggie Broth
1 cup Spinach Leaves, packed
1 cup Kale Leaves, packed
¼ cup Parmesan Cheese, grated
¼ cup diced Onion
3 tbsp Butter
2 tsp Olive Oil
1 ½ cups Arborio Rice
4 Sun-dried Tomatoes, chopped

A pinch of Nutmeg
Salt and Pepper, to taste

Directions

1. Heat oil and cook onions until soft, about 3 minutes. Add rice and cook for 3-5 minutes, on SAUTÉ at High. Pour in broth. Seal the lid, and cook for 9 minutes on PRESSURE COOK/MANUAL at High.

2. Do a quick pressure release. Stir in the remaining ingredients. Leave for a 1-2 minutes, or until greens wilt.

Nutritional Values Per serving:

Calories 272
Carbs 40g
Fat 11g
Protein 6g

426. Tropical Salsa Mash

Preparation Time: 10 minutes
Serves: 4

Ingredients

¼ cup Red Onions, chopped
1 cup Mango, chopped
1 cup Apples, chopped
1 cup Tomatoes, chopped
1 cup Pineapples, diced
2 tbsp chopped Mint
2 Jalapenos, minced
1 Garlic Clove, minced
2 tbsp Cilantro, chopped
¼ cup Lime Juice
1 tbsp Olive Oil
¼ tsp Sea Salt
¼ tsp Pepper

Directions

1. Heat oil on SAUTÉ at High, add the onions and cook for 2 minutes, until translucent. Add apples, pineapples, tomatoes, and mangos, and cook for 3 more minutes.

2. Stir in the garlic, salt, and pepper, and cook for another minute. Transfer the mixture to a bowl. Stir in the remaining ingredients.

Remove the mixture to a food processor.

3. Pulse for two seconds. The mixture should not be smooth, but chunky. Serve and enjoy!

Nutritional Values Per serving:

Calories 122
Carbs 24g
Fat 4g
Protein 2g

427. Roasted Potatoes with Gorgonzola

Preparation Time: 20 minutes
Serves: 4

Ingredients

1 ½ pounds Fingerling Potatoes,
1 cup Gorgonzola Cheese, grated
½ cup Vegetable Broth
4 tbsp Butter, melted
½ tsp Kosher Salt
½ tsp Thyme
½ tsp Cayenne Pepper

Directions

1. In your pressure cooker, add the butter, potatoes and broth. Seal the lid and switch the pressure release valve to close. Set on PRESSURE COOK/MANUAL mode and cook for 15 minutes at High pressure10 minutes.

2. Do a quick release. Sprinkle with cayenne pepper, thyme and grated Gorgonzola cheese. Serve hot.

Nutritional Values Per serving:

Calories 377
Carbs 28g
Fat 12g
Protein 11g

428. White Wine Red Peppers

Preparation Time: 15 minutes
Serves: 6

Ingredients

1 ½ pounds Red Bell Peppers, deveined and sliced
1 cup Tomato Puree
½ cup Vegetable Broth
½ tbsp miso paste
1 tbsp Garlic, crushed
½ cup Green Onions, chopped
3 tbsp Butter, melted
Sea Salt and freshly ground Black Pepper
2 tbsp White Wine

Directions

1. Melt butter on SAUTÉ at High and sauté onions, until soft, for about 3 minutes. Add garlic and stir for about a minute, until fragrant. Pour broth, tomato and pesto sauce, salt, and pepper.

2. Seal the lid, press PRESSURE COOK/MANUAL and cook for 10 minutes at High pressure. When ready, do a quick release. Season with salt, and black pepper. Serve drizzled with white wine.

Nutritional Values Per serving:

Calories 97
Carbs 7g
Fat 8g
Protein 2g

429. Leek and Swiss Chard Relish

Preparation Time: 15 minutes
Serves: 4

Ingredients

½ pound Leek, chopped
3 cups Swiss chard, chopped
2 ½ cups stock
½ cup Onions, chopped
2 Cloves Garlic, crushed
1 tbsp dry Thyme
Sea Salt and ground Black Pepper, to taste

Directions

1. Fry the leek for about 4 minutes, on SAUTÉ at High. Add in garlic and onions, and cook for 2 more minutes. Add the rest of the ingredients and seal the lid.

2. Select PRESSURE COOK/MANUAL and cook for 5 minutes at High. Do a quick release the pressure, and serve.

Nutritional Values Per serving:

Calories 324
Carbs 4g
Fat 24g
Protein 22g

430. Cheesy Acorn Squash Relish

Preparation Time: 15 minutes
Serves: 6

Ingredients

1 cup Water
1 tsp baking soda
1 cup Parmesan cheese, grated
¼ cup Milk
1 tsp Sesame Seeds, toasted
½ tsp Sea Salt
¼ tsp Black Pepper
½ cup Butter, melted
1 pound Acorn Squash, halved
2 tbsp Apple Cider Vinegar

Directions

1. Select STEAM mode, and add water and acorn squash. Drizzle with apple cider and stir in the remaining ingredients. Seal the lid, switch the pressure release valve to close and cook for 10 minutes on .

2. When it goes off, quick release the pressure. Put the squash in a food processor along with parmesan cheese, and blend until smooth, then add in the milk while the machine is running.

3. Spoon the dip into a serving bowl and sprinkle with sesame seeds to serve.

Nutritional Values Per serving:

Calories 167
Carbs 8g
Fat 15g
Protein 1g

431. Pickled Pepperoncini and Parmesan Dip

Preparation Time: 15 minutes
Serves: 10

Ingredients

1 tbsp minced pickled Pepperoncini Peppers
12 ounces Parmesan cheese, shredded
1 ½ tbsp Flour
1 cup Tomato paste
2 tsp Olive Oil
1 cup Milk
½ tsp Cayenne Pepper
½ tsp basil
Salt and Black Pepper, to taste

Directions

1. Heat oil on SAUTÉ at High. Slowly stir in flour and keep stirring until you obtain a paste. Pour the milk and stir until the mixture thickens, then bring to a boil. Add the cheese and stir until melted.

2. Add the remaining ingredients. Seal the lid, press PRESSURE COOK/MANUAL and cook for 5 minutes at High Pressure. Do a quick release the pressure.

Nutritional Values Per serving:

Calories 146
Carbs 5g
Fat 11g
Protein 8g

432. Instant Pot Vegan Jackfruit with Potato Curry

Preparation Time: 30 min, 8 servings

Ingredients

2 tablespoonscoconut oil
2 tablespoons currypowder
1 teaspoon paprika
1 teaspoon cumin
1 teaspoon turmericpowder
2 sprigs fresh thyme, or 1 teaspoon dried
1 cuponion, finely chopped
4 cloves garlic, mince
1 teaspoon fresh ginger, grated
2 green onions, chopped
20 ouncecan green jackfruit, drained and rinsed
4 medium potatoes, cubed
1 medium carrot, diced
15 ounce can coconut milk
2 cups vegetable broth, or 2 cubes vegetable bouillon plus water
1 teaspoon Italian seasoning
1/4 -1/2 teaspoon Cayennepepper, or 1 whole Scotch Bonnet pepper
1 batch dumpling optional, recipe below
1/4 cup chopped cilantro leaves, or parsley
Salt to taste, optional

Directions

1. Plug in your Instant Pot and press saute mode button. Add oil, once heated add dry spices, currypowder, paprika, cumin, turmeric, thyme and cook for a minute stirring constantly.

2. Add onion, garlic, ginger, spring onion and cook until for 2 minutesor until onionsaresoft. Add jackfruit, potato, carrots and stir to coat.

3. Add coconut milk, vegetable broth or bouillon plus water, Italian seasoning, cayenne pepper, and dumplings stir.

4. Close Instant Pot lid and press manual mode for 10 minutes. When finished, allow Instant Pot to natural release for 10 minutes. Carefully release the knob to release the remaining pressure. Remove lid, stir in cilantro leaves, crush someof thepotatoes to thicken curry and check seasonings.

Nutritional Values Per serving

267 kcal
Fat: 17 g
Protein: 5 g

Carbohydrate: 27 g

433. Vegan Baked Beans

Prep+Cook Time:1 hr 25 mins,
Servings: 10 servings

Ingredients

Beans:

> *1 pound 16 oz dried small navy beans, rinsed and drained*
> *6 cups water*

Sauce:

> *3/4 cup molasses*
> *1/2 cup brown sugar*
> *3/4 cup ketchup*
> *3/4 teaspoon salt*
> *2 tablespoons apple cider vinegar*
> *1 1/2 tablespoons vegan Worcestershire sauce*
> *2 teaspoons Sriracha hot sauce*

Other:

> *1 medium yellow onion, chopped*
> *4 cloves garlic, minced*

Directions

1. Put the rinsed beansand 6 cups of water into your Instant Pot. Put the lid on, closesteam valve and set to the "bean" setting for 60 minutes. Do a natural release when done and carefully drain the beans. Set aside.
2. Whisk all sauce Ingredients together in a bowl. Set aside.
3. Pour a few tablespoonsof water or olive oil into the Instant Pot. Turn the saute setting, and add theonion and garlic. Stir frequently for 2-3 minutes, until the onions have softened.
4. Turn off the saute, and add thesauceand drained beans to the Instant Pot. Give everything a □uick stir.
5. Put on the lid, close thesteam valve and set to "bean" setting for 15 minutes. Once done, do a natural releaseand lift the lid carefully.

Let sit for 15-30 minutes if possible before serving, as they will thicken up as they sit. Enjoy!

Nutrition Info:

Calories: 285 kcal

434. Vegan Carrot Giger Soup

Preparation Time: 30 minutes,
Servings: 5

Ingredients

> *1.5 tablespoonsgrapeseedoilorpreferredoil*
> *1 medium onion , diced*
> *4 cloves garlic , minced*
> *1.5 tablespoons fresh ginger , grated*
> *1 teaspoon dried thyme*
> *1/2 teaspoon ground coriander*
> *1/2 teaspoon crushed red pepper *optional*
> *2 bay leaves*
> *2 pounds carrots about 6 large, rough chopped*
> *4 cups vegetable broth , low sodium*
> *1 teaspoon sea salt , more to taste*
> *Fresh cracked pepper to taste *optional*
> *1 cupcanned coconut milk , full-fat*
> *1-2 tablespoons lime juice sub lemon*

Directions

1. Turn on the sauté feature of your Instant Pot and add the oil. When heated, add the onions and sauté until slightly translucent, about 2-3 minutes.
2. Add the garlic and ginger, sauté for 1-2 minutes.
3. Now add the thyme, coriander and crushed red pepper. Sauté for 30-60 seconds.
4. Cancel the sauté function and add the broth, carrots, bay leaves, salt, and cracked pepper.
5. Closeand secure the lid. Turn the steam release handle to the Sealing position. Push the Pressure Cooker Manual Setting button

to high pressure and set the time to 6 minutes by using the + or - button. Thescreen will then display ON while thepreheating is in progress thiscould take 8-12 minutes. When the Instant Pot hascome to pressure, you'll see the 6 minutes displayed on thescreen again.

6. Thecooker will beep when the time is up. Don't touch anything, just let the pressure naturally release for 2-3 minutes. Now carefully turn thesteam release handle to the Venting position It will loudly spurt out lots of steam and some water. Once the Float Valve goes down you can carefully open the lid.

7. Remove the bay leaves and add thecoconut milk & lime juice.

8. Using an immersion blender or regular blender, blend until creamyand smooth. Taste for seasoning and add more if needed.

9. If thesoup is too thick for your taste, you can add a small amount of vegetable broth to thin it out.

Nutrition Info: *Serving: 2cups,*

Calories: 268kcal
Carbohydrates: 26g
Protein: 7g
Fat: 16g

435. Vegan Black Eyed Peas Curry

Preparation Time: 30 mins,

Servings: 5 servings

Ingredients

1 cupdriedblackeyedpeas , soakedinwaterforabout 1-2 hoursseenotesbelow
2 cupswater
3 driedcurryleaves
1/8 teaspmustardseeds
4 cloves garlic
1/2 medium white onion , finely chopped
2.5 tbsp tomatopaste , from can
1 teasp ground cumin

1 teasp ground coriander
1/4 teasp ground turmeric
3 teasp jaggery , or brown sugar
2 teasp fresh lemon juice
chili powder , optional to taste
cooking oil , such as grapeseed or avocado oil
salt
fresh cilantro , finelychopped

Directions

1. Select the Saute button normal on the Instant Pot and add 2 teasp cooking oil.

2. Once the oil is hot, add the mustard seeds and curry leaves. Fry for a few seconds until fragrant.

3. Add the onions and garlic. Saute until fragrant and the onions start to become translucent. Be sure not to burn either. If you see this happening add moreoil or turn down thesaute heat.

4. Quicklyadd the tomato paste, ground cumin, and ground coriander. Combineand cook for a minute mixing frequently.

5. Drain the soaked black eyed peasand add them into the Instant Pot.

6. Mix in the water, turmeric, chili powder if using, jaggery, fresh lemon juice, and 1 teasp salt.

7. Close the Instant Pot lid, select the Pressure Cook button to cook on high. Set the timer for about 13-15 minutes be sure to turn the 'keep warm' button off unless enjoying immediately.

8. When the time is up, allow thepressure to release naturally.

9. Once the pressure has been released, remove the lid, and press the Saute normal-low button again on the Instant Pot. The black eyed peas should be fully cooked.

10. Simmer for a few more minutes until thecurry becomes thick.

11. Add salt to taste. Also feel free to adjust the amount of lemon juice and jaggery as needed.

12. Turn the Instant Pot off. Add freshlychopped cilantro and serve hot as is, over cooked rice, or alongside some Naan

or fresh roti!

Nutrition Info:

Calories 131
Sodium 75mg
Potassium 485mg
TotalCarbohydrates 24g
DietaryFiber 4g
Sugars 4g
Protein 8g

436.5 Ingredient Vegan Queso

Preparation Time: 10 mins
Serves: 10 servings

Ingredients

*2 cups raw cashew pieces, soaked in hot water
for 5 minutes*
1/2 cup water
*4 tablespoons fresh lemon juice; from about 2
small lemons*
2 teaspoonssalt, or to taste
*1/2 cup **Nutrition** Infoal yeast*
28 ouncecanned Rotel tomatoesand green chiles

Directions

1. Add the drained soaked cashews, water, lemon juice, salt and **Nutrition** Infoal yeast to a high powered blender. Drain the juice from the tomatoesand green chilesand add the liquid to the blender as well don't add the tomatoesand green chilesyet. Blend on high for a few minutes until very smooth.

2. Add the "cheese" sauce and the Rotel tomatoes and green chiles to a medium pot. Stir well and warm gentlyover low-medium heat. Becareful not to burn the□ueso; stir frequently while warming. The mixture will thicken slightly.

3. Serve while warm with tortillachipsand enjoy!

Nutritional Values Per serving

Calories: 160 kcal

437. Instant Pot Vegan Refried Beans

Prep+Cook Time:45 mins,
Servings: 8 people

Ingredients

1 mediumonion, chopped
4 clovesgarlic, minced
1 pounddrypintobeans
6 cups water
1 teaspoon chili powder
1 teaspoon cumin
2 teaspoonssalt, or to taste

Directions

1. In the Instant Pot, turn on the Saute feature. Add the onion, garlic and a few tablespoons of water. Cook for 4-5 minutes, until translucent and fragrant. Turn off the Instant Pot for a moment.

2. Add the dry pinto beans, water, spices and salt to the pot. Give it a little stir.

3. Place the lid on the Instant Pot and make sure the valve is set to "sealing". Set to manual, high pressure for 35 minutes.

4. Once the timer goes off, allow the pressure to release naturally for at least 10 minutes. Then, you may manually release the rest of the pressure.

5. Drain about 2 cups of the liquid, but reserve it in a bowl.

6. Use an immersion blender to blend the beans to the desired consistency. Add in more of the cooking li□uid if you need it. The beans will appear runny at first, but will thicken considerably as they cool.

Recipe Notes :

1. The beans freeze well. Freeze in containers glass or plastic, leavingalittle roomontopfor expansion.

2. Ifyouwantthickerrefriedbeans, drain evenmore liquidbefore blending, butreserve it so you can addmoreifthey are

too thick.

Nutritional Value Per Serving:

Calories: 200 kcal

438. Instant Pot Vegetable Soup

Preparation Time: 17 minutes,
Servings 8 2 cup servings

Ingredients

1 teaspoon canola oil
1 medium onion finely diced
2 teaspoons minced garlic
2 teaspoons Italian seasoning
2 teaspoonssalt
1/4 teaspoon black pepper
6 cups low sodium chicken broth
1 lb potatoes chopped about 3-4 medium
3 largecarrotspeeled and chopped
2 ribs celerysliced
1 1/2 cups fired roasted diced tomatoesor other flavor -- 398ml/13oz
1 cup fresh green beans cut in thirds
1 cup finelychopped spinach

Directions

1. Heat oil in Instant Pot on saute mode. Add onion, cook and stir until softened.

2. Turn the Instant Pot off and add the garlic, Italian seasoning, salt and pepper. Stir and cook for 1 minute on the residual heat.

3. Add chicken broth to the still hot pan, and scrape the bottom with a spoon to remove any left behind bits.

4. Add potatoes, carrots, celery, tomatoes and green beans and stir.

5. Put the lid on, turn the valve to sealing, and select Manual or Pressure Cook for 2 minutes. It will take about 15 minutes to come to pressure and begin counting down.

6. Once the cook time is over, let pressure release naturally for 8-10 minutes before opening the valve and removing the lid this is to prevent the splatter that can come

when pressure cooking soup.

7. Stir in the spinach, adjust seasonings to taste and serve.

Nutrition InfoL:

Calories 101 CaloriesfromFat 9
TotalFat 1g
Sodium 743mg
Potassium 566mg
TotalCarbohydrates 17g
DietaryFiber 3g
Sugars 3g
Protein 6g

439. Instant Pot Vegan Butter Chicken with Tofu

Preparation Time: 30 mins,
Servings: 6 servings

Ingredients

1 medium onion chopped
4 cloves garlic chopped
1-inch piece ginger chopped
2 tsp paprika Kashmiri chili powder is a good substitute
1 cup water or vegetablestock
1 16 oz block superfirm tofu, cut into 1/2-inch cubes extra firm tofu is fine. Press out all of the water before use
1 tsp vegetable oil
2 cupsor a 14.5 oz can pureed tomatoes or puree two large tomatoes
2 tsp coriander powder
1/2 tspcayenne use more or less based on your preference
Salt to taste
2 tbsp kasoori methi dry fenugreek leaves -- you can leave this out, but tryand use it for the best flavor
2 tsp garam masala
1 tsp maple syrup or sugar
2 tbsp raw cashews If nut-free, use 2 tbsp vegan butter instead of thecashew cream
2 tbsp lemon or lime juice
2 tbsp coriander leaves for garnish

Directions

1. Blend the cashews with 1/4 cup water or vegetable stock into a smooth paste and set aside.

2. Blend the onions, garlic, ginger and the paprika with 3/4 cup water or vegetable stock. Place the tofu cubes in a bowl and add half a cup of the onion-ginger-garlic-paprika puree to the bowl. Toss the tofu cubes in the puree.

3. Set the Instant Pot to the saute function. Add the oil and when it's hot, add the tofu cubes. Saute, stirring fre□uently, about 2-3 minutes. Then add the remaining onion-ginger-garlic-paprika puree, the tomato puree, coriander powder, cayenne and kasoori methi. Add salt to taste, give it a stir, and put the lid on. Set the Instant Pot to cook at high pressure for 10 minutes.

4. After cooking is complete,release pressure manually after 10 minutes. Open the lid.

5. If the butter tofu is too thick, you can thin it out with more vegetable stock or water. Stir in the garam masala, cashew cream or vegan butter, maple syrup or sugar and lemon or lime juice. Add more salt if needed. Heat the butter chicken tofu, especially if you added more stock or water, by turning the saute function back on. Once it's warmed through, remove to a bowl, garnish with coriander leaves, and serve hot with naan or roti or rice.

Recipe Notes

Make this □uick and easy butter tofu in a saucepan. Saute the tofu and the onion-ginger-garlic mixture in oil for about five minutes over medium-high heat, then add the tomatoes, saute until they turn a coupleof shades darker and moisture hasevaporated, then add spicesand proceed. Let thecurrycook about 10 minutes, then proceed with step 5.

Nutrition Info:

Calories 183
CaloriesfromFat 71
TotalFat 7.9g
Potassium 455mg

TotalCarbohydrates 15.3g
DietaryFiber 2.5g
Sugars 5.9g
Protein 14.7g

440. Chickpea Potato Soup in Instant Pot

Prep+Cook Time: 30 mins,
Servings: 3

Ingredients

1/4 cup water or broth
1/2 onion chopped
3 cloves of garlic
1/2 cupchopped tomato
1/8 tsp fennel seeds
1/2 tsp onion powder
1/4 tsp garlic powder
1/8 to 1/4 tsp cinnamon
1/2 tsp oregano
1/2 tsp thymeor use a tsp fresh rosemary
1 largepotato cubed smalll use yukon gold or white,
3/4 cup carrots
1/2 cup other veggies likepeppers mushrooms, zucchini, broccoli
1.25 cupscooked chickpeasor 1 15 oz can chickpeas drained
1/2 to 3/4 tspsalt
1 cup water
1 cup non dairy milk such ascoconut milk almond milk or cashew milk
2 cups Spinach
freshly ground black pepper for garnish , lemon juice optional

Directions

1. Add broth in the Instant Pot on saute. Add onion and garlic cook until golden. Deglaze with a tbsp of water in between if needed. See Stove top Saucepan instructions in Recipe note section below.

2. Add the chopped tomato and mix. Add the spices and herbs and mix in.

3. Add veggies, chickpeas, salt, non dairy milk ** and water and mix.

4. Pressure cook for manual, hi 5 minutes, let

the pressure release naturally.

5. Fold in spinach and saute for a minute. Add thick cashew cream for creamier soup and mix in. Add black pepper and lemon juice. Taste and adjust salt and flavor. Serve with crackers, garlic rolls or garlic bread.

Recipe Notes

1. Variations: Use other cooked beans or lentils of choice. If using kale, add it with the potatoes. If using red lentils, use 1/3 cup dried.

2. Saucepan: Follow steps 1 to 3 in a saucepan over medium heat. Add 1.5 cups of water instead of 1 cup. Partially over and cook for 12 to 15 mins or until potatoes are tender. Add in the spinach and continue to simmer for 2 mins.

3. Certain non dairy milks or brands tend to separate under pressure, so use all water or broth and add some cashew cream in the end or blend up a portion of the soup to make a creamy thick soup.

4. Or mix in 2 tsp flour into the milk and then add to the instant pot.

Nutritional Values Per serving

Calories 157
Calories from Fat 18
Total Fat 2g
Sodium 569mg
Sugars 4g
Protein 7g

441. Instant Pot Vegan Curried Butternut Squash Soup

Prep+Cook Time: 50 mins
Serves: 4 people

Ingredients

Soup

1 teaspoon extra-virgin oliveoil
1 large onion , chopped
2 cloves garlic , minced

1 tablespoon currypowder
1 3 pound butternut s□uash, peeled and cut into 1-inch cubes or use frozen
1 1/2 teaspoons fine seasalt
3 cups water
1/2 cup coconut milk coconut cream is fine, too

Optional Toppings:

Hulled pumpkin seeds
Dried cranberries

Instructions

1. Hit the "sauté" button on the Instant Pot. Add in the olive oil and onion, and sauté until tender, about 8 minutes. Add in the garlic and curry powder sauté just until fragrant, about one more minute.

2. Turn the Instant Pot off for a moment, then add the butternut s□uash, salt, and water into the pot. Cover with the lid and be sure to seal the top for pressure cooking. Select the "soup" setting, and let the soup cook at high pressure for 30 minutes.

3. When the soup is done, I like to wait 10 minutes before releasing the pressure, but I don't think that's necessary if you're in a hurry-- feel free to use the "□uick release" method by turning the valve on the lid from sealing to venting. Whichever method you use, just be sure that the pressure is totally released before attempting to remove the lid. It releases very easily when the pressure is removed.

4. Use an immersion blender to puree the soup directly in the pot, or transfer the cooked soup to a blender or food processor to blend until smooth. If using a blender, be sure to lightly cover the vent in your blender lid with a dish towel, to help the pressure from the steam release without splattering. The pressure from hot li□uids can blow the lid off your blender otherwise, and cause burns.

5. Return the blended soup to the pot and stir in the coconut milk. You can use coconut cream, if you don't mind a slightly creamier soup. Adjust any seasoning to taste at this point, I usually add a touch

more salt, and serve warm. Top with hulled pumpkin seeds and dried cranberries, if desired.

6. Leftovers can be stored in an airtight container for up to a week in the fridge.

Nutrition Info: Per Serving:

Calories: 282
Fat: 4g
Carbohydrates: 66g
Fiber: 10g
Protein: 4g

442. Instant Pot Mac and Cheese

Prep+Cook Time: 15 minutes,
Servings: 6 people

Ingredients

1 lb. macaroni
4 cups water
2 tsp prepared yellow mustard
1 tsp salt
12 oz. evaporated milk
8 oz. sharp cheddar cheese grated
¾ cup grated parmesan cheese
2 Tbsp butter
¼ tsp nutmeg
Salt and pepper to taste

Directions

1. Mix the macaroni, water, mustard, and salt in your Instant Pot. Close and lock the lid of the Instant Pot. Press "Manual" and adjust the timer to 4 minutes or half the time on the macaroni cooking Instructions. Check that the cooking pressure is on "high" and that the release valve is set to "Sealing".

2. When time is up, open the IP using "Quick Pressure Release". Stir the pasta to break it up. Add the evaporated milk, cheese, butter and nutmeg; stir until completely incorporated the and cheese has melted and coated the pasta.

3. Season to taste with salt and pepper, then serve immediately.

Nutritional Value Per Serving:

Calories 598
CaloriesfromFat 225
Protein 28g

443. Instant Pot Vegan Quinoa Burrito Bowls

Preparation Time: 25 mins
Serves: 5

Ingredients

1 teaspoon extra-virgin olive oil
1/2 red onion , diced
1 bell pepper , diced
1/2 teaspoon salt
1 teaspoon ground cumin
1 cup quinoa , rinsed well
1 cup prepared salsa
1 cup water
1 1/2 cups cooked black beans , or 1 15 oz. can, drained and rinsed
Optional toppings: Avocado , guacamole, fresh cilantro, green onions, salsa, lime wedges, shredded lettuce

Directions

1. Heat the oil in the bottom of the Instant Pot, using the "saute" setting. Saute the onions and peppers until start to soften, about 5 to 8 minutes, then add in cumin and salt and saute another minute. Turn of the Instant Pot for a moment.

2. Add in the ￼uinoa, salsa, water, and beans, then seal the lid, making sure that the switch at the top is flipped from venting to sealing. Press the "rice" button, or manually cook at low pressure for 12 minutes. Let the pressure naturally release once the cooking is over, to make sure the ￼uinoa completely absorbs the li￼uid. This takes 10 to 15 minutes.

3. Remove the lid, being careful to avoid any steam releasing from the pot, and fluff the ￼uinoa with a fork. Serve warm, with any toppings you love, such as avocado, diced onions, salsa, and shredded lettuce.

4. Leftovers can be stored in an airtight container in the fridge for up to a week. You can ꓳuickly reheat on the stove top, or serve cold!

Nutritional Values Per serving Per Serving:

Calories: 163
Fat: 2g
Carbohydrates: 28g
Fiber: 3g
Protein: 6g

444. Easy Ratatouille

Preparation Time: 16 minutes
Serves: 4

Ingredients

2 large zucchinis; sliced
4 cloves garlic; diced
2 tbsp. of thyme leaves
2 tbsp. balsamic vinegar
2 medium eggplants; sliced
4 medium tomatoes; sliced
2 small red onions; sliced
4 tbsp. olive oil
2 cups water
2 tsp. sea salt
1 tsp. black pepper

Directions:

1. Line a 6-inch springform pan with foil and place chopped garlic in the bottom.
2. Now arrange the vegetable slices, alternately, in circles,
3. Sprinkle the thyme, pepper and salt over the vegetables, Top with oil and vinegar.
4. Pour a cup of water into the instant pot and place the trivet inside,
5. Secure the lid and cook on *Manual* function for 6 minutes at high pressure,
6. Release the pressure naturally and remove the lid.
7. Remove the vegetables along with the

tin foil. Serve on a platter and enjoy.

Nutrition Values Nutritional Values Per serving

Calories:- 250
Carbohydrate:- 29.2g
Protein:- 6g
Fat:- 15.1g
Sugar:- 14.5g
Sodium:- 0.97g

445. Vegetable Teriyaki

Preparation Time: 28 minutes
Serves: 4

Ingredients

1 pound white potatoes; peeled and diced
3/4 large yellow or white onion; chopped.
1/2 tbsp. paprika
1 tsp. fresh rosemary
3/4 cups peas
1/4 cup fresh parsley; chopped.
1 ½ medium carrots; diced
1 ½ ribs celery; chopped
1 medium portabella mushroom; diced
3/4 tbsp. garlic; chopped
2 cups water
1/4cup tomato paste
1/2 tbsp. sesame oil
2 tsp. sesame seeds

Directions:

1. Put the oil, sesame seeds and all the vegetables in the instant pot and *Sauté* for 5 minutes,
2. Stir in the remaining Ingredients and secure the lid.
3. Cook on *Manual* function for 13 minutes at high pressure,
4. When it beeps; *Natural Release* the steam and remove the lid. Garnish with fresh parsley and sesame seeds and serve hot.

Nutrition Values Nutritional Values Per serving

Calories:- 202
Carbohydrate:34.5g
Protein:- 6.2g
Fat:- 5.3g
Sugar:- 9.2g
Sodium:- 54mg

446. IP Vegetable Barley

Preparation Time: 23 minutes
Serves: 6

Ingredients

10 baby Bella mushrooms; quartered
2 tbsp. oil
6 cloves garlic; minced
6 cups vegetable broth
1 cup onions; chopped.
1 cup carrots; chopped.
4 celery stalks; chopped.
1 cup water
2 bay leaves
1/2 tsp. dried thyme
1 large potato; shredded
⅔ cup pearl barley; rinsed
Salt and pepper to taste

Directions:

1. Put the onions, mushrooms, carrot and celery in the pot and cook for 5 minutes stirring constantly.
2. Add the garlic and cook for another minute,
3. Now add the thyme, bay leaves, water and broth and secure the lid.
4. Cook the mixture on the *manual* function at high pressure for 3 minutes,
5. Natural release the steam and remove the lid.
6. Stir in the potatoes and barley then cover the lid.
7. Cook on *Manual* for 5 minutes at high pressure Remove the lid and serve hot.

Nutrition Values Nutritional Values Per serving

Calories:- 245
Carbohydrate:- 37.7g
Protein:- 10.7g
Fat:- 6.5g
Sugar:- 4.5g
Sodium:- 0.79g

447. BBQ Mushroom Tacos

Preparation Time: 23 minutes
Serves: 3

Ingredients

8-ounce mushrooms chopped.
4 large guajillo chilies
2 tsp. oil
2 bay leaves
2 large onions; sliced
2 garlic cloves
2 chipotle chilies in adobo sauce
2 tsp. ground cumin
3/4 cup vegetable broth
1 tsp. apple cider vinegar
3 tsp. lime juice
1/4 tsp. sugar
1 tsp. dried oregano
1 tsp. smoked hot paprika
1/2 tsp. ground cinnamon
Salt to taste
Tacos to serve

Directions:

1. Put the oil, onion, garlic, salt and bay leaves into the instant pot and *Sauté* for 5 minutes,
2. Blend half of this mixture, in a blender, with all the spices and chilies,
3. Add the mushrooms to the remaining onions and *Sauté* for 3 minutes,
4. Pour the blended mixture into the pot and secure the lid.
5. Cook on *Manual* function for 5 minutes at high pressure,
6. *Quick Release* the steam and remove the lid. Stir well and serve with tacos,

Nutrition Values Nutritional Values

Per serving

Calories:- 160
Carbohydrate:- 22.9g
Protein:- 4.1g
Fat:- 6.7g
Sugar:- 8.2g
Sodium:- 0.51g

448. Delicious Potato Scallion Stew

Preparation Time: 13 minutes
Serves: 8

Ingredients

2 lbs. medium potatoes; diced
2 large brown onions; finely diced
4 tbsp. olive oil
1/2 tsp. ground turmeric
2 tsp. paprika
4 cups chopped; tinned tomatoes
3 cups water
2 cups vegetable stock
Cilantro garnish
4 large garlic cloves; diced
4 medium length scallions; chopped.
4 tsp. ground cumin
4 tsp. salt

Directions:

1. Put the oil and onions in the instant pot and *Sauté* for 5 minutes,
2. Stir in the remaining Ingredients and secure the lid.
3. Cook on *Manual* function for 3 minutes at high pressure,
4. *Quick Release* the steam and remove the lid.
5. Garnish with cilantro and lemon juice, Serve,

Nutrition Values Nutritional Values Per serving

Calories:- 496
Carbohydrate:- 99.9g
Protein:- 9.4g
Fat:- 7.6g

Sugar:- 4.4g
Sodium:- 1.28g

449. Spaghetti Squash.

Preparation Time: 40 minutes
Serves: 2

Ingredients

1 large spaghetti squash
1/2 tbsp. olive oil
1/4 small yellow onion; chopped.
1 jalapeño pepper; chopped
1/2 cup green onions; chopped.
1/2 cup carrots; chopped.
1/4 cup cabbage; chopped.
1 garlic clove; minced
1/2 6 oz. can sugar-free tomato sauce
1/2 tbsp. chili powder
1/2 tbsp. ground cumin
2 cups water
1/4 cup cheddar cheese; shredded
Salt and freshly ground black pepper to taste

Directions:

1. Pour the water into the instant pot and place the trivet inside,
2. Slice the squash into 2 halves and remove the seeds,
3. Place them over the trivet; skin side down and sprinkle some salt and pepper over.
4. Secure the lid and cook on *Manual* for 15 minutes at high pressure,
5. Release the pressure naturally and remove the lid. Empty the pot.
6. Shred the squash with a fork and keep the shredded pieces to one side,
7. Now put the oil, onion and garlic in the instant pot and *Sauté* for 5 minutes,
8. Stir in the remaining vegetables and stir-fry for 3 minutes,
9. Add the remaining Ingredients and secure the lid.
10. Cook on *Manual* function for 2 minutes at high pressure,
11. When it beeps; *Natural Release* the steam

and remove the lid.

12. Stir in the spaghetti squash shreds, Garnish with herbs and cheese, Serve warm.

Nutrition Values Nutritional Values Per serving

Calories:- 194
Carbohydrate:- 19.4g
Protein:- 5.4g
Fat:- 9g
Sugar:- 4.1g
Sodium:- 145mg

450.Cauliflower and Broccoli Florets

Preparation Time: 12 minutes
Serves: 3

Ingredients

1/2 pound frozen cauliflower
1/2 cup tomato paste
1/2 medium onion; diced
2 tsp. oil
1 garlic clove; minced
1/2 pound broccoli florets
1/2 cup vegetable broth
1/2 tsp. paprika
1/4 tsp. dried thyme
2 pinches sea salt

Directions:

1. Put the oil, onion and garlic into the instant pot and *Sauté* for 2 minutes,

2. Add the broth, tomato paste, cauliflower, broccoli and all the spices, to the pot.

3. Secure the lid. Cook on the *Manual* setting at with pressure for 5 minutes,

4. When it beeps; *Quick Release* the steam and remove the lid. Stir well and serve hot.

Nutrition Values Nutritional Values Per serving

Calories:- 124
Carbohydrate:- 19.7g
Protein:- 6.6g

Fat:- 3.9g
Sugar:- 9.4g
Sodium:- 0.37g

451. Awesome Vegetable Lasagne

Preparation Time: 22 minutes
Serves: 4

Ingredients

1/2 box of lasagne noodles small pieces
2 tbsp. olive oil
1 medium zucchini; chopped.
1 medium onion; chopped.
1/2 green pepper; chopped.
2 carrots; chopped.
1 tsp. black pepper
1 tsp. oregano
1 cup bell pepper sliced
1 large can diced tomatoes
3 cups vegetable stock
1/2 tsp. onion powder
Sea salt to taste

Directions:

1. Put the oil, green pepper, onion and carrots in the instant pot and sauté for 5 minutes,

2. Stir in the zucchini and all the spices to cook for 3 minutes

3. Add the broth, tomatoes and lasagne noodles to the cooker and secure the lid.

4. Cook on the *Manual* setting at high pressure for 4 minutes,

5. When it beeps; *Quick Release* the steam and remove the lid. Serve hot.

Nutrition Values Nutritional Values Per serving

Calories:- 468
Carbohydrate:- 90.6g
Protein:- 10.3g
Fat:- 8.3g
Sugar:- 8.4g
Sodium:- 194mg

452. Veg Bean Rice

Preparation Time: 23 minutes
Serves: 4

Ingredients

- 1/2 cup chickpeas; soaked
- 1 cup long-grain white rice
- 1/2 tbsp. ginger paste
- 1/2 tsp. garlic paste
- 1/2 tbsp. Worcester Sauce
- 1/2 tsp. coriander
- 1/2 tsp. parsley
- 1/2 large onion; chopped.
- 2 large carrots; diced
- 2 celery sticks; chopped.
- 1/2 small leek; chopped.
- 1 tbsp. olive oil
- 2 ½ cups water
- Salt and pepper; to taste

Directions:

1. Put the oil, onion, ginger and garlic paste in the instant pot and *Sauté* for 5 minutes,
2. Stir in the remaining vegetables and stir-fry for 3 minutes,
3. Add the remaining Ingredients and secure the lid.
4. Cook on *Manual* function for 5 minutes at high pressure,
5. When it beeps; *Natural Release* the steam and remove the lid. Stir well and serve warm.

Nutrition Values Nutritional Values Per serving

Calories:- 341
Carbohydrate:- 64.1g
Protein:- 9.1g
Fat:- 5.5g
Sugar:- 6g
Sodium:- 58mg

453. Instant Veg Quinoa

Preparation Time: 33 minutes
Serves: 5

Ingredients

- 1/4 cup quinoa
- 1 cup onion; diced
- 2 cloves garlic; minced
- 1/2 tsp. olive oil
- 1/2 green bell pepper; diced
- 1/2 red bell pepper; diced
- 1/2 cup corn kernels
- 1/2 can spicy chili beans in sauce
- 1/2 can black beans; drained and rinsed
- 1 ¼ tbsp. chili powder
- 3/4 tbsp. cumin
- 1/2 tsp. dried oregano
- 1/4 tsp. smoked paprika
- 1/4 cup dried red lentils
- 1 ¼ cups vegetable broth
- 1 cup crushed tomatoes
- Salt and pepper to taste

Directions:

1. Put the oil and the onions into the instant pot and *Sauté* for 5 minutes,
2. Add the remaining vegetables to the pot and stir-fry for 3 minutes,
3. Stir in the remaining Ingredients and secure the lid.
4. Cook on the *Manual* function for 15 minutes at high pressure,
5. When it beeps; *Natural Release* the steam and remove the lid.
6. Stir well and garnish with cilantro. Serve hot.

Nutrition Values Nutritional Values Per serving

Calories:- 232
Carbohydrate:- 38.6g
Protein:- 12.1g
Fat:- 3.9g
Sugar:- 6.1g
Sodium:- 0.44g

454. Fruit Stew Recipe

Preparation Time: 15 minutes
Serves: 4

Ingredients

20-ounce green Jackfruit drained and rinsed
2 tsp. oil
1 tsp. cumin seeds
1 tsp. mustard seeds
1 tsp. nigella seeds
2-inch ginger; chopped.
2 tsp. coriander powder
2 tsp. turmeric
2 bay leaves
4 dried red chilies
2 small onions; chopped.
5 cloves of garlic; chopped.
1/2 tsp. black pepper
3 cups tomato puree
Salt to taste
3 cups water

Directions:

1. Put the oil, onions, garlic, ginger, bay leaves, salt and red chili into the instant pot.
2. *Sauté* for 2 minutes, Stir in the remaining ingredients,
3. Secure the lid and cook on *Manual* for 8 minutes at high pressure,
4. When it beeps; *Natural Release* the steam and remove the lid. Stir well and serve hot.

Nutrition Values Nutritional Values Per serving

Calories:- 319
Carbohydrate:- 70.2g
Protein:- 5.4g
Fat:- 4.8g
Sugar:- 1.8g
Sodium:- 50mg

Chapter 9 – Stocks and sauces

455. Elderberry Sauce

Preparation Time: 10 minutes
Cooking Time: 10 minutes
Serves: 20

Ingredients:

4 cups water
1 cup elderberries
1-inch ginger piece, grated
1 cinnamon stick
1 vanilla bean, split
5 cloves
1 cup honey

Directions:

In the Instant Pot, mix the elderberries with the water, ginger, cinnamon, vanilla and cloves, stir, cover and cook on the Manual setting for 10 minutes. Release the pressure, strain the sauce and keep in a jar until needed.

Nutritional Values Per serving

Calories: 55
Fat: 0
Fiber: 0
Carbs: 13
Protein: 0

456. Fennel Sauce

Preparation Time: 10 minutes
Cooking Time: 10 minutes
Serves: 6

Ingredients:

1 fennel bulb, cut into pieces
2 pints grape tomatoes, cut into halves
¼ cup dry white wine
5 thyme sprigs
3 tablespoons olive oil
Sugar

Salt and ground black pepper, to taste

Directions:

Set the Instant Pot in Sauté mode, add the oil and heat it up. Add the fennel, tomatoes, thyme, sugar, salt, and pepper, stir, and sauté for 5 minutes. Add the white wine, cover the Instant Pot, and cook for 4 minutes. Release the pressure, uncover, discard the thyme, stir the sauce, and serve.

Nutritional Values Per serving

Calories: 76
Fat: 0.6
Fiber: 0.6
Carbs: 4
Protein: 5

457. Melon Sauce

Preparation Time: 5 minutes
Cooking Time: 10 minutes
Serves: 6

Ingredients:

Flesh from 1 small melon
1 ounce sugar
1 cup sweet wine
1 tablespoon butter
1 teaspoon starch
Juice of 1 lemon

Directions:

Put the melon and sweet wine into the Instant Pot, cover, and cook on the Manual setting for 7 minutes. Release the pressure, transfer the sauce to a blender, add the lemon juice, sugar, butter, and starch and blend very well. Return the sauce to the Instant Pot, set it on Manual mode, cook the sauce until it thickens for 3 minutes, and serve.

Nutritional Values Per serving

Calories: 68
Fat: 0.3
Carbs: 1
Protein: 1

458. Peach Sauce

Preparation Time: 5 minutes
Cooking Time: 3 minutes
Serves: 6

Ingredients:

10 ounces peaches, pitted and chopped
1/8 teaspoon nutmeg
2 tablespoons cornstarch
3 tablespoons sugar
½ cup water
Salt
1/8 teaspoon ground cinnamon
1/8 teaspoon almond extract

Directions:

In the Instant Pot, mix the peaches with the nutmeg, cornstarch, sugar, cinnamon, and salt, stir, cover, and cook on the Manual setting for 3 minutes. Release the pressure, uncover the Instant Pot, add the almond extract, stir, and serve sauce.

Nutritional Values Per serving

Calories: 100
Fat: 1
Fiber: 0.6
Carbs: 4
Protein: 6

459. Parsley Sauce

Preparation Time: 10 minutes
Cooking Time: 7 minutes
Serves: 6

Ingredients:

2 cups chicken stock
1 yellow onion, peeled and diced

2 tablespoons butter
2 tablespoons flour
¾ cup whole milk
4 tablespoons fresh parsley, chopped
1 egg yolk
¼ cup heavy cream
Salt and ground white pepper, to taste

Directions:

Put the stock and onion into the Instant Pot, set the Instant Pot on Manual mode, and bring to a boil. Heat up a pan with the butter over medium heat, add the flour and stir well to combine. Combine this mixture and whole milk with the stock and stir well. Bring to a boil, add the parsley, stir, cover, and cook on the Manual setting for 2 minutes. Release the pressure, uncover the Instant Pot, and set it back on Manual mode. In a bowl, mix the cream with egg yolk and some of the sauce from the Instant Pot. Stir this well, mix with the sauce, and whisk. Add the salt and pepper, stir again, cook for a couple of minutes until it thickens, and serve with chicken and rice.

Nutritional Values Per serving

Calories: 70
Fat: 2.5
Fiber: 0.5
Carbs: 7.3
Protein: 2.5

460. Cilantro Sauce

Preparation Time: 5 minutes
Cooking Time: 6 minutes
Serves: 6

Ingredients:

3 garlic cloves, peeled and minced
1 tablespoon olive oil
2 red chilies, minced
3 shallots, peeled and minced
3 scallions, chopped
3 tomatoes, cored and chopped
Salt and ground black pepper, to taste
2 tablespoons fresh cilantro, chopped
¼ cup water

Directions:

Set the Instant Pot on Sauté mode, add oil and heat it up. Add garlic, shallots and chilies, stir and cook for 3 minutes. Add scallions, tomatoes, water, salt, pepper and cilantro, stir, cover and cook on High for 3 minutes. Release the pressure, uncover the Instant Pot, blend using an immersion blender, and serve.

Nutritional Values Per serving

Calories: 67
Fat: 1
Fiber: 0.4
Carbs: 1
Protein: 0.5

461. Peach and Whiskey Sauce

Preparation Time: 10 minutes
Cooking Time: 10 minutes
Serves: 6

Ingredients:

1 cup brown sugar
3 cups peaches, pureed
6 tablespoons whiskey
1 cup white sugar
2 teaspoons lemon zest, grated

Directions:

In the Instant Pot mix the peaches with brown sugar, white sugar, whiskey, and lemon zest, stir, cover, and cook on the Manual setting for 10 minutes. Release the pressure, uncover the Instant Pot, stir the sauce, and transfer it to jars. Serve when needed.

Nutritional Values Per serving

Calories: 100
Fat: 0.7
Fiber: 0.6
Carbs: 7
Protein: 7

462. Leek Sauce

Preparation Time: 5 minutes
Cooking Time: 7 minutes
Serves: 8

Ingredients:

2 leeks, sliced thin
2 tablespoons butter
1 cup whipping cream
3 tablespoons lemon juice
Salt and ground black pepper, to taste

Directions:

Set the Instant Pot on Sauté mode, add the butter and melt it. Add the leeks, stir and cook for 2 minutes. Add the lemon juice, stir, cover, and cook on the Manual setting for 3 minutes. Release the pressure, uncover the Instant Pot, transfer the sauce to your blender, add whipping cream and blend everything together. Return the sauce to the Instant Pot, set on Manual mode, add the salt and pepper, stir, and cook for 2 minutes. Serve with fish.

Nutritional Values Per serving

Calories: 140
Fat: 13
Fiber: 0.4
Carbs: 5
Protein: 1

463. Chestnut Sauce

Preparation Time: 10 minutes
Cooking Time: 20 minutes
Serves: 6

Ingredients:

11 ounces sugar
11 ounces water
1½ pounds chestnuts, cut into halves and peeled
⅛ cup rum liquor

Directions:

In the Instant Pot, mix the sugar with the water,

rum, and chestnuts. Stir, cover, and cook on the Manual setting for 20 minutes. Release the pressure for 10 minutes, uncover the Instant Pot, and blend everything with an immersion blender. Serve when needed.

Nutritional Values Per serving

Calories: 50
Fat: 0
Fiber: 0
Carbs: 10
Protein: 0
Sugar: 12

464. Quince Sauce

Preparation Time: 10 minutes
Cooking Time: 15 minutes
Serves: 6

Ingredients:

2 pounds grated quince
Juice of 1 lemon
10 cloves
2 pounds sugar
¼ cup water

Directions:

In the Instant Pot, mix the quince with the sugar and stir well. Add the water and stir again. Tie the cloves in cheesecloth and add to the Instant Pot. Cover and cook on the Manual setting for 10 minutes. Release the pressure for 10 minutes, uncover the Instant Pot, stir the sauce again, and transfer to jars .Serve on top of sweet pastries.

Nutritional Values Per serving

Calories: 60
Fat: 0
Fiber: 1
Carbs: 16
Sugar: 9
Protein: 1

465. Corn Sauce

Preparation Time: 10 minutes
Cooking Time: 6 minutes
Serves: 4

Ingredients:

1 yellow onion, peeled and chopped
1 tablespoon olive oil
1 teaspoon white flour
1¾ cups chicken stock
¼ cup white wine
1 thyme sprig
2 cups corn kernels
Salt and ground black pepper, to taste
2 teaspoons butter
1 teaspoon thyme, diced

Directions:

Set the Instant Pot on Sauté mode, add the oil and heat it up. Add the onion, stir, and cook for 3 minutes. Add the flour, stir well, and cook for 1 minute. Add the wine, stir, and cook for 1 minute. Add the thyme sprig, stock, and corn, stir, cover, and cook on the Manual setting for 1 minute. Release the pressure, uncover the Instant Pot, discard the thyme sprig, transfer the sauce to a blender, add salt, pepper, butter, and chopped thyme, and blend well. Return to pot set it on Sauté mode again and cook 1-2 minutes. Serve when needed.

Nutritional Values Per serving

Calories: 100
Fat: 4.5
Fiber: 2
Carbs: 13
Protein: 3

466. Rhubarb Sauce

Preparation Time: 10 minutes
Cooking Time: 13 minutes
Serves: 6

Ingredients:

8 ounces rhubarb, trimmed and chopped
1 tablespoon cider vinegar
1 small onion, peeled and chopped

Ground cardamom
1 garlic clove, peeled and minced
2 jalapeño peppers, chopped
⅓ cup honey
¼ cup raisins
¼ cup water

Directions:

In the Instant Pot, mix the rhubarb with the vinegar, onion, cardamom, garlic, jalapeños, honey, water, and raisins, stir, cover, and cook on the Manual setting for 7 minutes. Release the pressure, uncover the Instant Pot, set it on Manual mode and cook for 3 minutes. Serve when needed.

Nutritional Values Per serving

Calories: 90
Fat: 0
Fiber: 1
Carbs: 23
Protein: 1

467. Instant Pot Vegetable Stock

Preparation Time: 30 mins
Serves: 4

Ingredients

4-5 carrots
1 cup mushrooms
1 onion
3-4 stalks of celery

Directions

1. Roughly slice/chop your veggies.
2. Add the vegetables and 10 cups of water to your Instant Pot.
3. Set the Instant Pot on manual mode for 30 minutes. Make sure the vent is sealed.
4. Once the 30 minutes are up, the Instant Pot will automatically go to "warm" mode and begin to naturally de-pressurize. I recommend letting it naturally de-pressurize as opposed to opening the vent because the hot stock liⵎuid may spurt out.

It should naturally de-pressurize within an hour, mine took about 40 minutes.

5. Let the stock cool and then strain using a fine mesh strainer.
6. Store the stock. I prefer to store it in mason jars in the freezers. Make sure to leave a couple of inches of space at the top of your jars so they don't break when the stock expands as it freezes.

Nutrition Info:

Calories: 101 cal

468. Instant Pot Marinara Fresh Tomato Sauce

Prep+Cook Time: 1 hr 20 mins,
Servings: 10 cups

Ingredients

4 TbspOliveOil
1 small Onion, chopped
5 cloves Garlic, minced
5 lbs Tomatoes*, chopped, about 9 1/2 cups any variety or mix
1/2 cup Red Wine
1/2 cup Water** optional see Notes
3 tsp Kosher Salt
1/2 tsp Pepper
1 Tbsp Cocoa Powder, unsweetened cuts acidity and adds a complexity. You won't notice it
2 tsp Basil, dried
2 1/2 Tbsp Italian Seasoning
1/4 - 1/2 tsp Red Pepper Flakes or more for spicier
2 tsp Oregano, dried
2 Tbsp Parsley Flakes, dried
3 6 oz cans Tomato Paste

Add Only if the Sauce is too Acidic After Pressure Cooking

2 tsp Sugar optional, if needed
1/4 - 1/2 tsp Baking Soda optional, if neede

Directions

1. Before you begin the cooking process, have all of your veggies chopped & ingredients

measured and ready to go.

2. Turn on the Sauté setting. When the pot is Hot, add the olive oil. Don't add the oil to a cold pot. Then add the onion and cook, stirring occasionally, until turning translucent.

3. Add the minced garlic and cook, stirring constantly, for about 30 seconds.

4. Add the chopped tomatoes and stir.

5. Add the red wine, salt, pepper, cocoa powder, basil, Italian seasoning, red pepper flakes, oregano, and parsley flakes. Stir well to combine.

6. Add the tomato paste, but do not stir it in. Leave it sitting on top. If you stir it in it will be too thick and the pot may scorch and not come to pressure.

7. Also, you will not have to add any additional li☐uid as the red wine and juice from the tomatoes is plenty to get the pot to pressure.

8. Close the lid and set the steam release knob to the Sealing position. Then press the Pressure Cook or Manual button or dial to select 25 minutes You can cook less time, but I tested and liked this time best.

9. After the cook cycle is finished, turn the pot off so it doesn't go to the Warm setting. Then leave it to Naturally Release the pressure until the pin in the lid drops down. Then open the lid and give the sauce a stir. Careful of the hot sauce splattering, so stir slowly!

10. Taste, and if the sauce is too acidic, either add the sugar, or add the baking soda. Stir it in and let it sit a while. Then taste and adjust as necessary.

11. Let the sauce cool, then use an immersion blender, food processor, or blender to puree it nice and smooth. It is best to do this when the sauce has cooled.

12. Transfer the sauce to jars with lids and keep in the fridge for up to 5 days. You can freeze it as well.

Nutritional Values Per serving

Calories: 97 kcal

469. Instant Pot Lasagna

Preparation Time: 1 hr 2 mins, **Servings:** 4 - 5

Ingredients

Meat Mixture

> 1/2 lb Lean Ground Beef to lean You can useall ground beef
> 1/2 lb Ground Italian Sausage you can use all sausage
> 1/2 tsp Coarse Salt 1/4 tsp table salt
> 1/4 tsp Pepper
> 1/2 tsp Onion Powder
> 1/2 tsp Garlic Powder
> 1/2 tsp Italian Seasoning

Cheese Mixture

> 1 cup Ricotta Cheese or Cottage Cheese
> 1 Egg
> 1/2 cup Mozzarella Cheese, shredded
> 1/2 cup Parmesan Cheese, grated
> 1 1/2 tsp Garlic Powder
> 1 1/4 tsp Onion Powder
> 1 1/4 tsp Italian Seasoning
> 1/2 tsp Oregano
> 1/2 tsp Salt if your pasta sauce is salty, decrease to 1/4 tsp
> 1/2 tsp Pepper
> 1/4 cup Chopped Fresh Parsley

Remaining Layers

> 1 24oz jar Pasta Sauceabout 3 cups I prefer marinara, or use your favorite brand
> 1/2 cup Chopped Spinach Leaves, optional fresh, or frozen, thawed
> 5-6 No Boil Lasagna Noodles or regular uncooked lasagna noodles that have been soaked in very hot water for 15 minutes
> 1/2 cup Mozzarella Cheese, shredded
> 1/2 cup Parmesan Cheese, grated

Directions

Cook Meat

1. Set pot to Sautéand add the beef, sausage, salt, pepper, onion powder, garlic powder,

and Italian seasoning. Cook, stirring, until the meat iscooked.

2. Remove meat, drain, and set aside. Clean out pot and add 1 1/2 cups water to it.

Mix the Cheese Mixture

In a mixing bowl combine the ricotta, egg, mozzarella, parmesan, garlic powder, onion powder, Italian seasoning, oregano, salt, pepper, and parsley. Use a fork to mix thoroughly. Set aside.

Make the Lasagna

1. In a 7" x 3" or 6"x3" springform or push pan, make a layer of the no-boil noodles by breaking them and fitting them like a mosaic to cover the bottom of thepan.

2. Spread 1/3 of thepastasauceover the noodles, covering them all.

3. Spread 1/2 of the meat mixture over the sauce evenly.

4. Spread 1/2 of the cheese mixture evenlyover the meat.

5. Sprinkle thespinach if using over the cheese mixtureevenly.

6. Add another layer of noodles, press down on them a little.

7. Add another layer of 1/3 of the sauce.

8. Add thesecond half of the meat.

9. Add the second half of thecheese mixture.

10. Add another layer of noodles, the last 1/3 of sauce, 1/2 cupof mozzarella, and 1/2 cup of parmesan.

11. Spray a piece of foil with nonstick spray and lightly cover the pan with the foil, enough that water can't get in.

12. Set the pan on a trivet with handles and lift them into the inner pot that has 1 1/2 cups of water in it. You can also use a sling to set thepan on the trivet in the pot.

13. Close the lid and lock in place. Turn the steam release knob to the Sealing position.

14. Press the Pressure Cook or Manual button or dial and choose 22 minutes. It will takeabout 5 minutesor so for the pot tocome topressure.

15. When the cook cycle hasended, let the pot sit undisturbed for 10-15 minutes 10-15 minute Natural Release. Then, turn the knob to the Venting position to release any remaining steam.

16. When the pin in the lid drops down, open the lid. Use silicone mitts, sling, or good pot holders that can get wet to lift the rack with the hot pan out of the pot to a cooling rack. Be VERY careful as it could slipoff the rack.

17. Carefully remove the foil. Turn on your broiler to 450° with the oven rack in the middle to top 1/3 position in the oven.

18. Set the pan on the oven rack and let thecheeseon top brown toyour desired amount. Watch it closely as it doesn't take very long. Every oven is different!

19. Let the lasagna rest for a few minutes before releasing from thepan. This will help it maintain its shape and cool down just a bit.

20. Carefully pan and lasagna very hot release the lasagna from the springform pan while it ison a plate.

21. If you used a push pan, set a largecan of soupor veggies on a plate and set thepush pan on top of thecan. gently, and carefully push thesidesof the pan straight down. Wear oven mitts or some kind of hand protection. The pan and the lasagna will be very hot.

22. Then slide another plate under the lasagna. You might need to use a spatula to helpslide it over.

23. Serve with salad and some crusty bread!

Nutritional Value Per Serving:

Total Fat 32g
Sodium 1576mg
Potassium 1041mg
Total Carbohydrates 35g
Dietary Fiber 3.9g

470. Instant Pot Spaghetti and Meatballs

Prep+Cook Time: 29 mins
Serves: 4

Ingredients

1 lb Meatballs, cooked, frozen
8 oz Spaghetti Noodles
14 oz can Diced Tomatoes optional, with juice
24 oz jar Spaghetti Sauce
3 cups Water fill the 24 oz jar once or use broth

Garnishes

Grated Parmesan Cheese
Shredded Mozzarella Cheese
Parsleyor Basil

Directions

1. Put meatballs in the bottom of the inner liner pot.
2. Break the spaghetti in half and sprinkle over meatballs in a random pattern, so not too manyare side by side. This helps prevent them sticking together.
3. Pour the water/broth over the noodles.
4. Pour the diced tomatoes, if using over the noodles, and then the spaghetti sauce over the noodles, and cover as much of them as you can with the sauce. This helps them all get cooked.
5. Put on the lid and set the steam release knob to the Sealing position.
6. Press the Pressure Cook Manual button or dial and then the +/- button or dial to select 9 minutes 7 minutes for al dente. The pot will takeseveral minutes to come topressure. Cook time begins when pot isat pressure.
7. After cook time has finished, turn off the pot and turn the steam release knob to the Venting position, and do a Quick Release of the steam so the pasta doesn't overcook.
8. Watch it closely, and if saucestarts tospew out with thesteam, close the vent and release thesteam in bursts until it looks like no more sauce will bespewing out.
9. After the pin in the lid drops down, open the lid and give the spaghetti a stir. If any

noodlesstuck together, just use a fork to separate them.
10. Serve with some bread, and garnish with parmesan cheese, mozzarella, or whatever you like!

Recipe Notes

If you choose to use the diced tomatoes thesauce will be a little thinner, but not too much as this isa thick sauce.

Nutritional Values Per serving

Calories: 382 kcal

471. Instant Pot Meatball Pasta Dinner

Preparation Time: 40 mins,
Servings: 6 - 8

Ingredients

2 lbsFrozenCookedMeatballs
1 lb Pasta I likepenneor rotini best
1 24 oz Jar of Pasta Sauce I use Marinara
1 14.5 oz can Diced Tomatoes, undrained
1 1/4 Jars 24 oz size Broth or Water fill thesauce jar 1 and 1/4 times with broth or water 3 3/4 cups

If you use Marinara, Season it with These Spices - Your Chosen Sauce May Not Need Seasoning

2 tsp Italian Seasoning
2 tsp Garlic Powder
3 tsp Dehydrated Onion
1/2 tsp Salt
1/2 tsp Pepper

Optional Toppings

1 cup Grated Parmesan cheese
1 1/2 cups Mozzarella Cheese shredded optional

Directions

Layer theIngredients in the Pot - Do Not Stir!

1. Put the meatballs in thepot.

2. Pour pasta on topand spread out in an even layer.

3. Pour thecan of tomatoes over the pasta, evenly.

4. Pour the jar of pasta sauce over, evenly, covering thepastaentirely.

5. Pour the jar with the broth or water along the insideof the pot, making sureyou don't pour it over the sauce and expose the pasta. Exposing thepasta may cause it to be undercooked in those areas Remember to use 1 1/4 jars of li□uid, which is 3 3/4 cups.

6. Sprinkle thespicesover the contents.

Cooking

1. Put the lid on the Pot and set the knob to Sealing.

2. Press the Pressure Cook or Manual button or dial, and then the + or - button to choose 5 minutes or half of thecooking time on thepasta package Instructions.

3. Thepot may take up to 20 minutes to get topressure, due to the frozen meatballs!

4. When the cooking cycle hasended, do a Controlled Quick Releaseof thepressure until thepin drops.

5. A controlled quick release means you release the steam in short bursts, then longer bursts, until you can be sure noneof thesauce spews out of the vent with the steam from the intensepressure. Then fully open the vent and let it go.

6. Carefully open the lid, facing it away from you.

7. Stir contentsand mix in the Parmesan cheese.

8. Tasteand add moresalt & pepper if needed.

9. Top with the Mozzarella cheese, if using, and cover thepot with a lid or just use a plate to help the cheese melt.

10. Serve!

Nutritional Values Per serving

Calories: 582 kcal

472. Instant Pot Spaghetti and Meat Sauce

Prep+Cook Time: 30 minutes
Serves: 6 servings

Ingredients

1 teaspoon olive oil
1 pound lean ground turkey
1/2 small yellow onion, diced about 1/2 cup
1 pound 16 oz whole wheat spaghetti
1 jar 24 oz spaghetti sauce of your choice
36 oz water 1 1/2 jars
1 can 14.5 oz diced tomatoes
A few handfuls of Spinach, optional

Directions

1. Heat Instant Pot to Saute. Add oliveoil and when it's shimmering and hot, add turkeyand onion. Cook, breaking up turkey with spatula, until browned and cooked through.

2. Break pieces of spaghetti in half and add on top of cooked meat. Pour spaghetti sauce, water, and tomatoes over the pasta. Movepastaaround a little with a spoon or spatula toseparate the pieces of pasta to prevent them from clumping. Make sure they'reall submerged in the sauce.

3. Secure lid of Instant Pot and turn valve to"seal." Set on Manual for 8 minutes on high.

4. After cooking timeelapses, □uick releasepressure. Remove lid and pileon spinach. Set lid back on you don't have to lock it on and let spinach steam for 2-3 minutesor until wilted. Stir as needed tospeed up thisprocess.

5. Serve immediately, or let set 5-10 minutes in Instant Pot for sauce to thicken slightly before serving.

Notes

1. You may use ground beef or Italian sausage in place of ground turkey. You may wish to drain fat off after browning the meat if needed.

2. If you wish toadd more vegetables bell peppers, carrots, mushrooms, you'll want tosaute them with the meat. Broccoli would be good if you added it at the same timeas the pasta. Put it on top of thesauce/pastaso that thepasta is all still submerged in the sauce.

Nutritional Values Per serving Amount Per Serving:

Calories: 257
TotalFat: 2g

473. Instant Pot Sunday Sauce

Preparation Time: 2 hr 25 min, Serving: 6 to 8 servings

Ingredients

Sauce:

> 1 tablespoon oliveoil
> 2 bone-in beef short ribs about 2 pounds
> 2 countrystylepork ribs about 1 pound
> 1 largeonion, finelychopped
> 6 cloves garlic, finelychopped
> 1/2 cup tomatopaste
> 1/2 cup dry red wine
> One 28-ounce can whole peeled tomatoes
> 4 links sweet or hot Italian sausages
> Kosher salt and freshly ground black pepper
> Crushed red pepper flakes, optional

Meatballs:

> 1 pound ground beef sirloin
> 1/2 cup grated Parmesan
> 1/4 cup plain breadcrumbs
> 1/4 cup milk
> 1/4 cupchopped fresh flat-leaf parsley
> 2 cloves garlic, grated
> 1 large eg
> Kosher salt and freshly ground black pepper

Serving suggestions:

> pastaor polenta

Directions

1. For thesauce: Add the oil to a 6-☐uart Instant Pot®and set tosautesee Cook's Note. Add theshort ribs and brown well. Transfer to a plate, then add the pork ribs and brown well. Transfer to a plate. Add theonions and garlicand cook, stirring often, until theonions are golden and the garlic is soft, about 5 minutes. Add the tomato pasteand stir well tocoat all the onions. Pour in the wineand scrape upany browned bitson the bottom of thepot. Bring to a boil and let cook until reduced by half, about 2 minutes.

2. Stir in the tomatoes, then add the beef, pork, sausages, 1 tablespoon salt, several grindsof black pepper and a pinch of pepper flakes, if using.

3. Follow the manufacturer's guide for locking the lid and preparing tocook. Set to pressure cook on manual high setting for 50 minutes.

4. For the meatballs: Meanwhile, combine thesirloin, Parmesan, breadcrumbs, milk, parsley, garlic, egg, somesalt and a few grinds of pepper in a medium bowl and mix well with a wooden spoon. Form into 1- to 2-inch balls.

5. After thepressure cook cycle is complete, follow the manufacturer's guide for quick release and wait until the☐uick releasecycle is complete. Be careful of any remaining steam and unlock and remove the lid.

6. Carefully remove the beef, pork and sausage. Skim any excess fat from the sauce and discard. When cool enough to handle, remove and discard any bones and excess fat from the meat. Chop the meat and sausage in to bite-sized pieces. Return the meat to thesauceand add the meatballs to the pot. Seal the pot and cook at manual high pressure for 5 minutes.

7. After the pressurecook cycle is complete, follow the manufacturer's guide for ☐uick release and wait until the☐uick releasecycle iscomplete. Becareful of any remaining steam and unlock and remove the lid. Season with salt and pepper. Serve over pastaor polenta.

Nutrition Info:

Calories: 259 cal

474. Beef Bacon Stock Recipe

Preparation Time: 2 hours 14 minutes
Serves: 10

Ingredients

4 lbs. beef stock bones
6 bacon strips
2 tbsp. olive oil
1 celery stalk; chopped into thirds
1 small onion; unpeeled and halved
2 garlic cloves; chopped
1/2 tsp. whole black peppercorns
1 tsp. kosher salt

Directions:

1. Grease the baking tray with olive oil and place the beef bones on it.

2. Roast the bones for 30 minutes in an oven at 420o F. Flip the bones over and roast for another 20 minutes

3. Add the bacon and the rest of the oil to the instant pot and *Sauté* for 3 minutes,

4. Now fill the instant pot with water up to one inch below the max line.

5. Put all the ingredients; including the roasted beef bones, into the water.

6. Secure the lid and turn the pressure release handle to the *sealed* position.

7. Select the *Manual* function. Set to high pressure and adjust the time to 75 minutes,

8. When it beeps; *Natural Release* the steam for 10 minutes and remove the lid.

9. Strain the prepared stock through a fine mesh strainer and discard all the solids, Skim off all the surface fats and serve hot.

Nutrition Values Nutritional Values Per serving

Calories:- 397
Carbohydrate:- 2g

Protein:- 50.1g
Fat:- 20.7g
Sugar:- 0.2g
Sodium:- 0.38g

475. Chicken with Herbs Stock Recipe

Preparation Time: 66 minutes
Serves: 8

Ingredients

2 ½ lbs. chicken bones only
1 small onion; unpeeled and halved
1/4 tsp. oregano
1/4 tsp. dried basil
1 tsp. dried bay leaf
1 sprig fresh parsley
1/2 tsp. whole black peppercorns
8 cups water
1 tsp. sea salt

Directions:

1. Pour the water into the instant pot.

2. Put all the Ingredients into the water.

3. Secure the lid and turn the pressure release handle to the *sealed* position.

4. Select the *Manual* function; set on high pressure and adjust the timer to 60 minutes,

5. When it beeps; *Natural Release* the steam for 10 minutes and remove the lid.

6. Strain the prepared stock through a mesh strainer and discard all the solids, Skim off all the surface fats and serve hot.

Nutrition Values Nutritional Values Per serving

Calories:- 221
Carbohydrate:- 3.3g
Protein:- 41.2g
Fat:- 4.6g
Sugar:- 0.1g
Sodium:- 0.37g

476. Pork Bone Stock Recipe

Preparation Time: 26 minutes
Serves: 8

Ingredients

3 lbs. pastured pork bones
1 small onion; unpeeled and halved
1 celery stalk; chopped into thirds
1 tsp. dried bay leaf
1 sprig fresh parsley
1/2 tsp. whole black peppercorns
8 cups water
1 tsp. kosher salt

Directions:

1. Pour the water into the instant pot.
2. Add all the Ingredients to the water.
3. Secure the lid and turn the pressure release handle to the *sealed* position.
4. Select the *Manual* function; set to high pressure and adjust the timer to 20 minutes,
5. When it beeps; *Natural Release* the steam for 10 minutes and remove the lid.
6. Strain the prepared stock through a mesh strainer and discard all the solids, Skim off all the surface fats and serve hot.

Nutrition Values Nutritional Values Per serving

Calories:- 445
Carbohydrate:7g
Protein:- 22.1g
Fat:- 36g
Sugar:- 0.4g
Sodium:- 1.60g

477. Mushroom Sauce Recipe

Preparation Time: 10 minutes
Serves: 3

Ingredients

2 ½ cups portabella mushrooms; sliced

1/2 tbsp. butter
1 tbsp. oil
1 sprig fresh thyme
1 garlic clove; crushed
1/2 cup cream
1/2 cup milk
1 tbsp. chopped parsley
3 tsp. corn starch
1 tbsp. lemon juice
1/2 cup water
Salt and pepper to taste

Directions:

1. Select the *Sauté* function on the instant pot and heat the oil and butter.
2. Add the garlic, mushrooms and thyme to the oil. Stir-fry for 5 minutes,
3. Add the salt, pepper, cream and water to the mushrooms,
4. Secure the lid and turn the pressure release handle to the *sealed* position.
5. Select the *Manual* function; set to high pressure and adjust the timer to 3 minutes,
6. When it beeps; *Quick Release* the steam and remove the lid.
7. Prepare a slurry by mixing the cornstarch with half a cup of milk. Add this slurry to the mushroom sauce, Stir in the parsley and lemon juice then serve.

Nutrition Values Nutritional Values Per serving

Calories:- 69
Carbohydrate:5.3g
Protein:- 1.8g
Fat:- 4.9g
Sugar:- 2g
Sodium:- 29mg

478. Super Quick Garlic Sauce Recipe

Preparation Time: 8 minutes
Serves: 2

Ingredients

1 cup water; divided as explained in Preparation

below
4 tbsp. chopped garlic
2 tsp. garlic powder
4 cups heavy cream
2 tbsp. chopped fresh parsley
4 tbsp. cornstarch
Salt and pepper to taste

Directions:

1. Put half the water, garlic, garlic powder, cream, salt and pepper in the instant pot.
2. Secure the lid and turn the pressure release handle to the *sealed* position.
3. Select the *Manual* function; set to high pressure and adjust the timer to 3 minutes,
4. When it beeps; *Quick Release* the steam and remove the lid.
5. Mix the cornstarch with the remaining water. Add this slurry to the garlic sauce, Stir in the parsley and serve.

Nutrition Values Nutritional Values Per serving

Calories:- 231
Carbohydrate:- 7.3g
Protein:- 1.7g
Fat:- 22.2g
Sugar:- 0.3g
Sodium:- 26mg

479. Green Hot Sauce Recipe

Preparation Time: 7 minutes
Serves: 8

Ingredients

16-ounce green chilies
1 green bell pepper; chopped
8 garlic cloves; peeled and smashed
1 cup white vinegar
1/4 cup apple cider vinegar
1/2 cup water
1 tbsp. sea salt

Directions:

1. Put all the Ingredients into the instant pot.

2. Secure the lid and turn the pressure release handle to the *sealed* position.
3. Select the *Manual* function. Set to high pressure and adjust the timer to 2 minutes,
4. When it beeps; *Quick Release* the steam and remove the lid.
5. Transfer the sauce to a blender and blend well to form a smooth mixture, Use immediately or save in a bottle for later use.

Nutrition Values Nutritional Values Per serving

Calories:- 34
Carbohydrate:- 6.2g
Protein:- 0.3g
Fat:- 0.1g
Sugar:- 2.8g
Sodium:- 0.93g

480. Beef Pepper Stock Recipe

Preparation Time: : 2 hours 11 minutes
Serves: 10

Ingredients

4 lbs. beef stock bones
1 cup red bell pepper
2 tbsp. olive oil
1 celery stalk; chopped into thirds
1 small onion; unpeeled and halved
2 garlic cloves; chopped
1/4 tsp. red pepper flakes
1/4 tsp. turmeric ground
1 tsp. kosher salt
1/2 tsp. whole black peppercorns

Directions:

1. Grease the baking tray with olive oil and place the beef bones on it.
2. Roast the bones for 30 minutes in an oven at 420o F. Flip the bones over and roast for another 20 minutes
3. Fill the instant pot with water up to one inch below the max line.
4. Add all the ingredients; including the

roasted beef bones to the water.

5. Secure the lid. Turn the pressure release handle to the *sealed* position.

6. Select the *Manual* function; set to high pressure and adjust the time to 75 minutes,

7. When it beeps; *Natural Release* the steam for 10 minutes and remove the lid.

8. Strain the prepared stock through a mesh strainer and discard all the solids, Skim off all the surface fats and serve hot.

Nutrition Values Nutritional Values Per serving

Calories:- 378
Carbohydrate:- 2.1g
Protein:- 48.6g
Fat:- 18.3g
Sugar:- 0.4g
Sodium:- 0.35g

481. Chicken Green Beans Stock Recipe

Preparation Time: 66 minutes
Serves: 8

Ingredients

1 cup green beans; sliced
2 ½ lbs. chicken bones only
1 celery stalk; chopped into thirds
1/2 tsp. whole black peppercorns
8 cups water
1 small onion; unpeeled and halved
1 tsp. dried bay leaf
1 sprig fresh parsley
1 tsp. kosher salt

Directions:

1. Pour the water into the instant pot.

2. Add all the Ingredients to the water.

3. Secure the lid and turn the pressure release handle to the *sealed* position.

4. Select the *Manual* function; set to high pressure and adjust the timer to 20 minutes,

5. When it beeps; *Natural Release* the steam for 10 minutes and remove the lid.

6. Strain the prepared stock through a mesh strainer and discard all the solids, Skim off all the surface fats and serve hot.

Nutrition Values Nutritional Values Per serving

Calories:- 480
Carbohydrate:- 2g
Protein:- 30.8g
Fat:- 9.5g
Sugar:- 0.6g
Sodium:- 0.49g

482. Bolognese Eggplant Sauce Recipe

Preparation Time: 45 minutes
Serves: 6

Ingredients

1 pound ground beef
1 28 oz. can crushed tomatoes
1/2 6 oz. can tomato paste
1 eggplant; diced
1/2 large onion; finely chopped
1 carrot; finely chopped.
1 ½ celery stalk; finely chopped.
1 ½ garlic clove; minced or pressed
1/2 tbsp. olive oil
1/2 tsp. black pepper
3/4 tsp. dried thyme
1 tsp. dried oregano
1 cup whole milk
1 cup dry red wine
1/2 tbsp. salt

Directions:

1. Pour the oil into the instant pot. Select the *Sauté* function.

2. Put all the vegetables into the oil and stir-fry for 10 minutes,

3. Stir in the tomato paste and all the spices, Use an immerse blender to blend the sauce,

4. Now put all the remaining Ingredients in

the instant pot.

5. Secure the lid and turn the pressure release handle to the *sealed* position.

6. Select the *Manual* function; set to high pressure and adjust the timer to 35 minutes,

7. When it beeps; *Quick Release* the steam and remove the lid. Stir well and serve with pasta.

Nutrition Values Nutritional Values Per serving

Calories:- 259
Carbohydrate:- 14.7g
Protein:- 26.5g
Fat:- 7.5g
Sugar:- 8.8g
Sodium:- 0.71g

483. Chicken Corn Stock Recipe

Preparation Time: 66 minutes
Serves: 8

Ingredients

2 ½ lbs. chicken bones only
1 cup corn kernels
1/2 cup green onion; chopped.
1/2 cup carrots; chopped.
1/2 tsp. whole black peppercorns
8 cups water
1/2 tsp. white pepper
1 tsp. kosher salt

Directions:

1. Pour the water into the instant pot.

2. Put all the Ingredients into the water.

3. Secure the lid and turn the pressure release handle to the *sealed* position.

4. Select the *Manual* function; set on high pressure and adjust the timer to 60 minutes,

5. When it beeps; *Natural Release* the steam for 10 minutes and remove the lid.

6. Strain the prepared stock through a mesh

strainer and discard all the solids, Skim off all the surface fats and serve hot.

Nutrition Values Nutritional Values Per serving

Calories:- 243
Carbohydrate:- 7.8g
Protein:- 45.1g
Fat:- 5.3g
Sugar:- 0.2g
Sodium:- 0.43g

484. Watermelon BBQ Sauce Recipe

Preparation Time: 35 minutes
Serves: 8

Ingredients

1/2 cup watermelon juice
2 cups watermelon pulp
2 cups dark corn syrup
1/2 cup Heinz ketchup
1/2 cup distilled vinegar
1/2 tsp. crushed red pepper flakes
1 tsp. liquid smoke
1/2 tsp. freshly ground black pepper

Directions:

1. Put the diced, red part of the watermelon into a food processor and blend.

2. Strain the watermelon pulp from its water. Keep it aside for later use.

3. Put all the ingredients; including 1 cup watermelon pulp, in the instant pot.

4. Secure the lid and turn the pressure release handle to the *sealed* position.

5. Select the *Manual* function, set to high pressure and adjust the timer to 20 minutes,

6. When it beeps; *Natural Release* the steam for 10 minutes and remove the lid.

7. Let it simmer for 5 minutes, Use immediately or save in a jar for later use.

Nutrition Values Nutritional Values

Per serving

Calories:- 244
Carbohydrate:- 64.9g
Protein:- 0.3g
Fat:- 0.1g
Sugar:- 25.6g
Sodium:- 172mg

485. Bolognese Lentil Sauce Recipe

Preparation Time: 35 minutes
Serves: 6

Ingredients

1/2 cup lentils; soaked, rinsed and drained
1/2 large onion; finely chopped.
1 carrot; finely chopped.
1 ½ celery stalks; finely chopped.
1 ½ garlic cloves; minced or pressed
1/2 tbsp. olive oil
1/2 can tomato paste 6 oz.
1/2 tsp. black pepper
3/4 tsp. dried thyme
1 tsp. dried oregano
1 can crushed tomatoes 28 oz.
1 cup whole milk
1 cup dry red wine
1/2 tbsp. salt

Directions:

1. Pour the oil into the instant pot and select the *Sauté* function.

2. Put all the vegetables into the oil and stir-fry for 10 minutes,

3. Stir in the tomato paste and all the spices, Use an immerse blender to blend the sauce,

4. Now put all the remaining Ingredients into the instant pot.

5. Secure the lid and turn the pressure release handle to the *sealed* position.

6. Select the *Manual* function; set to high pressure and adjust the timer to 20 minutes,

7. When it beeps; *Quick Release* the steam and remove the lid. Stir well and serve with pasta.

Nutrition Values Nutritional Values Per serving

Calories:- 156
Carbohydrate:- 19.8g
Protein:- 6.9g
Fat:- 2.8g
Sugar:- 6.8g
Sodium:- 0.66g

486. Red Hot Sauce Recipe

Preparation Time: 7 minutes
Serves: 4

Ingredients

6 garlic cloves; peeled and smashed
1 pound Fresno peppers
1/4 cup carrot; shredded
1 roasted red pepper; chopped.
1 cup white vinegar
1/4 cup apple cider vinegar
1/2 cup water
1 tbsp. sea salt

Directions:

1. Put all the Ingredients into the instant pot.

2. Secure the lid and turn the pressure release handle to the *sealed* position.

3. Select the *Manual* function. Set to high pressure and adjust the timer to 2 minutes,

4. When it beeps; *Quick Release* the steam and remove the lid.

5. Transfer the sauce to a blender and blend well to form a smooth mixture, Use immediately or save in a bottle for later use.

Nutrition Values Nutritional Values Per serving

Calories:- 43
Carbohydrate:9.5g
Protein:- 0.5g
Fat:- 0.1g
Sugar:- 1.4g
Sodium:- 0.45g

487. Fish Anchovy Stock Recipe

Preparation Time: 25 minutes
Serves: 8

Ingredients

2-ounce dried anchovies
1 celery stalk; chopped into thirds
6 small pieces kombu
1/2 tsp. whole black peppercorns
8 cups water
1 tsp. kosher salt

Directions:

1. Pour the water into the instant pot.
2. Put all the Ingredients into the water.
3. Secure the lid and turn the pressure release handle to the *sealed* position.
4. Select the *Manual* function. Set to high pressure and adjust the timer to 20 minutes,
5. When it beeps; *Natural Release* the steam for 10 minutes and remove the lid.
6. Strain the prepared stock through a mesh strainer and discard all the solids, Skim off all the surface fats and serve hot.

Nutrition Values Nutritional Values Per serving

Calories:- 20
Carbohydrate:0.9g
Protein:- 2.3g
Fat:- 0.7g
Sugar:- 0g
Sodium:- 0.63g

488. Beef Vegetable Stock Recipe

Preparation Time: 2 hours 11 minutes
Serves: 10

Ingredients

4 lbs. beef stock bones
2 tbsp. olive oil
1 celery stalk; chopped into thirds
1 small onion; unpeeled and halved
2 garlic cloves; chopped.
1/2 cup bell peppers; sliced
1/4 cabbage; chopped.
1/2 tsp. whole black peppercorns
1 sprig fresh parsley
1 tbsp. apple cider vinegar
1 cup carrots; chopped.
1 tsp. kosher salt

Directions:

1. Grease the baking tray with olive oil and place the beef bones on it.
2. Roast the bones for 30 minutes in an oven at 420o F. Flip the bones over and roast for another 20 minutes
3. Fill the instant pot with water up to one inch below the max line.
4. Add all the ingredients; including the roasted beef bones to the water.
5. Secure the lid. Turn the pressure release handle to the *sealed* position.
6. Select the *Manual* function; set to high pressure and adjust the time to 75 minutes,
7. When it beeps; *Natural Release* the steam for 10 minutes and remove the lid.
8. Strain the prepared stock through a mesh strainer and discard all the solids, Skim off all the surface fats and serve hot.

Nutrition Values Nutritional Values Per serving

Calories:- 396
Carbohydrate:- 1.3g
Protein:- 48.4g
Fat:- 18.9g
Sugar:- 0.4g
Sodium:- 0.36g

489. Chicken Bone Broth

Serves: 4
Cooking Time: 70 minutes

Ingredients:

1 chicken bones
6 cups water

¼ cup apple cider vinegar
1 tbsp sea salt

Directions for Cooking:

1. Add all ingredients into the instant pot.
2. Seal pot with lid and cook on manual mode for 60 minutes.
3. Allow to release pressure naturally for 10 minutes then release using quick release method.
4. Strain the broth and store.

Nutrition information Nutritional Values Per serving:

Calories: 38
Carbohydrates: 0.9g
Protein: 4.9g
Fat: 1.4g
Sugar: 0.7g
Sodium: 763mg

490. Leftover Turkey Stock

Serves: 4
Cooking Time: 70 minutes

Ingredients:

1 lb leftover turkey carcass
6 cups water
2 garlic cloves
1 cup carrots, sliced
1 cup celery, sliced
1 cup onion, diced

Directions for Cooking:

1. Add all ingredients into the instant pot.
2. Seal pot with lid and cook on manual mode for 60 minutes.
3. Allow to release pressure naturally for 10 minutes then release using quick release method.
4. Strain the stock and store.

Nutrition information Nutritional Values Per serving:

Calories: 10
Carbohydrates: 0.9g
Protein: 2g
Fat: 0g
Sugar: 0.9g
Sodium: 990mg

491. Bolognese Sauce

Serves: 4 | **Cooking Time:** 8 minutes

Ingredients:

1 lb ground beef
1 ½ tsp garlic, minced
3 tbsp fresh parsley, chopped
14 oz marinara sauce

Directions for Cooking:

1. Add all ingredients into the instant pot and stir well.
2. Seal pot with lid and cook on high for 8 minutes.
3. Release pressure using quick release method than open the lid.
4. Stir well and serve.

Nutrition information Nutritional Values Per serving:

Calories: 300
Carbohydrates: 14.2g
Protein: 36.3g
Fat: 9.8g
Sugar: 8.8g
Sodium: 483mg

492. Spicy Beef Stock

Serves: 6
Cooking Time: 45 minutes

Ingredients:

2 lbs beef bones
½ tsp red pepper flakes
2 tsp chili pepper
3 tbsp red wine vinegar

¼ cup onions, chopped
¼ cup celery, chopped
¼ cup celery stalk, chopped
3 garlic cloves
3 chili peppers
1 tsp salt

Directions for Cooking:

1. Add all ingredients to the pot and pour enough water to cover.
2. Seal pot with lid and cook on high for 35 minutes.
3. Allow to release pressure naturally for 10 minutes then release using quick release method.
4. Strain stock and store.

Nutrition information Nutritional Values Per serving:

Calories: 17
Carbohydrates: 1.7g
Protein: 2g
Fat: 0.4g
Sugar: 0.6g
Sodium: 396mg

493. Chicken Thyme Stock

Serves: 4
Cooking Time: 35 minutes

Ingredients:

2 lbs chicken neck
1 tsp peppercorn
1 tsp dried thyme
½ cup fresh parsley, chopped
2 chicken thighs
2 tsp sea salt

Directions for Cooking:

1. Add all ingredients to the pot and pour enough water to cover.
2. Seal pot with lid and cook on high for 25 minutes.

3. Allow to release pressure naturally for 10 minutes then release using quick release method.
4. Strain stock and store.

Nutrition information Nutritional Values Per serving:

Calories: 12
Carbohydrates: 1g
Protein: 0.8g
Fat: 0.6g
Sugar: 0.1g
Sodium: 941mg

494. Spicy Lamb Stock

Serves: 5
Cooking Time: 6 hours 10 minute

Ingredients:

2 lbs lamb bones
½ tsp white pepper
1 tsp red pepper flakes
2 tsp chili powder
¼ cup red wine vinegar
¼ cup celery, chopped
5 garlic cloves
1 onion, sliced
1 tsp salt

Directions for Cooking:

1. Add all ingredients into the instant pot and pour enough water to cover.
2. Seal pot with lid and cook on slow cook mode for 6 hours.
3. Allow to release pressure naturally for 10 minutes then release using quick release method.
4. Strain stock and store.

Nutrition information Nutritional Values Per serving:

Calories: 24
Carbohydrates: 4.2g
Protein: 2.5g
Fat: 0.7g

Sugar: 1.2g
Sodium: 620mg

495. Classic Beef Stock

Serves: 4
Cooking Time: 45 minutes

Ingredients:

2 lbs beef bones
½ tsp dried basil
1 tsp peppercorns
4 garlic cloves
½ cup celery stalks, chopped
2 tbsp red wine vinegar
1 tsp sea salt

Directions for Cooking:

1. Add all ingredients into the instant pot and pour enough water to cover.
2. Seal pot with lid and cook on high for 35 minutes.
3. Allow to release pressure naturally for 10 minutes then release using quick release method.
4. Strain stock and store.

Nutrition information Nutritional Values Per serving:

Calories: 18
Carbohydrates: 1.8g
Protein: 2.3g
Fat: 0.4g
Sugar: 0.2g
Sodium: 479mg

496. Celery Lamb Stock

Serves: 4
Cooking Time: 15 minutes

Ingredients:

2 lbs lamb bones
1 tsp dried thyme
2 tbsp apple cider vinegar
½ cup celery leaves
2 celery stalks, chopped
2 onions, sliced
1 tsp salt

Directions for Cooking:

1. Add all ingredients into the instant pot and pour enough water to cover.
2. Seal pot with lid and cook on high for 15 minutes.
3. Release pressure using quick release method than open the lid.
4. Strain stock and store.

Nutrition information Nutritional Values Per serving:

Calories: 42
Carbohydrates: 6g
Protein: 3.4g
Fat: 0.6g
Sugar: 2.6g
Sodium: 773mg

497. Butter Cheese Sauce

Serves: 8
Cooking Time: 8 minutes

Ingredients:

1/3 cup butter
¼ tsp dried basil
1 tsp red chili flakes
1 cup vegetable stock
2 garlic cloves, crushed
¼ cup fresh parsley, chopped
2 tbsp parmesan cheese, grated
1 cup cottage cheese
2 cups cream cheese
½ tsp salt

Directions for Cooking:

1. Add butter, basil, red chili flakes, and salt to the instant pot and set pot on sauté mode.

2. Once butter is melted then add garlic and sauté for a minute.
3. Add parmesan cheese, cottage cheese, and cream cheese and cook for 2 minutes.
4. Add parsley and stock. Stir well. Seal pot with lid and cook on manual mode for 6 minutes.
5. Release pressure using quick release method than open the lid.
6. Once sauce is cool completely then store in a jar.

Nutrition information Nutritional Values Per serving:

Calories: 308
Carbohydrates: 3.2g
Protein: 9.2g
Fat: 29.3g
Sugar: 0.5g
Sodium: 617mg

498. Cheese Onion Sauce

Serves: 5
Cooking Time: 35 minutes

Ingredients:

1 onion, chopped
2 tsp dried parsley
1 tsp onion powder
2 tbsp olive oil
1 cup vegetable stock
2 cups cream cheese

Directions for Cooking:

1. Add oil into the instant pot and set the pot on sauté mode.
2. Add onion and sauté for 10 minutes.
3. Add remaining ingredients and stir well.
4. Seal pot with lid and cook manual mode for 15 minutes.
5. Allow to release pressure naturally for 10 minutes then release using quick release method.
6. Allow to cool completely then store.

Nutrition information Nutritional

Values Per serving:

Calories: 385
Carbohydrates: 5.3g
Protein: 7.3g
Fat: 3804g
Sugar: 1.7g
Sodium: 420mg

499. Enchilada Sauce

Serves: 8 | **Cooking Time:** 20 minutes

Ingredients:

14 oz can roasted tomatoes, diced
½ cup water
1 tsp red chili powder
2 chipotle chilies in adobo sauce
3 garlic cloves
½ jalapeno pepper, sliced
½ bell pepper, chopped
½ onion, chopped
1 tsp salt

Directions for Cooking:

1. Add all ingredients except tomatoes into the instant pot and stir well.
2. Add tomatoes on top. Seal pot with lid and cook on high for 10 minutes.
3. Allow to release pressure naturally for 10 minutes then release using quick release method.
4. Using blender blend the sauce and store.

Nutrition information Nutritional Values Per serving:

Calories: 20
Carbohydrates: 4.2g
Protein: 0.7g
Fat: 0.1g
Sugar: 1.9g
Sodium: 408mg

500. Curry Tomato Sauce

Serves: 8
Cooking Time: 13 minutes

Ingredients:

- 28 oz can tomatoes, crushed
- ½ cup can coconut milk
- ½ tsp black pepper
- 1 tbsp fresh thyme leaves
- ¼ tsp ground cinnamon
- ¼ tsp red pepper flakes
- ½ tsp turmeric
- ½ tsp garam masala
- 1 tbsp ginger, minced
- 3 garlic cloves
- ½ onion, diced
- 1 tsp sea salt

Directions for Cooking:

1. Add all ingredients into the instant pot and stir well.
2. Seal pot with lid and cook on high for 10 minutes.
3. Release pressure using quick release method than open the lid.
4. Using blender blend the sauce until smooth.
5. Transfer sauce in container and store.

Nutrition information Nutritional Values Per serving:

Calories: 58
Carbohydrates: 7.4g
Protein: 1.5g
Fat: 3.1g
Sugar: 3.7g
Sodium: 448mg

501. Parmesan Basil Sauce

Serves: 5
Cooking Time: 15 minutes

Ingredients:

- 1 tbsp parmesan cheese
- ¼ tsp dried thyme
- ¼ tsp black pepper
- 1 tbsp olive oil
- 1 garlic clove, crushed
- ½ cup fresh basil
- ½ cup feta cheese, crumbled
- 1 cup cream cheese
- ½ tsp salt

Directions for Cooking:

1. Add all ingredients into the heat-safe bowl and stir well.
2. Pour ½ cup of water into the instant pot than place a trivet in the pot.
3. Place bowl on top of the trivet. Seal pot with lid and cook on manual mode for 10 minutes.
4. Release pressure using quick release method than open the lid.
5. Remove bowl from the pot and set aside to cool completely.
6. Place in refrigerator for an hour. Serve chilled.

Nutrition information Nutritional Values Per serving:

Calories: 232
Carbohydrates: 2.2g
Protein: 6.1g
Fat: 22.5g
Sugar: 0.7g
Sodium: 555mg

502. Tomato Goat Cheese Sauce

Serves: 4
Cooking Time: 3 hours

Ingredients:

- 1 cup goat cheese, crumbled
- ¼ tsp chili powder
- 1 tsp dried rosemary
- ¼ cup apple cider vinegar
- 3 tbsp olive oil
- 3 garlic cloves, crushed
- 1 onion, chopped
- ½ cup mozzarella cheese, shredded
- 1 cup tomatoes, diced

Directions for Cooking:

1. Add all ingredients into the instant pot and stir well to combine.
2. Seal pot with lid and cook on slow cook mode for 3 hours.
3. Release pressure using quick release method than open the lid.
4. Allow to cool completely then serve.

Nutrition information Nutritional Values Per serving:

Calories: 207
Carbohydrates: 6.6g
Protein: 6.9g
Fat: 18.3g
Sugar: 2.4g
Sodium: 162mg

503. Marinara Sauce

Serves: 8
Cooking Time: 17 minutes

Ingredients:

¼ cup water
¼ tsp red pepper flakes
½ tsp oregano
½ tsp thyme
3 tbsp fresh basil
1 carrot, peeled and grated
1 ¼ lbs tomatoes, crushed
3 garlic cloves, chopped
1 onion, chopped
1 tbsp olive oil
Pepper
Salt

Directions for Cooking:

1. Add oil into the instant pot and set the pot on sauté mode.
2. Add garlic and onion and sauté for 2 minutes.
3. Add remaining ingredients and stir well.
4. Seal pot with lid and cook on high for 30 minutes.
5. Release pressure using quick release method than open the lid.
6. Using blender blend the sauce.

7. Allow to cool completely then store in a container.

Nutrition information Nutritional Values Per serving:

Calories: 39
Carbohydrates: 5.3g
Protein: 1g
Fat: 1.9g
Sugar: 2.8g
Sodium: 29mg

504. Onion Apple Sauce

Serves: 8
Cooking Time: 55 minutes

Ingredients:

1 onion, chopped
2 apples, chopped
¼ tsp liquid stevia
¼ cup fresh cilantro, chopped
1 cup vegetable broth
2 tbsp butter
¼ cup apple cider vinegar
½ tsp salt

Directions for Cooking:

1. Add butter into the instant pot and set the pot on sauté mode.
2. Add onion and apple to the pot and sauté for 10 minutes.
3. Add stevia, apple cider vinegar, and salt. Stir well.
4. Add broth and cilantro. Seal pot with lid and cook on manual mode for 35 minutes.
5. Allow to release pressure naturally for 10 minutes then release using quick release method.
6. Using blender puree the sauce until smooth.

Nutrition information Nutritional Values Per serving:

Calories: 66
Carbohydrates: 9g

Protein: 1g
Fat: 3.2g
Sugar: 6.5g
Sodium: 265mg

505. Pasta Sauce

Serves: 12
Cooking Time: 33 minutes

Ingredients:

8 cups tomatoes, diced
1 tsp sugar
1 tsp pepper
1 ½ tbsp Italian seasoning
4 garlic cloves, minced
1 onion, diced
3 cups water
2 tbsp olive oil
1 tsp salt

Directions for Cooking:

1. Add oil into the instant pot and set the pot on sauté mode.
2. Add garlic and onion and sauté for 2-3 minutes.
3. Add remaining ingredients and stir well. Seal pot with lid and cook on high for 30 minutes.
4. Release pressure using quick release method than open the lid.
5. Puree the sauce using a blender.
6. Serve over pasta and enjoy.

Nutrition information Nutritional Values Per serving:

Calories: 54
Carbohydrates: 6.5g
Protein: 1.3g
Fat: 3.1g
Sugar: 4g
Sodium: 203mg

Chapter 10 – Desserts

506. Maple Crème Brulee

Serves: 3
Preparation Time: 10 minutes
Cooking Time: 30 minutes

Ingredients

3 large egg yolks, beaten
½ cup packed brown sugar
¼ teaspoon ground cinnamon
1 1/3 cups heavy whipping cream, warm
½ teaspoon maple flavoring
1 ½ teaspoon sugar for topping

Directions

1. Place a steamer in the Instant Pot and pour a cup of boiling water.
2. In a bowl, whisk the yolks, sugar, and cinnamon. Stir in the warm cream to the yolk mixture.
3. Stir in the maple flavoring.
4. Ladle the mixture into ramekins and sprinkle sugar for the topping.
5. Place the ramekins in the steamer basket.
6. Close the lid and press the Steam button.
7. Adjust the cooking time to 30 minutes.
8. Do natural pressure release.
9. Remove the ramekins and allow to cool in the fridge for 10 minutes.

Nutritional Values Per serving:

Calories: 578
Carbohydrates: 44g
Protein: 5g
Fat: 44g
Fiber: 0g

507. Sweet Rice Pudding

Serves: 4
Preparation Time: 10 minutes
Cooking Time: 15 minutes

Ingredients

1 ¼ cups milk
½ cup uncooked rice
½ cups brown sugar
½ cup raisin
1 teaspoon ground cinnamon
1 teaspoon butter, melted
2 eggs, beaten
1 teaspoon vanilla extract
¾ teaspoon lemon extract
1 cup heavy whipping cream

Directions

1. Place all ingredients except the whipping cream in the Instant Pot.
2. Give a good stir to incorporate all ingredients.
3. Close the lid and press the Manual button.
4. Adjust the cooking time to 15 minutes
5. Allow to chill in the fridge before serving.
6. Serve with whipping cream

Nutritional Values Per serving:

Calories:437
Carbohydrates: 63g
Protein: 8g
Fat:17 g
Fiber: 1g

508. Coconut, Cranberry, And Quinoa Crockpot Breakfast

Serves: 4
Preparation Time: 5 minutes
Cooking Time: 20 minutes

Ingredients

- 2 ½ cups coconut water
- ¼ cup slivered almonds
- ½ cup coconut meat
- 1 cup quinoa, rinsed
- ½ cup dried cranberries
- 1 tablespoon vanilla
- ¼ cup honey

Directions

1. Place all ingredients except the whipping cream in the Instant Pot.
2. Give a good stir to incorporate all ingredients.
3. Close the lid and press the Manual button.
4. Adjust the cooking time to 20 minutes
5. Allow to chill in the fridge before serving.

Nutritional Values Per serving:

Calories: 478
Carbohydrates:66.1 g
Protein: 6.4g
Fat:25.8 g
Fiber: 8.1g

509. Caramel and Pear Pudding

Serves: 7
Preparation Time: 10 minutes
Cooking Time: 15 minutes

Ingredients

- ½ cup sugar
- ½ teaspoon ground cinnamon
- 1 ½ teaspoons baking powder
- 1/8 teaspoon ground cloves
- ¼ teaspoon salt
- 3/4 cup milk
- 4 medium pears, peeled and cubed
- ½ cup pecans, chopped
- ¾ cup brown sugar
- ¼ cup softened butter

Directions

1. Place all ingredients in the Instant Pot.

2. Give a good stir to incorporate all ingredients.
3. Close the lid and press the Manual button.
4. Adjust the cooking time to 15 minutes
5. Allow to chill in the fridge before serving.

Nutritional Values Per serving:

Calories:274
Carbohydrates:47 g
Protein: 3g
Fat: 9g
Fiber: 3g

510. Double Dark Chocolate Cake

Serves: 6
Preparation Time: 10 minutes
Cooking Time: 25 minutes

Ingredients

- 4 drops liquid stevia
- 2 tablespoon raw cacao nibs
- ¼ cups unsweetened applesauce
- 2 tablespoon almond milk, unsweetened
- ½ cup coconut milk, full fat
- 1 large egg
- ½ teaspoon vanilla
- ½ cup cacao powder
- ½ cup raw honey
- 2 tablespoon tapioca flour
- 1 cup almond flour

Directions

1. Place a steamer basket in the Instant Pot.
2. In a mixing bowl, combine all ingredients.
3. Pour into a baking dish that will fit in the Instant Pot.
4. Place aluminum foil on top.
5. Place on top of the steamer basket.
6. Close the lid and press the Steam button.
7. Adjust the cooking time to 30 minutes.
8. Do natural pressure release.

Nutritional Values Per serving:

Calories: 267
Carbohydrates: 15.6g
Protein: 18.1g
Fat: 46.6g
Fiber: 72.1g

511. Apple Cinnamon Cake

Serves: 6
Preparation Time: 10 minutes
Cooking Time: 30 minutes

Ingredients

1 teaspoon fresh nutmeg, grated
1 tablespoon vanilla
1 medium peeled apple, cored and diced
1 large egg
½ cup raw honey
¼ cup coconut oil, melted
1 teaspoon cinnamon
¼ cup arrowroot powder
½ teaspoon baking soda
½ teaspoon salt
2 cups almond flour

Directions

1. Place a steamer basket in the Instant Pot.
2. In a mixing bowl, combine all ingredients.
3. Pour into a baking dish that will fit in the Instant Pot.
4. Place aluminum foil on top.
5. Place on top of the steamer basket.
6. Close the lid and press the Steam button.
7. Adjust the cooking time to 30 minutes.
8. Do natural pressure release.

Nutritional Values Per serving:

Calories:204
Carbohydrates: 29.1g
Protein: 0.9g
Fat: 10.4g
Fiber: 1.2g

512. Fruit Salad Jam

Serves: 6
Preparation Time: 5 minutes
Cooking Time: 15 minutes

Ingredients

½ teaspoon cinnamon
1 medium apple, diced
1 medium oranges, peeled
1 cup blueberries
1 cup sugar
Zest of ½ lemon
1 ½ cups water

Directions

1. Place all ingredients in the Instant Pot.
2. Give a good stir.
3. Close the lid and press the Manual button.
4. Adjust the cooking time to 10 minutes.
5. Do natural pressure release.
6. Once the lid is open, press the Sauté button and simmer to reduce the sauce.

Nutritional Values Per serving:

Calories: 131
Carbohydrates: 33.6g
Protein: 0.7g
Fat: 0.2g
Fiber: 2.1g

513. Pumpkin Spice Chocolate Chip Cookies

Serves: 6
Preparation Time: 10 minutes
Cooking Time: 30 minutes

Ingredients

½ cup chocolate chips, semi-sweet
1 tablespoon pumpkin pie spice
1 teaspoon baking soda
2 teaspoons vanilla
¼ cup coconut oil
¼ cup raw honey

3 tablespoon almond butter
½ cup pumpkin puree
1 ½ cup all-purpose flour

Directions

1. Place a steamer basket in the Instant Pot.
2. In a mixing bowl, combine all ingredients.
3. Pour into a baking dish that will fit in the Instant Pot.
4. Place aluminum foil on top.
5. Place on top of the steamer basket.
6. Close the lid and press the Steam button.
7. Adjust the cooking time to 30 minutes.
8. Do natural pressure release.

Nutritional Values Per serving:

Calories: 489
Carbohydrates: 58.9g
Protein: 9.4g
Fat: 25.5g
Fiber: 3.2g

514. Instant Pot Sweetened Rhubarb

Serves: 6
Preparation Time: 5 minutes
Cooking Time: 15 minutes

Ingredients

½ cups strawberries, fresh and cleaned
2 medium lemon, juiced
1 teaspoon vanilla
1 medium orange, juiced
1 ½ pounds rhubarb, sliced into segments
1 cup water
2 cups raw honey

Directions

1. Place all ingredients in the Instant Pot.
2. Give a good stir.
3. Close the lid and press the Manual button.
4. Adjust the cooking time to 10 minutes.
5. Do natural pressure release.
6. Once the lid is open, press the Sauté button and simmer to reduce the sauce.

Nutritional Values Per serving:

Calories: 484
Carbohydrates: 130g
Protein: 0.9g
Fat: 0.3g
Fiber: 2.8g

515. Vanilla Mousse Cups

Preparation Time: 15 minutes
Serve: 6

Ingredients:

8 ounces1 block cream cheese, softened
1/2 cup sugar substitute such as Swerve or TruviaStevia
1 1/2 tsp vanilla extract
Dash of sea salt
1/2 cup heavy whipping cream

Directions:

1. Add the first four ingredients to a food processor or blender.
2. Blend until combined.
3. With blender running, slowly add the heavy cream.
4. Continue to blend until thickened, about 12 minutes. Consistency should be mousselike.
5. Prepare a cupcake or muffin tin with 6 paper liners and portion the mixture into the cups.
6. Chill in the fridge until set and enjoy!

Nutritional Value

Calories 170
Fats 16.9g
Carbohydrates: 1.6g
Protein 3.1g

516.Rich & Creamy Fat Bomb Ice Cream

Preparation Time: 20 minutes

Serve: 5

Ingredients:

4 whole pastured eggs
4 yolks from pastured eggs
⅓ Cup melted cocoa butter
⅓ Cup melted coconut oil
1520 drops liquid stevia
⅓ Cup cocoa powder
¼ cup MCT oil
2 tsp pure vanilla extract
810 ice cubes

Directions:

1. Add all ingredients but the ice cubes into the jug of your highspeed blender. Blend on high for 2 minutes, until creamy.

2. While the blender is running, remove the top portion of the lid and drop in 1 ice cube at a time, allowing the blender to run about 10 seconds between each ice cube.

3. Once all of the ice has been added, pour the cold mixture into a 9×5" loaf pan and place in the freezer. Set the timer for 30 minutes before taking out to stir. Repeat this process for 23 hours, until desired consistency is met.

4. Serve immediately. Top with chopped nuts or shaved dark chocolate, if desired.

5. Store covered in the freezer for up to a week.

Nutritional Value

Calories 448
Fats 48.1g
Carbohydrates: 4.1g
Protein 7.6g
Fiber 1.7g

517. English Toffee Treats

Preparation Time: 10 minutes
Serve: 24

Ingredients:

1 cup coconut oil

2 tbsp butter
1/2 block cream cheese, softened
3/4 tbsp cocoa powder
1/2 cup creamy, natural peanut butter
3 tbsp Davinci Gourmet SugarFree English Toffee Syrup

Directions:

1. Combine all ingredients in a saucepan over medium heat.

2. Stir until everything is smooth, melted, and combined.

3. Pour mixture into small candy molds or mini muffin tins lined with paper liners.

4. Freeze or refrigerate until set and enjoy!

5. Store in an airtight container in the fridge.

Nutritional Value

Calories 125
Fats 13.4g
Carbohydrates: 1.1g
Protein 1.3g

518. Fudgy Peanut Butter Squares

Preparation Time: 10 minutes
Serve: 12

Ingredients:

1 cup all natural creamy peanut butter
1 cup coconut oil
1/4 cup unsweetened vanilla almond milk
a pinch of coarse sea salt
1 tsp vanilla extract
2 tsp liquid steviaoptional

Directions:

1. In a microwavesafe bowl, soften the peanut butter and coconut oil together. About 1 minute on medlow heat.

2. Combine the softened peanut butter and coconut oil with the remaining ingredients into a blender or food processor.

3. Blend until thoroughly combined.

4. Pour into a 9X4" loaf pan that has been lined with parchment paper.
5. Refrigerate until set. About 2 hours.
6. Enjoy.

Nutritional Value

Calories 292
Fats 28.9g
Carbohydrates: 4.1g
Protein 6g

519.Lemon Squares & Coconut Cream

Preparation Time: 1 HR 5 minutes
Serve: 8

Ingredients:

Base:

> *3/4 cup coconut flakes*
> *2 Tbsp coconut oil*
> *1 Tbsp ground almonds*

Cream:

> *5 eggs*
> *1/2 lemon juice*
> *1 Tbsp coconut flour*
> *1/2 cup Stevia sweetener*

Directions:

For the base

1. Preheat oven to 360 F.
2. In a bowl put all base ingredients and with clean hands mix everything well until soft.
3. With coconut oil grease a rectangle oven dish. Pour dough into a baking pan. Bake for 15 minutes until golden brown. Set aside to cool.

For the cream

1. In a bowl or blender, whisk together: eggs, lemon juice, coconut flour, and sweetener. Pour over the baked caked evenly.
2. Put the pan in the oven and bake 20 minutes more.

3. When ready refrigerate for at least 6 hours. Cut into cubes and serve.

Nutritional Value

Calories 129
Fats 15g
Carbohydrates: 1.4g
Protein 5g

520.Rich Almond Butter Cake & Chocolate Sauce

Preparation Time: 10 minutes
Serve: 12

Ingredients:

> *1 cup almond butter or soaked almonds*
> *1/4 cup almond milk, unsweetened*
> *1 cup coconut oil*
> *2 tsp liquid Stevia sweetener to taste*
> *Topping: Chocolate Sauce*
> *4 Tbsp cocoa powder, unsweetened*
> *2 Tbsp almond butter*
> *2 Tbsp Stevia sweetener*

Directions:

1. Melt the coconut oil in room temperature.
2. Add all ingredients in a bowl and blend well until combined.
3. Pour the almond butter mixture into a parchment lined platter.
4. Place in refrigerator for 3 hours.
5. In a bowl, whisk all topping ingredients together. Pour over the almond cake after it's been set. Cut into cubes and serve.

Nutritional Value

Calories 273
Fats 23.3g
Carbohydrates: 2.4g
Protein 5.8g

521.Peanut Butter Cake Covered in Chocolate Sauce

Preparation Time: 10 minutes
Serve: 12

Ingredients:

1 cup peanut butter
1/4 cup almond milk, unsweetened
1 cup coconut oil
2 tsp liquid Stevia sweetener to taste
Topping: Chocolate Sauce
2 Tbsp coconut oil, melted
4 Tbsp cocoa powder, unsweetened
2 Tbsp Stevia sweetener

Directions:

1. In a microwave bowl mix coconut oil and peanut butter melt in a microwave for 12 minutes.
2. Add this mixture to your blender add in the rest of the ingredients and blend well until combined.
3. Pour the peanut mixture into a parchment lined loaf pan or platter.
4. Refrigerate for about 3 hours the longer, the better.
5. In a bowl, whisk all topping ingredients together. Pour over the peanut candy after it's been set. Cut into cubes and serve.

Nutritional Value

Calories 273
Fats 27g
Carbohydrates: 2.4g
Protein 6g

522.Mint Custard

Preparation Time: 35 minutes
Serves: 8

Ingredients:

1 cup almond milk, unsweetened
1 cup coconut milk, unsweetened
5 large eggs
1 tbsp. powdered stevia
1 tsp peppermint extract

Directions:

1. In a large mixing bowl, combine almond milk, coconut milk, eggs, stevia, and peppermint extract. Beat on high speed for 3 minutes or until well combined.
2. Plug in your instant pot and pour in 2 cups of water. Position a trivet in the stainless steel insert. Pour the mixture into 8 small ramekins and place on top. Cover each with an aluminum foil.
3. Seal the lid and adjust the steam release handle. Press the "Manual" button and set the timer for 30 minutes. Cook on high pressure.
4. When you hear the cooker's end signal, press "Cancel" button and release the pressure naturally. Open the lid and chill to a room temperature. Optionally, decorate with few mint leaves.
5. Refrigerate for 30 minutes before serving.

Nutritional Value

Calories 119
Fats 10.6g
Carbohydrates: 0.3g
Protein 4.8g

523.Keto Carrot Cake

Preparation Time: 55 minutes
Serves: 8

Ingredients:

2 cups almond flour
¼ cup almonds, chopped
1 small carrot, shredded
4 large eggs
½ cup heavy cream
1 tsp baking powder
1 tbsp. stevia powder
1 tsp apple pie seasoning

Directions:

1. In a large mixing bowl, combine all ingredients. Mix until all well combined and set aside. Pour the mixture into 6inches

springform pan and cover with aluminum foil.

2. Plug in your instant pot and pour in 2 cups of water. Position a trivet in the stainless steel insert. Place the springform pan on top and securely close the lid.

3. Adjust the steam release handle and press the "Manual" button. Set the timer for 40 minutes. Cook on high pressure.

4. When done, press "Cancel" button and turn off the pot. Release the pressure naturally.

5. Let it chill to a room temperature before serving.

Nutritional Value

Calories 126
Fats 10.1g
Carbohydrates: 2.7g
Protein 5.5g

524.Chocolate Bundt Cake

Preparation Time: 30 minutes
Serves: 10

Ingredients:

1 cup almond flour
½ cup cocoa powder, unsweetened
3 tbsp. walnuts, unsweetened
4 large eggs
4 tbsp. coconut oil, melted
½ cup heavy cream
1 tsp baking powder
1 tsp powdered stevia

Directions:

1. Combine all dry ingredients in large mixing bowl. Mix well and then add eggs, coconut oil, and heavy cream. Using a hand mixer, beat until well combined.

2. Grease a 6inches bundt pan with some cooking spray. Pour in the batter and set aside.

3. Plug in your instant pot and pour in 2 cups of water in the stainless steel insert.

Position a trivet and place the bundt pan on top. Securely close the lid and adjust the steam release handle.

4. Press the "Manual" button and set the timer for 20 minutes. Cook on high pressure.

5. When you hear the cooker's end signal, press "Cancel" button and release the pressure naturally.

6. Open the pot and let it chill to a room temperature before serving.
Enjoy!

Nutritional Value

Calories 137
Fats 12.9g
Carbohydrates: 1.9g
Protein 4.6g

525.Raspberry Mug Cake

Preparation Time: 15 minutes
Serves: 3

Ingredients:

1 cup almond flour
½ cup fresh raspberries
1 tbsp. dark chocolate chips, unsweetened
3 large eggs
1 tbsp. swerve
¼ tsp vanilla extract, sugarfree
¼ tsp salt

Directions:

1. Mix together all ingredients in a large mixing bowl. Grease 3 mason jars with some cooking spray and evenly divide the mixture between them.

2. Plug in your instant pot and pour in 2 cups of water. Position a trivet in the stainless steel insert and place the jars on top. Cover each jar with aluminum foil and lock the lid.

3. Adjust the steam release handle and press the "Manual" button. Set the timer for 10

minutes and cook on high pressure.

4. When you hear the cooker's end signal, press "Cancel" button and turn off the pot. Perform a quick release of the pressure by turning the valve to a venting position.

5. Remove the jars from the pot and let it chill to a room temperature before serving.

Enjoy!

Nutritional Value

Calories 151
Fats 10.2g
Carbohydrates: 4.4g
Protein 8.7g

526. Melon Cream

Preparation Time: 5 minutes
Cooking Time: 10 minutes
Serves: 6

Ingredients:

Flesh from 1 melon
1 ounce stevia
1 cup natural apple juice
1 tablespoon ghee
Juice of 1 lemon

Directions:

1. Put melon and apple juice in your instant pot, cover, cook on High for 7 minutes, transfer to a blender, add lemon juice, ghee and stevia, pulse well and return to your instant pot.

2. Set on simmer mode, cook for a couple more minutes, divide into dessert cups and serve.

3. Enjoy!

Nutritional Values Per serving

calories 73
fat 1
fiber 1
carbs 2
protein 2

527. Peach Cream

Preparation Time: 5 minutes
Cooking Time: 3 minutes
Serves: 6

Ingredients:

10 ounces peaches, stoned and chopped
A pinch of nutmeg, ground
2 tablespoons coconut flakes
3 tablespoons stevia
½ cup water
1/8 teaspoon cinnamon powder
1/8 teaspoon almond extract

Directions:

1. In your instant pot, mix peaches with nutmeg, coconut, stevia, almond extract and cinnamon, stir, cover and cook at High for 3 minutes.

2. Divide into small cups and serve.

Enjoy!

Nutritional Values Per serving

calories 90
fat 2
fiber 1
carbs 3
protein 5

528. Peaches and Sweet Sauce

Preparation Time: 10 minutes
Cooking Time: 10 minutes
Serves: 6

Ingredients:

4 tablespoons stevia
3 cups peaches, cored and roughly chopped
6 tablespoons natural apple juice
2 teaspoons lemon zest, grated

Directions:

1. In your instant pot mix peaches with stevia, apple juice and lemon zest, stir,

cover and cook at High for 10 minutes.

2. Divide into small cups and serve cold. Enjoy!

Nutritional Values Per serving

calories 80
fat 2
fiber 2
carbs 5
protein 5

529. Chestnut Cream

Preparation Time: 10 minutes
Cooking Time: 20 minutes
Serves: 6

Ingredients:

11 ounces stevia
11 ounces water
1 and ½ pounds chestnuts, halved and peeled

Directions:

1. In your instant pot, mix stevia with water and chestnuts, stir, cover and cook on High for 20 minutes.
2. Blend using your immersion blender, divide into small cups and serve. Enjoy!

Nutritional Values Per serving

calories 82
fat 1
fiber 0
carbs 5
protein 3

530. Cheesecake

Preparation Time: 60 minutes
Cooking Time: 50 minutes
Serves: 12

Ingredients:

For the crust:

4 tablespoons melted ghee
1 and ½ cups chocolate cookie crumbs

For the filling:

24 ounces cream cheese, soft
2 tablespoons coconut flakes
3 tablespoons stevia
3 eggs
1 tablespoon vanilla extract
Cooking spray
1 cup water
½ cup Greek yogurt
5 ounces white chocolate, unsweetened and melted
5 ounces bittersweet chocolate, melted

Directions:

1. In a bowl mix cookie crumbs with ghee, stir well, press on the bottom of a cake pan that you've greased with cooking spray, and lined with parchment paper.
2. In a bowl, mix cream cheese with coconut, stevia, eggs, vanilla and yogurt, whisk well and leave aside for a few minutes.
3. Put milk chocolate in a heatproof bowl and heat up in the microwave for 30 seconds.
4. Add white and bittersweet chocolate, stir well again and pour over cookie crust.
5. Add the water to your instant pot, add steamer basket, and cake, cover and cook on High for 45 minutes.
6. Slice and serve cold. Enjoy!

Nutritional Values Per serving

calories 267
fat 4
fiber 7
carbs 10
protein 7

531. Banana Cake

Preparation Time: 10 minutes
Cooking Time: 30 minutes

Serves: 6

Ingredients:

- 4 tablespoons stevia
- 1/3 cup ghee, soft
- 1 teaspoon vanilla extract
- 1 egg
- 2 bananas, peeled and mashed
- 1 teaspoon baking powder
- 1 and ½ cups coconut flour
- ½ teaspoons baking soda
- 1/3 cup coconut milk
- 1 and ½ teaspoons keto cream of tartar
- 2 cups water
- Olive oil cooking spray

Directions:

1. In a bowl, mix milk with cream of tartar, stevia, ghee, egg, vanilla and bananas and stir everything.
2. Add flour, baking powder and baking soda, stir well and pour into a cake pan that you've greased with cooking spray.
3. Add the water to your instant pot, add steamer basket, and cake pan, cover and cook on High for 30 minutes.
4. Slice and serve cold.

   Enjoy!

Nutritional Values Per serving

calories 214
fat 2
fiber 2
carbs 6
protein 8

532. Pumpkin Cake

Preparation Time: 10 minutes
Cooking Time: 35 minutes
Serves: 12

Ingredients:

- 2 cups coconut flour
- 1 teaspoon baking soda
- ¾ teaspoon pumpkin pie spice

- ¾ cup stevia
- 1 banana, mashed
- ½ teaspoon baking powder
- 2 tablespoons coconut oil
- ½ cup Greek yogurt
- 8 ounces canned pumpkin puree
- Cooking spray
- 1-quart water
- 1 egg
- ½ teaspoon vanilla extract
- 2/3 cup chocolate chips

Directions:

1. In a bowl, mix flour with baking soda, baking powder, pumpkin spice, stevia, oil, banana, yogurt, pumpkin puree, vanilla and egg and stir using a mixer.
2. Add chocolate chips, stir, pour into a cake pan greased with cooking spray and cover with some tin foil.
3. Add the water to your instant pot, add steamer basket, add cake pan inside, cover and cook on High for 35 minutes.
4. Slice cake and serve cold.

   Enjoy!

Nutritional Values Per serving

calories 200
fat 3
fiber 3
carbs 6
protein 8

533. Apple Cake

Preparation Time: 10 minutes
Cooking Time: 1 hour and 10 minutes
Serves: 6

Ingredients:

- 3 cups apples, cored and cubed
- 4 tablespoons stevia
- 1 tablespoon vanilla extract
- 2 eggs
- 1 tablespoon apple pie spice
- 2 cups coconut flour

2 tablespoons ghee, melted
1 tablespoon baking powder
1 cup water

Directions:

1. In a bowl mix egg with ghee, apple pie spice, stevia, apples, flour and baking powder, stir and pour into a cake pan.
2. Add the water to your instant pot, add steamer basket, add cake pan inside, cover and cook on High for 1 hour.
3. Leave the cake to cool down, slice and serve.
   Enjoy!

Nutritional Values Per serving

calories 89
fat 1
fiber 2
carbs 5
protein 4

534. Sticky Pudding

Preparation Time: 15 minutes
Cooking Time: 20 minutes
Serves: 8

Ingredients:

2 cups water
1¼ cups dates, chopped
¼ cup blackstrap molasses
¾ cup hot water
1 teaspoon baking powder
1¼ cups white flour
Salt
¾ cup brown sugar
⅓ cup butter, softened
1 teaspoon vanilla extract
1 egg

For the caramel sauce:

⅓ cup whipping cream
⅔ cup brown sugar
¼ cup butter
1 teaspoon vanilla extract

Directions:

In a bowl, mix the dates with the hot water and molasses, stir and set the dish aside. In another bowl, mix the baking powder with the flour and salt. In a third bowl, mix the sugar with the butter, egg, and 1 teaspoon vanilla extract and stir using a hand mixer. Add the flour and dates mixtures to this bowl and stir well. Divide this mixture into 8 ramekins that greased with some butter, cover, with aluminum foil, place them in the steamer basket of the Instant Pot. Add 2 cups water to the Instant Pot, cover, and cook on Manual for 20 minutes. Heat up a pan with the butter for the caramel sauce over medium high heat. Add the cream, vanilla extract, and brown sugar, stir, and bring to a boil. Reduce the temperature to medium-low and simmer for 5 minutes, stirring often. Release the pressure from the Instant Pot, uncover it, take the ramekins out, remove the foil, drizzle sauce over pudding, and serve them warm.

Nutritional Values Per serving

Calories: 260
Fat: 14
Fiber: 1
Carbs: 33
Protein: 2
Sugar: 21

535. Pina Colada Pudding

Preparation Time: 10 minutes
Cooking Time: 5 minutes
Serves: 8

Ingredients:

1 tablespoon coconut oil
Salt
1½ cups water
1 cup Arborio rice
14 ounces canned coconut milk
2 eggs
½ cup milk
½ cup sugar
½ teaspoon vanilla extract

8 ounces canned pineapple chunks, drained and halved

Directions:

In the Instant Pot, mix the oil, water, rice, and salt, stir, cover and cook on the Manual setting for 3 minutes. Release the pressure for 10 minutes, uncover the Instant Pot, add the sugar and coconut milk and stir well. In a bowl, mix the eggs with milk and vanilla, stir, and pour over rice. Stir, set the Instant Pot on Sauté mode and bring to a boil. Add the pineapple, stir, divide into dessert bowls, and serve.

Nutritional Values Per serving

Calories: 113
Fat: 3.2
Fiber: 0.2
Carbs: 15
Protein: 4.2

536. Quick Flan

Preparation Time: 10 minutes
Cooking Time: 15 minutes
Serves: 6

Ingredients:

For the caramel:

> *¼ cup water*
> *¾ cup sugar*

For the custard:

> *2 egg yolks*
> *3 eggs*
> *1½ cups water*
> *Salt*
> *2 cups milk*
> *⅓ cup sugar*
> *½ cup whipping cream*
> *2 tablespoons hazelnut syrup*
> *1 teaspoon vanilla extract*

Directions:

Heat up a pot over medium heat, add ¼ cup water¾ cup sugar, stir, cover, bring to a boil,

boil for 2 minutes, uncover, and boil for a few minutes. Pour this into custard cups and coat evenly their bottoms. In a bowl, mix the eggs with the yolks, a pinch of salt ⅓ cup sugar, and stir using your mixer. Put the milk in a pan and heat up over medium heat. Add this to the egg mixture and stir well. Add the hazelnut syrup, vanilla, and cream, stir, and strain the mixture. Pour this into custard cups, place them in the steamer basket of the Instant Pot, add the remaining water to the Instant Pot, cover and cook on the Steam setting for 6 minutes. Release the pressure, uncover the Instant Pot, remove the custard cups and set aside to cool. Keep in the refrigerator for 4 hours before you serve them.

Nutritional Values Per serving

Calories: 145
Fat: 4
Fiber: 0
Carbs: 23
Sugar: 20
Protein: 4.5

537. Rhubarb Compote

Preparation Time: 10 minutes
Cooking Time: 30 minutes
Serves: 8

Ingredients:

> *⅓ cup water*
> *2 pounds rhubarb, chopped*
> *3 tablespoon honey*
> *Fresh mint, torn*
> *1 pound strawberries, chopped*

Directions:

Put the rhubarb and water into the Instant Pot, cover, cook on the Manual setting for 10 minutes, release the pressure and uncover the Instant Pot. Add the strawberries and honey, stir, set the Instant Pot on Manual mode and cook the compote for 20 minutes. Add the mint, stir, divide into bowls, and serve.

Nutritional Values Per serving

Calories: 71
Fat: 0.1
Fiber: 1
Carbs: 18
Protein: 0.5
Sugar: 16

538. Simple Chocolate Cake

Preparation Time: 10 minutes
Cooking Time: 40 minutes
Serves: 6

Ingredients:

¾ cup cocoa powder
¾ cup white flour
½ cup butter
1 cup water
1½ cups white sugar
½ teaspoon baking powder
3 eggs, whites and yolks separated
1 teaspoon vanilla extract

Directions:

In a bowl, beat the egg whites with a mixer until soft peaks form. In another bowl, beat the egg yolks until foamy. In a third bowl, mix the flour with the baking powder, sugar, and cocoa powder. Add the egg white, the egg yolks, and vanilla extract and combine gently. Grease a springform pan with butter, line with parchment paper, pour the cake batter, arrange the pan in the steamer basket of the Instant Pot, add 1 cup water to the Instant Pot, cover and cook on Manual mode for 40 minutes. Release the pressure, uncover the Instant Pot, take the pan out, let cake to cool, transfer to a platter, cut, and serve.

Nutritional Values Per serving

Calories: 379
Fat: 5
Fiber: 2
Carbs: 53
Protein: 5

539. Poached Figs

Preparation Time: 10 minutes
Cooking Time: 7 minutes
Serves: 4

Ingredients:

1 cup red wine
1 pound figs
½ cup pine nuts, toasted
½ cup sugar

For the yogurt crème:

2 pounds plain yogurt

Directions:

Put the yogurt in a strainer, press well, transfer to a container, and keep in the refrigerator overnight. Put the wine into the Instant Pot, place the figs in the steamer basket, cover, and cook on Steam mode for 4 minutes. Release the pressure, uncover the Instant Pot, take the figs out, and arrange them on plates. Set the Instant Pot on Manual mode, add the sugar and stir. Cook until sugar melts and then drizzle this sauce over the figs. Add the yogurt mixture on top or the side, and serve.

Nutritional Values Per serving

Calories: 100
Fat: 0
Fiber: 1
Carbs: 13
Sugar: 0.6
Protein: 0

540. Lemon Crème Pots

Preparation Time: 30 minutes
Cooking Time: 5 minutes
Serves: 4

Ingredients:

1 cup whole milk
Zest from 1 lemon
6 egg yolks
1 cup fresh cream

1 cup water
⅔ cup sugar
Blackberry syrup, for serving
½ cup fresh blackberries

Directions:

Heat up a pan over medium heat, add the milk, lemon zest, and cream, stir, bring to a boil, take off heat and set aside for 30 minutes. In a bowl, mix the egg yolks with the sugar and cold cream mixture and stir well. Pour this into ramekins, cover them with aluminum foil, place them in the steamer basket of the Instant Pot, add the water to the Instant Pot, cover, and cook on the Manual setting for 5 minutes. Release the pressure for 10 minutes, uncover the Instant Pot, take the ramekins out, let them cool down, and serve with blackberries and blackberry syrup on top.

Nutritional Values Per serving

Calories: 145
Fat: 4
Fiber: 3
Carbs: 10
Protein: 1

541. Simple Carrot Pudding

Preparation Time: 10 minutes
Cooking Time: 1 hour
Serves: 8

Ingredients:

1½ cups water
Vegetable oil cooking spray
½ cup brown sugar
2 eggs
¼ cup molasses
½ cup flour
½ teaspoon allspice
½ teaspoon ground cinnamon
Salt
Nutmeg
½ teaspoon baking soda
⅔ cup shortening, frozen, grated
½ cup pecans, chopped

½ cup carrots, peeled and grated
½ cup raisins
1 cup bread crumbs

For the sauce:

4 tablespoons butter
½ cup brown sugar
¼ cup heavy cream
2 tablespoons rum
¼ teaspoon ground cinnamon

Directions:

In a bowl, mix the molasses with eggs½ cup sugar and stir. Add the flour, shortening, carrots, nuts, raisins, bread crumbs, salt, ½ teaspoon cinnamon, allspice, nutmeg, and baking soda and stir everything. Pour this into a Bundt pan that you've greased with some cooking spray, cover with aluminum foil, place in the steamer basket of the Instant Pot, add the water to the Instant Pot, cover and cook on the Manual setting for 1 hour. Release the pressure, uncover the Instant Pot, take the pudding out and set it aside to cool down. Heat up a pan with the butter for the sauce over medium heat. Add ½ cup brown sugar, stir, and cook for 2 minutes. Add the cream, rum, ½ teaspoon cinnamon, stir, and simmer for 2 minutes. Serve the pudding with the rum sauce.

Nutritional Values Per serving

Calories: 316
Fat: 16
Fiber: 5
Carbs: 44
Protein: 7
Sugar: 7

542. Corn Pudding

Preparation Time: 10 minutes
Cooking Time: 30 minutes
Serves: 4

Ingredients:

11 ounces canned creamed corn
2 cups water
2 cups milk

3 tablespoons sugar
2 eggs, whisked
2 tablespoons flour
Salt
1 tablespoon butter
Vegetable oil cooking spray

Directions:

Put the water into the Instant Pot, set on Manual mode, and bring to a boil. In a bowl, mix the corn with the eggs, milk, butter, flour, sugar, and a pinch of salt and stir well. Grease a baking dish with some cooking spray, pour the corn mixture into the pan, cover with aluminum foil and arrange in the steamer basket of the Instant Pot. Cover and cook on the Steam mode for 20 minutes. Release the pressure, uncover the Instant Pot, take the pudding out, set it aside to cool down, and serve.

Nutritional Values Per serving

Calories: 200
Fat: 5
Fiber: 2
Carbs: 12
Protein: 9

543. Eggnog Cheesecake

Preparation Time: 15 minutes
Cooking Time: 20 minutes
Serves: 6

Ingredients:

2 cups water
2 teaspoons butter, melted
½ cup ginger cookies, crumbled
16 ounces cream cheese, softened
2 eggs
½ cup sugar
1 teaspoon rum
½ teaspoon vanilla extract
½ teaspoon nutmeg

Directions:

Grease a pan with the butter, add the cookie crumbs, and spread them evenly. In a bowl,

beat the cream cheese with a mixer. Add the nutmeg, vanilla, rum, and eggs and stir well. Pour this in the steamer basket of the Instant Pot, add the water to the Instant Pot, cover, and cook on the Manual setting for 15 minutes. Release the pressure, uncover the Instant Pot, take the cheesecake out, set aside to cool down, and keep in the refrigerator for 4 hours before slicing and serving it.

Nutritional Values Per serving

Calories: 400
Fat: 25
Fiber: 0
Carbs: 30
Protein: 6
Sugar: 19

544. Super Sweet Carrots

Preparation Time: 10 minutes
Cooking Time: 16 minutes
Serves: 4

Ingredients:

1 tablespoon brown sugar
2 cups baby carrots
Salt
½ cup water
½ tablespoon butter

Directions:

Set the Instant Pot on Sauté mode, add the butter and melt it. Add the sugar, water, and salt, stir, and cook for 1 minute. Add the carrots, toss to coat, cover the Instant Pot, and cook on the Manual setting for 15 minutes. Release the pressure, uncover the Instant Pot, transfer the carrots to plates, and serve.

Nutritional Values Per serving

Calories: 80
Fat: 1
Fiber: 1
Carbs: 3
Protein: 4

545. Pineapple and Ginger Risotto Dessert

Preparation Time: 10 minutes
Cooking Time: 12 minutes
Serves: 4

Ingredients:

¼ cup candied ginger, chopped
20 ounces canned pineapple chunks
½ cup coconut , shredded
1¾ cups Arborio rice
4 cups milk

Directions:

In the Instant Pot, mix the milk with the rice, coconut, pineapple, and ginger, stir, cover the Instant Pot, and cook on the Rice setting for 12 minutes. Release the pressure naturally, uncover the Instant Pot, and serve.

Nutritional Values Per serving

Calories: 100
Fat: 2
Fiber: 3
Carbs: 3
Protein: 2

546. Chocolate Molten Lava Cake

Preparation Time: 20 minutes
Serves: 4

Ingredients

2 tbsp Butter, melted
1 cup Dark Chocolate, melted
6 tbsp Almond Flour
1 cup Water
1 tsp Vanilla
3 Eggs plus
1 Yolk, beaten
¾ cup Coconut Sugar

Directions

1. Combine all ingredients, except the water, in a bowl. Grease four ramekins with cooking spray. Divide the filling between the ramekins. Pour the water in your Pressure cooker.

2. Place the ramekins on the trivet. Seal the lid and cook for 10 minutes PRESSURE COOK/MANUAL at High pressure. When ready, do a quick pressure release. Serve immediately and enjoy.

Nutritional Values Per serving:

Calories 413
Carbs 48g
Fat 23g
Protein 8g

547. Buttery Banana Bread

Preparation Time: 45 minutes
Serves: 12

Ingredients

3 ripe Bananas, mashed
1 ¼ cups Sugar
1 cup Milk
2 cups all-purpose Flour
1 tsp Baking Soda
1 tsp Baking Powder
1 tbsp Orange Juice
1 stick Butter, room temperature
A pinch of Salt
¼ tsp Cinnamon
½ tsp Pure Vanilla Extract

Directions

1. In a bowl, mix together the flour, baking powder, baking soda, sugar, vanilla, and salt. Add in the bananas, cinnamon, and orange juice. Slowly stir in the butter and milk.

2. Give it a good stir until everything is well combined. Pour the batter into a medium-sized round pan.

3. Place the trivet at the bottom of the pressure cooker and fill with 2 cups of water. Place the pan on the trivet. Select MEAT/STEW and cook for 40 minutes at

High. Do a quick pressure release.

Nutritional Values Per serving:

Calories 295
Carbs 48g
Fat 14g
Protein 5g

548. Peaches with Chocolate Biscuits

Preparation Time: 20 minutes
Serves: 4

Ingredients

4 small Peaches, halved lengthwise and pitted
8 dried Dates, chopped
4 tbsp Walnuts, chopped
1 cup Coarsely Crumbled Cookies
1 tsp Cinnamon Powder
¼ tsp grated nutmeg
¼ tsp ground Cloves

Directions

1. Pour 2 cups of water into the pressure cooker and add a trivet. Arrange the peaches on a greased baking dish cut-side-up. To prepare the filling, mix all of the remaining ingredients.

2. Stuff the peaches with the mixture. Cover with aluminium foil and lower it onto the trivet. Seal the lid, press PRESSURE COOK/MANUAL and cook for 15 minutes at High. Do a quick pressure release.

Nutritional Values Per serving:

Calories 302
Carbs 39g
Fat 16g
Protein 7g

549. Apricots with Blueberry Sauce

Preparation Time: 15 minutes
Serves: 4

Ingredients

8 Apricots, pitted and halved
2 cups Blueberries
¼ cup Honey
1 ½ tbsp Cornstarch
½ Vanilla Bean, sliced lengthwise
¼ tsp ground Cardamom
½ Cinnamon stick
1 ¼ cups Water

Directions

1. Add all ingredients, except for the honey and the cornstarch, to your pressure cooker. Seal the lid, select RICE mode and cook for 8 minutes at High pressure. Do a quick pressure release and open the lid.

2. Remove the apricots with a slotted spoon. Choose SAUTÉ at High, add the honey and cornstarch, then let simmer until the sauce thickens, for about 5 minutes.

3. Split up the apricots among serving plates and top with the blueberry sauce, to serve.

Nutritional Values Per serving:

Calories 205
Carbs 45g
Fat 2g
Protein 2g

550. Hot Milk Chocolate Fondue

Preparation Time: 5 minutes
Serves: 12

Ingredients

10 ounces Milk Chocolate, chopped into small pieces
2 tsp Coconut Liqueur
8 ounces Heavy Whipping Cream
¼ tsp Cinnamon Powder
1 ½ cups Lukewarm Water
A pinch of Salt

Directions

1. Melt the chocolate in a heat-proof recipient. Add the remaining ingredients, except for the liqueur. Transfer this recipient to the metal trivet. Pour 1 ½ cups of water into

the cooker, and place a trivet inside.

2. Seal the lid, select PRESSURE COOK/MANUAL and cook for 5 minutes at High. Do a quick pressure release. Pull out the container with tongs. Mix in the coconut liqueur and serve right now with fresh fruits. Enjoy!

Nutritional Values Per serving:

Calories 198
Carbs 12g
Fat 16g
Protein 3g

551. Tutty Fruity Sauce

Preparation Time: 15 minutes
Serves: 2

Ingredients

1 cup Pineapple Chunks
1 cup Berry Mix
2 Apples, peeled and diced
¼ cup Almonds, chopped
¼ cup Fresh Orange Juice
1 tbsp Olive Oil

Directions

1. Pour ½ cup of water, orange juice, and fruits, in the pressure cooker. Give it a good stir and seal the lid. Press PRESSURE COOK/MANUAL and set the timer to 5 minutes at High pressure.

2. When it goes off, release the pressure quickly. Blend the mixture with a hand blender and immediately stir in the coconut oil. Serve sprinkled with chopped almonds. Enjoy!

Nutritional Values Per serving:

Calories 125
Carbs 16g
Fat 4g
Protein 1g

552. Delicious Stuffed Apples

Preparation Time: 20 minutes
Serves: 6

Ingredients

3 ½ pounds Apples, cored
½ cup dried Apricots, chopped
¼ cup Sugar
¼ cup Pecans, chopped
¼ cup Graham Cracker Crumbs
¼ tsp Cardamom
½ tsp grated Nutmeg
½ tsp ground Cinnamon
1 ¼ cups Red Wine

Directions

1. Lay the apples at the bottom of your cooker, and pour in the red wine. Combine the other ingredients, except the crumbs. Seal the lid, and cook PRESSURE COOK/MANUAL at High pressure for 15 minutes.

2. Once ready, do a quick pressure release. Top with graham cracker crumbs and serve!

Nutritional Values Per serving:

Calories 152
3g Fat
21g Carbs
2g Protein

553. Coconut Crème Caramel

Preparation Time: 20 minutes
Serves: 4

Ingredients

2 Eggs
7 ounces Condensed Coconut Milk
½ cup Coconut Milk
1 ½ cups Water
½ tsp Vanilla
4 tbsp Caramel Syrup

Directions

1. Divide the caramel syrup between 4 small ramekins. Pour water in the pressure cooker and add the trivet.

2. In a bowl, beat the rest of the ingredients. Divide them between the ramekins. Cover them with aluminum foil and lower onto the trivet. Seal the lid, and set on RICE for 13 minutes at High pressure. Do a quick pressure release. Let cool completely. To unmold the flan, insert a spatula along the ramekin' sides and flip onto a dish.

Nutritional Values Per serving:

Calories 121
Carbs 17g
Fat 3g
Protein 3g

554. Homemade Egg Custard

Preparation Time: 20 minutes
Serves: 4

Ingredients

1 Egg plus 2 Egg yolks
½ cup Sugar
½ cups Milk
2 cups Heavy Cream
½ tsp pure rum extract
2 cups Water

Directions

1. Beat the egg and the egg yolks in a bowl. Gently add pure rum extract. Mix in the milk and heavy cream. Give it a good, and add the sugar. Pour this mixture into 4 ramekins.

2. Add 2 cups of water, insert the trivet, and lay the ramekins on the trivet. Select PRESSURE COOK/MANUAL and cook for 10 minutes at High. Do a quick pressure release. Wait a bit before removing from ramekins.

Nutritional Values Per serving:

Calories 425
Carbs 48g
Fat 25g
Protein 11g

555. Poached Pears with Orange and Cinnamon

Preparation Time: 20 minutes
Serves: 4

Ingredients

4 Pears cut in half
1 tsp powdered Ginger
1 tsp Nutmeg
1 cup Orange Juice
2 tsp Cinnamon
¼ cup Coconut Sugar

Directions

1. Place the trivet at the bottom of the pressure cooker. Stir in the juice and spices. Lay the pears on the trivet. Seal the lid, cook on PRESSURE COOK/MANUAL for 7 minutes, at High pressure.

2. When ready, do a quick release. Remove pears onto a serving plate. Pour juice over to serve.

Nutritional Values Per serving:

Calories 170
Carbs 43g
Fat 1g
Protein 1g

Conclusion

Thanks for purchasingthis book. It's my firm belief that it will provide you with all the answers to your questions.

Made in the USA
Middletown, DE
15 May 2019